Payne and Ivamy's
Carriage of Goods by Sea

Payne and Ivamy's
Carriage of Goods by Sea

Thirteenth edition

E R Hardy Ivamy LLB, PhD, LLD
of the Middle Temple, Barrister
Emeritus Professor of Law in the University of London

Butterworths
London and Edinburgh
1989

United Kingdom	Butterworth & Co (Publishers) Ltd, 88 Kingsway, LONDON WC2B 6AB and 4 Hill Street, EDINBURGH EH2 3JZ
Australia	Butterworths Pty Ltd, SYDNEY, MELBOURNE, BRISBANE, ADELAIDE, PERTH, CANBERRA and HOBART
Canada	Butterworths Canada Ltd, TORONTO and VANCOUVER
Ireland	Butterworth (Ireland) Ltd, DUBLIN
Malaysia	Malayan Law Journal Sdn Bhd, KUALA LUMPUR
New Zealand	Butterworths of New Zealand Ltd, WELLINGTON and AUCKLAND
Singapore	Butterworth & Co (Asia) Pte Ltd, SINGAPORE
USA	Butterworths Legal Publishers, ST PAUL, Minnesota, SEATTLE, Washington, BOSTON, Massachusetts, AUSTIN, Texas and D & S Publishers, CLEARWATER, Florida

A CIP Catalogue record for this book is available from the British Library.

First edition 1914	William Payne
Second edition 1924	Roger S Bacon
Third edition 1925	Roger S Bacon
Fourth edition 1938	John Samuel
Fifth edition 1949	John Samuel-Gibbon
Sixth edition 1954	J Milnes Holden
Seventh edition 1963	E R Hardy Ivamy
Eighth edition 1968	E R Hardy Ivamy
Ninth edition 1972	E R Hardy Ivamy
Tenth edition 1976	E R Hardy Ivamy
Eleventh edition 1979	E R Hardy Ivamy
Twelfth edition 1985	E R Hardy Ivamy
Thirteenth edition 1989	E R Hardy Ivamy

ISBN 0 406 52560 9
Typeset, printed and bound in Great Britain by William Clowes Limited, Beccles and London

Preface

So many developments in case law have taken place since the last edition that some parts of the book have had to be largely rewritten and re-arranged. Further, a fundamental change has been brought about by the Merchant Shipping Act 1979, which is now in force.

Chapter 2 ('Charter-parties') has undergone the greatest alteration especially with reference to time charter-parties. The effect of the word 'about' being used in relation to a vessel's speed, eg 'about15.5 knots', is that some margin is to be recognised on either side of the stated figure: *Arab Maritime Transport Co v Luxor Trading Panama and Geogas Enterprise Geneva, The Al Bida* [1986] 1 Lloyd's Rep 142. 'Wages' does not mean remuneration in conformity with International Transport Workers Federation rates of pay unless those rates are made part of the agreement between the shipowners and the crew: *Sanko SS Co Ltd v Fearnley and Eger A/S, The Manhattan Prince* [1985] 1 Lloyd's Rep 140. *Summit Investment Inc v British Steel Corp, The Sounion* [1987] 1 Lloyd's Rep 230, CA, interprets the words 'grates and stoves' in a provision of fuel clause. *Alexandros Shipping Co v MSC Mediterranean Shipping Co SA, The Alexandros P* [1986] 1 Lloyd's Rep 421 and other cases consider the liability of the charterer to arrange loading and discharge. Where there is a difference between local time at the port of delivery and that at the port of redelivery, the shipowners are entitled to claim hire only in respect of the actual period which has elapsed from the moment of the delivery of the vessel: *Ove Skou v Rudolf A Oetker, The Arctic Skou* [1985] 2 Lloyd's Rep 478. The charterer is not entitled to make a deduction of hire where the master has failed to keep accurate logs for such a failure does not affect the use of the vessel: *Leon Corp v Atlantic Lines and Navigation Co Inc, The Leon* [1985] 2 Lloyd's Rep 470. *Navigas International Ltd v Trans-Offshore Inc, The Bridgestone Maru (No 3)* [1985] 2 Lloyd's Rep 62 and *CA Venezolana de Navegacion v Bank Line, The Roachbank* [1987] 2 Lloyd's Rep 498 are instances of the 'off-hire' clause, whilst *Newa Line v Erechthion Shipping Co SA, The Erechthion* [1987] 2 Lloyd's Rep 180 construes the 'employment and indemnity' clause. Where a vessel is redelivered to the shipowners prematurely, they are entitled to damages: *Armagas Ltd V Mundogas SA, The Ocean Frost* [1986] 2 Lloyd's Rep 109, HL. The measure of damages where a charterer wrongfully repudiates the charter-party is the subject of *SIB International SRL v Metallgesellschaft Corpn, The Noel Bay* [1989] 1 Lloyd's Rep 361, CA.

In chapter 3 ('Bills of lading') the question whether a clause in a charter-party was effectively incorporated into a bill of lading is referred to in *Paros Shipping Corpn v Nafta (GB) Ltd, The Paros* [1987] 2 Lloyd's Rep 269, *Navigazione Alta Italia SpA v Svenska Petroleum AB, The Nai Matteini* [1988] 1 Lloyd's Rep 452 and *Federal Bulk Carriers Inc v C Itoh & Co Ltd, The Federal Bulker* [1989] 1 Lloyd's Rep 103, CA. There is an implied obligation on the part of the shipper that the bills of lading which he presents for signature by the master should relate to the goods actually shipped: *Boukadoura Maritime Corpn v Société Anonyme Marocaine de l'Industrie du Raffinage, The Boukadoura* [1989] 1 Lloyd's Rep 393. New cases on the duty of the carrier to take care of the cargo include *The Lucky Wave* [1985] 1 Lloyd's Rep 80 (galvanised steel), *Gatoil International Inc v Panatlantic Carriers Corp, The Rio Sun* [1985] 1 Lloyd's Rep 350 (crude oil) and *The Saudi Prince (No 2)* [1988] 1 Lloyd's Rep 1, CA (tiles). In *The Aramis* [1989] 1 Lloyd's Rep 1, CA it was decided that under the Bills of Lading Act 1855 contractual rights and contractual liabilities could not pass to an indorsee of a bill of lading unless property in the goods passed upon or by reason of an indorsement.

In chapter 6 ('Loading, discharge and delivery') *Palm Shipping Inc v Vitol SA, The Universal Monarch* [1988] 2 Lloyd's Rep 483 indicates that if there are insufficient tugs at the port of discharge for the vessel concerned, the port is unsafe. Where a vessel waits off a port at the charterer's request, the shipowner is entitled to a reasonable remuneration for such a service: *Greenmast Shipping Co SA v Jean Lion et Cie SA, The Saronikos* [1986] 2 Lloyd's Rep 277. The master is not justified in delivering to any person who does not produce the bill of lading: *Mobil Shipping and Transportation Co v Shell Eastern Petroleum (Pte) Ltd, The Mobil Courage* [1987] 2 Lloyd's Rep 655. In *Indian Oil Corpn Ltd v Greenstone Shipping SA, The Ypatianna* [1987] 2 Lloyd's Rep 286 the issue was how the goods, which had become mixed and unidentifiable on the voyage, should be apportioned. *Ferruzzi France SA and Ferruzzi SpA v Oceania Maritime Inc, The*

Palmea [1988] 2 Lloyd's Rep 261 sets out the measure of damages where goods are delivered short of their destination.

In chapter 7 ('The exclusion and limitation of a shipowner's liability') *Empressa Cubana Importada de Alimentos Alimport v Iasmos Shipping Co SA, The Good Friend* [1984] 2 Lloyd's Rep 586 (quarantine); *The Lucky Wave* [1985] 1 Lloyd's Rep 80 (insufficiency of packing); *The Tilia Gorthon* [1985] 1 Lloyd's Rep 552 (perils of the sea); and *The Mekhanik Evgrafov and Ivan Derbenev* [1987] 2 Lloyd's Rep 634 (inherent vice) are illustrations of the exceptions from liability set out in the Carriage of Goods by Sea Act 1971, Sch, art IV, r 2. Also in this chapter is the change regarding the exclusion and limitation of liability brought about by the Merchant Shipping Act 1979, ss 17, 18 and Sch 4, which have replaced the Merchant Shipping. Act 1894, ss 502 and 503.

In chapter 10 ('Demurrage and despatch money') *President of India v Jebsens (UK) Ltd, The General Caninpin, Proteus, Free Wave and Dinara* [1987] 2 Lloyd's Rep 354 concerns the number of lay days, *Seacrystal Shipping Ltd v Bulk Transport Group Shipping Co Ltd, The Kyzikos* [1989] 1 Lloyd's Rep 1, HL, an 'arrived ship', *Eurico SpA v Philipp Bros, The Epaphus* [1987] 2 Lloyd's Rep 215, CA and *Transgrain Shipping BV v Global Transporte Oceanico Shipping BV, The Mexico I* [1988] 2 Lloyd's Rep 149, readiness to discharge, and *Plakoura Maritime Corpn v Shell Transport International Petroleum Co Ltd* [1987] 2 Lloyd's Rep 258, the security of moorings. There is also a considerable number of cases relating to the giving of notice of readiness, eg *President of India v Davenport Marine Panama SA, The Albion* [1987] 2 Lloyd's Rep 365 and *President of India v Diamantis Pateras (Hellas) Marine Enterprises Ltd, The Nestor* [1987] 2 Lloyd's Rep 649. Decisions such as *Associated Bulk Carriers Ltd v Shell International Petroleum Co Ltd, The Nordic Navigator* [1984] 2 Lloyd's Rep 182, *R Pagnan and Fratelli v Finagrain Compagnie Commerciale Agricole et Financière SA, The Adolf Leonhardt* [1986] 2 Lloyd's Rep 395 and *Société Anonyme Marocain de l'Industrie du Raffinage v Notos Maritime Corpn, The Notos* [1987] 1 Lloyd's Rep 503, HL are cases showing when lay time may be interrupted. *President of India v Lips Maritime Corpn, The Lips* [1987] 2 Lloyd's Rep 311, HL, is the latest authority on exchange rates in connection with the payment of demurrage. *Action SA v Britannic Shipping Corpn Ltd, The Aegis Britannic* [1987] 1 Lloyd's Rep 119, CA is a new case on 'cesser clauses'.

Chapter 11 ('Freight') now includes *Elena Shipping Ltd v Aidenfield Ltd, The Elena* [1986] 1 Lloyd's Rep 425, *Freedom Maritime Corpn v*

International Bulk Carriers SA and Mineral and Metals Trading Corpn of India, The Khian Captain (No 2) [1986] 1 Lloyd's Rep 429, which are both cases on freight on delivery, and *Bank of Boston Connecticut v European Grain and Shipping Ltd, The Dominique* [1989] 1 All ER 545, HL (advance freight).

In chapter 12 ('Liens') *Re Welsh Ferries Ltd, The Ugland Trailer* [1985] 2 Lloyd's Rep 372 and other cases state that where a shipowner is a company, sub-freights belonging to a time charterer are book debts, and any lien on them should be registered under the Companies Act 1985, s 395.

Chapter 13 ('Carriage of goods by hovercraft') has been re-written in the light of the many changes brought about by the Hovercraft (Civil Liability) Order 1986 (SI 1986/1305).

In Appendix A the form of a bill of lading is reproduced by courtesy of the New Zealand Tonnage Committee. The 'Gencon' charter-party and the 'Baltime 1939' charter-party are printed in Appendix B with the kind permission of the Baltic and International Maritime Conference.

I should like to thank the staff of Butterworths for undertaking the arduous job of preparing the Index and the Table of Cases and Statutes, and seeing the book through to press.

June 1989   E R HARDY IVAMY

Contents

Table of statutes

References in this Table to *Statutes* are to Halsbury's Statutes of England (Fourth Edition) showing the volume and page at which the annotated text of an Act may be found. Page references printed in bold type indicate where the Act is set out in part or in full.

List of cases

xix

PAGE

I

N

1 *List of cases*

lii   *List of cases*

PAGE

U

Chapter 1

Commercial practice

The branch of the law of contract which relates to the carriage of goods by sea will be better understood if one knows something of the general practice of merchants, shipowners, and bankers who carry on the commerce of the world. For the benefit, therefore, of those who have not had the advantage of practical experience in such matters it is proposed to examine, in very brief form, some of the steps which are usually taken by those wishing to carry goods from one portion of the globe to another. In the course of such examination familiarity with common shipping terms will also be gained.

When a manufacturer, exporter, or other person has sold goods to a customer overseas and has decided, on the grounds of cost and convenience, which shipping line will best carry them for him to their destination, he can obtain from the offices of that line, or from printers who make it their business to supply them, three or four copies of a document known as a **bill of lading**. Almost all shipping lines have their own special forms of bills of lading. These serve as (1) *documents of title* to the goods, once they are shipped; (2) *a receipt for the goods* delivered to the shipowner or **carrier**; and (3) *evidence of the contract* which has been entered into between the **shipper** of the goods and the **shipowner**.

Under modern conditions when a shipment is made by a regular line, there are usually agents on each side intervening between the shipper and the shipowner.[1] The shipper frequently employs a **forwarding agent** and the shipowner a **loading broker**.

The forwarding agent's normal duties are to ascertain the date and place of sailing, obtain a space allocation if that is required, and fill in the blank spaces in the printed bills of lading, each one in identical terms, indicating the name of the **consignee**, or person to whom the goods are to be delivered; a description of the goods,

---

1   See *Heskell v Continental Express Ltd* [1950] 1 All ER 1033.

including the **shipping marks** which have been put on the bales, cases, or bags for the purpose of identification; stipulations as to the time and place of payment of **freight** (ie the remuneration payable to the shipowner for the carriage of the goods), and various other details.

The three or four copies (the practice varies) of the bill of lading thus filled in are known as a **set**. The forwarding agent sends these documents to the loading broker for signature. He also arranges for the goods to be brought **alongside**, ie within reach of the ship's tackle, and makes the customs entry and pays any dues on the cargo. After shipment he collects all the copies of the bill of lading except one, and sends them to the shipper. The remaining copy is handed to the shipowner and forms part of the **ship's papers** for the voyage. The ship's **manifest** is made up from all the bills so collected.

All the regular shipping lines operating from the United Kingdom appear to employ a **loading broker**. His duties are normally as follows. He advertises the dates of sailings, and supervises the arrangements for loading, though the actual **stowage**, or packing of the goods in the ship's holds, is decided on by the **cargo superintendent**, who is in the direct service of the shipowner. The loading broker will also sign the bills of lading and issue them in exchange for the freight. He is paid by way of commission on the freight, and that doubtless induces him to carry out his primary function of securing enough cargo to fill the ship.

It will be realised from this account of their duties that the loading broker and the forwarding agent perform well-defined and separate functions. Nevertheless, in practice, the same firm is often both the loading broker and the forwarding agent. A firm usually acts as loading broker for only one shipping line and does all that line's business. It is free in respect of other business to act as it will.

The shipper normally insures the goods against marine and, sometimes, war risks, breakage or leakage. The consideration paid by him to the insurers is a **premium**, and the document embodying the contract is a **policy**. He than has the complete set of **shipping documents** consisting of a bill of lading, the policy of insurance, and the **invoice** (which shows the details of the goods bought and the price payable). In nearly all cases the documents are attached to a **draft** or bill of exchange drawn on the consignee or on a bank named by him[2] either at sight or at so many days or months. Almost invariably the shipper does one of three things with these documents:

2 The transaction is arranged by means of a Bankers' Commercial Credit. See

(1) He may send them direct to the consignee of the goods. This is most frequently done when the consignee is his agent or employee.

(2) He may hand them to his bank with a covering letter asking the bank to collect from the consignee, or the bank named by the consignee, the amount indicated on the invoice against delivery of the documents. This the bank will do in consideration of a commission.

(3) He may **discount** the bill of exchange with this bank, ie the bank credits him at one with the amount of the bill, less a commission.

The consignee himself may be a merchant, or a **factor** (a selling agent), who wishes to resell the goods. Often he is able to do so before they are landed at their destination. In such a case he makes the documents over by a suitable form of **indorsement** or signature on the reverse side of the bill of lading to the new owner of the goods, who becomes an **indorsee for value**.

An indorsement of the bill of lading made within the intention of transferring the ownership of the goods named in it to the indorsee has the effect of actually making him the owner of the goods. An **indorsement in blank** is merely the signature of the shipper written on the bank of the bill of lading. A **special indorsement** is made up of the shipper's signature and a direction to deliver to a particular person; eg, if a bill of lading is in favour of 'A B & Co or order' and the goods are bought from them by C D & Co, a suitable special endorsement would be 'Deliver to C D & Co or order. (Signed) A B & Co'.

Various forms of contract for the sale of goods to an overseas buyer have become stereotyped by usage, of which the commonest are the following;

(1) **A CIF contract.**[3] These letters stand for 'cost, insurance, and freight'. Here the seller contracts to deliver the goods to the buyer at the place named by the buyer as their destination, the seller paying the insurance premium and the freight. Sometimes the seller fulfils the contract by buying goods already

generally C M Schmitthoff, *The Export Trade* (7th edn 1980), pp 244–270; H C Gutteridge and M Megrah, *The Law of Bankers' Commercial Credits* (7th revised edn 1984).

3 See generally D M Sassoon. *C.I.F. and F.O.B. Contracts* (3rd end 1984) (published as *British Shipping Laws*, vol 5).

afloat which are bound for the proper destination, and transferring the ownership of them to the buyer.

(2) An **FOB contract**.[4] These letters stand for 'free on board'. Here the seller's obligation is to deliver the goods over the ship's rail. The buyer must pay the insurance premium and the freight and any other expenses which may be incurred by the goods in transit, and the goods travel at the buyer's risk.

(3) An **ex warehouse contract**. In this case the buyer purchases the goods on the understanding that he will be responsible for their removal from the warehouse in which they are lying at the time of sale, and for their carriage to their destination.

It may be that during the voyage the ship or some of the cargo suffers damage. Subject to various exceptions, any loss so sustained must be borne by the shipowner or by the cargo-owner (or by their respective insurers), as the case may be. Such a loss, known as **particular average**, lies where it falls.

The most important exception to this rule is where a grave peril, e g a hurricane, threatens the whole adventure and a sacrifice is made intentionally for the benefit of everyone concerned. Perhaps some of the cargo will be **jettisoned** or thrown overboard. When such a sacrifice, known as a **general average sacrifice**, has been made, the loss, called a **general average loss**, is imposed on all those for whose benefit the sacrifice was made. They must all bear the loss rateably, in proportion to the value of their respective interests.

On arrival at the port of destination the master will, provided that the freight has been paid, deliver the goods to the first holder of a bill of lading who presents himself and demands them. It would appear at first sight that the existence of a set of bills involves a great risk of fraud. In practice, however, the cases of persons who have no right to the goods becoming possessed of them are extremely rare. Without a copy of the bill of lading the consignee is usually unable to obtain delivery of the goods from the carrier, though sometimes, e g where the documents have been delayed in transmission, the carrier consents to deliver against an **indemnity**. This will be given by some person or company of high standing, e g a bank, and will cover the carrier in respect of any loss which he may suffer by handing over the goods without the production of a bill of lading.

As soon as the consignee accepts delivery of the goods on the quay, if he suspects that they have suffered any loss or damage

4 See generally ibid.

covered by the policy of insurance, he calls in the local agent of the insurers and asks him to make an official **survey** of the parcel and furnish a signed certificate. The consignee may also seek the assistance of an independent surveyor. He may then make his claim against the insurers themselves.

The importance of marine insurance to the merchant lies in the fact that by certain clauses in the bill of lading known as **exceptions** the shipowner avoids responsibility for a multitude of **excepted perils** or mishaps which may befall the cargo. If it were not for the risks undertaken by the insurers, the merchant would be faced with the impossibility of trading with anything like a prospect of gain. A person whose business it is to work out the respective liabilities of the parties concerned, where average has been incurred, is known as a **average adjuster**.

It may be, however, that for some reason, eg delay or neglect, the consignee fails to take delivery. In such a case the master may land and warehouse the goods, or, if that is impracticable, may elect to carry them, in the interests of their owner, to some other place.

One must now glance at alternative methods frequently employed by shippers of goods in place of the process, already noticed, of entering into a contract with a shipowner which is evidenced by a bill of lading.

It often happens that a shipper wishes either

(1) to hire a ship for a fixed time;
or (2) to hire a ship, or a portion of a ship, for a certain voyage;
or (3) to become for the time being the owner of a ship, by causing her to be leased to him.

The contract entered in any of these three cases is a **charter-party**. In case

(1) it is known as a **time charter-party**,
(2) as a **voyage charter-party**,
(3) as a **charter-party by demise**.

In some instances the shipper who has entered into the charter-party wishes himself to fill the ship with his own goods; in others he advertises that he has a certain amount of space and, for a consideration, ships other merchants' goods; sometimes he even charters a ship as a speculation, having no cargo himself to ship in her, hoping to make a profit by the demands of others for such space as he can offer.

Where a ship is used, either by the shipowner or by her charterer, to carry the goods of a number of persons under different bills of lading, she is said to be employed as a **general ship**.

This brings one to a consideration of the variations of the term 'freight', as commonly used. **Advance freight** is often agreed upon, ie freight to be paid before the goods are delivered by the carrier to the consignee; eg, it may be agreed that payment is to be made on shipment. Again, sometimes a charterer agrees to pay **lump sum freight**; this means that he binds himself to pay a fixed sum for the whole voyage or series of voyages covered by the charter-party, irrespective of the amount of goods carried. **Pro rata freight** is freight which may become payable proportionately to the part of the voyage accomplished or to the part of the cargo delivered. **Dead freight** is the name given to the damages payable, in certain circumstances, by a charterer who has failed to load a **full and complete cargo**, ie a cargo which will fill the holds of the ship as far as they can be filled with safety; for, except where lump sum freight is agreed upon, the shipowner generally stipulates for the loading of the largest cargo he can carry. The shipowner's remuneration for carrying the goods beyond their original destination, where the consignee has failed to take delivery or to forward instructions as to the disposal of the goods, is **back freight**.

Finally, acquaintance should be made with the following terms:

Barratry is any act of fraud or violence done by the master or crew, without the consent or privity of the shipowner, which either results in, or necessitates the risk of, loss of or damage to the ship or cargo.

A contract whereby in an emergency both ship and cargo are given as security for a loan to enable the ship to complete her voyage is a **bottomry bond**. Where only the cargo is given as security, the document is known as a **respondentia bond**. Both transactions are very rare at the present day.

The letters **DWC** stand for dead-weight capacity. This phrase, when it appears in a charter-party without any restrictive explanatory words, means the gross weight of goods of any kind which the ship can carry.

A charter-party generally fixes a number of days, called **lay-days**, within which the ship is to be loaded or discharged, as the case may be.

Demurrage is a sum named in the charter-party to be paid by the charterer as liquidated damages for delay beyond the lay-days.

When the lay-days have expired and demurrage has not been provided for, *or* when the time for loading or discharge is not agreed, *or* where demurrage is only to be paid for an agreed number of days and a further delay takes place, the shipowner is entitled to **damages for detention**; for clearly the earning-power of a ship depends upon her continuous employment with as little delay as possible between voyages.

A charter-party sometimes provides that **despatch money** will be payable to the charterer if he loads or discharges the vessel in a time which is shorter than the number of lay-days.

Apart from special customs, **working days** are all days on which work is generally done at the particular port in question. **Weather working days** are all working days on which the weather allows of work of the particular kind in question being done. **Running days** are all days on which a ship might be sailing at sea, ie every day in the year.

Deviation means departure from the prescribed or ordinary route which the ship should follow in fulfilment of a contract of carriage.

Inherent vice is a term applied to goods signifying any fault or characteristic of the goods or their packing which of itself causes them to be damaged or to deteriorate, without any negligence or wrongdoing by anyone.

A **mate's receipt** is a temporary form of receipt given by the mate of a ship for goods which have been received on board. This receipt is subsequently handed to the shipowner—or more usually to the loading broker—in exchange for the bills of lading.

Pilferage is a general term covering thefts of goods at any time during transit, or while lying in a warehouse.

Salvage is the remuneration payable to persons outside the contract of carriage who have saved the ship or cargo from loss or damage.

Wharfage is a charge made for receiving goods on a wharf, or for storing them there, or for removing them from there.

Chapter 2

Charter-parties

There are various types of charter-parties.[1] Of these the most important are voyage charter-parties[2] and time charter-parties.[3] When the shipowner and the charterer enter into the contract, the shipowner may have made representations on which the charterer has relied.[4] A charter-party may contain conditions and warranties.[5] In certain circumstances a charter-party may be frustrated.[6] In some cases a party to the contract may be released from his obligations under it.[7] The Unfair Contract Terms Act 1977 applies to charter-parties but only to a limited extent.[8]

THE TYPES OF CHARTER-PARTY

Unlike a bill of lading, a charter-party is always a contract (not merely evidence of a contract) and never anything more.[9]

There are three types of charter-party:

(1) *a voyage charter-party*, i e where the vessel is chartered for a certain voyage;

1　See infra.
2　See pp 11–25, post.
3　See pp 25–66, post.
4　See pp 66–70, post.
5　See pp 66–70, post.
6　See pp 70–79, post.
7　See p 79, post.
8　See p 79, post.
9　As to the functions of a bill of lading, see pp 81–92 post.

(2) *a time charter-party*, ie where the vessel is chartered for a certain period of time;[10]

(3) *a charter-party by demise*, ie a lease of the vessel.

A voyage or time charter-party confers on the charterer simply the right to have his goods carried by a particular vessel. Here the possession and control of the ship are not transferred to the charterer. The shipowner exercises this right through the master and crew who are employed by him.

But in the case of a charter-party by demise the charterer puts his

---

10　Another form of time charter-party is a 'consecutive voyage' charter-party under which a vessel is chartered for a period of time for a number of consecutive voyages. See e g *Sanko SS Co Ltd v Propet Co Ltd* [1970] 2 Lloyd's Rep 235, QBD (Commercial Court); *Suisse Atlantique Société d'Armement Maritime SA v Rotterdamsche Kolen Centrale NV* [1967] 1 AC 361, [1966] 2 All ER 61, HL; *Agro Co of Canada Ltd v Richmond Shipping Ltd, The Simonburn* [1973] 1 Lloyd's Rep 392, CA, which concerned the question whether an arbitrator had been appointed within the time stated in the charter-party; *Yoho Maru (Owners) v Agip SpA c/o SNAM SpA* [1973] 1 Lloyd's Rep 409, QBD where the question was the rate of freight payable; *Marmara Transport AS v Mobil Tankers SA, The Mersin* [1973] 1 Lloyd's Rep 532, QBD (Commercial Court), where the issue was as to the amount of freight payable; *Skibsaktieselskapet Snefonn, Skibsaksjeselskapet Bergehus and Sig Bergesen D Y & Co v Kawasaki Kisen Kaisha Ltd, The Berge Tasta* [1975] 1 Lloyd's Rep 422, QBD (Commercial Court), where the question was whether redelivery of the vessel was late; *Mitsui OSK Lines Ltd v Agip SpA, The Bungamawar* [1978] 1 Lloyd's Rep 263, QBD (Commercial Court) in which a freight clause was construed; *Intermare Transport GmbH v Tradax Export SA, The Oakwood* [1978] 2 Lloyd's Rep 10, CA, where the issue was whether the disponent owners of a vessel could require the charterers to perform a further voyage under the charter-party; *Pole Star Compania Naviera SA v Koch Marine SA, The Maritsa* [1979] 1 Lloyd's Rep 581, QBD (Commercial Court), where the question was whether the shipowners could claim the extra cost of bunkers; *Bravo Maritime (Chartering) Est v Baroom, The Athinoula* [1980] 2 Lloyd's Rep 481, QBD (Commercial Court), where an issue arose as to demurrage; *BTP Tioxide Ltd v Pioneer Shipping Ltd and Armada Marine SA, The Nema* [1981] 2 Lloyd's Rep 239, HL, where the question was whether a voyage for one season had been frustrated; *Agip Spa v Navigazione Alta Italia SpA, The Nai Genova and Nai Superba* [1984] 1 Lloyd's Rep 353, CA, where the question was whether an escalation clause should be rectified; *Rhodian River Shipping Co SA and Rhodian Sailor Shipping Co SA v Halla Maritime Corpn: The 'Rhodian River' and 'Rhodian Sailor'* [1984] 1 Lloyd's Rep 373, QBD (Commercial Court), where the question was whether the name of the owners of the vessel should be rectified; *Motor Oil Hellas (Corinth) Refineries A/S v Shipping Corpn of India: The 'Kanchenjunga'* [1989] 1 Lloyd's Rep 354, CA, where there was an issue whether the shipowners had elected to treat the charterers' nomination of a port as an improper one; *Rashtriya Chemicals and Fertilizers Ltd v Huddart Parker Industries Ltd: The 'Boral Gas'* [1988] 1 Lloyd's Rep 342, QBD (Commercial Court), where there was a delay in loading.

own stores, fuel oil, etc. on board and hires the crew. The master and crew are the charterer's servants, and the possession and control of the ship vest in him. Consequently, the shipowner has no responsibility in connection with goods shipped while the vessel is thus leased.

Whether the possession and control of the vessel are to pass to the charterer depends on the intention of the parties.

The main test for discovering their intention is whether the master is to be the servant of the charterer or of the shipowner.[11]

Contracts whereby the possession and control of a ship vest in the charterer are becoming more common to-day especially in the oil tanker trade, and MacKinnon LJ's dictum that 'a demise charter-party has long been obsolete'[12] is, therefore, too sweeping.[13]

The importance of the distinction between a charter-party by demise and other charter-parties is that under the former the master is the agent of the charterer, not of the shipowner.

Thus, in *Sandeman v Scurr*[14]

A ship was chartered to proceed to Oporto and there load a cargo. The charter-party gave the master power to sign bills of lading at any rate of freight without prejudice

---

11 *Page v Admiralty Comrs* [1921] 1 AC 137.
12 *Re an Arbitration between Sea and Land Securities Ltd v William Dickinson & Co Ltd, The Alresford* [1942] 2 KB 65 at 69, [1942] 1 All ER 503 at 504.
13 See eg *RM & R Log Ltd v Texada Towing Co Ltd, Minnette and Johnson, The Coast Prince* [1967] 2 Lloyd's Rep 290, where it was held that the charterer was in breach of an express and implied undertaking to redeliver the chartered vessel in as good a condition as when received; *Falmouth Docks and Engineering Co v Fowey Harbour Comrs, The Briton* [1975] 1 Lloyd's Rep 319, where a dredger was let out under a demise charter-party; *Attica Sea Carriers Corpn v Ferrostaal-Poseidon Bulk Reederei Gmbh, The Puerto Buitrago* [1976] 1 Lloyd's Rep 250, CA, where a clause in the charter-party stated that the vessel was to be redelivered in the same good order and condition as on delivery, and that before redelivery, the charterer must effect all repairs found to be necessary, and it was held that the charterer was entitled to redeliver her even though the repairs had not been effected, and that the shipowner's remedy lay in damages; *Howard Marine and Dredging Co Ltd v A Ogden & Sons (Excavations) Ltd* [1978] 1 Lloyd's Rep 334, CA, where there was a misrepresentation by the owners as to the deadweight capacity of two barges; *CN Marine Inc v Stena Line AB and Regie Voor Maritiem Transport, The Stena Nautica* [1982] 2 Lloyd's Rep 323, CA, where the charterers had an option to buy a vessel, and the shipowners had agreed to sell her to a third party, and the charterers applied for an injunction to stop the sale; *CN Marine Inc v Stena Line A/B and Regie Voor Maritiem Transport, The Stena Nautica (No 2)* [1982] 2 Lloyd's Rep 336, CA, where the charterers applied for a decree of specific performance.
14 (1866) LR 2 QB 86. Chorley and Tucker's *Leading Cases* (4th edn 1962), p 290.

to the charter-party. Goods were shipped at Oporto by persons ignorant of the charter-party, under bills of lading signed by the master.
Held, the charter-party did not amount to a demise. Consequently, the master's signature to the bill of lading bound the shipowner.

But, in *Baumvoll Manufactur Von Carl Scheibler v Furness*[15]

The charter-party provided for the hire of the ship for four months, the charterer to find the ship's stores and pay the master and crew, insurance and maintenance of the ship to be paid by the shipowner who reserved power to appoint the chief engineer.
Held, that the charter-party amounted to a demise because the possession and control of the ship vested in the charterer. Hence the shipowner was *not* liable to shippers ignorant of the charter-party for the loss of goods shipped under bills of lading signed by the master.

In view of the relative unimportance of charter-parties by demise, the following pages will deal only with those charter-parties which do not deprive the owner of possession of his ship.

VOYAGE CHARTER-PARTIES

(1) The principal clauses in voyage charter-parties

The shipowner and charterer[16] are quite free to make their contract[17] in any form that they choose. But usually they use charter-parties in a standard form, eg one of the many which are approved by the Documentary Committee of the Chamber of Shipping of the United Kingdom. The terms found in them vary according to the type of trade concerned. The approved forms are usually referred to by their

15 [1893] AC 8. Chorley and Tucker's *Leading Cases* (4th edn 1962), p 290.
16 For a case where it was alleged that a person signed a charter-party as an agent for the receivers of the cargo and it was held that he had incurred a personal liability under the charter-party, see *Etablissement Biret et Cie SA v Yukiteru Kaiun KK and Nissui Shipping Corpn, The Sun Happiness* [1984] 1 Lloyd's Rep 381, QBD (Commercial Court). (See the judgment of Lloyd J, Figli SNC ibid, at 384.)
17 Whether a contract has, in fact, been concluded is a matter of construction in each case. See eg *Asty Maritime Co Ltd v Rocco Giuseppe and Panagiotis Stravelakis Figli SNC, The Astyanax* [1985] 2 Lloyd's Rep 109, CA (exchange of telexes between brokers); *Hofflinghouse & Co Ltd v C-Trade SA, The Intra Transporter* [1986] 2 Lloyd's Rep 132, CA (exchange of telexes between parties); *Star Steamship Society v Beogradska Plovidba, The Junior K* [1988] 2 Lloyd's Rep 583, QBD (Commercial Court). For a case where the question was whether a charter-party entered into by an agent without authority had been ratified by the principal, see *Shell Co of Australia Ltd v Nat Shipping Bagging Services Ltd, The Kilmun* [1988] 2 Lloyd's Rep 1, CA.

'code names', eg 'Gencon',[18] 'Russwood'. The parties are, of course, entitled to make such amendments to the terms to be found in the printed forms as they think fit.[19]

In general, the following provisions are found in most voyage charter-parties:

(1) The shipowner agrees to provide a ship and states her position, her capacity and class on the register.

(2) As to the preliminary voyage to the port of loading, the shipowner promises that the ship shall proceed with reasonable despatch.[20]

(3) The shipowner makes certain representations of fact regarding the ship, eg that she is 'tight, staunch, and in every way fitted for the voyage'.[1]

(4) The shipowner undertakes to carry the goods to their destination.

(5) The charterer agrees to provide a full cargo.[2]

(6) The charterer agrees to pay freight.[3] This is usually so much per ton of goods or per cubic foot of space.[4]

(7) A list of excepted perils. These exceptions are often made mutually operative.[5]

(8) Provisions regulating the manner of loading and discharge,[6] and especially the time to be allowed for these operations,[7] and the rate of demurrage.[8]

(9) A cancelling clause, giving the charterer the right to cancel the contract in the event of non-arrival of the ship by a certain day at a certain port.[9]

(10) A 'general paramount clause', the purpose of which is to incorporate the Hague-Visby Rules.[10]

18 The 'Gencon' Form is reproduced in Appendix B by the courtesy of the Baltic and International Maritime Conference.
19 On the relation between the printed and the written words, see p 131, post.
20 See pp 140–141, post.   1 See p 18, post.
 2 See pp 150–153, post.   3 See pp 257–272, post.
 4 Ibid.
 5 See pp 181–189, post.
 6 See pp 149–150, 162–163, post.
 7 See pp 237–238, post.
 8 See pp 252–253, post.
 9 See pp 141–143, post.
10 See p 93, post. For a case where the charter-party incorporated the Rules as set out in the United States Carriage of Goods by Sea Act 1936, see *Seven Seas Transportation Ltd v Pacifico Union Marina Corpn, The Satya Kailash and Ocean Amity* [1984] 1 Lloyd's Rep 586, CA. (See the judgment of Robert Goff LJ, ibid, at 594.)

(11) The 'amended Jason clause'.[11]
(12) A 'both-to-blame collision clause'.[12]
(13) An arbitration clause.[13]
(14) A clause concerning payment of commission to the ship-broker for negotiating the charter-party.
(15) A 'cesser' clause.[14]
(16) A war clause.[15]
(17) A clause incorporating the York-Antwerp Rules 1974 relating to general average.[16]

---

11 See pp 224–226, post.   **12** See pp 186–187, post.

13 See eg *Liberian Shipping Corpn v A King & Sons Ltd* [1967] 2 QB 86, [1967] 1 All ER 934, CA, where the clause stated: 'Any claim must be made in writing and Claimants' Arbitrator appointed within 3 months of final discharge, and where this provision is not complied with the claim shall be deemed to be waived and absolutely barred'; *Det Dansk-Franske Dampskibsselskab A/S v Compagnie Financière d' Investissements Transatlantiques SA (Compafina), The Himmerland* [1965] 2 Lloyd's Rep 353, where it was held that an arbitration clause in the above form barred a claim even though the cause of action giving rise to the claim had not arisen or come to the knowledge of the claimant until too late to enable him to comply with the clause; *Tradax Export SA v Volkswagenwerk AG* [1970] 1 QB 537, [1970] 1 All ER 420, CA, where it was held that a person was not 'appointed' as an arbitrator where he had only been nominated and had not been actually informed of the nomination (see p 173, post); *Astro Vencedor Compania Naviera SA of Panama v Mabanaft GmbH* [1971] 2 QB 588, [1971] 2 All ER 1301, CA, where the arbitration clause was held to be wide enough to cover a dispute arising out of the arrest of a vessel; *Transamerican Ocean Contractors v Transchemical Rotterdam BV, The Ioanna* [1978] 1 Lloyd's Rep 238, CA, where a clause stating that 'general average and arbitration was to be settled according to the York–Antwerp Rules', and was held not to cover disputes as to demurrage, but only those relating to general average. For a case where a third party guaranteed that the charterers would pay such amount as was awarded by an arbitrator, see *Compania Sudamericana de Fletes SA v African Continental Bank Ltd, The Rosarina* [1973] 1 Lloyd's Rep 21, QBD (Commercial Court); *Furness Withy (Australia) Pty Ltd v Metal Distributors (UK) Ltd, The Amazonia* [1989] 1 Lloyd's Rep 403, QBD (Commercial Court), where the clause was void because it conflicted with the (Australian) Sea-Carriage of Goods Act 1924, s 9(1). (See the judgment of Gatehouse J, ibid at 406.)

14 See pp 254–256, post.

15 See eg 'Gencon' form, clause 16. Usually, the shipowner takes out a war risks insurance policy, but where the vessel is to enter certain areas, additional war risk premiums may be payable by the charterer. See eg *Islamic Republic of Iran Shipping Lines v P & O Bulk Shipping Ltd, The Discaria* [1985] 2 Lloyd's Rep 489, QBD (Commercial Court), where the voyage was wholly within the Persian Gulf.

16 See chapter 9, post.

(18) A clause relating to the duty of the master to sign bills of lading.[17]

The interpretation and effect of the above clauses are discussed in this chapter and the ones which follow, but first it is necessary to consider what undertakings are implied by law.

(2) Implied undertakings in voyage charter-parties

It is a general rule of law that the Courts will not imply a particular term in a contract merely because it would have been reasonable for the parties to have inserted such a term. Nevertheless, it is well recognised, as Lord Wright said,[18]

'that there may be cases where obviously some term must be implied if the intention of the parties is not to be defeated, some term of which it can be predicated that 'it goes without saying,' some term not expressed but necessary to give to the transaction such business efficacy as the parties must have intended.'

(A) ON THE PART OF THE SHIPOWNER

In the case of a voyage charter-party the shipowner impliedly undertakes:

(1) to provide a seaworthy ship;

---

17 See eg 'Gencon' form, clause 9. Where a clause states that the master is to sign bills of lading 'in the form appearing at the end of the charter-party for all cargo shipped', and a bill of lading with blank spaces (eg the date of the charter-party and the names of the parties) is presented to him for signature, he is under no duty to sign it; *Garbis Maritime Corpn v Philippine National Oil Co, The Garbis* [1982] 2 Lloyd's Rep 283, QBD (Commercial Court). (See the judgment of Robert Goff J, ibid, at 288.) Where a master signs a bill of lading without noticing that the date has been incorrectly inserted by the charterer, there is no implied promise by the shipowner to ensure that the bill does, in fact, bear the correct date, for the inclusion of a wrong date must have involved a want of care on the part of the charterer: *Rudolph A Oetker v IFA Internationale Frachagentur AG, The Almak* [1985] 1 Lloyd's Rep 557, QBD (Commercial Court); *Boukadoura Maritime Corpn v Marocaine de l'Industrie et du Raffinage SA, The Boukadoura* [1989] 1 Lloyd's Rep 393, QBD (Commercial Court), where the charter-party stated: 'Bills of lading shall be signed by the master as presented . . . the charterer shall indemnify the owner against all consequences or liabilities which may arise from . . . an irregularity in papers supplied by the charterer . . .', and the master rightly refused to sign a bill of lading unless it was claused as to the quantity he considered had been loaded, and the vessel was delayed in sailing. For the measure of damages, see the judgment of Evans J, ibid at 402).

18 In *Luxor (Eastbourne) Ltd v Cooper* [1941] AC 108 at 137, [1941] 1 All ER 33 at 52.

(2) that she shall proceed with reasonable despatch; and
(3) that she shall proceed without unjustifiable deviation.

These undertakings may, however, be varied or excluded by clear and unambiguous terms in the contract.

(1) *Seaworthiness*

The implied undertaking is that the ship shall, when the voyage begins, be seaworthy for that particular voyage and for the cargo carried.[19] Thus, the standard varies with every adventure. The shipowner undertakes not merely that he has taken every precaution, but that, in fact, the ship is seaworthy. It is no defence that he did not know of the existence of a defect.[20] But his undertaking relates merely to the ordinary perils likely to be encountered on such a voyage with the cargo agreed on. He does not guarantee that the ship will withstand any weather, however stormy. The following test has been laid down:[1]

Would a prudent owner have required the defect to be remedied before sending his ship to sea if he had known of it? If he would, the ship was unseaworthy.

Unseaworthiness includes lack of sufficient bunker fuel for the voyage, or, where the voyage is a long one and the ship will fuel at ports of call, for the particular stage of the voyage during which the loss occurs.[2]

Thus, in *The Vortigern*[3]

A vessel sailed on her voyage from the Philippines to Liverpool. The charter-party excluded liability for the negligence of the master and engineers. The voyage was divided into stages. She called at Colombo, but did not take on sufficient coal for the next stage to Suez. When she was near a coaling station, the master did not take on any more fuel for he was not warned by the engineer that supplies were running short. Some of the cargo had to be burned as fuel to enable her to get to Suez.
Held, the shipowners could not plead the exception clause for they had not made the vessel seaworthy at the commencement of each stage of the voyage.

Unseaworthiness also includes an avoidable excess of coal which makes it necessary for the ship to incur expenses for lightening.[4]

---

19 *Stanton v Richardson* (1874) LR 9 CP 390.
20 *The Glenfruin* (1885) 10 PD 103.
 1 *McFadden v Blue Star Line* [1905] 1 KB 697 at 706.
 2 *The Vortigern* [1899] P 140. See also *Northumbrian Shipping Co Ltd v E Timm & Son Ltd* [1939] AC 397, [1939] 2 All ER 648.
 3 [1899] P 140.
 4 *Darling v Raeburn* [1907] 1 KB 846.

Even though a shipowner has not installed the latest appliances, the vessel may still be held to be seaworthy.[5]

The shipowner's duty to provide a seaworthy ship comprises a duty to have her loading and discharging tackle available for the ordinary purposes of loading and discharging.[6]

Although a charter-party provides that stowing, trimming and discharging are to be performed and paid for by the charterers, the shipowner is still under an obligation to have the ship's gear available for their use.[7]

Since the ship must be seaworthy with reference to the cargo agreed on, proper appliances to deal with special cargoes are necessary.

Thus, it will be seen that in reality the undertaking is twofold:

(1) That the ship is fit to receive the particular cargo at the time of loading. A defect arising after the cargo has been shipped is no breach of this undertaking.[8]

(2) That she is seaworthy at the time of sailing.[9]

The effect of unseaworthiness. The undertaking to provide a seaworthy vessel is one of a complex character which cannot be categorised as being a 'condition' or a 'warranty'. It embraces obligations with respect to every part of the hull and machinery, stores, equipment and the crew. It can be broken by the presence of trivial defects easily and rapidly remediable as well as by defects which must inevitably result in a total loss of the vessel. Consequently the problem is not soluble by considering whether the undertaking is a 'condition' or a 'warranty'. The undertaking is an undertaking, one breach of which may give rise to an event which relieves the charterer of further performance of his part of the contract if he so elects, and another breach of which entitles him to monetary compensation in the form of damages.[10]

---

5   *Virginia Carolina Chemical Co v Norfolk and North American Steam Shipping Co* [1912] 1 KB 229, CA.

6   *Hang Fung Shipping and Trading Co Ltd v Mullion & Co Ltd* [1966] 1 Lloyd's Rep 511, where the shipowner did not make the necessary gear available, and the charterers were held to be entitled to claim reimbursement of the expenses which they had incurred in hiring additional labour.

7   Ibid.

8   *McFadden v Blue Star Line* [1905] 1 KB 697.

9   *Cohn v Davidson* (1877) 2 QBD 455.

10   *Hong Kong Fir Shipping Co Ltd v Kawasaki Kisen Kaisha Ltd* [1962] 1 All ER 474 at 487–488, CA (per Diplock LJ). (See also the judgment of Upjohn LJ, ibid, at 483–484.)

If the charterer or shipper discovers that the ship is unseaworthy before the voyage begins, and the defect cannot be remedied within a reasonable time, he may repudiate the contract. Thus, in *Stanton v Richardson*[11]

A ship was chartered to take a cargo including wet sugar. When the bulk of the sugar had been loaded, it was found that the pumps were not of sufficient capacity to remove the drainage from the sugar, and the cargo had to be discharged. Adequate pumping machinery could not be obtained for a considerable time, and the charterer refused to reload.

Held, the ship was unseaworthy for the cargo agreed on, and, as she could not be made fit within a reasonable time, the charterer was justified in refusing to reload.

After the voyage has begun, the charterer is no longer in a position to rescind the contract, but can claim damages for any loss caused by initial unseaworthiness.

Further, although the vessel is unseaworthy, the shipowner can still rely on the exception clauses in the charter-party, if the loss has not been caused by unseaworthiness.

Thus, in *The Europa*[12]

A ship was chartered for the carriage of a cargo of sugar from Stettin to Liverpool, and one of the excepted perils in the charter-party was 'collision'. On entering the dock at Liverpool the ship struck the dock wall. A water-closet pipe was broken and water got through it into the 'tween decks, and some sugar stowed there was damaged. In the 'tween decks near to the water-closet pipe were two scupper holes. The pipes which had originally been affixed to, and led from, these two scupper holes for the purpose of carrying off water from the 'tween decks to the bilges had been removed, and the scupper holes had been imperfectly plugged, with the result that water from the broken closet-pipe got through the scupper holes and passed into the sugar stowed in the lower hold. It was not disputed that this imperfect plugging existed before the cargo was loaded, and that thereby the ship was unseaworthy. The owners of the *Europa* did not therefore dispute their liability for the damage to the sugar in the lower hold, admitting that it was caused by the unseaworthiness. But they did dispute their liability for the damage to the sugar in the 'tween decks.

Held, that they were not liable for this damage. Once the cargo had been loaded the owners could be made responsible only in damages. The breach of the undertaking of seaworthiness did not displace the terms of the contract. The damage to the sugar in the 'tween decks was caused not by unseaworthiness, but by the collision, and so the owners were entitled to rely on the exception clause.

Where the ship is seaworthy when she sails, but becomes unseaworthy while at sea, the incidence of liability will be determined

---

11 (1874) LR 9 CP 390.
12 [1908] P 84. Chorley and Tucker's *Leading Cases* (4th edn 1962), p 303. See also *Smith, Hogg & Co Ltd v Black Sea and Baltic General Insurance Co Ltd* [1940] AC 997, [1940] 3 All ER 405; *Monarch SS Co Ltd v Karlshamns Oljefabriker AB* [1949] AC 196, [1949] 1 All ER 1.

not by reference to the undertaking (of which, of course, there has been no breach) but by reference to the cause of the loss. If the loss was due to an excepted peril, the shipowner will be protected, otherwise he will not.

It should, however, be observed that where fire results from unseaworthiness, the owner of the ship may be able to invoke the Merchant Shipping Act 1979, s 18,[13] and so escape liability.[14]

Express and implied undertakings as to seaworthiness. A clause in a charter-party stating that the ship is to be 'tight, staunch, and strong, and in every way fitted for the voyage', relates to the preliminary voyage to the port of loading. It refers to the time at which the contract is made[15] or to the time of sailing *for* the port of loading.

The undertaking of seaworthiness implied by law, on the other hand, relates to the time of sailing *from* the port of loading.

The express undertaking, therefore, does not displace the undertaking implied by law. Thus, in *Seville Sulphur Co v Colvils*[16]

Under a charter-party containing the above clause the ship was to proceed to Seville and there load. The ship was unseaworthy on leaving Seville.
Held, this was a breach of the undertaking implied by law.

A breach of the implied undertaking of seaworthiness at the port of loading entitles the charterer to refuse to load;[17] but a breach of the express undertaking does not, unless it is such as to frustrate the object of the charter-party.[18] This difference arises from the different times to which the express and the implied undertakings relate. The charterer's obligation to load is conditional on the ship being seaworthy at the port of loading, not on her being seaworthy at the time the contract was made.

Burden of proving unseaworthiness. The burden of proving unseaworthiness is on those who allege it, and there is no presumption of law that a ship is unseaworthy because she breaks down or even sinks from an unexplained cause. Nevertheless in rare cases the facts may raise an inference of unseaworthiness and so shift the burden of proof.

13   See pp 201–202 and Appendix D, post.
14   *Louis Dreyfus & Co v Tempus SS Co* [1931] AC 726.
15   *Scott v Foley* (1899) 5 Com Cas 53.
16   1888 25 SLR 437.
17   *Stanton v Richardson*, p 16, ante.
18   *Tarrabochia v Hickie* (1856) 26 LJEx 26.

Thus, in *Fiumana Societa di Navigazione v Bunge & Co Ltd*[19]

An unexplained fire in the coal bunkers occurred.
Held, it could be presumed that this was due to unfitness of the bunker coal at the time of loading of the cargo which amounted to a breach of the undertaking of seaworthiness.

Excluding liability for unseaworthiness. The shipowner can, however, exempt himself from liability for unseaworthiness, but if he wishes to do so, he must use clear and unambiguous language.[20]

Thus, in *Nelson Line (Liverpool) Ltd v James Nelson & Sons Ltd*[1]

Frozen meat had been shipped under an agreement which stated that the shipowner would not be liable for any damage 'which is capable of being covered by insurance'. The meat arrived in a damaged condition on account of the unseaworthiness of the vessel.
Held, that the clause was not sufficiently clear to exempt the shipowner from being liable to supply a seaworthy ship.

Sometimes the shipowner exempts himself from liability for unseaworthiness only where the loss or damage is caused by personal want of due diligence on his part or that of his employees to make the vessel in all respects seaworthy.

Thus, cl 2 of the 'Gencon'[2] charter-party provides:

'Owners are to be responsible for loss of or damage to goods . . . only in case the loss, damage has been caused . . . by personal want of due diligence on the part of the Owners or their Manager to make the vessel in all respects seaworthy . . .'

In *Itoh & Co Ltd v Atlantska Plovidba, The Gundulic*[3]

The vessel 'Gundulic' was chartered for a voyage under a charter-party containing the above clause. The cargo was damaged by the entry of seawater through the hatch covers. The charterers claimed damages from the shipowners.
Held, by the Queen's Bench Division (Commercial Court), that there would be judgment for the charterers. The condition of the hatch covers was such that any prudent surveyor ought to have seen a real risk that seawater would enter the holds through them, and would have called for repairs. The shipowners had failed to discharge the burden of showing that the damage had occurred without any personal want of due diligence on the part of a junior engineer superintendent employed by them.[4]

19 [1930] 2 KB 47.
20 See further for similar clauses in bills of lading, pp 111–112, post.
1 [1908] AC 16, [1904–7] All ER Rep 244, HL.
2 See Appendix B, post.
3 [1981] 2 Lloyd's Rep 418, QBD (Commercial Court).
4 See the judgment of Lloyd J, ibid, at 425.

(2) *Reasonable despatch*

The shipowner undertakes that the ship shall proceed on the voyage with reasonable despatch. Thus, in *M'Andrew v Adams*[5]

By the terms of a charter-party dated 20 October 1832, a vessel was to proceed from Portsmouth where she was then lying to St Michaels (in the Azores) and there load a cargo of fruit and return to London. On 7 November, instead of proceeding direct to St Michaels she went on an intermediate voyage to Oporto, and returned later to Portsmouth, from where she finally sailed for St Michaels on 6 December.
Held, that the shipowner was liable to the charterer for breach of the implied undertaking that the voyage should be commenced within a reasonable time.

Further, in the case of a consecutive voyage charter-party the shipowner's obligation to proceed with despatch applies to every voyage made under it.[6]

If the shipowner fails to carry out this undertaking, the shipper's remedy depends on whether the failure is such as to frustrate the venture as a commercial enterprise. If it is, he may repudiate the contract;[7] if it is not, he has an action for damages for the delay,[8] but to this the plea of excepted perils is a good answer.[9]

It should be noted that this rule of law is distinct from the doctrine which we shall notice,[10] whereby a contract of affreightment may be dissolved by implication on account of the frustration of the adventure due to unforeseen events *totally unconnected with any breach* of the contract by either party. For the effect of the frustration is different in the two cases: where there has been a breach of the implied undertaking of reasonable despatch resulting in frustration, only the shipper is released from his obligations; but where the frustration is independent of any breach, e g where war subsequently breaks out, the release is mutual.

The one rule is a particular application of the general principle that a failure to perform his part of the contract by one contractor may, according to the circumstances, be of so serious a nature as to justify the other contractor in treating it as a repudiation of the

5   (1834) 1 Bing NC 29.
6   *Suisse Atlantique Société d' Armement Maritime SA v Rotterdamsche Kolen Centrale NV* [1967] 1 AC 361, [1966] 2 All ER 61, HL.
7   *Freeman v Taylor* (1831) 1 LJCP 26.
8   *CHZ Rolimpex v Eftavrysses Compania Naviera SA, The Panaghia Tinnou* [1986] 2 Lloyd's Rep 586, QBD (Commercial Court), where it was not established that any except nominal damages were attributable to the shipowners' breach in failing to prosecute the voyage with reasonable despatch.
9   *Barker v M'Andrew* (1865) 18 CBNS 759.
10   See pp 70–78, post.

entire contract; the other rule is a modification[11] of an ancient and rigorous doctrine which excluded the grafting upon a contract, under any circumstances, of an exception which would operate as an excuse for its non-performance.[12]

(3) *No deviation*

It is an implied condition precedent in every voyage charter-party that the ship shall proceed on the voyage without departure from her proper course. If the route is not prescribed in the contract, the proper course is the ordinary trade route. 'If no evidence be given, that route is presumed to be the direct geographical route, but . . . evidence may always be given to show what the usual route is, unless a specific route be prescribed by the charter-party or bill of lading. . . . In some cases there may be more than one usual route'.[13]

It must, however, be observed that 'the essence of deviation is the voluntary substitution of another voyage for the contract voyage'. Hence, where the master, who was ill, unintentionally steered a wrong course, it was held that there had been no deviation.[14]

When deviation is justified at Common Law. In certain cases deviation will be justified, apart from any express terms of the contract, and will, therefore, not expose the shipowner to liability. These are:

(1) For purposes necessary for the prosecution of the voyage or for the safety of the adventure.

One of the main duties of the master is to use all reasonable care to bring the adventure to a successful conclusion, protecting the ship and cargo from undue risks, as agent for the shipowner. Considerable latitude is thus given to him in the matter of taking the ship off her proper course. If the ship sustains such damage that repairs are necessary, he must put into the nearest port at which such repairs can be effected.[15] The same doctrine applies in the case of any other grave peril threatening the ship or her cargo,[16] e g pirates, hurricanes, icebergs or heavy fog.

The deviation is still justified, even though necessitated by the

---

11 First clearly stated in *Taylor v Caldwell* (1863) 3 B & S 826.
12 The rule in *Paradine v Jane* (1647) Aleyn 26.
13 *Reardon Smith Lines Ltd v Black Sea and Baltic General Insurance Co Ltd, The Indian City* [1939] AC 562 at 584, [1939] 3 All ER 444 at 457, per Lord Porter.
14 *Rio Tinto Co v Seed Shipping Co* (1926) 42 TLR 381.
15 *James Phelps & Co v Hill* [1891] 1 QB 605.
16 *The Teutonia* (1872) LR 4 PC 171.

ship's unseaworthiness at the commencement of the voyage, if, in fact, it would be dangerous to keep her at sea without effecting such repairs.[17]

Thus, in *Kish v Taylor*[18]

The master of a vessel took on board an excessive load of deck cargo to such an extent that she was rendered unseaworthy. As a result of the unseaworthiness she was obliged to deviate from her normal route in order to proceed to a port for repairs. *Held*, that the deviation was justifiable.

Lord Atkinson said:[19]

'Must the master of every ship be left in this dilemma, that whenever, by his own culpable act, or a breach of contract by his owner, he finds his ship in a perilous position, he must continue on his voyage at all hazards, or only seek safety under the penalty of forfeiting the contract of affreightment? Nothing could, it would appear to me, tend more to increase the dangers to which life and property are exposed at sea than to hold that the law of England obliged the master of a merchant ship to choose between such alternatives.'

(2) To save human life.

Deviation to save human life is always justified, but not to save property, unless this is expressly stipulated. Thus, in *Scaramanga v Stamp*[20]

A ship deviated to assist another in distress, but instead of merely saving the crew, attempted to earn salvage by towing the distressed vessel into port, and, in the attempt, went ashore herself and was lost with her cargo. *Held*, that the shipowers was liable for the loss of the cargo although it was partly caused by 'perils of the sea' which were excepted by the charter-party.

Express clauses permitting deviation. The terms of the contract often give the shipowner the right to call at ports off the ordinary trade route. Vague general terms, however, will not be taken to confer an unlimited right to turn aside.

A clause[1] often gives liberty to the vessel to tow or assist vessels, or both, in all situations, and also to deviate for the purpose of saving life or property, or both, and to comply with any orders given by the government of the nation under whose flag she sails or by any other government.[2]

17 *Kish v Taylor* [1912] AC 604. Lord Porter expressed the opinion that the rule does not apply if the owners knew of the vessel's state on sailing: *Monarch SS Co Ltd v AB Karlshamns Oljefabriker* [1949] 1 All ER 1 at 5. This, with respect, seems open to question.
18 Supra.
19 [1912] AC at 618–19.
20 (1880) 5 CPD 295.
1 For an example, see the 'Gencon' charter-party, clause 3 (Appendix B).
2 See *Luigi Monta of Genoa v Cechofracht Co Ltd* [1956] 2 QB 552, [1956] 2 All ER 769.

The effect of unjustifiable deviation. In a leading case, Lord Atkin observed:[3]

'I venture to think that the true view is that the departure from the voyage contracted to be made is a breach by the shipowner of his contract, a breach of such a serious character that, however slight the deviation, the other party to the contract is entitled to treat it as going to the root of the contract, and to declare himself as no longer bound by any of the contract terms. . . . If this view be correct, then the breach by deviation does not automatically cancel the express contract, otherwise the shipowner by his own wrong can get rid of his own contract.'

The charterer, however, can elect to treat the contract as subsisting, and if he does this with knowledge of his rights, he must, in accordance with the general law of contract, be held bound.[4] But there must be acts which plainly show that he intended to treat the contract as still binding.[5]

If a charter-party, although for two consecutive voyages, is held to be one indivisible contract, a deviation on the first voyage entitles the charterer to treat the breach as a repudiation of the whole contract.[6]

Where there has been unjustifiable deviation, the shipowner cannot rely on the exception clauses in the charter-party, and is then only entitled to the benefit of the exceptions available to a common carrier, eg act of God, loss by the Queen's Enemies, if he can prove that the loss would have occured even if no deviation had taken place.[7]

Further, the shipowner cannot claim the contractual rate of freight payable under the charter-party, but may be entitled to a reasonable sum if the goods are carried to their destination safely.[8] Again, he cannot claim a general average contribution from the charterer unless the breach of contract by the deviation being made has been waived.[9]

Finally, where there has been an unjustified deviation, the

---

3 *Hain SS Co Ltd v Tate and Lyle Ltd* [1936] 2 All ER 597 at 601, HL.
4 Ibid.
5 *Hain SS Co Ltd v Tate and Lyle Ltd*, supra.
6 *Compagnie Primera de Navigaziona Panama v Compania Arrendataria de Monopolio de Petroleos SA, The Yolanda* [1940] 1 KB 362, [1939] 4 All ER 81, CA.
7 *James Morrison & Co Ltd v Shaw, Savill and Albion Co Ltd* [1916] 2 KB 783.
8 *Hain SS Co Ltd v Tate and Lyle Ltd*, supra.
9 Ibid.

shipowner cannot rely on any clause in the charter-party entitling him to limit his liability[10] or to claim demurrage.[11]

(B) ON THE PART OF THE CHARTERER NOT TO SHIP DANGEROUS GOODS

The charterer impliedly undertakes that he will not ship dangerous goods.[12] Even if the master accepts them on board, the charterer will be liable for any loss or damage they may cause,[13] unless the master has acted unreasonably in carrying them.[14]

Sometimes charter-parties expressly prohibit the loading of dangerous goods, but sometimes a charterer is entitled by an express term to load them provided that due notice is given to the master.

Goods may be 'dangerous' not merely by reason of the fact that they may endanger the safety of the vessel, e g (i) iron ore concentrate with a high moisture content;[15] (ii) copper concentrate,[16] but also because they are liable to cause her to be detained.

Thus, in *Mitchell, Cotts & Co v Steel Bros & Co Ltd*[17]

The charterers loaded a cargo of rice on board a vessel, and sent her to a port where they knew that it could not be discharged without the permission of the British Government. They did not inform the shipowners of this. Permission was refused and the ship was delayed.
Held, that the charterers were liable for damages for the delay.

Statutory provisions concerning dangerous goods. The following statutes make provision with regard to dangerous goods:

(1) The Merchant Shipping Act 1894, ss 446–50.[18] By s 446 a consignor of dangerous goods must indicate the nature of the

---

10   *Cunard SS Co Ltd v Buerger* [1927] AC 1, HL. As to limitation of liability, see pp 202–210, post.
11   *United States Shipping Board v Bunge y Born Ltda Sociedad* (1925) 134 LT 303, [1925] All ER Rep, 173, HL. As to demurrage, see pp 236–256, post.
12   For the meaning of 'dangerous goods', see infra.
13   *Chandris v Isbrandtsen-Moller Co Inc* [1951] 1 KB 240, [1950] 1 All ER 768.
14   *Compania Naviera Maropan SA v Bowaters Lloyd Pulp and Paper Mills* [1955] 2 QB 68, [1955] 2 All ER 241, CA (similar principle applied concerning safe port).
15   *Micada Compania Naviera SA v Texim* [1968] 2 Lloyd's Rep 57, QBD (Commercial Court). For the evidence on this point, see the judgment of Donaldson J, ibid, at 60, 62.
16   *Heath Steele Mines Ltd v The Erwin Schroder* [1969] 1 Lloyd's Rep 370, Exchequer Court of Canada, Nova Scotia Admiralty District. For the evidence on this point, see the judgment of Pottier J, ibid, at 373.
17   [1916] 2 KB 610, [1916–17] All ER Rep 578.
18   See Appendix D, post.

goods on the outside of the packages, and must give notice of the nature of the goods to the master or owner of the vessel at or before the time of shipment.

(2) The Merchant Shipping (Safety Convention) Act 1949, s 23 enables rules to be made by the Secretary of State for the Environment for regulating in the interests of safety the carriage of dangerous goods.[19] Goods declared by the rules to be dangerous are deemed to be 'dangerous goods' for the purposes of the 1894 Act.

(3) The Explosive Substances Act 1883, s 8 enables the master or owner of a vessel to search the cargo for dangerous goods, if he has reasonable grounds for suspecting that such goods are concealed on board.

TIME CHARTER-PARTIES

(A) The principal clauses in time charter-parties

Although the parties are entitled to make their contract in any manner that they like,[20] it is usual for them to adopt one of the forms of time charter-party approved by the Documentary Committee of the Chamber of Shipping of the United Kingdom, e g the 'Transitime' form or the 'Baltime 1939' form,[1] and then amend it as they think fit.

In general, the following provisions are found in most time charter-parties:

(1) The shipowner[2] agrees to provide a vessel[3] for a period of

---

19 The relevant rules are the Merchant Shipping (Dangerous Goods) Regulations 1981, SI 1981/1747.

20 Whether a contract has, in fact, been concluded is a matter of construction in each case. See e g *Orri v Seawind Navigation Co SA, The Winner* [1986] 1 Lloyd's Rep 36, QBD (Commercial Court).

1 The 'Baltime' form is reproduced in Appendix B by the courtesy of the Baltic and International Maritime Conference.

2 For a case where a clause in a charter-party stated the name of the owner/manager of a vessel and the charterers objected to the appointment of new managers, and it was held that the clause was never intended to deal with management except to record as a fact who was the owner/manager, see *European Banking Corpn v Total Transport Corpn, The Katingo Colocotronis* [1978] 1 Lloyd's Rep 388, QBD (Commercial Court). (See the judgment of Donaldson J, ibid, at 390.)

3 Or a substitute. see p 27, post.

time, and states her size, speed,[4] fuel consumption, and amount of fuel on board;

(2) the port of delivery and the time of delivery of the vessel to the charterer are stated;

(3) the charterer agrees to engage only in lawful trades and carry lawful merchandise,[5] and only use good and safe ports where the vessel can 'safely lie always afloat';

(4) the shipowner agrees to pay for the crew's wages,[6] for the vessel's insurance and her stores, and promises to maintain her in a thoroughly efficient state;[7]

(5) the charterer agrees to provide and pay for fuel,[8] to pay dock and harbour dues, and arrange and pay for loading and discharge;[9]

(6) the charterer agrees to pay a named sum for the hire of the vessel;[10]

(7) a clause concerns the redelivery of the vessel;[11]

(8) certain events are stated on the occurrence of which hire will cease to be payable;[12]

(9) the master is to be under the orders of the charterer;[13]

(10) a list of 'excepted perils';[14]

(11) the charterer agrees to indemnify the shipowner for loss or damage to the vessel by careless loading or discharge;[15]

(12) a cancelling clause;[16]

(13) a clause incorporates the York-Antwerp Rules 1974 relating to general average;[17]

4   *Steelwood Carriers Inc of Monrovia, Liberia v Evimeria Compania Naviera SA of Panama, The Agios Giorgis* [1976] 2 Lloyd's Rep 192, QBD (Commercial Court); *Cosmos Bulk Transport Inc v China National Foreign Trade Transportation Corpn, The Apollonius* [1978] 1 Lloyd's Rep 53, QBD (Commercial Court). See p 31, post.
5   See p 152, post.
6   See p 35, post.
7   See pp 36–37, post.
8   See p 37, post.
9   See p 38, post.
10 See pp 39–43, post.
11 See pp 59–64, post.
12 See pp 47–51, post.
13 See pp 52–56, post.
14 See pp 56–57, post.
15 See pp 57–58, post.
16 See pp 141–143, post.
17 See chapter 9, post.

(14) an arbitration clause;[18]
(15) a clause concerning payment of commission to the shipbroker for negotiating the charter-party;[19]
(16) a war clause.[20]

Some of the above clauses will now be examined in more detail.

SUBSTITUTION OPTION

A clause sometimes provides that the shipowner is entitled to substitute another vessel during the currency of the charter-party.[1]

Whether or not an option to substitute survives the total loss, actual or constructive, of the vessel currently in service depends on the words of the charter-party.[2]

PERIOD OF HIRE

A usual clause in a time charter-party states the period for which the vessel is let e g

'The Owners let and the Charterers hire the Vessel for a period of the number of calendar months indicated in Box 14 from the time (not a Sunday or a legal holiday unless taken over) the Vessel is delivered and placed at the disposal of the Charterers between 9 a m and 6 p m or between 9 a m and 2 p m if on Saturday at the port stated in Box 15. . . .'[3]

Sometimes the period of time is at the charterers' option, e g '24/30 calendar months in charterers' option at the end of the 22nd month

---

18 See pp 64–65, post.
19 See e g *Les Affréteurs Réunis Société Anonyme v Leopold Walford (London) Ltd* [1919] AC 801; *Christie and Vesey v Maatschappij Tot Exploitatie Van Schepen en Andere Zaken, The Helvetia* [1960] 1 Lloyd's Rep 540.
20 See e g *Ocean Tramp Tankers Corpn v Sovfracht V/O, The Eugenia* [1964] 2 QB 226, [1964] 1 All ER 161, CA, where a vessel was trapped in the Suez Canal during the Suez crises of 1956.
 1 *Maritime et Commerciale of Geneva SA v Anglo-Iranian Oil Co Ltd* [1954] 1 All ER 529, [1954] 1 WLR 492 (charter-party for series of voyages); *Niarchos (London) Ltd v Shell Tankers Ltd* [1961] 2 Lloyd's Rep 496; *Terkol Rederierne v Petroleo Brasileiro SA and Frota Nacional de Petroleiros, The Badagry* [1985] 1 Lloyd's Rep 395, CA.
 2 *Terkol Rederierne v Petroleo Brasileiro SA and Frota Nacional de Petroleiros, The Badagry*, supra. See the judgment of Sir John Donaldson, ibid at 397.
 3 'Baltime 1939' form, clause 1 (Appendix B).

with a margin of 15 days more or less at charterers' option from the time the vessel is delivered.'[4]

Sometimes the period of hire is expressed in a different way e g 'the period necessary to perform one time charter trip via safe port(s) East Coast Canada within [specified] trading limits'.[5]

In some charter-parties, the charterer is granted an option to extend the period after the normal expiry date.[6]

DELIVERY

A usual clause[7] states that the vessel is to be delivered at a specified port

'in such available berth where she can safely lie always afloat.'

Where the charter-party does not expressly provide for the time when the charterers have to give directions for the available berth to which the vessel is to go to make her delivery, the necessary inference is that directions have to be given either on arrival at the port or before arrival.[8]

A usual clause[9] relates to the payment for fuel oil and states:

---

4 See *Empresa Cubana de Fletes v Aviation and Shipping Co Ltd* [1969] 2 Lloyd's Rep 257, QBD (Commercial Court), where it was held that the period of 22 months after which the option was to be declared was not affected by another clause in the charter-party concerning time lost through circumstances beyond the charterers' control (see the judgment of Roskill J, ibid, at 261); *Atlantic Lines and Navigation Co Inc v Didymi Corpn and Leon Corpn, The Didymi and Leon* [1984] 1 Lloyd's Rep 583, CA, where a clause stated: '. . . owners agree to let and the . . . charterers to hire the . . . vessel from the time of delivery for 5 years time charter with 3 months more or less in charterers' option to be narrowed to 45 days more or less in charterers option latest by the end of the fourth year'.

5 *Segovia Compagnia Naviera SA v R Pagnan and Fratelli, The Aragon* [1977] 1 Lloyd's Rep 343, CA.

6 See e g *Marseille Fret SA v D Oltmann Schiffahrts GmbH & Co KG, The Trado* [1982] 1 Lloyd's Rep 157, QBD (Commercial Court), where the charter-party was for 6 months, and contained a clause which stated: 'Charterers' option further 6 months to be declared 60 days in advance; 20 days more or less in charterers' option on final period'.

7 See e g 'Baltime 1939' form, clause 1 (Appendix B). For a case where the shipowners failed to deliver a vessel to the charterers for a ninth voyage under a time charter-party, see *Yamashita Shinnihon SS Co Ltd v Elios SpA, The Lily Prima* [1976] 2 Lloyd's Rep 487, CA.

8 *Anders Utkilens Rederi A/S v Compagnie Tunisienne de Navigation of Tunis, The Golfstraum* [1976] 2 Lloyd's Rep 97 at 102 (per Mocatta J).

9 See e g 'Baltime 1939' form, clause 4 (Appendix B).

'The charterers at port of delivery . . . to take over and pay for all . . . fuel-oil remaining in the vessel's bunkers at current price at [that port].'

If the price is not mentioned, it is implied that the charterer must pay a reasonable price i e the market price.[10]

SEAWORTHINESS OF VESSEL

A clause in a charter-party often states:

'The Owners let, and the Charterers hire the Vessel . . . she being in every way fitted for ordinary cargo service.'[11]

A vessel is not in every way fitted for cargo service if at the time of her delivery to the charterers her engine room staff is incompetent and inadequate, and accordingly she is unseaworthy.[12]

Again, shipowners were held to be in breach of the clause set out above if at the time of the delivery of the vessel to the charterers she had not a deratisation certificate from the port health authorities or a deratisation exemption certificate, for without the certificate she could not trade as the charter-party provided or for the contemplated purpose.[13]

But the words 'fitted for ordinry service' do not require the provision of a 'blue' certificate demanded by some extra-legal grouping such as the International Transport Workers Federation which would not be granted unless the shipowners agreed to pay the crew a minimum wage.[14]

Thus, in *Alfred C Toepfer Schiffahrtgesellschaft mbH v Tossa Marine Co Ltd, The Derby*[15]

The owners of a Cypriot vessel whose crew were Filipinos let her out to the charterers under a time charter-party, which contained a clause stating that she was 'to be in

10 *Harmony Shipping Co SA v Saudi-Europe Line Ltd, The Good Helmsman* [1981] 1 Lloyd's Rep 377, CA. (See the judgment of Ackner LJ, ibid, at 418.)
11 See e g 'Baltime 1939' form, clause 1 (Appendix B). Sometimes, however, there is no absolute duty to provide a seaworthy vessel, for the clause may state: 'Vessel on delivery shall be, in so far as due diligence can make her so, seaworthy, tight, staunch, strong and in every way suitable . . .'. See e g *United States of America v The Marilena P and Marilena Compania Naviera SA* [1969] 2 Lloyd's Rep 641, US Court of Appeals, Fourth Circuit.
12 *Hong Kong Fir Shipping Co Ltd v Kawasaki Kisen Kaisha Ltd* [1962] 2 QB 26, [1962] 1 All ER 474, CA.
13 *Cheikh Boutros Selim El-Khoury v Ceylon Shipping Lines Ltd, The Madeleine* [1967] 2 Lloyd's Rep 224.
14 *Alfred C Toepfer Schiffahrtsgesellschaft GmbH v Tossa Marine Co Ltd, The Derby* [1985] 2 Lloyd's Rep 325, CA.
15 [1985] 2 Lloyd's Rep 325, CA.

every way fitted for the service'. The International Transport Workers Federation, which looked after the interests of seamen so as to procure the payment of Western levels of wages to all crews, halted her discharge until the shipowners produced a 'blue card' or signed a special agreement with the ITF regarding manning. The vessel did not possess a 'blue card'. The shipowners signed the manning agreement and discharge was resumed. The charterers claimed damages for delay on the ground that the absence of the 'blue card' was a breach of the clause set out above.

Held, by the Court of Appeal, that there would be judgment for the shipowners. The context in which the words 'in every way fitted for the service' occurred showed they related primarily to the physical state of the vessel. They required, however, the provision of a sufficient and competent crew and of documents relevant to the vessel's seaworthiness. But they did not require the provision of a 'blue card'.[16]

The words 'in every way fitted for cargo service' do not impose an absolute obligation on the shipowners to deliver the vessel in a fit condition but only to use reasonable diligence to do so.[17]

It is an inevitable presumption of fact that a vessel is unseaworthy if there is something about her which endangers the safety of her or her cargo or which may cause significant danger to the cargo or which renders it legally or practically impossible for her to go to sea or unload the cargo. Where the characteristic in question has none of those effects but is one which may only cause some delay to the movement of the vessel or to the loading or discharging of her cargo, what its likely effect may be and whether the effect is such as to render her unseaworthy or unfitted are all questions of fact. There is no rule of law having the effect that a defect of no significance nonetheless renders a vessel unseaworthy or unfitted.[18]

Accordingly, where a defect in a vessel's tank cleansing system was of no real significance from a commercial point of view, she was still fitted for the service.[19]

If the vessel is delivered in a damaged condition, the evidence may show that the charterers have waived any claim which they may have against the shipowners.[20]

---

16   See the judgment of Kerr LJ, ibid at 331, and that of Sir Denys Buckley, ibid, at 333.

17   *Marbienes Compania Naviera SA v Ferrostaal AG, The Democritos* [1976] 2 Lloyd's Rep 149, CA. (See the judgment of Lord Denning MR, ibid, at 152).

18   *Athenian Tankers Management SA v Pyrena Shipping Inc, The Arianna* [1987] 2 Lloyd's Rep 376, QBD (Commercial Court), at 389 per Webster J.

19   Ibid. (See the judgment of Webster J, ibid at 390.)

20   See eg *Marbienes Compania Naviera SA v Ferrostaal AG, The Democritos* [1975] 1 Lloyd's Rep 386, QBD (Commercial Court), where the case was remitted to the arbitrators so that they could consider whether there had been a waiver by the charterers. (See the judgment of Kerr J, ibid, at 398.) The case subsequently went to appeal on different points: [1976] 2 Lloyd's Rep 149, CA. See further, *Navigas*

VESSEL'S SPEED

The whole purpose of the description of the vessel containing a speed warranty is that when she enters on her service, she will be capable of the speed in question, subject, of course, to any protection which her owners may obtain if there has been some casualty between the date of the charter-party and the date of delivery affecting her speed which, under an exceptions clause, protects them from liability in relation to a failure to comply with the warranty.[1] Commercial considerations require the description as to the vessel's speed to be applicable as at the date of her delivery whether or not it is applicable at the date of the charter-party.[2]

Thus, in *Cosmos Bulk Transport Inc v China National Foreign Trade Transportation Corpn, The Apollonius*[3]

A vessel which was chartered under a time charter-party was described as capable of steaming at 14½ knots. Due to her bottom being fouled by being encrusted with molluscs, she was only capable of steaming at 10·61 knots.
Held, that the owners were guilty of a breach of warranty, but were protected by an exceptions clause.[4]

The effect of the word 'about' being used in relation to a vessel's speed, eg 'about 15·5 knots' is that some margin has to be recognised on either side of the stated figure. The size of the margin is a question of fact in each case.[5]

USE OF SAFE PORTS ONLY

A usual clause states:[6]

'The vessel to be employed . . . between good and safe ports or places where she can safely lie always afloat.'

International Ltd v Trans-Offshore Inc, The Bridgestone Maru (No 3) [1985] 2 Lloyd's Rep 62, QBD (Commercial Court), where there was an express clause stating 'Owners shall . . . exercise due diligence to make the vessel in every way fit for . . . service'.
1 *Cosmos Bulk Transport Inc v China National Foreign Trade Transportation Corpn, The Apollonius* [1978] 1 Lloyd's Rep 53, QBD (Commercial Court) at 64 (per Mocatta J).
2 Ibid, at 64 (per Mocatta J).
3 [1978] 1 Lloyd's Rep 53, QBD (Commercial Court).
4 As to the exception clause, see p 56, post.
5 *Arab Maritime Petroleum Transport Co v Luxor Trading Panama and Geogas Enterprise Geneva, The Al Bida* [1986] 1 Lloyd's Rep 142, QBD (Commercial Court). (See the judgment of Evans J, ibid, at 148).
6 'Baltime 1939' form, clause 2 (Appendix B, post). See eg *Anders Utkilens Rederi A/S v Lovisa Stevedoring Co O/Y AB, The Golfstraum* [1976] 1 Lloyd's Rep 547,

The phrase 'safely lie always afloat' is concerned exclusively with the marine characteristics of the loading or discharging place and requires that the vessel shall at all times be water-borne and shall be able to remain there without risk of loss or damage from wind, weather or other craft which are properly navigated. Thus, a place which dries out or one in which she might in certain winds or tides lie across the fairway would not be within the requirements of the clause.[7]

If the charterer sends a vessel to a unsafe port,[8] and she is damaged as a result, he will have to indemnify the shipowner.

Thus, in *Grace (G W) & Co Ltd v General Steam Navigation Co Ltd*[9]

A vessel under time charter was directed to Hamburg. The master complied with the charterer's order and she was damaged by ice in the approaches to the port.
Held, the charterer was liable for such damage.

Again, in *Tape Berglund v Montoro Shipping Corpn Ltd, The Dagmar*[10]

A vessel was directed to Cape Chat, Quebec. While she was loading there, the wind and swell increased and she was driven aground. The shipowners claimed damages on the ground that the port was unsafe in that the pier gave no shelter from a northerly wind, that there was no means of communicating an adverse weather forecast to the vessel, and that the charterers had failed to warn the master of the approach or risk of bad weather.
Held, that the port was unsafe unless the vessel was warned (a) that she would receive no weather information from the shore and must rely on her own resources for obtaining weather forecasts; and (b) that in strong winds and seas the port was unsafe for her to remain in it. The action succeeded because the charterers had given warning (b) but not (a), and had passed on no weather forecasts.[11]

But if the master has acted unreasonably, e g knowing of the danger

QBD (Commercial Court), where the vessel was directed to Commercial Wharf, Gravesend, took the ground and was severely damaged. (See the judgment of Donaldson J, ibid, at 548.) Sometimes a charter-party states that the wharf or place of loading or discharge must be safe. See eg *Venore Transportation Co v Oswego Shipping Corpn, Banco do Brasil (Third Party), The Santore* [1974] 2 Lloyd's Rep 236, US Court of Appeals, Second Circuit, where a berth at which there was only one pontoon was held to be unsafe. (See the judgment of Lumbard Ct J, ibid, at 239.)

7   *Vardinoyannis v Egyptian General Petroleum Corpn, The Evaggelos Th* [1971] 2 Lloyd's Rep 200, QBD (Commercial Court), at 204 (per Donaldson, J).
8   See pp 155–158, post.
9   [1950] 2 KB 383, [1950] 1 All ER 201; *Lensen Shipping Co Ltd v Anglo-Soviet Shipping Co Ltd* (1935) 40 Com Cas 320.
10   [1968] 2 Lloyd's Rep 563, QBD (Commercial Court).
11   See the judgment of Mocatta J, ibid, at p 586.

in the port has still proceeded to enter it, and damage results, the charterer will not be liable.[12]

Where the charter-party requires the vessel to use safe ports only, the port, at the time when the order is given, must be prospectively safe for her to get to, stay at, so far as necessary, and in due course leave. But if some unexpected and abnormal event thereafter suddenly occurs which creates conditions of unsafety where conditions of safety had previously existed and as a result the ship is delayed, damaged or destroyed, the charterer is not liable.[13]

Where the time charterer has performed his primary obligation by ordering the ship to a port which at the time of the order was prospectively safe, and while she is still proceeding to that port new circumstances arise which render the port unsafe, he is under a secondary obligation to cancel his original order and order her to go to another port which, at the time when the fresh order is given, is prospectively safe.[14]

Where the vessel has entered the port and new circumstances arise which render the port unsafe, the charterer is under no secondary obligation to nominate another port, if it is impossible for the vessel to avoid the danger by leaving the port. But if it is possible for her to avoid the danger by leaving the port, the charterer must order her to leave forthwith, whether or not she has completed loading and discharge and order her to go to another port.[15]

Thus, in *Kodros Shipping Corpn v Empresa Cubana de Fletes, The Evia (No 2)*[16]

A vessel under a time-charter-party which required the charterers to use safe ports only was ordered by them to proceed to Basrah. She arrived there on 20 August 1979, and discharge of the cargo was completed on 22 September, but she was unable to leave as a result of the outbreak of large-scale hostilities between Iran and Iraq. The shipowners claimed damages from the charterers.

Held, by the House of Lords, that there would be judgment for the charterers, for Basrah was prospectively safe at the time of nomination, and the unsafety was due to

---

12 *Grace (GW) & Co Ltd v General Steam Navigation Co Ltd*, supra. The same principle is applied in the case of voyage charter-parties: *Compania Naviera Maropan S/A v Bowaters Lloyd Pulp and Paper Mills* [1955] 2 QB 68, [1955] 2 All ER 241, CA; *Reardon Smith Lines Ltd v Australian Wheat Board* [1956] AC 266, [1956] 1 All ER 456, PC. See pp 160–161, post.

13 *Kodros Shipping Corpn v Empresa Cubana de Fletes, The Evia (No 2)* [1982] 2 Lloyds Rep 307 at 315, HL (per Lord Roskill).

14 Ibid, at 320 (per Lord Roskill).

15 Ibid, at 320 (per Lord Roskill).

16 [1982] 2 Lloyd's Rep 307, HL.

an unexpected and abnormal event after her arrival. They were not under a secondary obligation to make a fresh nomination for such an order would have been ineffective.[17]

TRADING LIMITS

Sometimes the charter-party specifies that the vessel must only use safe ports within a certain area, eg 'vessel to perform one time charter trip via safe port(s) East Coast Canada within . . . trading limits', the trading limits being defined as 'always within Institute Warranty Limits East Coast Canada, USA East of Panama Canal, UK Continent Gibraltar-Hamburg Range, Mediterranean . . .'.[18]

The charter-party may state that the charterers have the privilege of breaching the trading limits by paying an extra insurance premium.[19]

Where a charter-party states that 'loss of time caused by average due to breach of the Institute Warranty Limits[20] is to be for the charterers' account', this provision does not relate only to time lost on passage due to average (ie damage). The words are apt to include time wasted by the shipowner while the damage is being repaired.[1]

DETENTION OF VESSEL

A usual clause provides that:

'In the event of the Vessel being driven into port or to anchorage through stress of

---

17 See the judgment of Lord Roskill, ibid, at 319–320. See further, *Uni-Ocean Lines Pte Ltd v C-Trade SA, The Lucille* [1984] 1 Lloyd's Rep 244, CA, where the charterers were in breach in ordering the vessel to Basrah or in failing to countermand the previous order when Basrah became unsafe (see the judgment of Kerr LJ, ibid, at 250); *Idaho D/S A/S v Colossus Maritime SA, The Concordia Fjord* [1984] 1 Lloyd's Rep 385, QBD (Commercial Court), where the vessel was ordered to Beirut, which was then a safe port, but became unsafe while she was proceeding there, and the charterers were held to be in breach in not countermanding the order (see the judgment of Bingham J, ibid, at 388).

18 *Segovia Compagnia Naviera SA v R Pagnan and Fratelli, The Aragon* [1977] 1 Lloyd's Rep 343, CA, where it was held that the expression 'USA East of Panama Canal' meant that part of the USA which could be reached from Europe westbound without passing through the Panama Canal. (See the judgment of Lord Denning MR, ibid, at 345.)

19 *Tropwood AG v Jade Enterprises Ltd, The Tropwind* [1977] 1 Lloyd's Rep 397, QBD (Commercial Court); *St Vincent Shipping Co Ltd v Bock, Godeffroy & Co, The Helen Miller* [1980] 2 Lloyd's Rep 95, QBD (Commercial Court); *Maritime Transport Overseas GmbH v Unitramp, The Antaios* [1981] 2 Lloyd's Rep 284, QBD (Commercial Court); *Atlantic Lines and Navigation Co Inc v Hallam Ltd, The Lucy* [1983] 1 Lloyd's Rep 188, QBD (Commercial Court).

20 See Ivamy, *Marine Insurance* (4th edn 1985), pp 561–562.

 1 *St Vincent Shipping Co Ltd v Bock, Godeffroy & Co, The Helen Miller*, supra, at 100 (per Mustill J).

weather, trading to shallow harbours or to rivers or ports with bars or suffering an accident to her cargo, any detention of the Vessel and/or expenses resulting from such detention is to be for the Charterers' account even if such detention and/or expenses, or the cause by reason of which either is incurred, be due to, or be contributed to by, the negligence of the Owners' servants.'[2]

The word 'bars' in the above clause applies to rivers and ports, ie the clause relates to trading to rivers with bars and to trading to ports with bars.[3]

The River Plate is no less a 'river' for the purpose of the clause because it is made up of the River Uruguay and the River Parana.[4]

The Martin Garcia Bar in the River Plate is a 'bar', and the mere existence of a passageway or channel cut by artificial means through the barrier of sand or silt or whatever else the bar may be made of, does not prevent the Bar from being a 'bar'.[5]

To render the charterers liable under the clause, the shipowners must show that the proximate cause of detention or expense was trading to a river with a bar or to a port with a bar. It is not enough that the charterers should be trading geographically and in point of time to a river with a bar or to a port with a bar.[6]

WAGES

A usual clause states that the shipowners will pay the 'wages' of the crew. The word 'wages' means the remuneration to which the crew are entitled for their services. It does not mean remuneration in conformity with International Transport Workers Federation rates of pay unless those rates are made part of the agreement between the shipowner and the crew.[7]

INSURANCE

A usual clause in a time charter-party states

'The owners to provide and pay for . . . insurance of the vessel.'[8]

2 'Baltime 1939' form, clause 11 (B). See Appendix B, post.
3 *Court Line Ltd v Finelvet A-G, The Jevington Court* [1966] 1 Lloyd's Rep 683 at 691 (per Roskill J).
4 Ibid, at 690 (per Roskill J).
5 Ibid, at 695 (per Roskill J).
6 Ibid, at 697 (per Roskill J).
7 *Sanko SS Co Ltd v Fearnley and Eger A/S: The Manhattan Prince* [1985] 1 Lloyd's Rep 140, QBD (Commercial Court). (See the judgment of Leggatt J, ibid, at 146).
8 'Baltime 1939' form, clause 3 (Appendix B).

But a clause may provide that if the charterer wishes to go outside the trading limits[9] specified in the charter-party, it is he who has to pay the additional premium.[10]

The charter-party may provide that if the charterer orders the vessel to a war zone

'the owners to be entitled . . . to insure their interests in the vessel and/or hire against any of the risks likely to be involved . . . on such terms as they shall think fit, the charterers to make a refund to the owners of the premium on demand.'[11]

The phrase 'insure their interests in the vessel' is not confined to the insurance of the vessel against physical loss or damage. The ownership of the vessel gives the shipowners an interest to protect themselves and the vessel against all their potential liabilities to their master, officers and crew.[12]

A charter-party, however, may contain a clause stating that the basic war risk insurance premium is always to be for the shipowner's account while any extra war risk insurance premium due to the vessel's trading, eg to the Persian Gulf, is for the charterer's account.[13]

MAINTENANCE OF VESSEL IN AN EFFICIENT STATE

Under the usual type of clause[14] the shipowner is not under a duty to see that the vessel is absolutely fit at all periods of her service

---

9   See p 34, ante.
10   *Tropwood AG v Jade Enterprises Ltd, The Tropwind* [1977] 1 Lloyd's Rep 397, QBD (Commercial Court).
11   'Baltime 1939' form, clause 21 (Appendix B). See eg *Telfair Shipping Corpn v Athos Shipping Co SA, The Athos* [1981] 2 Lloyd's Rep 74, QBD (Commercial Court); *Maritime Transport Overseas GmbH v Unitramp, The Antaios* [1981] 2 Lloyd's Rep 284, QBD (Commercial Court); *Schiffahrtsagentur Hamburg Middle East Line GmbH v Virtue Shipping Corpn, The Oinoussian Virtue (No 2)* [1981] 2 Lloyd's Rep 300, QBD (Commercial Court); *Ocean Star Tankers SA v Total Transport Corpn, The Taygetos* [1982] 2 Lloyd's Rep 272, QBD (Commercial Court); *Phoenix Shipping Corpn v Apex Shipping Corpn, The Apex* [1982] 2 Lloyd's Rep 407, QBD (Commercial Court); *Empresa Cubana de Fletes v Kissavos Shipping Co SA, The Agathon (No 2)* [1984] 1 Lloyd's Rep 183, QBD (Commercial Court); *Ocean Star Tankers SA v Total Transport Corpn, The Taygetos (No 2)* [1988] 2 Lloyd's Rep 474, QBD (Commercial Court).
12   *Empresa Cubana de Fletes v Kissavos Shipping Co SA, The Agathon (No 2)*, supra, where it was held that the shipowners had been reasonable in including the liabilities to the crew in the war risk cover.
13   *Pacific Navigators Corpn v Islamic Republic of Iran Shipping Lines, The El Campion, El Challenger and El General*, supra; *World Magnate Shipping Ltd v Rederi AB Soya* [1975] 2 Lloyd's Rep 498, QBD (Commercial Court).
14   See 'Baltime 1939' form, clause 3. See Appendix B, post. In *Splosna Plovba of*

under the charter-party, but he must take reasonable steps to rectify defects as soon as they are brought to his notice.[15] But if he does not keep the vessel in an efficient state, this only entitles the charterer to sue him for damages, and not to repudiate the charter-party,[16] though sometimes the failure to remedy the defect within a reasonable time may amount to frustration of the contract.[17]

PROVISION OF AND PAYMENT FOR FUEL

A usual clause[18] states:

'The charterers to provide and pay for all coals including galley coal, oil fuel . . .'

Where a charter-party stated that 'fuel used by the vessel for cooking, condensing water, or for grates and stoves' was to be allowed for by the shipowners, it was held that the combination of 'grates and stoves' with 'cooking' showed that the clause was intended to cover domestic use generally, whether that was lighting, heating, cooking or crew 'indulgences'.[19] There was no logic in seeking the precise modern equivalent of 'grates and stoves'.[20]

Where a clause stated that if the vessel's warranted speed[1] of 13 knots was reduced by a 'defect' in her hull, machinery or equipment, the cost of any extra fuel consumed was to be for the shipowners' account, and she was delivered with her bottom fouled, there was a 'defect' in her hull.[2] Consequently, the charterers could claim for the extra fuel consumed.[3]

Piran v Agrelak Steamship Corpn, The Bela Krajina [1975] 1 Lloyd's Rep 139, QBD (Commercial Court) the shipowners were held not to have broken the obligation to keep the vessel in a thoroughly efficient state, for it had not been shown that they had failed to ensure that her holds were ready to receive a cargo of grain.

15 *Tynedale Steam Shipping Co Ltd v Anglo-Soviet Shipping Co Ltd* [1936] 1 All ER 389, CA.

16 *Hong Kong Fir Shipping Co Ltd v Kawasaki Kisen Kaisha Ltd* [1962] 2 QB 26, [1962] 1 All ER 474, CA.

17 Ibid. As to frustration, see pp 70–78, post.

18 'Baltime 1939' form, clause 4 (Appendix B).

19 *Summit Investment Inc v British Steel Corp: The Sounion'* [1987] 1 Lloyd's Rep 230, CA. See the judgments of Sir John Donaldson MR, ibid at 234, and of Lloyd LJ, ibid at 235.

20 Ibid at 235 (per Lloyd LJ).

1 For speed warranties, see p 31, ante.

2 *Ocean Glory Compania Naviera SA v A/S PV Christensen, The Ioanna* [1985] 2 Lloyd's Rep 164, QBD (Commercial Court).

3 See the judgment of Staughton J, ibid at 167. 'Extra fuel' meant fuel oil and diesel oil: ibid at 167 (per Staughton J). The 'cost of any extra fuel consumed' meant the net cost of extra fuel oil and diesel oil taken together. If there was an extra

LOADING AND DISCHARGE

A usual clause states

'The owners to provide one winchman per hatch. If further winchmen are required, or if the stevedores refuse or are not permitted to work with the crew, the charterers to provide and pay qualified shore-winchmen.'[4]

A further clause states

'The charterers to arrange and pay for loading, trimming, stowing . . . unloading . . .'[5]

Sometimes, however, there is a clause stating

'Charterers are to load, stow and trim and discharge the cargo at their expense under the supervision and responsibility of the Captain.'[6]

The words 'and responsibility' in such a clause and the transfer of risk comprehended by it relate to the entire operation of loading, stowing, trimming and discharging the cargo. Specifically they cover not only the mechanical process of handling the ship's gear and cargo but also matters of stevedores' negligence in the strategic planning of loading and discharge of the cargo.[7]

The effect of the addition of the words 'and responsibility' is therefore to effect a prima facie transfer of liability for damage caused by the stevedores' negligence in the loading, stowing, trimming and discharge of the cargo. Of course, if the charterers' intervention in such operations causes the loss, the charterers will be liable.[8]

Whether the charterers have, in fact, interfered is a matter of fact in each case.[9]

consumption of diesel oil but a saving in fuel oil, it was only the net balance which was recoverable by the charterers. If the fuel oil saved exceeded the extra diesel oil, the charterers could claim nothing under the head 'cost of extra fuel', but they did not have to give credit for anything: ibid at 167 (per Staughton J).

4 See 'Baltime 1939' form, clause 3. (Appendix B).

5 See 'Baltime 1939' form, clause 4. (Appendix B).

6 See eg New York Produce Exchange Form, clause 8.

7 *Alexandros Shipping Co v MSC Mediterranean Shipping Co SA, The Alexandros P* [1986] 1 Lloyd's Rep 421, QBD (Commercial Court), at 424 (per Hirst J).

8 Ibid at 424 (per Hirst J); *AB Marintrans v Comet Shipping Co Ltd, The Shinjitsu Maru (No 5)* [1985] 1 Lloyd's Rep 568, QBD (Commercial Court), at 575 (per Neill LJ); *MSC Mediterranean Shipping Co SA v Alianca Bay Shipping Co Ltd, The Argonaut* [1985] 2 Lloyd's Rep 216, QBD (Commercial Court), at 224 (per Leggatt J).

9 *AB Marintrans v Comet Shipping Co Ltd, The Shinjitsu Maru (No 5)*, supra; *MSC Mediterranean Shipping Co SA v Alianca Bay Shipping Co Ltd, The Argonaut*, supra; *Alexandros Shipping Co v MSC Mediterranean Shipping Co, The Alexandros P*, supra.

THE PAYMENT OF HIRE

The charter-party usually states the amount of hire which must be paid,[10] eg

'The charterers to pay as hire the rate stated in Box 19 per 30 days commencing in accordance with Clause 1 until her redelivery to the Owners.'[11]

Where there is a difference between local time at the port of delivery and that at the port of redelivery, the shipowners are entitled to claim hire only in respect of the actual period which has elapsed from the moment of the delivery of the vessel.[12]

Thus, in *Ove Skou v Rudolf A Oetker, The Arctic Skou*[13]

The vessel was delivered at Angra dos Reis, Brazil at 1600 hours local time on 12 August 1982 and redelivered at Bilbao, Spain, at 1303 hours local time on 9 September 1982. Local time at Bilbao was 5 hours ahead of local time in Brazil. The shipowners claimed hire for 27 days 21 hours.

Held, by the Queen's Bench Division (Commercial Court), that the charterers were liable for hire for 27 days 16 hours only for that was the actual period which had elapsed from the moment of delivery. There was nothing in the charter-party to indicate that it was by reference to the local time at the respective ports of delivery and redelivery that the period of hire was to be calculated.[14]

Sometimes, however, the rate is calculated according to a standard scale such as the International Tanker Nominal Freight Scale. Thus, in the case of a consecutive voyage charter-party a clause stated that the hire was to be calculated 'in accordance with the dollar rates

10   For a case where a person who controlled the charterers agreed to guarantee that he would pay their obligations not only in regard to the hire due but for any other sums which became due under the charter-party, see *Thermistocles Navegacion SA v Langton, The Queen Frederica* [1978] 2 Lloyd's Rep 164, CA. For a case where the question was whether a guarantor was entitled to set off and to equitable set off, see *Aliakmon Maritime Corpn v Transocean Continental Shipping Ltd and Frank Truman Export Ltd, The Aliakman Progress* [1978] 2 Lloyd's Rep 499, CA. For a case where there was no concluded agreement as to the rate of hire, see *Harmony Shipping Co SA v Saudi-Europe Line Ltd, The Good Helmsman* [1981] 1 Lloyd's Rep 377, CA (see the judgment of Waller LJ, ibid, at 409, and that of Watkins LJ, ibid, at 418). For a case as to whether the guarantee was valid, see *Clipper Maritime Ltd v Shirlstar Container Transport Ltd, The Anemone* [1987] 1 Lloyd's Rep 546, QBD (Commercial Court).
11   See 'Baltime 1939' form, clause 6 (Appendix B).
12   *Ove Skou v Rudolf A Oetker, The Arctic Skou* [1985] 2 Lloyd's Rep 478, QBD (Commercial Court). As to redelivery, see pp 59–64, post.
13   [1985] 2 Lloyd's Rep 478, QBD (Commercial Court).
14   See the judgment of Leggatt, ibid at 480.

provided in the International Tanker Nominal Freight Scale minus
31¼ per cent'.[15]

The charter-party may state that the charterers must provide a
letter of undertaking from their bank that it will pay the hire if the
owners state to it that the hire is due and unpaid.[16]

A clause in a charter-party sometimes provides that the hire may
be increased or decreased if there is an alteration in the wages paid
to the crew.[17] Further, there may be a clause to the effect that hire
will be reduced if the vessel cannot accommodate all the goods
intended to be shipped.[18] Again, a clause may provide that the
amount of hire is to be adjusted if the vessel falls below or exceeds
the performance guaranteed in respect of her speed or bunker
consumption stated in the charter-party.[19] Similarly a clause may

---

15   *Achille Lauro fuo Gioacchino & Co v Total Societa Italiana per Azioni* [1969] 2
Lloyd's Rep 65, CA, where the question was whether hire was to be based on a
notional ballast voyage via the Cape of Good Hope or via the Suez Canal; *Agenor
Shipping Co Ltd v Société des Petroles Miroline* [1968] 2 Lloyd's Rep 359, QBD,
where the question was whether the accounting currency was the Pound Sterling
or the United States Dollar; *Total Societa Italiana per Azioni v Liberian Transocean
Navigation Corpn, The Alexandra I* [1972] 1 Lloyd's Rep 339, CA, where a similar
question arose in the case of a consecutive voyage charter-party; *Yoho Maru
(Owners) v Agip SpA c/o SNAM SpA* [1973] 1 Lloyd's Rep 409, QBD, where the
question in a consecutive voyage charter-party was whether the 1971 or the 1972
'Worldscale' schedule of rates should be applied; *Marmara Transport A/S v Mobil
Tankers SA, The Mersin* [1973] 1 Lloyd's Rep 532, QBD (Commercial Court),
which concerned an amendment to the 'Intascale' rate after a consecutive voyage
charter-party had been entered into; *Mitsui OSK Lines Ltd v Agip SpA, The
Bungamawar* [1978] 1 Lloyd's Rep 263, QBD (Commercial Court), where the
question in a consecutive voyage charter-party was whether the term 'Worldscale
as amended' related to Worldscale as amended as at the date of the accrual of the
obligation to pay freight.

16   See e g *Aurora Borealis Compania Armadora SA and Buenamar Compania Naviera
SA v Marine Midland Bank NA, The Maistros* [1984] 1 Lloyd's Rep 646, QBD
(Commercial Court).

17   *W Bruns & Co of Hamburg v Standard Fruit and SS Co of New Orleans, The
Brunsrode* [1976] 1 Lloyd's Rep 501, CA.

18   *Oceanic Freighters Corpn v MV Libyaville Reederei und Schiffahrts GmbH, The
Libyaville* [1975] 1 Lloyd's Rep 537, QBD (Commercial Court), where there was
a dispute as to the number of trailers a 'roll-on roll-off' vessel could carry on her
trailer deck, and a new clause was added to the charter-party to the effect that if
she was only able to accommodate 16 trailers (as against 17), the daily hire was
to be reduced by 1½ per cent.

19   *Showa Oil Tanker Co Ltd of Japan v Maravan SA of Caracas, The Larissa* [1963] 2
Lloyd's Rep 325, QBD (Commercial Court); *Petroleo Brasileiro S/A v Elounda
Shipping Co, The Evanthia M* [1985] 2 Lloyd's Rep 154, QBD (Commercial Court),
where the consumption of fuel was less while the vessel was being used for

state that in the event of a failure of a derrick, winch or winches, the hire is to be reduced pro rata to the number of winches and/or derricks available for the period of such inefficiency.[20]

Where the charter-party states that payment of hire is to be made 'without discount', this merely means that there is to be no discount for early payment.[1]

Where hire is payable in advance at so much per ton on the deadweight capacity of the vessel, there is an implied obligation on the shipowner to inform the charterer correctly as to the deadweight capacity.[2]

If on the due date for payment the vessel is 'off-hire', the charterer's obligation to make payment of the next monthly instalment of hire is suspended until immediately before the vessel is again at his service.[3]

Where a charter-party confers on the charterers an express right to deduct certain items from the hire, e g in respect of the value of bunkers remaining on board at redelivery or in respect of disbursements incurred by the charterers for the shipowner's account, the amount to be deducted can only be an estimated sum. An estimate can, of course, only be justified if it can be shown to have been made in good faith and on reasonable grounds.[4]

By virtue of the principle of equitable set-off a charterer may set-

storage; *Didymi Corpn v Atlantic Lines and Navigation Inc, The Didymi* [1988] 2 Lloyd's Rep 108, CA.

20 See e g New York Produce Exchange form, clause 56; *Alexandros Shipping Co v MSC Mediterranean Shipping Co SA, The Alexandros P* [1986] 1 Lloyd's Rep 421, QBD (Commercial Court).

1 *Compania Sud Americana de Vapores v Shipmair BV, The Teno* [1977] 2 Lloyd's Rep 289, QBD (Commercial Court) at 292 (per Parker J).

2 *Kawasaki Kisen Kabushiki Kaisha v Bantham SS Co Ltd* [1938] 2 K B 790, [1938] 3 All ER 600.

3 *Tradax Export SA v Dorada Compania Naviera SA, The Lutetian* [1982] 2 Lloyd's Rep 140, QBD (Commercial Court). (See the judgment of Bingham J, ibid, at 149, 150 and 153.)

4 *SL Sethia Liners Ltd v Naviagro Maritime Corpn, The Kostas Melas* [1981] 1 Lloyd's Rep 18, QBD (Commercial Court) at 25 (per Robert Goff J); *Tropwood AG of Zug v Jade Enterprises Ltd, The Tropwind* [1982] 1 Lloyd's Rep 232, CA, where the charterers made a bona fide and reasonable estimate and paid accordingly. (See the judgment of Lord Denning MR, ibid, at 236–237.) For a case where the shipowners and the charterers had entered into a compromise agreement concerning the deduction of hire and the charterers applied for rectification of the agreement, see *Olympia Sauna Shipping Co SA v Shinwa Kaium Kaisha Ltd, The Ypatia Halcoussi* [1985] 2 Lloyd's Rep 364, QBD (Commercial Court).

off certain claims against hire, even where the contract does not expressly give him the right to do so.[5]

If the shipowner wrongly and in breach of contract deprives the charterer for a time of the use of the vessel, the charterer can deduct a sum equivalent to the hire for the time so lost. But this right to deduct does not extend to other breaches or default of the shipowner, e g damage to cargo arising from the negligence of the crew.[6]

Further, the charterer is not entitled to make a deduction where the master has failed to keep accurate logs and to disclose them to the charterer or has been a party to the creation of false documentation by the bunker supplier or there has been a breach of the shipowner's duty as a bailee of the bunkers to use them in accordance with the charterer's orders[7]. None of these breaches affect the use of the vessel.[8]

In the absence of agreement the shipowner and the charterer regarding the payment of interest on unpaid hire, the shipowner has no remedy by way of a claim for general damages in respect of such interest if the amount due is paid late but before proceedings for its recovery have been commenced.[9] But the shipowner may be entitled to special damages if he can show e g that he has had to pay interest on an overdraft as a result of the charterer's late payment of hire even though the amount is paid before the commencement of proceedings for its recovery.[10]

Where hire remains unpaid, the Court may grant an ex parte application by the shipowners for an interim injunction to restrain

---

5   *SL Sethia Liners Ltd v Naviagro Maritime Corpn, The Kostas Melas,* supra, at 25 (per Robert Goff J).
6   *Federal Commerce and Navigation Ltd v Molena Alpha Inc, Same v Molena Beta Inc, Same v Molena Gamma Inc, The Nanfri, Benfri and Lorfri* [1978] 2 Lloyd's Rep 132, CA. (See the judgment of Lord Denning MR, ibid, at 141.) Cf *Compania Sud Americana de Vapores v Shipmair BV, The Teno* [1977] 2 Lloyd's Rep 289, QBD (Commercial Court), where it was held that the charterers could set off a claim for unliquidated damages for cargo shut out due to the breakdown in a ballast pipe line. (See the judgment of Parker J, ibid, at 297.) *Federal Commerce and Navigation Ltd v Molena Beta Inc, Same v Molena Gamma Inc, The Nanfri, Benfri and Lorfri* (supra) subsequently went to the House of Lords where the decision was affirmed without affecting the question as to whether a deduction could be made from the hire: [1979] 1 All ER 307.
7   *Leon Corp v Atlantic Lines and Navigation Co Inc, The Leon* [1985] 2 Lloyd's Rep 470, QBD (Commercial Court).
8   See the judgment of Hobhouse J, ibid, at 474.
9   *President of India v La Pintada Cia Navegacion SA* [1985] AC 104, [1984] 3 All ER 773, HL (a case on the late payment of demurrage).
10 Ibid.

the charterers from removing any of their assets out of the jurisdiction.[11]

RIGHT OF WITHDRAWAL

A usual clause states that payment must be made in cash without discount every 30 days in advance, and that in default of payment the shipowners have the right to withdraw the vessel from the charterer's service.[12]

Sometimes a charter-party contains an 'anti-technicality' clause stating e g

'If hire not received when due, Owners to give Charterers 48 hours' notice in order to rectify the cause for delay before exercising their [right of withdrawal].'[13]

The latest point of time which constitutes punctual payment of an instalment of hire is midnight of the day in question.

Thus, in *Afovos Shipping Co SA v R Pagnan and F Lli, The Afovos*[14]

A vessel was chartered under a time charter-party. Clause 31 stated: 'When hire is due and not received the owners before exercising the option of withdrawing the vessel . . . will give charterers 48 hours' notice'. An instalment of hire became due on 14 June 1979. The shipowners gave notice of withdrawal at 1640 hours on that day. The charterers contended that the notice was premature and therefore of no effect.
Held, by the House of Lords, that the notice was of no effect because the charterers had until midnight of 14 June before the instalment had to be paid.

Where the hire has been paid by cheque instead of in cash and always accepted by the shipowners, they cannot insist on payment in cash unless they first give the charterers notice to that effect.

Thus, in *Tankexpress A/S v Compagnie Financière Belge de Petroles SA, The Petrofina*[15]

11 *Nippon Yusen Kaisha v G & J Karageorgis* [1975] 2 Lloyd's Rep 137, CA; *Mareva Compania Naviera SA v International Bulkcarriers SA* [1975] 2 Lloyd's Rep 509, CA. See further, the Supreme Court Act 1981, s 37(3).
12 See e g 'Baltime 1939' form, clause 6.
13 As in *Italmare Shipping Co v Ocean Tanker Co Inc, (No 2), The Rio Sun* [1982] 1 Lloyd's Rep 404, QBD (Commercial Court), where the notice which was sent was held not to be clear (see judgment of Parker J, ibid, at 407); *Afovos Shipping Co SA v R Pagman and F Lli, The Afovos* [1983] 1 Lloyd's Rep 335, HL, where it was held that the notice could not be given until after the last moment for payment had arrived (see the judgment of Lord Hailsham of St Marylebone LC, ibid, at 339).
14 [1983] 1 Lloyd's Rep 335, HL (see the judgment of Lord Hailsham of St Marylebone LC, ibid, at 339).
15 [1949] AC 76, [1948] 2 All ER 939, HL. See also *Zim Israel-Navigation Co Ltd v Effy Shipping Corpn, The Effy* [1972] 1 Lloyd's Rep 18, QBD (Commercial Court).

A clause in a time charter-party provided that payment of hire was to be made 'in cash monthly in advance in London'. In default of such payment the shipowners had the right to withdraw the vessel from the charterers' service. In accordance with the practice which had always been followed the charterers had sent a cheque every month to the shipowners instead of paying cash. A cheque was delayed in transmission, and the shipowners claimed that they were entitled to withdraw the vessel because payment had not been made in cash.

Held, that the claim failed for if the shipowners wanted to insist on payment in cash, they must give reasonable notice of such intention.

Where payment of the hire is to be made 'in cash', the charterer is not considered to have paid unless what the shipowner receives is the equivalent of cash or as good as cash.[16]

Thus, in *Awilco A/S v Fulvia SpA di Navigazione, The Chikuma*[17]

By the terms of a time charter-party the payment of the hire was to be made in cash monthly in advance, otherwise the shipowners could withdraw the chartered vessel from the service of the charterers. One instalment of the hire fell due on 22 January 1976. On that date the sum due was credited to the shipowners' bank account, but interest could not run on it until 26 January. On January the shipowners withdrew the vessel. The charterers claimed damages for wrongful withdrawal.

Held, by the House of Lords, that there would be judgment for the shipowners, for the payment which had been made was not payment 'in cash' or its equivalent because the money could not immediately earn interest.[18]

A right to withdraw a vessel from the service of the charterers 'failing the punctual and regular payment of the hire' cannot be defeated by a late tender of the hire.

Thus, in *Mardorf Peach & Co Ltd v Attica Sea Carriers Corpn of Liberia, The Laconia*[19]

A vessel was chartered to the charterers under a time charter-party which stated that hire was to be paid in cash semi-monthly in advance, and that 'failing the punctual and regular payment of the hire' the shipowners were to be at liberty to withdraw the vessel from the charterers' service. The charterers tendered payment one day late, and the shipowners withdrew the vessel.

Held, by the House of Lords, that the shipowners were entitled to do so. The breach of the obligation to pay in advance could not be cured by the late tender.

Where the withdrawal clause is in the usual form, the shipowners are not entitled to effect a partial or temporary suspension or

---

16 *Awilco A/S v Fulvia Sp A di Navigazione, The Chikuma* [1981] 1 Lloyd's Rep 371, HL.
17 [1981] 1 Lloyd's Rep 371, HL.
18 See the judgment of Lord Bridge of Harwich, ibid, at 375.
19 [1977] AC 850, [1977] 1 All ER 545, HL.

withdrawal eg by instructing the master to stop the discharge of cargo.[20]

The shipowners must within a reasonable time after the default give notice of withdrawal to the charterers. What is a reasonable time depends on the circumstances.[21] In many cases it will be a short time, ie the shortest time reasonably necessary to enable the shipowners to hear of the default and issue instructions.[1]

If, of course, the charter-party contains an express provision regarding notice, that provision must be applied.[2]

The shipowners may be held to have waived the default if when a late payment is tendered, they choose to accept it as if it were timeous, of if they do not within a reasonable time give notice that they have rejected it.[3]

In order to prove a waiver on the part of the shipowners the charterers must establish

(a) that the shipowners had represented unequivocally that they

---

20 *Steelwood Carriers Inc of Monrovia, Liberia v Evimeria Compania Naviera SA of Panama, The Agios Giorgis* [1976] 2 Lloyd's Rep 192, QBD (Commercial Court); *Aegnoussiotis Shipping Corpn of Monrovia v Kristian Jebsens Rederi of Bergen A/S, The Aegnoussiotis* [1977] 1 Lloyd's Rep 268, QBD (Commercial Court); *International Bulk Carriers (Beirut) SARL v Evlogia Shipping Co SA and Marathon Shipping Co Ltd, The Mihalios Xilas* [1978] 2 Lloyd's Rep 186, QBD (Commercial Court).

21 *China Foreign Trade Transportation Corpn v Evlogia Shipping Co SA, The Mihalios Xilas* [1979] 2 Lloyd's Rep 303, HL, where the shipowners were held to be entitled to a reasonable time to ascertain whether the amounts comprising deductions from hire made by the charterers were correct before deciding to exercise a right of withdrawal which would accrue only if the deductions were wrong. (See the judgment of Lord Diplock, ibid, at 307.)

1 *Mardorf Peach & Co Ltd v Attica Sea Carriers Corpn, The Laconia* [1977] 1 All ER 545, HL at 552 (per Lord Wilberforce).

2 Ibid, at 552 (per Lord Wilberforce). See *Oceanic Freighters Corpn v MV Libyaville Reederei und Schiffahrts GmbH, The Libyaville* [1975] 1 Lloyd's Rep 537, QBD (Commercial Court), where Mocatta J, said (ibid, at 554) that the clause showed a praiseworthy effort to reduce the technicalities inappropriate to a commercial relationship which so often arose in connection with the right to withdraw a ship under a time charter-party.

3 *Mardorf Peach & Co Ltd v Attica Sea Carriers Corpn, The Laconia,* supra, at 552 (per Lord Wilberforce); *China National Foreign Trade Corpn v Evlogia Shipping Co SA, The Mihalios Xilas,* supra; *Scandinavian Trading Tanker Co AB v Flota Petrolera Ecuatoriana, The Scaptrade* [1983] 1 Lloyd's Rep 146, CA, where the mere fact that late payments of hire had been accepted by the shipowners without protest was held not to be a waiver. (The decision was subsequently affirmed by the House of Lords on another point without affecting the present one: [1983] 2 Lloyd's Rep 253, HL.)

would not enforce their strict legal right to withdraw the vessel
from the charterers' service; and
(b) that in the circumstances it would be inequitable to allow the
shipowners to enforce their strict legal right, having regard to
the dealings which had taken place between the parties.[4]

The former requirement may be fulfilled if a reasonable man in
the shoes of the charterers would have inferred from the shipowners'
conduct that they were making such a representation.[5]

As to the latter requirement, it could only be unconscionable for
the shipowners to enforce their strict legal right if the charterers'
conduct had been so influenced by the representation as to call for
the intervention of equity.[6] Whether or not the charterers' conduct
had been so influenced must depend on the evidence.[7]

The Court has no jurisdiction to grant relief against the exercise
by a shipowner of his contractual right under a withdrawal clause to
withdraw the vessel from the service of the charterer on the
charterer's failure to make payment of an instalment of the hire in
the manner and at a time which is not later than that for which the
clause provides.[8]

Thus, in *Scandinavian Trading Tanker Co AB v Flota Petrolera
Ecuatoriana, The Scaptrade*[9]

A vessel was chartered under a time charter-party. One month's hire became due on
8 July 1979, but the charterers failed to pay it. So the shipowners withdrew her from
the charterers' service. The charterers applied for relief against forfeiture.
Held, that no relief would be granted.

There are practical reasons of legal policy for declining to create
any such new jurisdiction out of sympathy for charterers. The freight
market is notoriously volatile. If it rises during the period of a time
charter-party, the charterer is the beneficiary of the windfall which
he can realise, if he wants to, by sub-chartering at the then market
rates. What withdrawal of the vessel does is to transfer the benefit of
the windfall from the charterer to the shipowner.[10]

---

4   *Scandinavian Trading Tanker Co AB v Flota Petrolera Ecuatoriana, The Scaptrade*
    [1983] 1 Lloyd's Rep 146 at 149, CA (per Robert Goff LJ).
5   Ibid, at 150 (per Robert Goff LJ).
6   Ibid, at 150 (per Robert Goff LJ).
7   Ibid, at 150 (per Robert Goff LJ).
8   *Scandinavian Trading Tanker Co AB v Flota Petrolera Ecuatoriana, The Scaptrade*
    [1983] 2 Lloyd's Rep 253, HL.
9   [1983] 2 Lloyd's Rep 253, HL.
10 Ibid, at 256 (per Lord Diplock).

THE 'OFF-HIRE' CLAUSE

A usual clause[11] provides that:

'In the event of drydocking[12] or other necessary measures to maintain the efficiency of the vessel, deficiency of men or Owners' stores, breakdown of machinery, damage to hull or other accident, either hindering or preventing the working of the vessel and continuing for more than 24 consecutive hours, no hire to be paid in respect of any time lost thereby[13] during the period in which the vessel is unable to perform the service immediately required.[14]

'Deficiency of men' relates to the numerical deficiency[15] and not their unwillingness to work, eg refusal to proceed to sea in time of war except in convoy.[16] The word 'men' means 'crew', and not

---

11 For similar clauses in American forms of charter-party, see *Heinrich C Horn v Cia de Navegacion Fruca SA and J R Atkins (Trading as Alabama Fruit and Produce Co), The Heinz Horn* [1970] 1 Lloyd's Rep 191, US Ct of Appeals, Fifth Circuit; *United States of America v The Marilena P and Marilena Compania Naviera SA* [1969] 2 Lloyd's Rep 641, US Ct of Appeals, Fourth Circuit; *Mareva Navigation Co Ltd v Canaria Armadora SA, The Mareva AS* [1977] 1 Lloyd's Rep 368, where the words were 'detention by average accidents to ship or cargo preventing the full working of the vessel', and it was held that 'detention' was intended to refer to some physical or geographical constraint on the vessel's movements in relation to her service under the charter-party, and that 'average accident' meant an accident which caused damage. (See the judgment of Kerr J, ibid, at 381–382.)

12 For a drydocking clause in a tanker time charter-party, see *A K Fernstoms Rederi v Transportes Maritimos Internacionals Ltda* [1960] 1 Lloyd's Rep 669.

13 Whether time has been lost 'thereby' will depend on the circumstances: *Eastern Mediterranean Maritime (Liechtenstein) Ltd v Unimarine SA, The Marika M* [1981] 2 Lloyd's Rep 622, QBD (Commercial Court), where time was not lost 'from' the grounding of a vessel nor 'thereby' but from the Bahrain port system of a strict berthing turn; *Western Sealanes Corpn v Unimarine SA, The Pythia* [1982] 2 Lloyd's Rep 160, QBD (Commercial Court), where Robert Goff J (ibid, at 168) pointed out the difference between 'period' off-hire clauses and 'net loss of time' off-hire clauses. As to the difference, see p 51, post.

14 'Baltime 1939' form, clause 11(A). See Appendix B, post. For a case where the charterers were held liable to pay overtime to the officers and crew even when the vessel was off-hire, see *Court of Line Ltd v Finelvet AG, The Jevington Court* [1966] 1 Lloyd's Rep 683 at 698. For a case where the vessel was not off-hire on account of rust in her holds, see *Splosna Plovba of Piran v Agrelak SS Corpn, The Bela Krajina* [1975] 1 Lloyd's Rep 139, QBD (Commercial Court).

15 See eg *Harmony Shipping Co SA v Saudi-Europe Line Ltd, The Good Helmsman* [1981] 1 Lloyd's Rep 377, CA, where a member of the crew was missing, and the vessel was prevented by the port authorities from sailing, but there was no evidence as to whether the 'deficiency of men' was the cause of the detention. (See the judgment of Ackner LJ, ibid, at 422.)

16 *Royal Greek Government v Minister of Transport, The Ilissos* [1949] 1 KB 525, [1949] 1 All ER 171, CA.

additional gunners needed to protect a merchant ship in time of war against attacks by enemy submarines.[17]

Although damage to the ship's machinery may have been sustained at an earlier date, it will not be held to have 'broken down' within the meaning of the clause until it is necessary for her to proceed to port for repairs to be effected.[18]

'Or other accident' includes running aground in a river,[19] but if a crew refuses to sail except in convoy, that is not an 'accident', and hire continues to be payable.[20]

Where a vessel's bottom became encrusted with molluscs during a long stay at a port where the water was fresh or slightly brackish, and her speed was reduced, hire ceased to be payable for the encrustation fell within the words 'or other accident' for molluscs preferred salt water.[1]

But where a clause provided that if on the voyage the vessel's speed was reduced by a defect in her hull, the time so lost was to be deducted from the hire, and her hull was fouled by marine growth, hire was still payable for the accumulation of such growth was not a 'defect'.[2]

Where a charter-party stated that hire was to be reduced in the event of a breakdown of a Munck crane or cranes, with which the vessel was fitted, 'by reason of disablement', and the trolley of No 1 crane fell overboard, and No 2 and No 3 cranes were taken out of service for examination, hire was held not to be payable in respect of No 1 crane but was payable in respect of the other two cranes, for there had not been a breakdown 'by reason of disablement'.[3]

'The working of the vessel' may be prevented by a delay in the granting of free pratique.

Thus, in *Sidermar SpA v Apollo Corpn, The Apollo*[4]

---

17 *Radcliffe & Co v Compagnie Generale Transatlantique* (1918) 24 Com Cas 40, CA.
18 *Giertsen v Turnbull & Co* (1908) SC 1101.
19 *SS Magnhild v McIntyre Bros & Co* [1921] 2 KB 97, [1921] All ER Rep 359.
20 *Royal Greek Government v Minister of Transport, The Ilissos* [1949] 1 KB 7, [1948] 1 All ER 904 (at first instance).
 1 *Cosmos Bulk Transport Inc v China National Foreign Trade Transportation Corpn, The Apollonius* [1978] 1 Lloyd's Rep 53, QBD (Commercial Court). (See the judgment of Mocatta J, ibid, at 66.)
 2 *Santa Martha Baay Scheepvaart and Handelsmaatschappij NV v Scanbulk A/S, The Rijn* [1981] 2 Lloyd's Rep 267, QBD (Commercial Court). (See the judgment of Mustill J, ibid, at 272.)
 3 *Canadian Pacific (Bermuda) Ltd v Canadian Transport Co Ltd, The HR Macmillan* [1974] 1 Lloyd's Rep 311. (See the judgment of Lord Denning MR, ibid, at 314.)
 4 [1978] 1 Lloyd's Rep 200, QBD (Commercial Court).

Hire was to cease to be payable in the event of loss of time from certain specified causes 'or any other cause whatsoever preventing the full working of the vessel'.[5] The port health authorities tested and inspected her after cases of suspected typhus amongst her crew were discovered. Free pratique was not granted for 29½ hours.

Held, the obtaining of free pratique in the present case was not a mere formality, and the vessel was prevented from working. No hire was payable in respect of the 29½ hours.[6]

Where the ship in herself remains an efficient ship, hire is still payable.[7]

Thus, where the ship is delayed by a boom across a river, the charterers are still liable to pay hire.[8]

Again, in *Actis Co Ltd v Sanko SS Co Ltd, The Aquacharm*[9]

The 'Aquacharm' was chartered under a time charter-party, which contained a clause stating that 'in the event of the loss of time from deficiency of men or stores, fire, breakdown or damage to hull, machinery or equipment or by any other cause preventing the full working of the vessel, the payment of hire shall cease for the time thereby lost.' Whilst on a voyage from Baltimore to Tokyo she had to pass through the Panama Canal. The Canal authorities would not allow her to proceed because she exceeded the permitted draught as she had too much coal on board. Some of the coal had to be transhipped on to another vessel, which followed her through the Canal. The cargo was then reloaded at the other end. The operation took 9 days. The charterers contended that the vessel was 'off-hire' for this period as her full working was prevented.

Held, by the Court of Appeal, that she was not 'off-hire' for she remained at all times in herself fully efficient in all respects.[10]

In *Sanko SS Co Ltd v Fearnley & Eger A/S, The Manhattan Prince*[11]

A vessel was blockaded by the International Transport Workers Federation and no tugs would help her until the shipowners agreed to pay her Filipino crews the rates enjoyed by Western crews. The charterers refused to pay hire during the period of the blockade.

Held, by the Queen's Bench Division (Commercial Court), that hire was still payable because the vessel was capable of efficient physical working. The vessel worked even

---

5 As to the exclusion of the *ejusdem generis* rule in this case, see p 133, post.
6 See the judgment of Mocatta J: [1978] 1 Lloyd's Rep at 205, where he said that where the obtaining of health clearance was a mere formality, the very minor delays, if any, involved in obtaining it would not bring the off-hire clause into play, since the ship would be able to render the service then required of her.
7 *Actis Co Ltd v Sanko SS Co Ltd, The Aquacharm* [1982] 1 Lloyd's Rep 7 at 9, CA (per Lord Denning MR).
8 *Court Line Ltd v Dant and Russel Inc* (1939) 64 Ll L Rep 212.
9 [1982] 1 Lloyd's Rep 7, CA.
10 See the judgment of Lord Denning MR, ibid, at 9, and that of Griffiths LJ, ibid, at 11.
11 [1985] 1 Lloyd's Rep 140, QBD (Commercial Court).

though she was prevented by the action of the ITF from working in the way the charterers would have wished.[12]

In *CA Venezolana de Navegacion v Bank Line, The Roachbank*[13]

While in the South China Sea a vessel sighted a boat containing a number of Vietnamese refugees and picked them up. When she arrived at Kaohsiung the port authorities, at first, refused to allow her into the port. She was held up for 9 days, and the charterers contended that she was off-hire for this period.

Held, by the Queen's Bench Division (Commercial Court), that the vessel was not off-hire. On the evidence, the presence of the refugees did not prevent her from being fully worked if port facilities had been made available.[14]

On the other hand, where a vessel is arrested and therefore prevented from leaving port, no hire is payable for no one can use her.[15]

Again, where a booster pump had been fitted to a vessel to assist the discharge of cargo, and the harbour master refused to allow her to discharge because the pump had failed to comply with a classification society's regulations in that it was unfixed, the crew could not use the relevant part of the machinery. The working of the vessel had been prevented, and she was off-hire.[16]

'The working of the vessel' is considered to be hindered even if there is only a partial interference with her working. Thus, in *Hogarth v Miller Bros & Co*[17]

The vessel's high-pressure engine broke down. But she managed to get into port with the assistance of a tug and partly by using her own low-pressure engine.

Held, hire was not payable during this period, because the working of the vessel had been hindered.

But as long as she is capable of performing the service immediately required, hire will continue to be payable, eg if the vessel is

---

12 See the judgment of Leggatt J, ibid, at 146.
13 [1987] 2 Lloyd's Rep 498, QBD (Commercial Court).
14 See the judgment of Leggatt J, ibid, at 508.
15 *Belcore Maritime Corpn v F Lli Moretti Cereali SpA, The Mastro Giorgis* [1983] 2 Lloyd's Rep 66, QBD (Commercial Court). Sometimes there is a combination of causes preventing the work of the vessel and then it may be necessary to go behind the immediate cause to find the underlying cause: ibid, at 69 (per Lloyd J).
16 *Navigas International Ltd v Trans-Offshore Inc, The Bridgestone Maru No 3* [1985] 2 Lloyd's Rep 62, QBD (Commercial Court). See the judgment of Hirst J, ibid, at 83.
17 [1981] AC 48, HL.

discharging and fit for that purpose, it does not matter if she was not in a fit state to put to sea.[18]

If the vessel breaks down and puts into port for repairs, hire will cease to be payable, but will become payable again when she is fit to sail again from that place, and not from the time when she reaches again the spot at which the breakdown occurred.[19]

TYPES OF OFF-HIRE CLAUSES

An off-hire clause may be a 'period' clause or a 'net loss of time' clause. It is a matter of construction in each case into which category it falls.[20]

It is generally construed as a 'period' clause if it states that hire ceases to be due from the off hire event *until* the vessel is again in an

18 Ibid. See further, *Court Line Ltd v Finelvet A-G, The Jevington Court* [1966] 1 Lloyd's Rep 683, where a vessel which was refloated after grounding still remained able to perform the service required, viz, to unload and reload the charterers' cargo (see the judgment of Roskill J, ibid, 698); *Mareva Navigation Co Ltd v Canaria Armadora SA, The Mareva A/S* [1977] 1 Lloyd's Rep 368, where the vessel was capable of discharging cargo from all her holds (see the judgment of Kerr J, ibid, at 383); *Compania sud Americana de Vapores v Shipmair BV, The Teno* [1977] 2 Lloyd's Rep 289, QBD (Commercial Court), where the vessel's ballast pipe line system broke down when loading was nearing completion and deballasting could not continue and the vessel reached the maximum draught when she was still short of the declared cargo and it was held that the vessel was 'off-hire'. (See the judgment of Parker J, ibid, at 292.)

19 *Vogemann v Zanzibar SS Co* (1902) 7 Com Cas 254, CA, unless there is a clause to the contrary. See eg *Eastern Mediterranean Maritime (Liechtenstein) Ltd v Unimarine SA, The Marika M* [1981] 2 Lloyd's Rep 622, QBD (Commercial Court; *Chilean Nitrate Sales Corpn v Marine Transportation Co Ltd and Pansuiza Compania de Navegacion SA, The Hermosa* [1982] 1 Lloyd's Rep 570, CA, where a clause stated: 'Should the veseel put back whilst on voyage by reason of an accident . . . the hire shall be suspended from the time of the inefficiency until vessel is again efficient in the same position and voyage resumed therefrom and all expenses incurred . . . shall be for owners' account.'; *Tradax Export SA v Dorada Compania Naviera SA, The Lutetian* [1982] 2 Lloyd's Rep 140, QBD (Commercial Court); *Western Sealanes Corpn v Unimarine SA, The Pythia* [1982] 2 Lloyd's Rep 160, QBD (Commercial Court); *Sanko SS Co Ltd v Fearnley & Eger A/S, The Manhattan Prince* [1985] 1 Lloyd's Rep 140, QBD (Commercial Court), where a clause stated: 'Hire shall cease to be . . . payable until the vessel is again ready and in an efficient state to resume her service from a position not less favourable to charterers than that at which such loss of time commenced'.

20 See eg *Western Sealanes Corpn v Ultramarine SA, The Pythia* [1982] 2 Lloyd's Rep 160, QBD (Commercial Court) ('net loss of time' clause); *Navigas International Ltd v Trans-Offshore Inc, The Bridgestone Maru No 3* [1985] 2 Lloyd's Rep 62, QBD (Commercial Court) ('period clause').

efficient state to resume service. In such a clause it is the efficiency of the vessel which is the relevant consideration.

In a 'net loss of time' clause the loss of efficiency as such is irrelevant. The key question is how much time, in fact, has been lost as a result of the off-hire event, enabling the Court to go backwards as well as forwards in time in order to answer that question.

The Courts have always leaned strongly in favour of construing clauses as 'period' ones in order to avoid the complexities of calculating minutiae of lost time under the 'net loss of time' approach.[1]

LOSS OF VESSEL CLAUSE

A further clause[2] usually sets out the position if the vessel is lost, e g

'Should the vessel be lost or missing, hire to cease from the date when she was lost. If the date of loss cannot be ascertained, half-hire to be paid from the date the vessel was last reported until the calculated date of arrival at the destination. Any hire paid in advance to be adjusted accordingly.'[3]

THE 'EMPLOYMENT AND INDEMNITY' CLAUSE

A clause usually provides that:

'The master to be under the orders of the charterers as regards employment, agency or other arrangements. The charterers to indemnify the owners against all consequences or liabilities arising from the master ... signing bills of lading or otherwise complying with such orders.'[4]

Under the 'employment and indemnity' clause the charterers are entitled to present to the master for signature by him on behalf of the shipowners bills of lading which contain or evidence contracts between the shippers of goods and the shipowners, provided that

1   *Navigas International Ltd v Trans-Offshore Inc, The Bridgestone Maru No 3*, supra, at 84.
2   'Baltime 1939' form, clause 16.
3   For a case where a clause stated that 'money paid in advance and not earned' was to be repaid to the charterers, see *Meling v Minos Shipping Co Ltd, The Oliva* [1972] 1 Lloyd's Rep 458, QBD (Commercial Court).
4   'Baltime 1939' form, clause 9. See Appendix B, post. For a case where a claim by the shipowner for an indemnity in respect of money paid to a stevedore who was injured during the discharge of cargo was statute-barred, see *Anchor Line Ltd v Star Shipping Co A/S, The Star Assyria* [1980] 2 Lloyd's Rep 365, QBD (Commercial Court). Sometimes, even where there is no express clause, the shipowners may be entitled to claim an implied indemnity: *Telfair Shipping Corpn v Inersea Carriers SA, The Caroline P* [1984] 2 Lloyd's Rep 466, QBD (Commercial Court).

the bills of lading do not contain extraordinary terms or terms manifestly inconsistent with the charter-party. The master is obliged, on presentation to him of such bills of lading, to sign them on the shipowners' behalf.[5]

The charterers, however, may, instead of presenting the bills of lading to the master for signature by him on behalf of the shipowners, sign them themselves on the same behalf. In either case the signature binds the shipowners as principals to the contract contained in or evidenced by the bills of lading.[6]

In *Milburn v Jamaica Fruit Importing and Trading Co of London*[7]

The master had signed bills of lading which omitted a clause excepting liability for negligence. The vessel was damaged and by reason of the absence of the clause, the shipowners could not obtain a general average contribution from the owners of the cargo.
Held, since the charterers had ordered the master to sign the bills, they must indemnify the shipowners for the loss they had suffered in not recovering the contribution.

The shipowner, however, is entitled to an indemnity under the 'employment and indemnity' clause only if he can show that there was a causal connection between the loss and his compliance with the charterer's instructions.

Thus, in *The White Rose: Helsingfors SS Co Ltd AB v Rederiaktiebolaget Rex*[8]

Under a time charter-party containing the usual 'employment and indemnity' clause the charterers ordered the vessel to Duluth, Minnesota, to load a cargo and arranged for the loading to be carried out by a stevedoring company. One of the company's employees was injured when he fell through a 'tween deck hatch. The shipowners settled his claim against them, and now claimed an indemnity from the charterers under the 'employment and indemnity' clause. It was proved that the accident was caused partly by the employee's failure to have regard for his own safety and partly

---

5 *The Berkshire* [1974] 1 Lloyd's Rep 185, QBD (Admiralty Court) at 188 (per Brandon J).
6 Ibid, at 188 (per Brandon J).
7 [1900] 2 QB 540, CA. See further *Gesellschaft Burgerlichen Rechts v Stockholms Rederiaktiebolag Svea (SS Brabant)* [1967] 1 QB 588, [1966] 1 All ER 961, where it was held that the shipowners could not claim an indemnity from the charterers in respect of damage to the owners of cargo caused by coal dust because the charter-party contined a clause stating: 'The decks and holds and other spaces to be properly cleaned at Owners' risk and expense before loading.'
8 [1969] 2 Lloyd's Rep 52, QBD (Commercial Court). See the judgment of Donaldson J, ibid, at 59. See further, *Vardinoyannis v Egyptian General Petroleum Corpn, The Evaggelos Th* [1971] 2 Lloyd's Rep 200, QBD (Commercial Court), where the question was whether the charterers were responsible for the loss of a vessel by shell fire at Suez in the war between Egypt and Israel in 1967.

because there was no fencing round the hatch, and that the charterers had not been negligent.
Held, that the action failed, for, on the evidence, there was no causal connection between the order to load the cargo and the loss incurred by the shipowners.

The meaning of the expression 'to indemnify against all liabilities' is that it imposes the obligation to indemnify against the incurring of a liability, not the discharge of that liability by payment or determination of that liability by judicial process.[9]

Consequently the shipowner should make certain that his claim against the charterer is not statute-barred under the Limitation Act 1980, s 5, which allows him 6 years in which to sue.[10]

Thus, in *Bosma v Larsen*[11]

A charter-party contained a clause stating that the charterers would indemnify the shipowners 'against all liabilities arising from the master signing bills of lading'. The bill of lading was signed by the master on the charterers' orders in respect of some fish carried from Iceland to Italy. The fish arrived damaged on 17 March 1956. On 10 March 1962, the cargo insurers were awarded damages against the shipowners by an Italian Court. On 17 December 1963, the shipowners paid the insurers under a compromise settlement. On 12 March 1965, the shipowners issued a writ claiming to be indemnified under the indemnity clause.
Held, that the action was statute-barred. The cause of action arose on 17 July 1956. It was not dependent upon the determination of liability by the Italian Court or payment under the compromise settlement.

The clause set out above does not entitle the charterer to give orders concerning navigation. This remains the responsibility of the master, and he is the judge, e g of whether it is safe for his vessel to proceed to sea, even if directed to do so by the charterer.[12]

Thus, in *Larrinaga SS Co Ltd v R*[13]

A time charter -party stated that the master was to obey the orders of the charterer 'as regards employment'. The vessel was ordered by the charterer's representative to leave port. The master did so although the weather was very bad. In consequence of a storm the vessel stranded and sustained serious damage.
Held, by the House of Lords, that the charterer was not liable. The order which had been given was one as to navigation and not one as to employment.

The 'employment' referred to in the clause is 'employment of the ship' i e 'the services which she is ordered to perform e g the voyages

---

9   *Bosma v Larsen* [1966] 1 Lloyd's Rep 22. (See especially the judgment of McNair J, ibid, at 28.)
10   See p 172 post.
11   [1966] 1 Lloyd's Rep 22.
12   *Larrinaga SS Co Ltd v R* [1945] AC 246, [1945] 1 All ER 329, HL.
13   [1945] AC 246, [1945] 1 All ER 329, HL.

to or from particular ports with particular cargoes or in ballast.[14] 'An order to sail from port A to port B is in common parlance an order as to employment but an order that a ship shall sail at a particular time is not an order as to employment because its object is not to direct how the ship shall be employed, but how she shall act in the course of that employment'.[15]

Where it was the intention of the parties that a vessel should lighten at an anchorage in the Bonny River, Nigeria, by discharging part of her cargo, the charterers' order that she should proceed there was an order as to 'employment'.[16] But if they had specified the particular spot in the anchorage at which she should anchor, that would have been an order as to navigation.[17]

It is the duty of the master to act reasonably upon receipt of orders. Some orders are of their nature such that they would, if the master were to act reasonably, require immediate compliance. Others would require a great deal of thought and consideration before a reasonable master would comply with them.[18]

Thus, in *Midwest Shipping Co Ltd Inc v D I Henry (Jute) Ltd*[19]

A time charter-party stated that the master was to be 'under the orders and directions of the charterers as regards employment and agency'. The vessel sailed from Chalna on 10 October. On 12 October he received a cable from the charterers ordering him to return there. He informed them that he could not cross the bar there until 20 October, and continued on his voyage. On 13 October he was again ordered to return and wait until there was sufficient water over the bar. He still continued on the voyage because the bills of lading showed that the vessel had sailed for Singapore instead of for Durban and the port authorities might cause difficulties if he returned. He pointed this out to the charterers, who on 14 October again ordered him to return despite the fact that the bills of lading stated that the vessel was bound for Singapore. The master turned round and arrived at Chalna on 19 October. The charterers claimed that his failure to return when ordered constituted a breach of the charter-party, and that they were entitled to deduct 5 days while the vessel was off-hire and the cost of 5 days' fuel which was wasted.

Held, that the action failed. There had been no breach of the charter-party, for, on the evidence,[20] the master had acted reasonably.

If a shipowner threatens to send the vessel on a voyage which is

---

14 Ibid, at 333 (per Lord Wright).
15 Ibid, at 336 (per Lord Porter).
16 *Newa Line v Erechthion Shipping Co SA, The Erechthion* [1987] 2 Lloyd's Rep 180, QBD (Commercial Court). (See the judgment of Staughton J, ibid, at 185).
17 Ibid, at 185 (per Staughton J).
18 *Midwest Shipping Co Ltd Inc v D I Henry (Jute) Ltd* [1971] 1 Lloyd's Rep 375, QBD (Commercial Court) at 379 (per Donaldson J).
19 [1971] 1 Lloyd's Rep 375, QBD (Commercial Court).
20 Set out ibid, at 378–380.

entirely inconsistent with the terms of the time charter-party, the charterer is entitled to apply for an injunction to restrain him from doing so.[1]

Where the charterer orders the master to deliver the cargo to a person who is not entitled to receive it, the order is not one which he is bound to obey nor is it one which the charterer is entitled to give.[2] But the act which the order required is not manifestly illegal in itself nor is it something which would have excited the suspicion of the master or caused him to refuse to act.[3] The question is whether the order caused loss to the shipowner or whether the master in obeying it without further inquiry was a *novus actus interveniens*.[4]

EXCEPTED PERILS

A usual clause states:

'The owners only to be responsible for delay in delivery of the vessel or for delay during the currency of the charter and for loss or damage to goods on board, if such delay or loss has been caused by want of due diligence on the part of the owners or their manager in making the vessel seaworthy and fitted for the voyage or any other personal act or omission or default of the owners or their manager. The owners not to be responsible in any other case nor for damage or delay whatsoever and howsoever caused even if caused by the neglect or default of their servants. The owners not to be liable for loss or damage arising or resulting from strikes, lock-outs or stoppage or restraint of labour (including the master, officers or crew) whether partial or general.'[5]

Thus, in *Cosmos Bulk Transport Inc v China National Foreign Trade Transportation Corpn, The Apollonius*[6]

A time charter-party contained a clause in the above form. The vessel was delayed by her bottom being encrusted with molluscs, which reduced her speed, and by the reluctance of her engineers to operate the main engine at full output relative to safe

1   *Empresa Cubana de Fletes v Lagonisi Shipping Co Ltd, The Georgios C* [1971] 1 Lloyd's Rep 7, CA. The same principle applies in the case of an intermittent voyage charter-party: *Associated Portland Cement Manufacturers Ltd v Teigland Shipping A/S, The Oakworth* [1975] 1 Lloyd's Rep 581, CA. (See the judgment of Lord Denning MR, ibid, at 583.)
2   *Hansen-Tangens Rederi III A/S v Total Transport Corpn, The Sagona* [1984] 1 Lloyd's Rep 194, QBD (Commercial Court), at 205 (per Staughton J).
3   Ibid, at 205 (per Staughton J).
4   Ibid, at 205 (per Staughton J). In this case it was held that the master followed the usual practice in the oil tanker trade in not insisting on the production of a bill of lading and there were no circumstances to arouse his suspicion, so the charterer's order caused the shipowner's loss and the shipowner was entitled to an indemnity. (See the judgment of Staughton J, ibid, at 205–206.)
5   'Baltime 1939' form, clause 13. See Appendix B, post.
6   [1978] 1 Lloyd's Rep 53, QBD (Commercial Court).

working temperatures in periods of moderate weather. The charterers claimed damages for delay.

Held, that the action failed, for the word 'delay' in the clause applied both to the reduction of the vessel's speed and the engineers' conduct.[7]

The clause set out above does not protect the shipowners against a claim for financial loss suffered by the charterers by reason of the shipowners' breaches of the charter-party.[8]

Thus, in *Tor Line AB (Renamed Investment AB Torman) v Alltrans Group of Canada Ltd, The TFL Prosperity*[9]

A vessel was let under a time charter-party containing (i) cl 13, which was in the form of the clause set out above; and (ii) cl 26 which stated that the free height of her main deck was 6·10 m. In fact, the free height was only 6·05 m at a critical point, and a trailer double stacked with 40 ft containers could not be loaded on to the main deck. The charterers claimed damages from the shipowners in respect of the financial loss which they had suffered. The shipowners contended that they were exempted from liability by cl 13.

Held, by the House of Lords, that on its true construction cl 13 did not afford the shipowners a defence to the claim.[10]

The burden of proving that such delay or loss falls within the exception clause lies on the shipowners.[11]

CARELESS LOADING OR DISCHARGE

A clause usually provides that:

'The charterers to be responsible for loss or damage caused to the vessel or to the owners by goods being loaded contrary to the terms of the charter or by improper bunkering or loading, stowing or discharge of goods or any other improper or negligent act on their part or that of their servants.'[12]

7 Ibid, at 65 (per Mocatta J). As to the time when a speed warranty applied, see p 31, ante.
8 *Tor Line AB (Renamed Investment AB Torman) v Alltrans Group of Canada Ltd, The TFL Prosperity* [1984] 1 Lloyd's Rep 123, HL.
9 [1984] 1 Lloyd's Rep 123, HL.
10 See the judgment of Lord Roskill, ibid, at 127, 128 and 130, disapproving *Nippon Yusen Kaisha v Acme Shipping Corpn* [1972] 1 All ER 35, CA.
11 *International Bulk Carriers (Beirut) SARL v Evlogia Shipping Co SA and Marathon Shipping Co Ltd, The Mihalios Xilas* [1978] 2 Lloyd's Rep 186, QBD (Commercial Court), where the shipowners failed to prove that the delay was not caused by their 'personal act or default'. (See the judgment of Donaldson J, ibid, at 192.)
12 'Baltime 1939' form, clause 13. See Appendix B, post. For a case where a clause in a charter-party entitled the charterers to limit their liability in respect of claims arising from improper handling during discharging, see *Filikos Shipping Corpn of Monrovia v Shipmair BV, The Filikos* [1983] 1 Lloyd's Rep 9, CA. For a case where a vessel loaded a cargo of scrap causing damage to a tank top and the charterers were held liable, see *Atlantis Shipping (CI) Ltd v J Wharton (Shipping) Ltd, The Sea Humber* [1984] 2 Lloyd's Rep 355, QBD (Commercial Court). (See the judgment of Neill J, ibid, at 362.)

The indemnity afforded by this clause is wide enough to cover a reasonable settlement of a claim made by a stevedore against the shipowners in respect of injuries sustained by him in loading a vessel, but the charterers are under no liability to indemnify the shipowners unless there has been improper or careless loading on their part and this caused the injuries.[13]

A charter-party sometimes states that the charterers are 'to load, stow and trim the cargo under the supervision and responsibility of the master'.[14]

The effect of the words 'and responsibility' is to effect a prima facie transfer of liability for damage to the vessel or cargo by the negligence of stevedores in the loading or discharge of the cargo.[15] If, however, the charterers intervened in such operations, they themselves would be liable for the damage caused.[16]

Where a shipowner chooses to withdraw his vessel from her profit-earning function in order to undertake necessary wrongful damage repairs, he is entitled to take advantage of the period of repair to do other work of his own which is desirable although not immediately necessary, and to recover the whole cost of detention from the charterer.[17]

WAR CLAUSE

A clause in a time charter-party often states:[18]

'The vessel, unless the consent of the owners be first obtained, not to be ordered nor continue to any place or on any voyage nor be used on any service which will bring

---

13   *Helsingfors SS Co Ltd AB v Rederiaktiebolaget Rex, The White Rose* [1969] 2 Lloyd's Rep 52, QBD (Commercial Court). See the judgment of Donaldson J, ibid, at 60. For a case where a charter-party provided that the charterers were to bear 1s. per gross registered ton 'on any one cargo' of claims arising from improper stowage or short delivery, see *Clan Line Steamers Ltd v Ove Skou Rederi A/S* [1969] 2 Lloyd's Rep 155, QBD (Commercial Court) where Roskill J, held (ibid, at 163) that the words 'any one cargo' meant any one parcel of cargo identifiable by a separate bill of lading.

14   *Alexandros Shipping Co of Piraeus v MSC Mediterranean Shipping Co SA of Geneva, The Alexandros P* [1986] 1 Lloyd's Rep 421, QBD (Commercial Court).

15   Ibid. The words were held to cover specifically not only the mechanical process of handling the ship's gear and cargo but also matters of the negligence of the stevedores in the strategic planning of loading and discharging the cargo: ibid.

16   Ibid.

17   *Elpidoforos Shipping Corpn v Furness Withy (Australia) Pty Ltd, The Oinoussian Friendship* [1987] 1 Lloyd's Rep 258, QBD (Commercial Court), where the vessel suffered damage due to ranging while lightening.

18   See e g 'Baltime 1939' form, clause 21 (Appendix B).

her within a zone which is dangerous as the result of any actual or threatened act of war, war hostilities, warlike operations. . . .'

Whether a zone is dangerous is a matter of fact in each case. Thus, in *Ocean Tramp Tankers Corpn v Sovfracht V/O*[19]

During the Suez Canal crisis of 1956 the charterers ordered a vessel, which was chartered under a charter-party containing a war clause in the form set out above, to Port Said and allowed her to remain in the Canal.
Held, that the zone was 'dangerous'[20] and that the charterers were in breach of the clause.

Where a charter-party stated that a crew war bonus was to be paid by the charterers, it was held that it was recoverable by the shipowners if in all the circumstances it was reasonable for them to agree to pay such a bonus to the crew having regard to the risks involved to the vessel.[1]

REDELIVERY

(i) *Place and time of redelivery*
A usual clause states that

'The vessel is to be redelivered at an ice-free port in the charterers' option at the place or within the range stated in [the charter-party] between 9 am and 6 pm, and 9 am and 2 pm on Saturday, but the day of redelivery shall not be a Sunday or legal holiday.'[2]

In *Reardon Smith Line Ltd v Sanko Steamship Co Ltd, The Sanko Honour*[3]

A vessel was to be redelivered at a port 'not further in distance than the Persian Gulf is from Japan' at the charterers' option. She was redelivered at Honolulu. The shipowners claimed damages for wrongful redelivery on the ground that Honolulu was further from the Persian Gulf than Japan was.
Held, by the Queen's Bench Division (Commercial Court), that the charterers were not in breach, for the words indicated that Japan, and not the Persian Gulf, was to be

---

19 [1963] 2 Lloyd's Rep 381, CA.
20 The evidence on this point is set out ibid, at 387–8.
1 *Ocean Star Tankers SA v Total Transport Corpn of Liberia Ltd, The Taygetos (No 2)* [1988] 2 Lloyd's Rep 474, QBD (Commercial Court). See the judgment of Hamilton QC, ibid, at 478. In this case there was a clear danger of attacks on vessels navigating in the sea routes to the ports to which the vessel was ordered during the Iran/Iraq war (ibid, at 479).
2 See eg 'Baltime 1939' form, clause 7 (Appendix B).
3 [1985] 1 Lloyd's Rep 418, QBD (Commercial Court).

treated as the central point from which the obligation of redelivery was to be regarded. Honolulu, therefore, was within the redelivery range.[4]

Where a vessel is redelivered at the wrong port, the measure of damages varies according to the circumstances in each case.[5]

Thus, in *Malaysian International Shipping Corpn v Empresa Cubana de Fletes, The Bunga Kenanga*[6]

The vessel 'Bunga Kenanga' was redelivered to her owners at Rotterdam instead of at a port in the Far East. The owners claimed damages for breach of contract. *Held*, by the Queen's Bench Division (Commercial Court), that the measure of damages was the difference between the net return under the charter-party and the net return of her actual employment.[7]

A clause[8] usually provides that

'The charterers to give the owners not less than ten days' notice at which port and on about which day the vessel will be redelivered.'

Where a vessel is redelivered to the shipowners prematurely, they are entitled to damages.[9]

(ii) *Condition of the vessel on redelivery*

Usually the charterer has to redeliver the ship in the same good order as when delivered (fair wear and tear excepted).[10]

Breach of such a clause entitles the shipowner to claim damages

4   See the judgment of Hobhouse J, ibid, at 420.
5   *Malaysian International Shipping Corpn v Empresa Cubana de Fletes, The Bunga Kenanga* [1981] 1 Lloyd's Rep 518, QBD (Commercial Court); *Santa Martha Baay Scheepvaart and Handelsmaatschappij NV v Scanbulk A/S, The Rijn* [1981] 2 Lloyd's Rep 267, QBD (Commercial Court). (See the judgment of Mustill J, ibid, at 270.)
6   [1981] 1 Lloyd's Rep 518, QBD (Commercial Court).
7   See the judgment of Parker J, ibid, at 519.
8   'Baltime 1939' form, clause 7. (Appendix B).
9   *Armagas Ltd v Mundogas SA, The Ocean Frost* [1986] 2 Lloyd's Rep 109, HL, where, however, the charterers were held not to be bound by the charter-party because their agent had no authority to enter into it. See the judgment of Lord Keith of Kinkel, ibid, at 116.
10 *Chellew Navigation Co v A R Appelquist Kolimport AG* (1933) 38 Con Cas 218. For a case where the holds of the vessel were unclean on redelivery, see *Aurora Borealis Compania Armadora SA and Buenamar Compania Naviera SA v Marine Midland Bank NA, The Maistros* [1984] 1 Lloyd's Rep 646, QBD (Commercial Court). (See the judgment of Staughton J, ibid, at 651.) For a case where the shipowners were to take redelivery of a vessel with the damage unrepaired but damage affecting her class was to be repaired before redelivery, see *Somelas Corpn v Gerrards Rederi A/S, The Pantelis A Lemos* [1980] 2 Lloyd's Rep 102, QBD (Commercial Court).

only, and not to insist on the charterer effecting the repairs before redelivery.[11]

Where a vessel is redelivered to the shipowner and is not in the same good order as when delivered due to the charterer's fault, and repairs to her have to be effected in order to restore her to that condition, the shipowner can claim the cost of repairs and any loss of profit whilst she is being repaired. But he cannot claim hire for this period.[12]

(iii) *Fuel-oil*
Often there is a clause stating the amount of fuel-oil which must be left in the vessel's bunkers on redelivery.

A usual clause[13] states:

'... the owners at port of redelivery to take over and pay for all ... fuel-oil remaining in the vessel's bunkers at current price at [that port].'

Where a charter-party states that the owners must take over and pay for all fuel remaining on board at the port of redelivery, the charterers are not entitled to take on board fuel which is in no way required for charter-party purposes.[14]

Thus, in *Mammoth Bulk Carriers Ltd v Holland Bulk Transport BV, The Captain Diamantis*[15]

By a clause in a time charter-party the owners were to take over and pay for all fuel remaining on board the vessel at the port of redelivery. The charterers informed the owners that the vessel would be redelivered with full bunkers aboard and that the

---

11 *Attica Sea Carriers Corpn v Ferrostaal-Poseidon Bulk Reederei GmbH, The Puerto Buitrago* [1976] 1 Lloyd's Rep 250, CA (charter-party by demise).
12 *Wye Shipping Co v Compagnie Paris-Orleans* [1922] 1 KB 617. See also *Attica Sea Carriers Corpn v Ferrostaal-Poseidon Bulk Reederei GmbH*, supra, where the shipowners' remedy, where the vessel was let out under a demise charter-party and redelivered in bad condition, lay in damages only, and they could not claim hire until the repairs were affected.
13 See e g 'Baltime 1939' form, clause 4 (Appendix B). A similar clause in the New York Produce Exchange form of charter-party has been held to be wholly inapt to apply to termination of the contract otherwise than on its expiry; the bunkers while aboard the vessel were at all material times the property of the charterers; and on cancellation of the charter-party the shipowners' right to consume the bunkers remaining on board the vessel terminated: *Stellar Chartering and Brokerage Inc v Efibanca-Ente Finanziario Interbancario SpA* [1984] 1 Lloyd's Rep 119, HL. (See the judgment of Lord Diplock, ibid, at 122).
14 *Mammoth Bulk Carriers Ltd v Holland Bulk Transport BV, The Captain Diamantis* [1978] 1 Lloyd's Rep 346, CA.
15 [1978] 1 Lloyd's Rep 346, CA. (See the judgment of Lord Denning MR, ibid, at 349.)

owners would be required to purchase all the fuel, although it was in excess of their requirements. The owners instructed the master not to accept further bunkers.
Held, that they were entitled to do so. Although no upper limits on the bunkers for which the owners had to pay was fixed by the clause, the charter-party did not confer any power on the charterers to take on board fuel which was in no way required for charter-party purposes, for the minimum quantity of fuel to reach the nearest main bunkering port was already on board when the vessel reached the port of redelivery.

Where there is a clause in the charter-party stating that on redelivery the owners are to pay for fuel remaining on board, and no price is mentioned, it is implied that they must pay a reasonable one i e the market price.[16]

(iv) *Sending vessel on last voyage*

If the charterer sends the vessel on her last voyage at a time when there is no expectation that she will be redelivered within a reasonable time of the end of the period of the charter-party, and she is, in fact, redelivered late, he is guilty of a breach of contract.[17]

When a charter-party is for a stated period, eg 3 or 6 months, without any express margin or allowance, the Court may imply a reasonable margin or allowance because it is impossible for anyone to calculate exactly the day on which the last voyage may end.[18] But it is open to the parties to provide that there is to be no margin or allowance.[19] It is also open to them to fix expressly what the margin or allowance will be, and then the vessel must be redelivered within the permitted margin or allowance.[20]

If the charterer sends the vessel on a voyage which it is reasonably expected will be completed by the end of the charter period, the shipowners must obey the directions. If she is delayed by causes for

16   *Harmony Shipping Co SA v Saudi-Europe Line Ltd, The Good Helmsman* [1981] 1 Lloyd's Rep 377, CA. (See the judgment of Ackner LJ, ibid, at 419.)

17   *Alma Shipping Corpn of Monrovia v Mantovani, The Dione* [1975] 1 Lloyd's Rep 115, CA; *Marbienes Compania Naviera SA v Ferrostaal AG, The Democritos*[1976] 2 Lloyd's Rep 149, CA; *Skibsaktieselskapet Snefonn, Skibsaksjeselskapet Bergehus and Sig Bergesen D Y & Co v Kawasaki Kisen Kaisha Ltd, The Berge Tasta* [1975] 1 Lloyd's Rep 422, QBD (Commercial Court), which concerned late redelivery of a vessel chartered under a consecutive voyage charter-party.

18   *Alma Shipping Corpn of Monrovia v Mantovani, The Dione*, supra, at 117 (per Lord Denning MR).

19   Ibid, at 117 (per Lord Denning MR).

20   Ibid, at 117 (per Lord Denning MR). See *Gulf Shipping Lines Ltd v Compania Naviera Alanje SA, The Aspa Maria* [1976] 2 Lloyd's Rep 643, CA ('6 months, 30 days more or less at charterers' option'); *Mareva Navigation Co Ltd v Canaria Armadora SA, The Mareva A/S* [1977] 1 Lloyd's Rep 368 ('5 months, 20 days more or less at charterers' option').

which neither party is responsible, hire is payable at the charter rate until redelivery even though the market rate may have gone up or down.[1]

Thus, in *Timber Shipping Co SA v London and Overseas Freighters Ltd*[2]

A vessel was chartered 'for 12 months, 15 days more or less in charterers' option' from 29 December 1967. Discharge of her cargo was delayed by reason of strikes and she was not redelivered to the shipowners until 24 April 1969. The charterers contended that damages were the only remedy available to the shipowners, and should be assessed on the basis of the current market rate.
Held, that the charterers were liable to pay the contractual rate of hire from 29 December 1968 until 24 April 1969.

A firm intention on the part of the charterer is by itself insufficient to fix the date when the legitimacy of a last voyage must be established.[3]

If the charterer sends the vessel on a voyage which she cannot reasonably be expected to complete within the charter period, the shipowner is entitled to refuse that direction and call for another one. If the charterer refuses to give it, the shipowner can accept his conduct as a breach going to the root of the contract, fix a fresh charter for the vessel, and sue for damages.[4]

If the shipowner agrees to the voyage originally ordered by the charterer, he is entitled to be paid hire at the current market rate for the excess period.[5]

Thus, in *Alma Shipping Corpn of Monrovia v Mantovani, The Dione*[6]

A vessel was chartered 'for a period of 6 months, 20 days more or less in charterers' option' from 8 March 1970. The charterers sent her on her last voyage on 2 August. It could not reasonably be expected to be completed until the middle of October. In fact, the vessel was redelivered on 7 October.

---

1   *Alma Shipping Corpn of Monrovia v Mantovani, The Dione*, supra, at 117 (per Lord Denning MR); *Jadranska Slobodna Plovidba v Gulf Shipping Line Ltd, The Matija Gubec* [1983] 1 Lloyd's Rep 24, QBD (Commercial Court) ('12 months, 45 days more or less in charterers' option').
2   [1971] 1 Lloyd's Rep 523, HL. See the judgment of Lord Reid, ibid, at 528, and that of Lord Morris of Borth-y-Gest, ibid, at 529.
3   *Jadranska Slobodna Plovidba v Gulf Shipping Line Ltd, The Matija Gubec* [1983] 1 Lloyd's Rep 24, QBD (Commercial Court), at 28 (per Staughton J).
4   *Alma Shipping Corpn of Monrovia v Mantovani, The Dione* [1975] 1 Lloyd's Rep 115 at 118, CA (per Lord Denning MR).
5   Ibid, at 118 (per Lord Denning MR). For the method of calculating the market rate, see *Arta Shipping Co Ltd v Thai Europe Tapioca Service Ltd, The Johnny* [1977] 2 Lloyd's Rep 1, CA. (See the judgment of Orr J, ibid, at 4, and that of Sir David Cairns, ibid, at 4.)
6   [1975] 1 Lloyd's Rep 115, CA.

Held, by Court of Appeal, she should have been redelivered by 28 September. Hire was payable at the charter rate until that date, but thereafter at the market rate.

The charter-party, of course, may contain an express clause relating to the sending of a vessel on her last voyage eg

'Should the vessel be ordered on a voyage by which the charter period will be exceeded the charterers to have the use of the vessel to enable them to complete the voyage provided it could be reasonably calculated that the voyage would allow redelivery about the time fixed for the termination of the charter, but for any time exceeding the termination date the charterers to pay the market rate if higher than the rate stipulated herein.'[7]

REPUDIATION OF CHARTER-PARTY BY SHIPOWNER

Where a time charter-party is wrongfully repudiated, the charterer is entitled to claim damages amounting to the difference between the contract rate for the balance of the period of the charter-party and the market rate for chartering a substitute vessel.[8]

Thus, in *Koch Marine Inc v D'Amico di Navigazione ARL, The Elena d' Amico*[9]

The owners of the vessel 'Elena d'Amico' let her out to the charterers under a time charter-party for a period of 3 years from 10 January 1972. The charter-party stated that the owners should maintain her class during and throughout the period. In March 1973 they informed the charterers that due to substantial repairs being necessary there was no chance of her resuming her service. On 30 March the charterers accepted the owners' conduct as a repudiation of the charter-party and claimed damages.
Held, by the Queen's Bench Division (Commercial Court), that the measure of damages was the difference between the contract rate for the balance of the period of the charter-party and the market rate for chartering a substitute vessel.[10]

ARBITRATION CLAUSE

A usual clause[11] states:

'Any dispute arising under the Charter to be referred to arbitration in London (or

---

7 'Baltime 1939' form, clause 7. (Appendix B).
8 *Koch Marine Inc v D'Amico Societa di Navigazione ARL, The Elena d'Amico* [1980] 1 Lloyd's Rep 75, QBD (Commercial Court).
9 [1980] 1 Lloyd's Rep 75, QBD (Commercial Court).
10 See the judgment of Robert Goff J, ibid, at 89. For a case where the shipowners failed to secure the release from arrest and were held not to have wrongly repudiated the charter-party in insisting on the charterers putting up satisfactory security to bring about her release, see *Richmond Shipping Ltd v Vestland D/S and A/S, The Vestland* [1980] 2 Lloyd's Rep 171, QBD (Commercial Court).
11 'Baltime 1939' form, clause 23. For a case in which a charter-party contained an arbitration clause stating that arbitration under it was to take place in London,

such other place as may be agreed) one arbitrator to be nominated by the Owners and the other by the Charterers, and in case the Arbitrators shall not agree then to the decision of an Umpire to be appointed by them, the award of the Arbitrators or the Umpire to be final and binding upon both parties.'

The charter-party may state that the claimant's arbitrator must be appointed within a specified time otherwise the claim will be deemed to be waived and absolutely barred.[12]

The Court has power to extend the time for commencing arbitration proceedings if it is of the opinion that in the circumstances of the case undue hardship would otherwise be caused.[13]

(B) Implied undertakings in time charter-parties

In the case of a time charter-party certain undertakings are implied by law, *viz.*

(1) *On the part of the shipowner*: that the vessel is seaworthy[14] at the commencement of the period of the hiring.[15] But unseaworthiness by itself does not entitle the charterer to repudiate the contract. He can only do so if the delay in putting the defects right is such as to amount to a frustration of the charter-party.[16]

and that the contract was governed by Spanish law, and it was held that the clause was valid under that law, see *Cia Maritima Zorroza SA v Sesostris SAE, The Marques de Bolarque* [1984] 1 Lloyd's Rep 652, QBD (Commercial Court). (See the judgment of Hobhouse J, ibid, at 659.)

12 See e g *Intermare Transport GmbH v Naves Transoceanicas Armadora SA, The Aristokratis* [1976] 1 Lloyd's Rep 552, QBD (Commercial Court), where the claimant's arbitrator was to be appointed 'within 12 months of final discharge, and these words meant within 12 months from discharge at the end of a cargo-carrying voyage'. (See the judgment of Mocatta J, ibid, at 555.)

13 Arbitration Act 1950, s 27. See e g *Intermare Transport GmbH v Naves Transoceanicas Armadora SA, the Aristokratis*, supra. (See the judgment of Mocatta J, ibid, at 557.) *Casillo Grani v Napier Shipping Co, The World Ares* [1984] 2 Lloyd's Rep 481, QBD (Commercial Court). (See the judgment of Neill J, ibid, at 489.)

14 As to seaworthiness, see pp 29–30, ante.

15 *Giertsen v Turnbull* 1908 SC 1101; *Hong Kong Fir Shipping Co Ltd v Kawasaki Kisen Kaisha Ltd* [1962] 2 QB 26, [1962] 1 All ER 474, CA.

16 See p 16, ante.

(2) *On the part of the charterer*:

(a) that he will only use the vessel between good and safe ports.[17]

(b) that he will not ship dangerous goods.[18]

REPRESENTATIONS, CONDITIONS AND WARRANTIES

If the charterer has entered into a charter-party on the strength of statements made to him by the shipowner, certain courses are open to him if the statements turn out to be untrue. Certain remedies are also available to him if there has been a breach of condition or a breach of warranty on the part of the shipowner.

The legal effect

(1) *Representations*[19]

If the shipowner makes an innocent misrepresentation which induces the charterer to sign the contract, the charterer may be entitled to rescind the charter-party.[20]

Where an innocent misrepresentation has been made, the person making it will be liable to pay damages unless he proves that he had reasonable ground to believe and did believe up to the time when the contract was made that the facts represented were true.[1]

But in lieu of rescission of the contract on the ground of innocent misrepresentation, the Court may declare the contract subsisting and award damages if it is of opinion that it would be equitable to do so, having regard to the nature of the misrepresentation and the loss that would be caused by it if the contract were upheld, as well as to the loss that rescission would cause to the other party.[2]

If the misrepresentation is fraudulent, the charterer can rescind the contract and claim damages for deceit.[3]

---

17 *Vardinoyannis v Egyptian General Petroleum Corpn, The Evaggelos Th* [1971] 2 Lloyd's Rep 200, QBD (Commercial Court), at 205 (per Donaldson J).

18 See pp 24–25, ante. The statutes relating to the shipment of dangerous goods there mentioned also apply to time charter-parties.

19 See generally Chitty, *The Law of Contracts* (25th edn 1983), volume 1, chapter 6. This subject is primarily a matter of the law of contract, and a full discussion would appear out of place in an introductory book on the carriage of goods by sea.

20 Ibid, paras 438–458.

1 Misrepresentation Act 1967, s 2(1).

2 Ibid, s 2(2).

3 Chitty, op cit, paras 433–437.

No remedy is available to him if the misrepresentation, whether innocent or fraudulent, does not induce him to enter the contract.[4]

(2) *Conditions*

Certain terms in a charter-party go to the root of the contract and amount to a condition. If there has been a breach of a condition, the charterer can refuse to load, and can claim damages as well.[5]

(3) *Warranties*

Some terms in the charter-party do not go to its root, and for breach of them a charterer can claim damages only.[6]

If a representation has been made a term of the contract, then it may amount to a condition or a warranty, as the case may be.[7]

Is the term a condition or a warranty?

Whether the term amounts to a condition or a warranty is a matter of construction, depending on the intention of the parties and the whole of the circumstances.[8]

(A) EXAMPLES OF CONDITIONS

The following express terms are usually held to be conditions:

(i) the position of the ship at the date of the charter-party;

Thus, in *Behn v Burness*[9]

A charter-party stated that a vessel was 'now in the port of Amsterdam'. In fact, she was 62 miles away from that port.
Held, the statement was a condition and, since it had been broken, the charterer was entitled to refuse to load when the vessel arrived at the port of loading.

4 ibid, paras 405–406.
5 Ibid, para 746.
6 Ibid, para 746.
7 Ibid, para 733.
8 See eg *Compagnie General Maritime v Diakan Spirit SA, The Ymnos* [1982] 2 Lloyd's Rep 574, QBD (Commercial Court), where the charter-party in respect of a container vessel stated: 'Owners guarantee the loading of the containers in the stowage plan without any stability problem', and the Court refused to construe the clause as a condition, the word 'guarantee' meaning no more than that any stability problem during loading of the contractual number of containers would result in a breach of contract by the shipowners. (See the judgment of Robert Goff J, ibid, at 584.)
9 (1863) 3 B & S 751. See also *Ollive v Booker* (1847) 1 Exch 416.

(ii) her time of sailing:
    Thus, in *Bentsen v Taylor, Sons & Co (No 2)*[10]

A vessel was described as 'now sailed or about to sail from a Pitch Pine Port to the United Kingdom'. The charter-party was dated 29 March but in fact the vessel did not leave the port concerned until 23 April.
Held, the phrase 'now sailed or about to sail' was a condition, and the charterers would have been able to repudiate the charter-party, but were not entitled to do so since, on the evidence, they had waived the breach of the condition.[11]

(iii) her nationality;[12]
(iv) her class on the register;[13]
(v) her capacity for a particular cargo;[14]
(vi) the date when she is 'expected ready to load'.

Thus, in *Maredelanto Compania Naviera SA v Bergbau-Handel GmbH, The Mihalis Angelos*[15]

A vessel was chartered under a charter-party dated 25 May 1965 which stated that she was 'expected ready to load' at Haiphong on 1 July. She arrived at Hong Kong on 23 June and began discharging, but did not complete it until 23 July. In order to maintain her class on the register she would have to undergo a general examination in less than 2 days. It would have taken her 2 days to get from Hong Kong to Haiphong. The charterers repudiated the charter-party on 17 July on the ground that there had been a breach of the clause set out above, and that the clause was a condition. Evidence was given that on 25 May 1965 the shipowners could not reasonably have estimated that the vessel would arrive at Haipong 'about 1 July'.
Held, that the clause was a condition and the charterers were entitled to repudiate the charter-party.

10   [1893] 2 QB 274, CA. See also *Glaholm v Hays* (1841) 2 Man & G 257.
11   As to waiver of a breach of a condition, see p 70, post.
12   *Lothian v Henderson* (1803) 3 Bos & P 499. During the currency of the charter-party there is an implied condition that the ship's flag will not be changed, e g by a British ship being sold to an alien: *Isaacs & Sons Ltd v McAllum & Co Ltd* [1921] 3 KB 377. The amount of damages will depend on the circumstances of each case and may only be nominal: ibid.
13   *Routh v Macmillan* (1863) 2 H & C 750.
14   *Louis Dreyfus et Cie v Parnasa Cia Naviera SA, The Dominator* [1960] 2 QB 49, [1960] 1 All ER 759, CA.
15   [1970] 2 Lloyd's Rep 43, CA. See the judgment of Lord Denning MR at 47. See also *R Pagnan and Fratelli v N G J Schouten NV, The Filipinas I*, [1973] 1 Lloyd's Rep 349 QBD (Commercial Court) [1973] 1 Lloyd's Rep 349, where an arbitration award was remitted to an arbitrator for him to consider whether the statement that the vessel was expected ready to load by a certain date was based on reasonable grounds. In *Sanday & Co v Keighley, Maxted & Co* (1922) 91 LJKB 624 and *Finnish Government (Ministry of Food) v H Ford & Co Ltd* (1921) 6 Ll L Rep 188, which were both cases concerning the sale of goods, the phrase 'expected ready to load' was also held to be a condition.

(vii) the date by which the vessel is to be nominated by the shipowner.[16]

(B) EXAMPLES OF WARRANTIES

(i) Maintenance of vessel
If the shipowner has failed to carry out a term of a time charter-party whereby he undertakes to maintain the vessel in a seaworthy state, this only entitles the charterer to sue him for damages, and not to repudiate the charter-party.[17] But he can repudiate if the defect cannot be remedied in a reasonable time.[18]

(ii) Size of bunkers
A statement as to the size of a vessel's bunkers has been held to be a warranty.[19]

Thus, in *Efploia Shipping Corpn Ltd v Canadian Transport Co Ltd, The Pantanassa*[20]

A vessel was chartered for a voyage from 'North Pacific Coast to South and/or East Africa', and was to be placed at the disposal of the charterers at a safe port in South Korea. A clause in the charter-party stated that the charterers were to take over the fuel on board 'expected about 6/700 tons'. The vessel was delivered at Pusan with 936 tons of fuel on board. The shipowners claimed the price of the oil, but the charterers claimed, by way of set-off or counterclaim, damages for breach of warranty by the shipowners in delivering a larger quantity of oil.
Held, by the Queen's Bench Division (Commercial Court), that the counterclaim succeeded. By the words 'expected about 6/700 tons' the shipowners warranted that they honestly expected the bunkers to be about 600 to 700 tons, and that they had reasonable grounds for that expectation. They had acted honestly, but had not made their estimate on reasonable grounds because the master had been negligent in taking proper measurements, and in consequence they were ignorant of the amount of the oil on board when she sailed for Pusan.[1]

---

16 *Mitsui OSK Lines v Garnar Grain Co Inc, The Myrtos* [1984] 2 Lloyd's Rep 449, QBD ('vessel to be nominated 20 days prior to the vessel's ETA'); *Greenwich Marine Inc v Federal Commerce Navigation Co Ltd, The Mavro Vetranic* [1985] 1 Lloyd's Rep 580, QBD ('20 days prior to ETA the owners are to nominate performing vessels').

17 *Hong Kong Fir Shipping Co Ltd v Kawasaki Kisen Kaisha Ltd* [1962] 2 QB 26, [1962] 1 All ER 474.

18 Ibid.

19 *Efploia Shipping Corpn Ltd v Canadian Transport Co Ltd, The Pantanassa* [1958] 2 Lloyd's Rep 449, QBD (Commercial Court).

20 [1958] 2 Lloyd's Rep 449, QBD (Commercial Court).

1   See the judgment of Diplock J, ibid, at 455.

(iii) Redelivery of vessel

A clause in a charter-party by demise stating that the charterer was
to redeliver the vessel to the shipowner in the same good order and
condition as on delivery, and before redelivery make all such repairs
found to be necessary, was held not to be a condition precedent to
the right to redeliver, but merely to give the shipowner a remedy in
damages for the cost of the repairs.[2]

(iv) Vessel's speed

Where a time charter-party stated that a vessel was capable of
steaming at 14½ knots, and in fact could only do 10·61 knots, this was
held to be a breach of warranty for which the owners would have
been liable had it not been for an exception clause in their favour.[3]

Waiver of breach of condition

If the party who has a right to repudiate the contract elects to go on
with it, so that the position of the parties is changed, he must abide
by the contract, but can sue for damages for any loss he has
sustained.[4]

Thus, in *Pust v Dowie*[5]

A ship was chartered for a lump sum freight[6] on condition that she took a cargo of
1000 tons. In the special circumstances of the voyage she could not take that amount,
but the charterers loaded her and she sailed. The shipowner claimed the freight.
Held, that there was no breach of the condition, and, even if there had been, the
charterers had waived their right to repudiate. They must pay the freight.[7]

FRUSTRATION OF A CHARTER-PARTY

Both the shipowner and the charterer will be discharged from their
obligations under the charter-party if it becomes frustrated.

2   *Attica Sea Carriers Corpn v Ferrostaal-Poseidon Bulk Reederei GmbH, The Puerto
Buitrago* [1976] 1 Lloyd's Rep 250, CA.
3   *Cosmos Bulk Transport Inc v China National Foreign Trade Transportation Corpn,
The Apollonius* [1978] 1 Lloyd's Rep 53, QBD (Commercial Court). As to the time
when the warranty applied, see p 31, ante. As to the exception clause in that case
see p 56, ante.
4   See *Fraser v Telegraph Construction and Maintenance Co* (1872) LR 7 QB 566.
5   (1864) 5 B & S 20.
6   As to lump sum freight, see pp 261–262, post.
7   See also *Bentsen v Taylor, Sons & Co (No) 2* [1893] 2 QB 274.

Causes giving rise to frustration

Frustration of the charter-party may arise from various causes:

(1) impossibility of performance;
(2) delay;
(3) subsequent change in the law.

(1) *Impossibility of performance*

The doctrine of impossiblity of performance applies to contracts in general. For present purposes it is sufficient to note that it affects all contracts of affreightment. But its scope is not unlimited; unless certain well-defined circumstances exist the Court will refuse to apply it.

When performance of a contract depends upon the continued existence of a given person, thing or set of circumstances,[8] a condition will generally be implied that if, without the fault of either party, performance becomes impossible owing to the fact that that person, thing or set of circumstances has ceased to exist, each of the parties to the contract shall be discharged from liability for further performance.[9]

The fact that a charter-party becomes more expensive for a party to perform is not sufficient to bring about its frustration.

Thus, in *Ocean Tramp Tankers Corpn v Sovfracht V/O, The Eugenia*[10]

A vessel had been chartered under a time charter-party in September 1956 'for a trip out to India via Black Sea' from Genoa. The Suez Canal was blocked in the Suez crisis of tht year.

Held, in the circumstances the blockage of the Canal did not bring about such a fundamentally different situation as to frustrate the adventure for (i) the voyage via

---

8 See e g *Occidental Worldwide Investment Corpn v Skibs Avanti A/S, Skibs Glarona A/S, Skibs Navalis A/S, The Siboen and the Sibotre* [1976] 1 Lloyd's Rep 293, QBD (Commercial Court), where it was contended that the charter-parties were frustrated because the charterers had chartered the vessel as a reserve in case they could not get their oil supplies from Libya, and that had not arisen.

9 On the theory of frustration generally, see Chitty, *The Law of Contracts* (25th edn 1983), volume 1, *Taylor v Caldwell* (1863) 3 B & S 826; *Joseph Constantine SS Line Ltd v Imperial Smelting Corpn Ltd, The Kingswood* [1942] AC 154, [1941] 2 All ER 165. A somewhat different view of the basis of the rule was expressed by Goddard J, in *W J Tatem Ltd v Gamboa* [1939] 1 KB 132, [1938] 3 All ER 135. But the point was left open by Lord Wright in the *Joseph Constantine* case [1941] 2 All ER 165 at 186, as being wholly academic. See further, *Davis Contractors Ltd v Fareham UDC* [1956] AC 696, [1956] 2 All ER 145, HL.

10 [1964] 2 QB 226, [1964] 1 All ER 161, CA, overruling *Société Franco Tunisienne d'Armement v Sidermar SpA, The Messalia* [1961] 2 QB 278, [1960] 2 All ER 529.

the Suez Canal would normally take 108 days, and via the Cape of Good Hope, 138 days; (ii) the cargo would not have been adversely affected by the longer voyage; and (iii) the voyage via the Cape made no great difference except that it would be more expensive.

Again, in *Palmo Shipping Inc v Continental Ore Corpn, The Captain George K*[11]

A vessel was chartered in April 1967 for a voyage from Coatzacoalcos, Mexico, to Kandla, India. At that time the Suez Canal was open. The distance between the two ports via the Canal was 9,700 miles. When the vessel was approaching the Canal in June 1967, war broke out and the Canal was closed. She turned back and went to Kandla via the Cape of Good Hope and sailed 18,400 miles in consequence.
Held, in the circumstances the closure of the Canal did not frustrate the charter-party, and the charterers were not liable to the shipowners for the additional costs incurred in sailing via the Cape.

In the absence of exceptions clauses,[12] there is an absolute obligation to supply a cargo of the contractual description and quantity. The inability to do so or difficulties or delays in the country of shipment is not capable of bringing the doctrine of frustration into operation.[13]

Thus, in *Kawasaki Steel Corpn v Sardoil SpA, The Zuiho Maru*[14]

An oil company carried out the Saudi Arabian Government's policy of cutting oil production by rationing the supply of oil to individual tankers. As a result the charterers of the 'Zuiho Maru' could only load 93 per cent instead of a full and complete cargo.
Held, that the charter-party was not frustrated.

Where, however, the charterer seeks to rely on destruction of the intended cargo as giving rise to frustration, it would seem that he must show that the contract was for shipment of a *specific* cargo and

---

11 [1970] 2 Lloyd's Rep 21, QBD (Commercial Court). See the judgment of Mocatta J, ibid, at 32, where he said that the difference between the contemplated voyage via the Canal and the voyage via the Cape amounted only to a difference in expense, and for that reason was insufficient to produce frustration. See also *American Trading and Production Corpn v Shell International Marine Ltd, The Washington Trader* [1972] 1 Lloyd's Rep 463, District Court for the Southern District of New York, where the Suez Canal was closed in 1967, and it was held that the added expense involved in the Cape of Good Hope route was insufficient to make out a case of frustration. (See the judgment of Tyler DJ, ibid, at 467.)

12 See pp 180–189, post.

13 *Kawasaki Steel Corpn v Sardoil SpA, The Zuiho Maru* [1977] 2 Lloyd's Rep 552, QBD (Commercial Court), at 555 (per Kerr J).

14 [1977] 2 Lloyd's Rep 552, QBD (Commercial Court).

that that cargo has become substantially a total loss and cannot be replaced.[15]

Although, however, this principle is common to the general law of contract, the warning by Viscount Simon LC in *Joseph Constantine SS Line Ltd v Imperial Smelting Corpn Ltd, The Kingswood*[16] should always be borne in mind:

'Discharge by supervening impossibility is not a Common Law rule of general application, like discharge by supervening illegality; whether the contract is terminated or not depends on its terms and the surrounding circumstances in each case.'

It follows that, where an implied term of the kind set out above would be inconsistent with some express terms of the contract, the doctrine of frustration cannot be invoked.

So, in *Isles Steam Shipping Co Ltd v Theodoridi & Co*[17]

The charter-party contained a clause that, in the event of export of grain from the loading port being prohibited, the contract should be null and void.
Held, that the doctrine of frustration could not be invoked, since impossibility of performance was dealt with in an express clause; *expressum facit cessare tacitum*.

The application of the maxim *expressum facit cessare tactitum* will, however, exclude the doctrine of frustration only in cases where the express term relied on deals with *total* impossibility of performance: where a limited interruption only is contemplated by the express term, the doctrine will not be excluded by that term.

Thus, in *Fibrosa Spolka Akcyjna v Fairbairn Lawson Combe Barbour Ltd*[18]

The contract contained an express provision that 'should dispatch be hindered or delayed by . . . any cause beyond our reasonable control including . . . war . . . a reasonable extension of time shall be granted'. Performance of the contract by an English company to deliver machinery to a Polish company was rendered impossible by the outbreak of war in 1939.
Held, that the contention that that express term precluded the existence of an implied term would be rejected. Viscount Simon LC said: 'The ambit of the express condition is limited to delay in respect of which a reasonable extension of time might be granted. That might mean a minor delay as distinguished from a prolonged and indefinite interruption of prompt contractual performance which the present war manifestly

---

15 See *E B Aaby's Rederi A/S v Lep Transport Ltd* (1948) 81 Ll L Rep 465, where the finding of the fact was against the charterers on all three points and the actual decision was negative in form. Whether it is in all circumstances necessary to prove non-replaceability, and if so in what sense, does not appear to have been decided.
16 [1942] AC at 163.
17 (1926) 24 Ll L Rep 362.
18 [1943] AC 32, [1942] 2 All ER 122.

and inevitably brings about. . . . The principle is that where supervening events, not due to the fault of either party, render the performance of a contract indefinitely impossible, and there is no undertaking to be bound in any event, frustration ensues, even though the parties may have expressly provided for the case of a limited interruption.'[19]

It will be noted that the doctrine does not apply in cases where performance becomes impossible by reason of the default of one of the parties to the contract. When, therefore, one of the parties relies upon frustration as releasing him from further contractual liability, the onus of proof as to whether or not the impossibility was due to his default may be important.

Thus, in *Joseph Constantine SS Line Ltd v Imperial Smelting Corpn Ltd, The Kingswood*[20]

Where damages for failure to load a cargo were claimed by the charterers, the shipowners relied on the explosion which had occurred in the ship as having frustrated the chartered voyage. The cause of the explosion, however, could not be established. *Held,* the onus was upon the charterers to establish neglect or default on the part of the shipowners; the latter, having shown that the voyage was frustrated by the explosion, had established a prima facie defence and were not bound to prove further that neglect or default on their part had not caused the explosion.

The fact that it has become more onerous or more expensive for one party than he thought is not sufficient to bring about a frustration. It must be more than merely more onerous or more expensive. It must be positively unjust to hold the parties bound. It is often difficult to draw the line. But it must be done, and it is for the Courts to do it as a matter of law.[1]

(2) *Delay*

Discharge from liability on this ground was explained by Bailhache J, thus:

'The commercial frustration of an adventure by delay means, as I understand it, the happening of some unforeseen delay without the fault of either party to a contract, of such a character as that by it the fulfilment of the contract, in the only way in which fulfilment is contemplated and practicable, is so inordinately postponed that its fulfilment when the delay is over will not accomplish the only object or objects which both parties to the contract must have known that each of them had in view at the

---

19 [1943] AC 32 at 40, [1942] 2 All ER 122 at 125.
20 [1942] AC 154, [1941] 2 All ER 165.
 1 *Ocean Tramp Tankers Corpn v Sovfracht V/O, The Eugenia* [1963] 2 Lloyd's Rep 381 at 390, CA (per Lord Denning MR).

time they made the contract, and for the accomplishment of which object or objects the contract was made.'[2]

The burden of proving that a sufficiently serious interruption has occurred to put an end to the contract is, of course, on the party who asserts it.[3] At one time it was thought that the doctrine did not apply if the contract was partly executed, but it is now well settled that this is not so.[4]

In *Jackson v Union Marine Insurance Co Ltd*[5]

Frustration was due to stranding on rocks. The charterers, judging that the delay would be considerable, threw up the charter-party before the ship was refloated.
Held, the charterers were not liable to load the ship, the jury having found that the time necessary for repairing was unreasonably long.

But in *Trade and Transport Inc v Iino Kaiun Kaisha Ltd, The Angelia*[6]

A cargo of phosphate rock was not available at the loading port due to lack of transport. The lack of transport existed at the time the voyage charter-party for the carriage of the cargo was entered into. No enquiry was made by the charterers. The charterers failed to supply a cargo and cancelled the charter-party on the ground that the cargo would not be available before the expiry of a frustrating time.
Held, by QBD (Commercial Court) that, on the evidence, the delay was not sufficient to frustrate the charter-party.

The following cases illustrate the doctrine of frustration in relation to time charter-parties.

In *Admiral Shipping Co Ltd v Weidner, Hopkins & Co*[7]

A ship was hired under a time charter-party for 'two Baltic rounds'. She was not allowed to leave a Russian port on account of the outbreak of war between Germany and Russia. The charter contained an exception of 'restraints of princes'.[8]
Held, that the delay was such as completely to frustrate the adventure and the charterers were not liable for hire.

On the other hand, it should be noted that the doctrine of frustration:

---

2 Per Bailhache J, in *Admiral Shipping Co Ltd v Weidner, Hopkins & Co* [1916] 1 KB 429 at 436, cited with approval in the CA, [1917] 1 KB 222 at 242.
3 *Metropolitan Water Board v Dick, Kerr & Co* [1917] 2 KB 1 at 31, per Scrutton LJ.
4 *Embiricos v Sydney Reid & Co* [1914] 3 KB 45; *Bank Line Ltd v Arthur Capel & Co* [1919] AC 435 at 455.
5 (1874) LR 10 CP 125. See further *Universal Cargo Carriers Corpn v Citati* [1957] 3 All ER 234, [1957] 1 WLR 979, CA.
6 [1972] 2 Lloyd's Rep 154, QBD (Commercial Court). (See the judgment of Kerr J, ibid, at 163.)
7 [1917] 1 KB 222.
8 As to the exception of 'restraints of princes', see pp 182–183, post.

'does not apply when the time charterer has the use of the vessel for some purpose for which he is, under the terms of the time charter-party, entitled to use her, even though that purpose is not the particular purpose for which he desires to use her.'[9]

In other words, the interruption must be such as to destroy the whole basis of the contract. The learned Judge went on to say that as to when a party is entitled to claim that frustration has taken place, the test is the estimate which a reasonable man of business would make of the probable period during which the vessel's services would be lost to the charterer, 'and it will be immaterial whether his anticipation is justified or falsified by the event'.[10]

Thus, in *Port Line Ltd v Ben Line Steamers Ltd*[11]

In November 1954 a vessel was chartered for 30 months. In August 1956 she was requisitioned in view of the Suez Canal crisis, the period of requisition being estimated to be 3 or 4 months. She was released in late November 1956.
Held, the charter-party was not frustrated.

Further, in *Hong Kong Fir Shipping Co Ltd v Kawasaki Kisen Kaisha Ltd*[12]

A vessel was chartered for 24 months from February 1957. Her engines kept breaking down and in June 1957 major repairs had to be effected. These were estimated to take until September, and she was redelivered to the charterers in that month.
Held, the charter-party was not frustrated.

Again, frustration may occur where a vessel is 'trapped' as a result of the outbreak of a war.[13]

Except in the case of supervening illegality, arising from the fact that the contract involves a party in trading with someone who has become an enemy, a declaration of war does not prevent the performance of a contract. It is the acts done in furtherance of the war which may or may not prevent performance, depending on the individual circumstances of the case. If there is any presumption at all, it relates to the duration of the state of war, not to the effects which the war may have on the performance of the contract. The war itself and its effects are by no means necessarily co-terminous.

---

9   Per Bailhache J, in *Anglo-Northern Trading Co Ltd v Emlyn Jones and Williams* [1917] 2 KB 78 at 84.
10   [1917] 2 KB 78 at 85.
11   [1958] 2 QB 146, [1958] 1 All ER 787.
12   [1962] 2 QB 26, [1962] 1 All ER 474, CA.
13   See *International Sea Tankers Inc v Hemisphere Shipping Co Ltd, The Wenjiang (No 2)* [1983] 1 Lloyd's Rep 400, QBD (Commercial Court) and *Finelvet AG v Vinava Shipping Co Ltd, The Chrysalis* [1983] 1 Lloyd's Rep 503, QBD, where in each case vessels were trapped in the Shatt-el-Arab waterway by the outbreak of war between Iran and Iraq.

Any presumption as to the indefinite duration of the war is capable of being rebutted.[14]

(3) *Subsequent change in the law*
Again, both parties are released by a supervening change in the law which renders the contract illegal either by English law or by the law of the country in which performance was to have taken place.[15]

It must be stressed that discharge by supervening illegality, unlike frustration by supervening impossibility, abrogates the contract quite independently of its terms, or of the presumed intention of the parties to it.[16]

Effect of frustration

The effect of frustration upon the rights and liabilities of the parties will depend on whether the charter-party is a voyage charter-party, a time charter-party or a demise charter-party.

(i) *Voyage charter-parties*
In the case of frustration of a voyage charter-party, two results follow:[17]—

(1) the charter-party automatically comes to an end, and each of the parties is released from any further liability to perform his part of the bargain.
(2) If either party has, in pursuance of the charter-party, made a payment to the other in consideration of a consideration which had wholly failed the money so paid could be recovered as money had and received.

An important exception to the above effects is the principle that freight paid in advance[18] is not returnable if frustration supervenes.

---

14 *Finelvet AG v Vinava Shipping Co Ltd, The Chrisalis,* supra, at 511 (per Mustill J).
15 *Ralli Bros v Compania Naviera Sota y Aznar* [1920] 2 KB 287.
16 Per Viscount Simon LC in *Joseph Constantine SS Line Ltd v Imperial Smelting Corpn Ltd, The Kingswood* [1942] AC 154 at 163, [1941] 2 All ER 165 at 171.
17 *Fibrosa Spolka Akcyjna v Fairbairn Lawson Combe Barbour Ltd* [1943] AC 32; [1942] 2 All ER 122, HL.
18 As to advance freight, see pp 262–265, post.

This principle

'should . . . be regarded as a stipulation introduced into such contracts by custom, and not as a result of applying some abstract principle'.[19]

(ii) *Time charter-parties and demise charter-parties*
Time charter-parties and demise charter-parties are governed by the Law Reform (Frustrated Contracts) Act 1943.
   If either of these types of charter-party is frustrated:
   (1) All sums paid or payable to any party in pursuance of the contract before the time of discharge are, in the case of sums so paid, recoverable from him as money received by him to the use of the party by whom the sums were paid, and, in the case of sums so payable, cease to be payable;[20]
   (2) If the party to whom the sums were so paid or payable incurred expenses before the time of discharge in, or for the purpose of, the performance of the contract, the Court may, if it considers it just to do so having regard to all the circumstances of the case, allow him to retain or, as the case may be, recover the whole or any part of the sums so paid or payable, not being an amount in excess of the expenses so incurred.[21]
   (3) Where any party to the contract has, by reason of anything done by any other party, in, or for the purpose of, the performance of the contract, obtained a valuable benefit (other than a payment of money), such sum (if any), not exceeding the value of the benefit, is recoverable from him by the other

---

19 *Fibrosa Spolka Akcyjna v Fairbairn Lawson Combe Barbour Ltd*, supra, at 126 and 43 of the respective reports.
20 Law Reform (Frustrated Contracts) Act 1943, s 1(2).
21 Ibid, s 1(2) proviso. In estimating the amount of an expenses incurred by any party to the contract, the Court may include such sum as appears to be reasonable in respect of overhead expenses and in respect of any work or services performed personally by him: ibid, s 1(5). In considering whether any sum ought to be recovered or retained by any party to the contract, the Court must not take into account any sums which have, by reason of the circumstances giving rise to the frustration of the contract, become payable to that party under any contract of insurance unless there was an obligation to insure imposed by an express term of the frustrated contract or by or under any enactment: ibid, s 1(5).

party, as the Court considers just, having regard to all the circumstances of the Case.[1]

RELEASE OF ONE PARTY FROM HIS OBLIGATIONS

One is now on fresh ground. There is no question of frustration. The principle is this: if either party, before the time for performance of the contract, renounces the contract, the other is released;[2] but if that other elects to treat the contract as still subsisting, he will have his remedy for the breach which has been committed;[3] in so electing, however, he runs the risk of the offending party escaping all liability by reason of a subsequent change of circumstances which renders performance within the agreed time impossible.[4]

Again, either party is released if, before the time for performance, the other has by his conduct made it impossible for him to perform his part.[5]

THE UNFAIR CONTRACT TERMS ACT 1977

By the Unfair Contract Terms Act 1977, s 2(1), which is expressly stated to apply to charter-parties,[6] a person cannot by reference to

1 Ibid, s 1(6). The Court must take into consideration in particular: (*a*) the amount of any expenses incurred before the time of discharge by the benefited party in, or for the purpose of, the performance of the contract, including any sums paid or payable by him to any other party in pursuance of the contract and retained or recoverable by that party; and (*b*) the effect, in relation to the benefit, of the circumstances giving rise to the frustration of the contract: ibid, s 1(3).

2 *SIB International SRL v Metallgesellschaft Corpn, The Noel Bay* [1989] 1 Lloyd's Rep 361, CA, where the charterers repudiated the charter-party and the shipowners entered into a substitute charter-party with a third party. As to the measure of damages, see the judgment of Staughton LJ, ibid, at 366–367.

3 *Danube and Black Sea Railway and Kustenjie Harbour Co Ltd v Xenos* (1863) 13 CBNS 825.

4 *Avery v Bowden* (1856) 6 E & B 953 at 962.

5 *Budgett & Co v Binnington & Co* [1981] 1 QB 35. See also *Alexander & Sons v Akt Dampskibet Hansa* [1920] AC 88.

6 Unfair Contract Terms Act 1977, Sch 1, A detailed discussion of the terms of this Act is outside the scope of this book.

any contract term or to a notice given to persons generally or to particular persons exclude or restrict his liability for death or personal injury resulting from negligence.[7]

Subject to this, sections 2,[8] 3,[9] 4[10] and 7[11] do not extend to charter-parties except in favour of a person dealing as consumer.[12]

7   For the meaning of 'negligence', see Unfair Contract Terms Act 1977, s 1.
8   Which relates to 'negligence liability'.
9   Which relates to 'liability arising in contract'.
10   Which relates to 'unreasonable indemnity clauses'.
11   Which relates to 'miscellaneous contracts under which goods pass'.
12   Unfair Contract Terms Act 1977, Sch 1. As to the meaning of 'dealing as consumer', see ibid, s 12.

Chapter 3

Bills of lading

THE FUNCTIONS OF A BILL OF LADING

A bill of lading has, in the eyes of the law, various aspects:—

(1) It is very good evidence of the contract of affreightment, though not the contract itself, for the contract is usually entered into before the bill of lading is signed.[1]
(2) It is a receipt for the goods shipped and contains certain admissions as to their quantity and condition when put on board.
(3) It is a document of title, without which delivery of the goods cannot normally be obtained.

It is in the second and third of these functions that a bill of lading differs entirely from a charter-party. In the first there is some similarity. A charter-party is always a contract, and nothing more. Where the charterer is also the shipper, the bill of lading is usually only a receipt for the goods and a document of title.[2] In no case, however, does a bill of lading fail to function as a document of title.

(1) Evidence of the contract

Where the charterer is also the shipper, the rights of the shipowner and the charterer as such will be governed by the charter-party

---

1 See per Lord Bramwell in *Sewell v Burdick* (1884) 10 App Cas 74 at 105, and *Ardennes SS (Owner of Cargo) v Ardennes SS (Owners)* [1951] 1 KB 55, [1950] 2 All ER 517, where evidence was admitted of the contract which was made before the bill of lading was signed and which contained a different term. See also *Rambler Cycle Co Ltd v Peninsular and Oriental Steam Navigation Co, Sze Hai Tong Bank Ltd (First Third Party), Southern Trading Co (Second Third Party)* [1968] 1 Lloyd's Rep 42 (Malaysia Federal Court) at 47 (per Thomson LP).
2 See *Rodocanachi v Milburn* (1886) 18 QBD 67.

alone.³ The bill of lading cannot vary or add to the terms of that charter-party unless it contains an express provision to that effect.

But where the charterer puts the ship up as a general ship, the contract of carriage will in each case be evidenced by the bill of lading given to each shipper, irrespective of the terms of the charter-party, except where there is an express agreement to the contrary.⁴

Further, in the case of a general ship, if a shipper knew of the existence of a charter-party, he is taken to have contracted with the charterer and can sue or be sued by him; if he did not, his contract is with the shipowner.⁵

Where the shipper of goods in the chartered ship indorses a bill of lading to the charterer, the relations between the shipowner and the charterer are still governed by the charter-party, at any rate when the master is only authorised to sign bills of lading without prejudice to the charter-party.⁶

Where the charterer indorses a bill of lading so as to transfer the rights and obligations evidenced by it, the indorsee will not be affected by the terms of the charter-party unless:

(1) there is a clause in the bill of lading incorporating some or all of the terms of the charter-party in itself; such clause must be clear and express;⁷

---

3 These statements should be read as painting a general picture in broad outline only. It seems clear that a charterer who is also the shipper may well be liable for freight under the bill of lading notwithstanding a cesser clause in the charter-party: see *Rederi Aktiebolaget Transatlantic v Board of Trade* (1925) 30 Com Cas 117 at 125–6: and *Hill Steam Shipping Co v Hugo Stinnes Ltd* 1941 SC 324.

4 *Pearson v Goschen* (1864) 17 CBNS 352.

5 *Sanderman v Scurr* (1866) LR 2 QB 86; Chorley and Tucker's *Leading Cases* (4th edn 1962), p 290; *The Berkshire* [1974] 1 Lloyd's Rep 185, QBD (Admiralty Court), where the contract was held to be one between the shipowners and the shippers. (See the judgment of Brandon J, ibid, at 188.); *Associated Metals and Minerals Corpn v The Ship Evie W, Aris SS Co Inc and Worldwide Carriers Ltd, The Evie W* [1978] 2 Lloyd's Rep 216, Federal Ct of Appeal of Canada, where it was held that the master signed the bill of lading as the agent of the shipowners. (See the judgment of Jackett CJ, ibid, at 219.)

6 *Love and Steward Ltd v Rowtor SS Co Ltd* [1916] 2 AC 527, HL; *President of India v Metcalfe Shipping Co Ltd, The Dunelmia* [1969] 1 QB 289, [1969] 3 All ER 1549, CA, distinguishing *Calcutta SS Co Ltd v Andrew Weir & Co* [1910] 1 KB 759.

7 As to the effect of the clause 'all other conditions as per charter-party' see *Serraino v Campbell* [1891] 1 QB 283, and *Vergottis v Robinson David & Co* (1928) 31 Ll L Rep 23. Whether the terms of a charter-party have been incorporated into the bill of lading is in each case a matter of construction. See, eg *The Merak* [1965] P 223, [1965] 1 All ER 230, CA (arbitration clause in charter-party *held* to be incorporated into bill of lading); *Atlas Levante-Linie Aktiengesellschaft v*

or (2) the bill of lading is one which the master could not have legally given on account of the terms of the charter-party.

The Courts have taken a benevolent view of the use of general words to incorporate by reference standard terms to be found elsewhere.[8] But where a bill of lading purports to incorporate the terms of a charter-party, a different and stricter rule has developed, especially where the incorporation of arbitration clauses is concerned.[9] The Courts have, in general, defended this rule with some tenacity in the interests of commercial certainty.[10]

Where in a bill of lading there is a clause which purports to incorporate the terms of a specified charter-party, there is not any rule of construction that clauses in that charter-party which are directly germane to the shipment, carriage or delivery of goods and impose obligations on the 'charterer' under that designation, are presumed to be incorporated in the bill of lading with the substitution of (where there is a cesser clause[11]), or inclusion in (where there is

---

Gesellschaft Fuer Getreidhandel AG and Becher, The Phonizien [1966] 1 Lloyd's Rep 150 (arbitration clause in charter-party *held* not to be incorporated into bill of lading); *The Annefield* [1971] P 168, [1971] 1 All ER 394, CA (arbitration clause in charter-party *held* not to be incorporated into bill of lading); *Pacific Molasses Co and United Molasses Trading Co Ltd v Entre Rios Compania Naviera SA, The San Nicholas* [1976] 1 Lloyd's Rep 8, CA (charter-party governed by English *held* to be incorporated into bill of lading, even though blanks were left in charter-party); *Miramar Maritime Corpn v Holborn Trading Ltd, The Miramar* [1984] 2 Lloyd's Rep 129, HL (clause in charter-party relating to demurrage *held* not to be incorporated into bill of lading); *Paros Shipping Corpn v Nafta (GB) Ltd, The Paros* [1987] 2 Lloyd's Rep 269, QBD (Commercial Court), where the bill of lading did not incorporate the terms of the charter-party, and the references to a charter-party were left blank; *Navigazione Alta Italia SpA v Svenska Petroleum AB, The Nai Matteini* [1988] 1 Lloyd's Rep 452, QBD (Commercial Court) (arbitration clause in charter-party *held* not to be incorporated into bill of lading); *Federal Bulk Carriers Inc v C., Itoh & Co Ltd, The Federal Bulker* [1989] 1 Lloyd's Rep 103, CA (arbitration clause in charter-party *held* not to be incorporated into bill of lading). In *Denny, Mott and Dickson Ltd v Lynn Shipping Co Ltd* [1963] 1 Lloyd's Rep 339, it was held that an arbitration clause in a charter-party had been effectively incorporated into the bill of lading, but that the clause did not apply in the events which happened. As to this point, see p 172, post.

8   *Federal Bulk Carriers Inc v C Itoh & Co Ltd, The Federal Bulker*, supra, at 105 (per Bingham LJ).
9   Ibid, at 105 (per Bingham LJ).
10   Ibid, at 105 (per Bingham LJ).
11   As to cesser clauses, see pp 254–256, post.

no cesser clause), the designation 'charterer', the designation 'consignee of the cargo' or 'bill of lading holder'.[12]

Exceptional terms are sometimes introduced, and the question, familiar in the law of contract, arises: How far is an acceptor of an offer in common form bound by conditions contained in it? The question has arisen mainly in connection with tickets issued to passengers containing stipulations limiting the liability of the carrying company. The answer is that the acceptor is bound by such terms, whether he read them or not[13] provided reasonable notice of them was given him.[14] 'If a shipowner wishes to introduce into his bill of lading so novel a clause as one exempting him from general average contribution . . . he ought not only to make it clear in words, but also to make it conspicuous by inserting it in such type and in such part of the document that a person of ordinary capacity and care should not fail to see it.'[15]

(2) The bill of lading as a receipt

Under modern conditions the bill of lading is usually signed by the loading broker,[16] but sometimes by the master, acknowledging the quantity and condition of the goods when put on board. The precise effect of this acknowledgement is most important in view of the rule of law that the ship must deliver 'what she receives as she received it, unless relieved by the excepted perils'.[17]

Sometimes the bill of lading refers to the 'leading marks' inscribed on the goods, and sometimes there is a statement as to their quality.

(A) RECEIPT AS TO QUANTITY

(i) At common law

The bill of lading is prima facie evidence that the quantity of goods alleged to have been shipped has been shipped in fact. But the shipowner is entitled to show that the goods were never shipped.[18] If he does so, he escapes liability in respect of them.

---

12   *Miramar Maritime Corpn v Holborn Oil Trading Ltd, The Miramar*, supra, at 134 (per Lord Diplock).
13   *Watkins v Rymill* (1883) 10 QBD 178.
14   *Richardson, Spence & Co and Lord Gough SS Co v Rowntree* [1894] AC 217.
15   Per Lush J, in *Crooks v Allan* (1879) 5 QBD 38 at 40.
16   See p 2, ante.
17   Per Lord Sumner in *Bradley & Sons Ltd v Federal Steam Navigation Co Ltd* (1927) 137 LT 266 at 267.
18   *Smith & Co v Bedouin Steam Navigation Co* [1896] AC 70.

Thus, in *Grant v Norway*[19]

A bill of lading was signed by the master for twelve bales of silk, which the shipowner proved had not been put on board.

Held, that the master had no authority to sign for goods not shipped, and the holders of the bill of lading had no claim against the shipowner for non-delivery of these bales.

If the bill of lading contains the words 'weight and quantity unknown', it is not even prima facie evidence, and to succeed in an action for non-delivery the shipper must show that the goods were, in fact, shipped.[20]

Where a bill of lading stated that it would be prima facie evidence of the total amount of 'containers, packages or other units specified on the face of the bill', the reference to 'packages' was held to mean packages where no container was used and not to packages within a container.[21]

There is an implied obligation on the part of the shipper that the bills of lading which he presents for signature by the master, should relate to the goods actually shipped and that they shall not contain a misdescription of the goods which is known to be incorrect.[1]

(ii) Under the Carriage of Goods by Sea Act 1971
Under the Carriage of Goods by Sea Act 1971,[2] a shipper can demand that a bill of lading be issued to him showing 'either the

---

19   (1851) 10 CB 665.
20   *New Chinese Antimony Co Ltd v Ocean SS Co Ltd* [1917] 2 KB 664; *A-G of Ceylon v Scindia Steam Navigation Co Ltd* [1962] AC 60, [1961] 3 All ER 684, PC; *Rederiaktiebolaget Gustav Erikson v Ismail, The Herroe and Askoe* [1986] 2 Lloyd's Rep 281, QBD (Commercial Court), where a charter-party stated that the shipowners were to be responsible for the number of bags of potatoes as signed for in the bills of lading and the bills of lading contained a 'quantity unknown' clause in respect of some of the voyages undertaken and accordingly the shipowners were not liable.
21   *Ace Imports Pty Ltd v Companhia de Navegacio Lloyd Brasilero, The Esmeralda 1* [1988] 1 Lloyd's Rep 206, Supreme Court of New South Wales (Commercial Division), where the bill of lading had on its face the words 'Container 20 with 437 cardboard boxes', and it was held that no representation was made by the carriers as to the accuracy of the statement that the container contained 437 boxes, and that the statement was not prima facie evidence against them.
 1   *Boukadoura Maritime Corpn v Marocaine de l'Industrie et du Raffinaige SA, The Boukadoura* [1989] 1 Lloyd's Rep 393, QBD (Commercial Court) at 399 (per Evans J). There was also in this case an express clause in the charter-party giving the shipowner an indemnity, if the charterer tendered a bill of lading which was inaccurate. As to this point, see p 14, ante.
 2   For the circumstances in which the Act applies, see pp 95–98, post.

number of packages or pieces, or the quantity, or weight, as the case may be, as furnished in writing by the shipper'.[3]

Such bill of lading is prima facie evidence of the receipt of the goods as therein described.[4] But proof to the contrary is not admissible when the bill of lading has been transferred to a third party acting in good faith.[5]

The shipper is deemed to have guaranteed the accuracy at the time of shipment of the quantity and weight as furnished by him, and must indemnify the shipowner against all loss, damages and expenses arising from inaccuracies in such particulars.[6] It should be observed that the master is not bound to show *both* the number of packages *and* the weight; if the number is stated, the phrase 'weight unknown' may properly be inserted, and will have full effect.[7]

Thus, in *Oricon Waren-Handels GmbH v Intergraan NV*[8]

A bill of lading to which the Hague Rules applied acknowledged receipt of 2000 packages containing copra cake. A clause in it stated: 'Contents and condition of contents ... measurement ... weight ... unknown, any reference in this Bill of Lading to these particulars is for the purpose of calculating Freight only.' The bill of lading also stated under the heading 'Description of Goods': 'Said to Weigh Gross, 105,000 Kg...'

Held, the bill of lading was prima facie evidence of the number of packages shipped, but was no evidence whatever of their weight.

(iii)   Under the Bills of Lading Act 1855

Although he may not have a remedy as against the shipowner, the consignee or indorsee for value of a bill of lading can make use of the Bills of Lading Act 1855, s 3. This section states that in his hands the bill of lading is conclusive evidence, *as against the master or other person*[9] *signing it*, that the goods represented to have been shipped were actually shipped. But this does not apply where:

(*a*) the holder of the bill of lading knew when he took it that the goods had not been shipped;

or (*b*) the person signing can show that the misrepresentation was

---

3   Carriage of Goods by Sea Act 1971, Sch Art III, r 3 (Appendix E, post).
4   Sch, Art III, r 4 (Appendix E, post).
5   Ibid, Art III, r 4.
6   Sch. Art III, r 5 (Appendix E, post).
7   *Pendle and Rivet v Ellerman Lines* (1927) 33 Com Cas 70.
8   [1967] 2 Lloyd's Rep 82.
9   In *Rasnoimport V/O v Guthrie & Co Ltd* [1966] 1 Lloyd's Rep 1, it was assumed that ship's agents who had signed the bill of lading were 'other persons' for the purpose of s 3. (See the judgment of Mocatta J, ibid, at 18.)

due to the fraud of the shipper, the holder of the bill of lading, or someone under whom the holder claims.

Section 3 does not make such a person liable for non-delivery of any goods represented as having been shipped. It only gives the consignee or indorsee for value a statutory estoppel to rely on to show that the goods were shipped. It does not give him a separate cause of action.[10]

The person who signs the bill of lading without the authority of the shipowner stating that goods have been shipped, when they have, in fact, not been shipped at all, is liable to an indorsee of the bill of lading, who has relied on that statement, for damages for breach of warranty of authority.[11]

(B) RECEIPT AS TO CONDITION

Where goods are described in the bill of lading as being 'shipped in good order and condition', the position is as follows:

(1) *As between the shipowner and a charterer who was also the shipper*
Here the position is governed by the charter-party, which cannot be varied by the bill of lading.[12] Subject to this, the position appears to be the same as in (2) *infra*.

(2) *As between the shipowner and a shipper other than the charterer*
Here the admissions in the bill of lading, though not conclusive, afford some evidence against the shipowner.[13] The mere fact, however, that the goods have been delivered in a damaged condition does not suffice to render the shipowner liable. The shipper must show that the damage was due to fault on the part of the shipowner, or else that the goods were in fact shipped in good condition internally.[14]

Both (1) and (2) above must be read subject to this qualification, that it is, of course, open to the parties to agree, by an express clause in the document which governs their respective rights, that the statements in the bill of lading shall be conclusive. A 'conclusive

---

10 *Rasnoimport V/O v Guthrie & Co Ltd*, supra.
11 Ibid. As to the measure of damages, see ibid, pp 7, 18.
12 *Sugar Supply Commission v Hartlepools Seatonia SS Co Ltd* [1927] 2 KB 419; *Rodocanachi v Milburn* (1886) 18 QBD 67.
13 *The Peter der Grosse* (1875) 1 PD 414; *Crawford and Law v Allan Line SS Co Ltd* [1912] AC 130.
14 *The Ida* (1875) 32 LT 541; *J Kaufman Ltd v Cunard SS Co Ltd* [1965] 2 Lloyd's Rep 564.

evidence' clause of this type will bind the shipowner, unless there has been fraud on the part of the shipper.[15]

(3) *As between the shipowner and an indorsee for value of the bill of lading*

(i) **At Common Law.** Here, unless there is evidence to show that the indorsee did not act to his detriment on the faith of the bill,[16] the shipowner will be estopped by the admissions contained in it.[17]

To found such an estoppel, however, the statement in the bill of lading must be clear and unambiguous: if the words 'received in apparent good order and condition' are qualified by other clauses in the document, this may prevent the bill from being a clean bill, and in such a case estoppel will not arise.

15   *Crossfield & Co v Kyle Shipping Co Ltd* [1916] 2 KB 885. Cf *Oricon Waren-Handelsgesellschaft mbH v Intergraan NV* [1967] 2 Lloyd's Rep 82, where a clause in a cif contract which stated 'Weighing.—Final settlement shall be made on the basis of gross delivered weight and the goods shall be weighed at place of discharge at port of destination herein named', was not a conclusive evidence clause, but made it mandatory upon the buyers to see that the goods were weighed at the place of discharge. It did not provide that the gross delivered weight should only be arrived at in the manner specified in the clause. See the judgment of Roskill J, on this point, ibid, at 95.

16   *The Skarp* [1935] P 134; *Peter Cremer, Westfaelische Central Genossenschaft GmbH and Intergraan NV v General Carriers SA, The Dona Mari* [1973] 2 Lloyd's Rep 366, QBD (Commercial Court), where it was shown that the bills of lading would have been rejected by the buyers of some tapioca stated to be 'shipped in good order and condition' but actually in moist condition, if the bills of lading had been claused. (See the judgment of Kerr J, ibid, at 373.)

17   *Silver v Ocean SS Co Ltd* [1930] 1 KB 416; *Cummins Sales and Service Inc v Institute of London Underwriters, The Goldenfels* [1974] 1 Lloyd's Rep 292, US Court of Appeals, Fifth Circuit, where the shipowners were estopped from showing pre-shipment damage to some component parts of a pre-fabricated metal building. Sometimes the shipowner is willing to issue to the shipper of the goods a clean bill of lading even though they are not in good condition, provided that the shipper is willing to indemnify him against any claim by a holder of the bill. But he runs the risk of the indemnity being held to be illegal because the bill of lading contains a false representation and therefore to be unenforceable: *Brown Jenkinson & Co Ltd v Percy Dalton (London) Ltd* [1957] 2 QB 621, [1957] 2 All ER 844, CA. See further, *Hellenic Lines Ltd v Chemoleum Corpn* [1972] 1 Lloyd's Rep 350, New York Supreme Court (Appellate Division), where it was held that a letter of guarantee against a clean bill of lading issued in respect of bagged fertilizer in a leaky condition contravened public policy as expressed in the United States Carriage of Goods Act 1936, s 3(8) and could not be enforced.

So, in *Canadian and Dominion Sugar Co Ltd v Canadian National (West Indies) Steamships Ltd*[18]

A bill of lading relating to a shipment of sugar contained the qualifying words 'signed under guarantee to produce ship's clean receipt' and the ship's receipt was not clean, in that it contained the phrase 'many bags stained, torn and re-sewn'.
Held, that the bill was not a clean bill and the shipowners were not estopped.

An admission as to the condition of goods on shipment will bind the shipowner only as to defects which ought to be apparent on a reasonable inspection.

Thus, in *Compania Naviera Vasconzada v Churchill and Sim*,[19]

Timber, although obviously stained with petroleum, was stated in the bill of lading to be 'shipped in good order and condition'.
Held, the indorsee of the bill of lading could sue the shipowner for damages, and the latter was estopped from denying that the timber was shipped in good condition.

Again, in *The Peter der Grosse*[20]

A bill of lading acknowledged the receipt of goods 'shipped in good order and condition . . . weight, contents, and value unknown'. The goods were delivered both externally and internally damaged.
Held, that the bill of lading was evidence that the goods had been shipped in good condition externally, and that there was no obligation on the consignees to show how the damage had arisen. The shipowners were, therefore, liable.

But, if estoppel is established, it will operate in favour of an innocent indorsee even if the master has been induced to sign by the shipper's fraud.[1]

Of course, the fact that an indorsee of the bill of lading happens also to be the charterer will not affect the position; in such circumstances he sues not qua charterer, but qua indorsee of the bill.[2]

---

18 [1947] AC 46, PC. See also *Tokio Marine and Fire Insurance Co Ltd v Retla SS Co* [1970] 2 Lloyd's Rep 91, US Ct of Appeals, Ninth Circuit, where it was held that no estoppel arose in the case of a bill of lading concerning some steel pipes damaged by rust before shipment for the bill of lading, although stating that the goods were shipped in apparent good order and condition, stated 'The term "apparent good order and condition" when used in this bill of lading with reference to iron, steel or metal products does not mean that the goods, when received, were free of visible rust or moisture'. See the judgment of Jameson DJ, ibid, at 96.
19 [1906] 1 KB 237.
20 (1875) 1 PD 414.
1 *Evans v James Webster & Bros Ltd* (1928) 45 TLR 136.
2 *United Molasses Co Ltd v National Petroleum Co* (1934) 50 TLR 266.

(ii) Under the Carriage of Goods by Sea Act 1971. Where the Carriage of Goods by Sea Act 1971 applies,[3] any shipper[4] can insist upon the bill of lading containing a statement as to the 'apparent order and condition' of the goods.[5]

Where the bill of lading contains such a statement, the statement will be prima facie evidence of the receipt by the carrier of the goods as therein described.[6] But proof to the contrary is not admissible when the bill of lading has been transferred to a third party acting in good faith.[7]

(C) RECEIPT AS TO 'LEADING MARKS'

(i) At Common Law. The Bills of Lading Act 1855, s 3, does not preclude the person who has signed the bill of lading from showing that the goods shipped were marked otherwise than as stated, unless the marks are material to the description of the goods. Thus, in *Parsons v New Zealand Shipping Co*[8]

Frozen carcases of lamb were put on board, and the bills of lading, signed by the defendants, described the goods as '622X, 608 carcases. 488X, 226 carcases.' On arrival, some carcases were found to be marked 522X and others 388X. The indorsee of the bill of lading argued that the defendants were estopped from denying this statement in the bill of lading and were liable for failing to deliver the carcases shipped.

Held, by the majority of the Court of Appeal, that the marginal description of the goods in the bills of lading and the numbers of packages stated therein did not affect or denote the nature, quality, or commercial value of the goods. The Act protected persons who had acted on a misrepresentation that goods had been shipped when they had not. Here the marks were quite immaterial as far as the purchaser was concerned, because the carcases delivered were of the same character and value as those shipped.

(ii) Under the Carriage of Goods by Sea Act 1971. Where the

---

3   See pp 95–98, post.
4   The carrier is under no duty to issue a bill of lading showing the apparent good order and condition of the goods unless the shipper actually demands such a bill of lading: *Canada and Dominion Sugar Co Ltd v Canadian National (West Indies) Steamships Ltd* [1947] AC 46 at 57, PC; *Tokio Marine and Fire Insurance Co Ltd v Retla SS Co,* supra, at 96.
5   Carriage of Goods by Sea Act 1971, Sch, Art III, r 3. In *Tokio Marine and Fire Insurance Co Ltd v Retla SS Co,* supra, it was held that the 'rust' clause which qualified the meaning of 'apparent good order and condition' was not invalid under Art III, r 3.
6   Carriage of Goods by Sea Act 1971, Sch, Art III, r 4.
7   Ibid, Sch, Art III, r 4.
8   [1901] 1 KB 548.

Carriage of Goods by Sea Act 1971 applies,[9] a shipper can insist on the bill of lading showing 'the leading marks necessary for the identification of the goods'.[10]

The master can refuse to show them in the bill of lading if the goods if uncovered, or the cases or coverings in which they are contained are not clearly marked 'in such a manner as should ordinarily remain legible until the end of the voyage'.[11]

Further, he can refuse to incorporate them in the bill of lading if he has reasonable grounds for suspecting that the information relating to them supplied by the shipper is inaccurate or he has had no reasonable means of checking it.[12]

If the leading marks are inserted, the bill of lading is prima facie evidence of the receipt by the shipowner of the goods as therein described.[13] But proof to the contrary is not admissible when the bill of lading has been transferred to a third party acting in good faith.[14]

The Act, however, is careful to provide that the shipper shall be deemed to have guaranteed to the carrier the accuracy at the time of shipment of the information furnished by him, and that he must indemnify the carrier against any loss due to that information being inaccurate.[15]

If, therefore, inaccurate information concerning marks or quantities is incorporated in the bill of lading, and an indorsee for value makes a claim against the carrier as a result, the carrier, though liable to the indorsee, has a remedy against the shipper.

(D) RECEIPT AS TO QUALITY

A master does not generally bind the shipowners by a description in the bill of lading of the *quality* of the goods.

Thus, in *Cox v Bruce* (1886) 18 QBD 147

Bales of jute were shipped with marks indicating the quality of the jute. The bill of lading wrongly described the bales as bearing other marks indicating a better quality. The holders of the bill of lading claimed the difference in value from the shipowner. *Held*, the shipowner was not estopped from denying the statement in the bill of lading as to quality. It was not the captain's duty to insert quality marks; hence, if he stated

---

9 See pp 95–98, post.
10 Carriage of Goods by Sea Act 1971, Sch, Art III, r 3.
11 Ibid, Sch, Art III, r 3.
12 Ibid, Sch, Art III, r 3.
13 Ibid, Sch, Art III, r 4.
14 Ibid, Sch, Art III, r 4.
15 Sch, Art III, r 5.

them incorrectly, that did not prevent the shipowner from showing that goods of that quality were not put on board.[16]

(E) RECEIPT AS TO DATE OF SHIPMENT

Where the date of the bills of lading is to be accepted as proof of the date of shipment, and the bills of lading are indorsed, the indorsees are entitled to claim damages from the shipowners on discovering that the shipowners' agents were authorised to insert the date and had inserted a false one.[17]

(3) The bill of lading as a document of title

For many purposes possession of a bill of lading is equivalent in law to possession of the goods. It enables the holder to obtain delivery of the goods at the port of destination[18] and, during the transit, it enables him to 'deliver' the goods by merely transferring the bill of lading. These rules are particularly important in c i f contracts.

Thus, in *Clemens Horst Co v Biddell Bros*[19]

A contract was made for the sale of hops to be shipped from San Francisco to London, c i f net cash. The buyer refused to pay for the goods until they were actually delivered. *Held,* that possession of the bill of lading was in law equivalent to possession of the goods, and that under a c i f contract the seller was entitled to payment on shipping the goods and tendering to the buyer the documents of title.

In *Sanders Bros v Maclean & Co*[20]

The buyer refused to pay because only two out of the three bills of lading were tendered to him.
Held, apart from a special stipulation, the tender of one bill of lading was sufficient.[1]

A bill of lading, unlike a bill of exchange, is not a negotiable instrument. The holder of a bill of lading who indorses it to an indorsee, cannot therefore give a better title than he himself has. Thus, if he has no title, he cannot pass one.

When the word 'negotiable' is used in relation to a bill of lading, it merely means transferable.[2]

---

16   (1886) 18 QBD 147.
17   *The Saudi Crown* [1986] 1 Lloyd's Rep 261, QBD (Admiralty Court).
18   *Erichsen v Barkworth* (1858) 3 H & N 894.
19   [1912] AC 18.
20   (1883) 11 QBD 327.
 1   See also *Shepherd v Harrison* (1871) LR 5 HL 116.
 2   *Kum v Wah Tat Bank Ltd* [1971] 1 Lloyd's Rep 439 at 446, PC (per Lord Devlin).

It has never been settled, however, whether delivery of a bill of lading which is marked 'non-negotiable' transfers title at all.[3]

INTERNATIONAL CONVENTIONS

The various Conventions

In September 1921 a meeting of the International Law Association was held at The Hague with the object of securing adoption by the countries represented of a set of rules relating to bills of lading, so that the rights and liabilities of cargo-owners and shipowners respectively might be subject to rules of general application. Previously those rights and liabilities had been differently defined in different countries, with consequent embarrassment to overseas trade.

The rules agreed upon, thenceforth known as the 'Hague Rules', were revised and were embodied in the articles of an International Convention signed at Brussels in August 1924. In the same month an Act of Parliament was passed—The Carriage of Goods by Sea Act 1924— which gave statutory force to the Rules so far as this country is concerned.

The International Convention which was signed at Brussels in 1924 was amended by a Protocol signed there on 23 February 1968, and new rules known as the 'Hague–Visby Rules' were adopted. The United Kingdom was a signatory to this Protocol, and the Carriage of Goods by Sea Act 1971[4] was passed in order to give effect to it.

A United Nations Conference on the Carriage of Goods by Sea was held at Hamburg in March 1978. The Conference adopted a Convention embodying new rules to be known as the 'Hamburg Rules',[5] which may eventually replace the 'Hague Rules' and the 'Hague–Visby Rules', as the case may be. As far as this country is concerned these new Rules are not in force.

---

3 Ibid, where Lord Devlin said that this was not surprising for when consignor and consignee were also seller and buyer, as they most frequently were, the shipment ordinarily served as delivery (Sale of Goods Act 1979, s 32(1)) and also as an unconditional appropriation of the goods (Sale of Goods Act 1979, s 18, r 5(2)) which passed the property, so as between seller and buyer it did not usually matter whether the bill of lading was a document of title or not.
4 See pp 94–105, post.
5 See pp 105–109, post.

Interpretation of the Rules

Since the Carriage of Goods by Sea Act 1924 was based on the Hague Rules, it was desirable to seek uniformity of interpretation in the many jurisdictions in which the Rules might arise for consideration.

Thus, Lord Atkin said in *Stag Line Ltd v Foscolo, Mango & Co Ltd*[6]

'For the purpose of uniformity it is, therefore, important that the Courts should apply themselves to the consideration only of the words used without any predilection for the former law, always preserving the right to say that words used in the English language which have already in the particular context received judicial interpretation may be presumed to be used in the same sense already judicially imputed to them.'

Again, Lord Macmillan observed in the same case,[7]

'As these Rules must come under the consideration of foreign Courts it is desirable in the interests of uniformity that their interpretation should not be rigidly controlled by domestic precedents of antecedent date, but rather that the language of the Rules should be construed on broad principles of general acceptation.'

The same principles apply in the case of interpretation of the Hague–Visby Rules as set out in the Carriage of Goods by Sea Act 1971.

Thus, in *The Morviken*[8] Lord Diplock said[9]

'[The provisions of the Hague–Visby Rules] should be given a purposive rather than a narrow literalistic construction, particularly wherever the adoption of a literalistic construction would enable the stated purpose of the international Convention viz. the unification of domestic laws of the contracting States relating to bills of lading to be evaded by the use of colourable devices that, not being expressly referred to in the Rules, are not specifically prohibited.'

THE CARRIAGE OF GOODS BY SEA ACT 1971

The principal provisions of the Act are as follows:

(1) REPEAL OF THE CARRIAGE OF GOODS BY SEA ACT 1924

The Act of 1971 repeals the earlier Act of 1924 in its entirety.[10]

6   [1932] AC 328 at 343, HL.
7   Ibid, at 350.
8   [1983] 1 Lloyd's Rep 1, HL.
9   Ibid, at 5.
10   Carriage of Goods by Sea Act 1971, s 6(3)(a).

(2) HAGUE RULES SET OUT IN REVISED FORM

The Hague Rules as revised by the Protocol are set out in the Schedule to the Act of 1971 and have the force of law.[11]

(3) GENERAL SCOPE OF ACT

The Act applies to certain types of contract only. There are special provisions relating to the carriage of live animals and deck cargo. Where a vessel is chartered and a bill of lading is issued under the charter-party, the Act applies only from a certain moment. The Act applies only to certain parts of the contract of carriage.

(a) *Types of contract concerned*
The Act applies to:

(i) any contract for the carriage of goods[12] by sea in ships where the port of shipment is a port in the United Kingdom and the contract expressly or by implication provides for the issue of a bill of lading or any similar document of title.[13]

(ii) any bill of lading if the contract contained in or evidenced by it expressly provides that the Hague Rules shall govern the contract.[14]

(iii) any receipt which is a non-negotiable document marked as such if the contract contained in or evidenced by it is a contract for the carriage of goods by sea which expressly

---

11 Ibid, s 1(2).
12 The word 'goods' includes goods, wares, merchandise and articles of every kind whatsoever except live animals and cargo which by the contract of carriage is stated as being carried on deck and is so carried: ibid, Sch, Art I(c). In *The Aegis Spirit* [1977] 1 Lloyd's Rep 93, District Court, Western District of Washington, containers supplied by time charterers and damaged by the entry of sea water were held not to be 'goods' in an action brought by them against the shipowner, for the containers were not cargo but were carrier-owned equipment designed to provide additional protection for cargo. (See the judgment of Beeks DJ, ibid, at 97.)
13 Carriage of Goods by Sea Act 1971, s 1(3). See also ibid, Sch, Art X.
14 Ibid, s 1(6)(a).

provides that the Rules are to govern the contract as if the receipt were a bill of lading.[15]

Where the goods are transhipped the Act applies to the whole voyage, unless, of course, there is an agreement between the parties to the contrary[16].

The Act does not apply to carriage or storage before the port of shipment or after the port of discharge, because that would be inland and not sea carriage.[17]

But where goods are shipped but are subsequently discharged and stored at an intermediate port prior to transhipment on to another vessel, the Act applies during the period of storage for the storage is an operation 'in relation to and in connection with the carriage of goods by sea in ships'.[18] The Act, of course, would not apply during a lengthy period of storage ashore between two voyages.[19]

(b)   *Carriage of live animals and deck cargo*
Where the shipment is made from a port in the United Kingdom, the Act does not apply to the carriage of live animals and cargo

15   Ibid, s 1(6)(b). See eg *McCarren & Co Ltd v Humber International Transport Ltd and Truckline Ferries (Poole) Ltd, The Vechscroon* [1982] 1 Lloyd's Rep 301, QBD (Commercial Court); *Browner International Transport Ltd v Monarch SS Co Ltd* [1989] Times, 17 April, where the words 'as if the receipt were a bill of lading' were not included in the receipt concerned, and accordingly the Carriage of Goods Act 1971 did not apply. In the case of such a non-negotiable document the Hague Rules apply subject to any necessary modifications and in particular with the omission of the second sentence of r 4 (concerning the bill of lading as prima facie evidence of receipt of the goods by the carrier) and of the omission of the whole of r 7 (concerning the issue of a 'shipped' bill of lading) of the Carriage of Goods by Sea Act 1971, Sch, Art III: ibid.

16   *The Anders Maersk* [1986] 1 Lloyd's Rep 483, Hong Kong High Court, where goods were shipped at Baltimore for delivery at Shanghai and were transhipped at Hong Kong, and it was held that the United States Carriage of Goods Act 1936 applied to the whole voyage and not merely until the goods were transhipped.

17   *Mayhew Foods Ltd v Overseas Containers Ltd* [1984] 1 Lloyd's Rep 317, QBD (Commercial Court) at 320 (per Bingham J).

18   Ibid, at 320 (per Bingham J). In this case a cargo of chicken and turkey portions was shipped in a refrigerated container at Shoreham for delivery at Jeddah, but was transhipped at Le Havre, where the contents decayed due to the temperature control on the container being wrongly set. (See the judgment of Bingham J, ibid, at 319).

19   *Captain v Far Eastern SS Co* [1979] 1 Lloyd's Rep 595, Supreme Court of British Columbia, where the shipper had been told at the time when the contract was made that there would be transhipment, and there were separate bills of lading for the two legs of the journey.

which by the contract of carriage is stated as being carried on deck and is so carried.[20]

But where the bill of lading expressly provides that the Hague Rules shall govern the contract,[1] or a non-negotiable receipt provides that the Rules are to govern the contract as if it were a bill of lading, the Act applies even though the cargo consists of live animals or deck cargo.[2]

(c) *Bills of lading issued under charter-party*
The Act does not apply at all to a charter-party.[3]

Where a vessel is chartered, a bill of lading[4] issued under the charter-party is merely a receipt and the Act does not apply to it. But

---

20 Ibid, Sch, Art I(c). A clause in a bill of lading stating that the 'steamer has liberty to carry goods on deck' does not amount to a statement that the goods *are* carried on deck; therefore the goods so shipped are subject to the Hague Rules: *Svenska Traktor Aktiebolaget v Maritime Agencies (Southampton) Ltd* [1953] 2 All ER 570; *Encyclopaedia Britannica Inc v The Hong Kong Producer and Universal Marine Corpn* [1969] 2 Lloyd's Rep 536, US Ct of Appeals, Second Circuit. See the judgment of Anderson CtJ, ibid, at 542.

1 See eg *The Tilia Gorthon* [1985] 1 Lloyd's Rep 522, QBD (Admiralty Court), where the bill of lading stated that deck cargo was to be carried subject to the Hague Rules with the exception that the 'carrier should not be liable for any loss or damage resulting from any act, neglect or default of his servants in the management of such deck cargo.'

2 Carriage of Goods by Sea Act 1971, s 1(7).

3 Ibid, Sch, Art V. But if bills of lading are issued in the case of a ship under a charter-party, they must comply with the terms of the Rules: ibid, Sch, Art V.

4 The term 'contract of carriage' applies only to contracts of carriage covered by a bill of trading or any similar document of title: ibid, Sch, Art I(b). In *The Maurice Desgagnes* [1977] 1 Lloyd's Rep 290, Federal Court of Canada, Trial Division, a document issued by a freight forwarder was held not to be a bill of lading but was a non-negotiable receipt. (See the judgment of Dube J, ibid, at 295.) In *The Aegis Spirit* [1977] 1 Lloyd's Rep 93, District Court, Western District of Washington, where containers were supplied by the time charterer for the carriage of cargo and they were damaged, and a claim was brought against the shipowner, it was held that the Hague Rules did not apply for the containers were in no way represented collectively or individually by 'documents of title'. (See the judgment of Beeks DJ, ibid, at 97.) Whenever a contract of carriage is concluded and it is contemplated that a bill of lading will in due course be issued, that contract is from its creation covered by a bill of lading: *Hugh Mack & Co Ltd v Burns and Laird Lines Ltd* (1944) 77 Ll L Rep 377; *Pyrene Co Ltd v Scindia Navigation Co Ltd* [1954] 2 QB 402, [1954] 2 All ER 158; *Anticosti Shipping Co v Viateur St Amand* [1959] 1 Lloyd's Rep 352 (Supreme Court of Canada); *Automatic Tube Co Pty Ltd and Email Ltd—Balfour Buzacott Division v Adelaide SS (Operations) Ltd, Adelaide SS Co Ltd and Adelaide SS Co Pty Ltd, The Beltana* [1967] 1 Lloyd's Rep 531 at 533 (per Nevile J); *Mayhew Foods Ltd v Overseas Containers Ltd* [1984] 1 Lloyd's Rep 317 at 320, QBD (Commercial Court) (per Bingham J).

the Act does apply 'from the moment at which such bill of lading or similar document of title regulates the relations between a carrier and a holder of the same',[5] i e if a bill of lading is issued to a charterer, and he indorses it to a third party, the bill of lading is the document which governs the relations between the carrier and the indorsee, and from the moment of indorsement the Act applies.

(d) *Portion of contract to which Act applicable*
The Act applies only to that part of the contract which relates to the carriage by sea,[6] and only to 'the period from the time when the goods are loaded on to the time when they are discharged from the ship'.[7]

A carrier or a shipper is entitled to enter into any agreement, stipulation, condition, reservation or exemption as to the responsibility and liability of the carrier or the ship for the loss of or damage to, or in connection with, the custody and care and handling of the goods prior to the loading on, and subsequent to the discharge from, the ship on which the goods are carried by sea.[8]

(4) ABOLITION OF ABSOLUTE WARRANTY OF SEAWORTHINESS

Where the Act applies, no absolute undertaking by the carrier to provide a seaworthy ship is implied.[9] But the carrier must before

5 Carriage of Goods by Sea Act 1971, Sch, Art I(b).
6 Ibid.
7 Ibid, Sch, Art I(e); *Pyrene Co Ltd v Scindia Navigation Co Ltd*, supra (loading); *Goodwin Ferreira & Co Ltd v Lamport & Holt Ltd* (1929) 141 LT 494 (discharge); *Rambler Cycle Co Ltd v Peninsular and Oriental Steam Navigation Co, Sze Hai Tong Bank Ltd (First Third Party), Southern Trading Co (Second Third Party)* [1968] 1 Lloyd's Rep 42, Malaysia Federal Court (discharge); *East and West SS Co v Hossain Bros* [1968] 2 Lloyd's Rep 145, Supreme Court of Pakistan (discharge); *Falconbridge Nickel Mines Ltd, Janin Construction Ltd and Hewitt Equipment Ltd v Chimo Shipping Ltd, Clarke SS Co Ltd and Munro Jorgensson Shipping Ltd* [1973] 2 Lloyd's Rep 469, Supreme Court of Canada, where it was held that as the shipowners carried barges on the vessel for use in lightering the cargo and were bound by the contract of carriage to use them, the lightering was part of the operation of 'discharge' and the Rules applied to it. See the judgment of Ritchie J, ibid, at 472.
8 Carriage of Goods by Sea Act 1971, Sch Art VII. See e g *Robert Simpson Montreal Ltd v Canadian Overseas Shipping Ltd, The Prins Willem III* [1973] 2 Lloyd's Rep 124, Court of Appeal, Province of Quebec, District of Montreal, where the cargo was pilfered after it had been discharged into a shed by the stevedores, and the carrier's liability was held to have been effectively excluded.
9 Carriage of Goods by Sea Act 1971, s 3.

and at the beginning of the voyage exercise due diligence to make her seaworthy.[10]

(5) EXTENSION OF RIGHT TO DEVIATE

Liberty to deviate is given in order to save property or where a deviation is reasonable.[11]

(6) PARTICULARS TO BE SHOWN IN BILL OF LADING

On the demand of the shipper the shipowner must issue a bill of lading giving certain particulars, eg the quantity of goods shipped, their apparent condition.[12]

(7) CARE OF CARGO

The carrier must 'properly and carefully load, handle, stow, carry, keep, care for and discharge the cargo'.[13]

But he is free to determine by the contract with the shipper which part each has to play in the loading. If, however, the carrier does the loading, then he must do it properly.[14]

There is some doubt as to the meaning of the word 'properly'.[15]

One view[16] is that 'properly' means 'in accordance with a sound system'. The obligation on the carrier is to adopt a system which is sound in the light of all knowledge which the carrier has or ought to have *about the nature of the goods*.

Another view[17] is that the word 'properly' presumably adds something to the word 'carefully', and means 'upon a sound system'.

---

10   Ibid, Sch, Art III, r 1. See pp 112–116, post.
11   Ibid, Sch, Art IV, r 4. See pp 117–119, post.
12   Ibid, Art III, r 3. See pp 85–86, 90, ante.
13   Ibid, Art III, r 2. 'Carry' does not mean 'transport', and the carriage begins the moment the goods are loaded, and before the ship has moved: *G H Renton & Co Ltd v Palmyra Corpn of Panama* [1957] AC 149, [1956] 3 All ER 957, HL.
14   *Pyrene Co Ltd v Scindia Navigation Co Ltd* [1954] 2 QB 402 at 419, [1954] 2 All ER 158 at 163–4 (per Devlin J); *G H Renton & Co Ltd v Palmyra Trading Corpn of Panama* [1957] AC 149 at 170, [1956] 3 All ER 957 at 966, HL (per Lord Morton).
15   *G H Renton & Co Ltd v Palmyra Trading Corpn of Panama* [1957] AC 149, [1956] 3 All ER 957, HL; *Albacora SRL v Westcott and Laurance Line Ltd* [1966] 2 Lloyd's Rep 53.
16   *Albacora SRL v Westcott and Luarance Line Ltd*, supra, at 58 (per Lord Reid). See further, *G H Renton & Co Ltd v Palmyra Trading Corpn of Panama* [1957] AC 149 at 166 (per Viscount Kilmuir LC).
17   *Albacora SRL v Westcott and Laurance Line Ltd*, supra, at 62 (per Lord Pearce).

A sound system does not mean a system suited to all the weaknesses and idiosyncrasies of a particular cargo, but a sound system under all the circumstances *in relation to the general practice of carriage of goods by sea*.

A further view[18] is that the word 'properly' means 'in an appropriate manner'. The word 'properly' adds something to 'carefully', if carefully has a narrow meaning of merely taking care. The element of skill or sound system is required in addition to taking care.

Whether the carrier has broken his obligation is a question of fact in each case, eg (i) whether a cargo of wet salted fish had been negligently stowed and ventilated;[19] (ii) whether a cargo of bags of cocoa had been negligently stowed, dunnaged and protected;[20] (iii) whether a cargo of coco yams had been negligently stowed and ventilated;[1] (iv) whether a cargo of melons, garlic and onions had been negligently stowed and badly ventilated because they had been stowed in a hold containing a cargo of fishmeal;[2] (v) whether an electric shovel had been properly stowed because there were gaps in the stowage;[3] (vi) whether the shipowner by entering a strike-bound port causing delay had damaged a cargo of oranges;[4] (vii) whether a cargo of lumber had been safely stowed;[5] (viii) whether boxes of bananas had been properly stowed;[6] (ix) whether the shipowners were negligent in securing the cargo on a barge to keep it from sliding, and in tethering the barge to the vessel;[7] (x) whether apple

---

18 Ibid, at 64 (per Lord Pearson).
19 Ibid.
20 *Jahn (Trading as C F Otto Weber) v Turnbull Scott Shipping Co Ltd and Nigerian National Line Ltd, The Flowergate* [1967] 1 Lloyd's Rep 1.
1 *Chris Foodstuffs (1963) Ltd v Nigerian National Shipping Line Ltd* [1967] 1 Lloyd's Rep 293, CA.
2 *David McNair & Co Ltd and David Oppenheimer Ltd and Associates v Santa Malta* [1967] 2 Lloyd's Rep 391.
3 *Blackwood Hodge (India) Private Ltd v Ellerman Lines Ltd and Ellerman and Bucknall SS Co Ltd* [1963] 1 Lloyd's Rep 454.
4 *Crelinsten Fruit Co v The Mormacsaga* [1969] 1 Lloyd's Rep 515, Exchequer Court of Canada.
5 *Charles Goodfellow Lumber Sales Ltd v Verreault, Hovington and Verreault Navigation Inc* [1968] 2 Lloyd's Rep 383, Exchequer Court of Canada, Quebec Admiralty District. See the judgment of Dumoulin J, ibid, at 389; reversed on other grounds, [1971] 1 Lloyd's Rep 185, Supreme Court of Canada.
6 *Heinrich C Horn v Cia de Navegacion Fruco SA and J R Atkins (trading as Alabama Fruit and Produce Co), The Heinz Horn* [1970] 1 Lloyd's Rep 191, US Ct of Appeals, Fifth Circuit. See the judgment of Rives, CtJ, ibid, at 196.
7 *Falconbridge Nickel Mines Ltd, Janin Construction Ltd and Hewitt Equipment Ltd*

concentrate in containers had been properly stowed because no additional dunnage had been used;[8] (xi) whether melons stowed in crates 17 high without air circulating in the hold had been properly stowed;[9] (xii) whether cars had been stowed too closely together;[10] (xiii) whether a cargo of apples and pears had been properly stowed in a refrigerated vessel;[11] (xiv) whether a cargo of plate glass should have been surrounded by dunnage fixed more securely;[12] (xv) whether a cargo of galvanised steel had been properly stowed;[13] (xvi) whether a cargo of crude oil had been heated;[14] and (xviii) whether a cargo of ceramic tiles had been stowed with sufficient care to fill up void spaces.[15]

The fact that the goods arrive damaged does not of itself constitute a breach of the carrier's obligation though it may well be in many cases sufficient to raise an inference of a breach of the obligation.[16]

(8) IMMUNITIES GIVEN TO CARRIER

The Act sets out a list of 'excepted perils',[17] and if loss or damage is caused by them, the shipowner will not be liable provided he has fulfilled his duties under the Act.

He is entitled to increase his liabilities,[18] but cannot add to the list of 'excepted perils'.[19]

The defences provided for in the Act apply in any action against

   v Chimo Shipping Ltd, Clarke SS Co Ltd and Munro Jorgensson Shipping Ltd[1973] 2 Lloyd's Rep 469, Supreme Court of Canada.

8 *Bruck Mills Ltd v Black Sea SS Co, The Grumant* [1973] 2 Lloyd's Rep 531, Federal Court of Canada, Trial Division.

9 *William D Branson Ltd and Tomas Alcazar SA v Jadranska Slobodno Plovidba (Adriatic Tramp Shipping), The Split* [1973] 2 Lloyd's Rep 535, Federal Court of Canada, Trial Division.

10 *Nissan Automobile Co (Canada) Ltd v Owners of the Vessel Continental Shipper, The Continental Shipper* [1976] 2 Lloyd's Rep 234, Court of Appeal of Canada.

11 *Crelinsten Fruit Co and William D. Branson Ltd v Maritime Fruit Carriers Co Ltd, The Lemoncore* [1975] 2 Lloyd's Rep 249, Federal Court of Canada, Trial Division.

12 *The Washington* [1976] 2 Lloyd's Rep 453, Federal Court of Canada, Trial Division.

13 *The Lucky Wave* [1985] 1 Lloyd's Rep 80, QBD (Admiralty Court).

14 *Gatoil International Inc v Panatlantic Carriers Corp, The Rio Sun* [1985] 1 Lloyd's Rep 350 (Commercial Court).

15 *The Saudi Prince (No 2)* [1988] 1 Lloyd's Rep 1, CA.

16 *Albacora SRL v Westcott and Laurance Line Ltd,* supra, at 63.

17 Carriage of Goods by Sea Act 1971, Sch, Art IV, r 2. See pp 194–199, post.

18 Ibid, Sch, Art V.

19 Ibid, Sch, Art III, r 8.

the carrier in respect of loss or damage to the goods whether the action be founded in contract or in tort.[20]

If an action is brought against a servant or agent of the carrier (such a servant or agent not being an independent contractor), such servant or agent is entitled to avail himself of the defences which the carrier is entitled to invoke under the Act.[1]

(9) RIGHTS GIVEN TO CARRIER

The carrier is entitled to throw overboard goods which are dangerous.[2] He can obtain an indemnity for loss caused to him by the shipper stating the particulars of the goods inaccurately.[3] But the shipper is not responsible for loss or damage sustained by the carrier arising or resulting from any cause without the act, fault or neglect of the shipper, his agents or his servants.[4]

(10) LIMITATION OF LIABILITY

The Act limits the liability of the carrier for any loss or damage to or in connection with the goods[5] to 666·67 units of account per package or unit or 2 units of account per kilogramme of gross weight of the goods lost or damaged, whichever is the higher.[6]

The limits of liability provided for in the Act apply in any action brought against the carrier in respect of loss or damage to goods whether the action is founded in contract or tort.[7]

If an action is brought against a servant or agent of the carrier (such servant or agent not being an independent contractor), such servant or agent is entitled to avail himself of the limits of liability set out above.[8]

---

20   Ibid, Sch, Art IV, bis, r 1.
1   Ibid, Sch, Art IV bis, r 2.
2   Ibid, Sch, Art IV, r 6.
3   Ibid, Sch, Art III, r 5. See p 91, ante.
4   Ibid, Art IV, r 3. The words 'loss or damage' refer to physical loss or damage and not to loss by delay in discharging: *Hellenic Lines Ltd v Embassy of Pakistan* [1973] 1 Lloyd's Rep 363, US Court of Appeals, Second Circuit. (See the judgment of Timbers Ct J, ibid, at 368.)
5   These words are not confined to physical damage, and are wide enough to cover, e g the loss caused by having to tranship goods because they have been delivered at a different port from that stated in the bill of lading: *G H Renton & Co Ltd v Palmyra Trading Corpn of Panama* [1957] AC 149, [1956] 3 All ER 957, HL.
6   Carriage of Goods by Sea Act 1971, Sch, Art IV, r 5(a). See pp 205–206, post.
7   Ibid, Sch, Art IV bis, r 1.
8   Ibid, Art IV bis, r 2.

(11) LIMITATION OF ACTION

The carrier is discharged from all liability if the action is not brought within one year from the date of the delivery of the goods or the date when they should have been delivered.[9]

But an action for indemnity against a third person may be brought after the expiration of the year if brought within the time allowed by the law of the Court seized of the case.[10]

(12) CONTRACTING OUT OF THE ACT

The Act of 1971 is intended mainly to protect holders of bills of lading, by ensuring to them certain rights of which they cannot be deprived. It is, therefore, laid down that, in cases to which the Act applies, the carrier should be able to avoid liability only in certain circumstances defined in the Act.[11]

It should be observed that the term 'carrier', as used in the Act, is defined as meaning 'the owner or the charterer who enters into a contract with the shipper',[12] ie the person liable to be sued by the holder of the bill of lading.

In general, the extent of the carrier's immunity, as laid down by the Act, cannot be increased by contract: any clause or contract purporting to relieve a carrier of his liabilities under the Act is expressly declared to be void and of no effect.[13]

Thus, a clause in a bill of lading stating that the carrier would not be liable for any damage unless the shipper proved negligence or lack of due diligence on the carrier's part was held to be void because it shifted the burden of proof from the carrier to the shipper.[14] Again, a clause excluding the carrier's liability 'for bags or bales burst, torn or stained and consequences arising therefrom' was held

---

9 Ibid, Art III, r 6. See pp 174–175, post.
10 Ibid, Art III, r 6 bis. See pp 176–177, post.
11 Carriage of Goods by Sea Act 1971, Sch, Arts II, III and IV.
12 Ibid, Sch, Art I(a). The word 'carrier' does not include stevedores: *Scruttons Ltd v Midland Silicones Ltd* [1962] AC 446, [1962] 1 All ER 1, HL. See also *Krawill Machinery Corpn v Robert C Herd & Co Inc* [1959] 1 Lloyd's Rep 305, United States Supreme Court. Nor does it include the master: *International Milling Co v The Perseus and Nicholson Transit Co* [1958] 2 Lloyd's Rep 272 (US District Court of Michigan).
13 Carriage of Goods by Sea Act 1971, Sch, Art III, r 8.
14 *Encyclopaedia Britannica Inc v The Hong Kong Producer and Universal Marine Corpn* [1969] 2 Lloyd's Rep 536, US Ct of Appeals, Second Circuit. See the judgment of Anderson Ct J, ibid, at 543.

to be void,[15] as also was a clause excluding liability for 'deterioration' of a cargo of melons.[16] Similarly, a clause purporting to relieve the shipowners of their obligation to load or unload, and to confer a mandate on them to appoint stevedores to carry out those functions on their behalf is void.[17]

On the other hand, the carrier may, by an express provision in the bill of lading, give up any of his rights under the Act and so increase his liabilities.[18] In order that such a clause may be effective it must be clearly worded. 'The surrender of a statutory immunity must be clearly stated'.[19]

The Act also contains a provision that where 'particular goods' are shipped, and the transaction is not an ordinary commercial shipment in the ordinary course of trade, the shipper and the carrier may make an agreement in any terms, provided certain conditions are complied with.[20]

The necessary conditions are that no bill of lading has been or shall be issued, and that the terms agreed shall be embodied in a receipt which is non-negotiable and marked as such.[1] Any such agreement has full legal effect, except in so far as an attempted limitation of the carrier's liability as to seaworthiness may be contrary to public policy.[2]

The precise meaning of the phrase 'particular goods' in this connection has not so far been judicially determined. The only assistance to be derived from the Act itself is the proviso that contracting out in the case of particular goods shall be allowed 'where the character or condition of the property to be carried, or the circumstances, terms and conditions under which the carriage is to be performed are such as reasonably to justify a special agreement',[3] but this proviso itself is somewhat obscure.

It is submitted, albeit with some hesitation, that the meaning is that where goods of a particular class are shipped, and the parties

---

15   *Bruck Mills Ltd v Black Sea SS Co, The Grumant* [1973] 2 Lloyd's Rep 531, Federal Court of Canada, Trial Division.
16   *William D Branson Ltd and Thomas Alcazar SA v Jadranska Slobodna Plovidba (Adriatic Tramp Shipping), The Split* [1973] 2 Lloyd's Rep 535, Federal Court of Canada, Trial Division.
17   *The Saudi Prince (No 2)* [1988] 1 Lloyd's Rep 1, CA.
18   Carriage of Goods by Sea Act 1971, Sch, Art V.
19   *The Touraine* [1928] P 58 at 66, per Hill J.
20   Carriage of Goods by Sea Act 1971, Sch, Art VI.
 1   Ibid, Sch, Art VI.
 2   Ibid, Sch, Art VI.
 3   Ibid, Sch, Art VI.

agree that the carrier shall perform, in relation to those goods, some service apart altogether from his usual duties as a carrier, then the carrier may insist, if he wishes, on a modification of those usual duties.

THE HAMBURG RULES

A United Nations conference on the carriage of goods by sea was held in Hamburg in March 1978. A Convention was adopted by the conference, and the rules contained in it are known as the 'Hamburg Rules'.[4] The Convention comes into force following the expiration of one year from the date of deposit of the 20th instrument of ratification, acceptance, approval or accession.[5] Each Contracting State must apply the provisions of the Convention to contracts of carriage by sea on or after the date of the entry into force of the Convention in respect of that State.[6]

The principal provisions of the Rules are:

(1) REPEAL OF THE HAGUE RULES

On becoming a Contracting State any State which is a party to the Hague Rules in their original or amended form must denounce the Convention when the Convention enters into force in respect of that State.[7]

(2) SCOPE OF APPLICATION

The provisions of the Convention are applicable to all contracts of carriage by sea[8] between two different States if:

(a) the port of loading provided for in the contract is in a Contracting State; or

4 The Rules are set out in Appendix H, post.
5 Annex I, Art 30(1).
6 Annex I, Art 30(3).
7 Annex I, Art 31. Power is given to defer the denunciation for a period of 5 years from the entry into force of the Convention: Annex I, Art 31(4).
8 'Contract of carriage by sea' means any contract whereby the carrier undertakes against payment of freight to carry goods by sea from one port to another. But a contract which involves carriage by sea and also carriage by some other means is deemed to be a contract of carriage by sea for the purpose of the Convention only in so far as it relates to the carriage by sea: Annex I, Art 1(6).

(b) the port of discharge provided for in the contract is in a Contracting State; or

(c) one of the optional ports of discharge provided for in the contract is the actual port of discharge and is in a Contracting State; or

(d) the bill of lading or other document evidencing the contract is issued in a Contracting State; or

(e) the bill of lading or other document evidencing the contract provides that the provisions of the Convention or the legislation of any State giving effect to them are to govern the contract.[9]

The provisions of the Convention are not applicable to charter-parties. But where a bill of lading is issued pursuant to a charter-party, the Convention applies to such a bill of lading if it governs the relation between the carrier and the holder of the bill of lading, not being the charterer.[10]

The Convention applies only to the carriage of goods. The term 'goods' includes live animals.[11] Where the goods are consolidated in a container, pallet or similar article of transport or where they are packed, 'goods' includes such article of transport or packaging if supplied by the shipper.[12]

(3) LIABILITY OF CARRIER

The responsibility of the carrier[13] for the goods covers the period during which the carrier is in charge of the goods[14] at the port of loading, during the carriage and at the port of discharge.[15]

The carrier is liable for loss resulting from loss or damage to the goods as well as from delay in delivery if the occurrence which caused the loss, damage or delay took place while the goods were in his charge unless the carrier proves that he, his servants or agents

---

9 Annex I, Art 2(1).

10 Annex I, Art 2(3).

11 Annex I, Art 1(5).

12 Annex I, Art 1(5).

13 'Carrier' means any person by whom or in whose name a contract of carriage of goods by sea has been concluded with a shipper: Annex I, Art 1(1).

14 As to 'the period during which the carrier is deemed to be in charge of the goods', see Annex I, Art 4(2).

15 Annex I, Art 4(1). For the purpose of Art 4(1) and (2) the term 'carrier' includes his servants or agents: Annex I, Art 4(3).

took all measures that could reasonably be required to avoid the occurrence and its consequences.[16]

The person entitled to make a claim for the loss of goods may treat them as lost if they have not been delivered within 60 consecutive days following the expiry of the time for delivery.[17]

The carrier is liable

(i) for loss of or damage to the goods or delay in delivery caused by fire, if the claimant proves that the fire arose from fault or neglect on the part of the carrier, his servants or agents;

(ii) for such loss, damage or delay in delivery which is proved by the claimant to have resulted from the fault or neglect of the carrier, his servants or agents, in taking all measures that could reasonably be required to put out the fire and avoid or mitigate its consequences.[18]

With respect to live animals, the carrier is not liable for loss, damage or delay resulting from any special risks inherent in that kind of carriage.[19]

The carrier is entitled to carry the goods on deck only if such carriage is in accordance with an agreement with the shipper or with the usage of the particular trade or is required by statutory rules or regulations.[20] If the carrier and the shipper have agreed that the goods shall or may be carried on deck, the carrier must insert in the bill of lading a statement to that effect. In the absence of such a statement the carrier has the burden of proving that an agreement for carriage on deck has been entered into.[1]

(4) LIABILITY OF SHIPPER

The shipper is not liable for loss sustained by the carrier or for damage sustained by the ship unless such loss or damage was caused by the fault of the shipper, his servants or agents.[2] A servant or

---

16 Annex I, Art 5(1).
17 Annex I, Art 5(3).
18 Annex I, Art 5(4).
19 Annex I, Art 5(5).
20 Annex I, Art 9(1).
1 Annex I, Art 9(2). But the carrier is not entitled to invoke such an agreement against a third party, including a consignee, who had acquired the bill of lading in good faith: Annex I, Art 9(2).
2 Annex I, Art 12.

agent of the shipper is not liable for such loss or damage unless the loss or damage was caused by fault or neglect on his part.[3]

The shipper must mark or label in a suitable manner dangerous goods as dangerous.[4]

(5) TRANSPORT DOCUMENTS

When the carrier takes the goods in his charge, he must, on demand of the shipper, issue to the shipper a bill of lading.[5]

It must include a number of particulars, eg the general nature of the goods, the leading marks necessary for identification, the number of packages or pieces, the weight of the goods or their quantity, the apparent condition of the goods, the names of the shipper and the consignee, the ports of loading and discharge.[6]

Where a 'shipped' bill of lading is issued, it is prima facie evidence of loading of the goods as described therein. Proof to the contrary by the carrier is not admissible if the bill of lading has been transferred to a third party, including a consignee, who in good faith has acted in reliance on the description of the goods.[7]

(6) NOTICE OF LOSS ETC

Unless notice of loss or damage specifying the general nature of such loss or damage, is given in writing by the consignee to the carrier not later than the working day after the day when the goods were handed over to the consignee, such handing over is prima facie evidence of the delivery by the carrier of the goods as described in the document of transport.[8]

Where the loss or damage is not apparent, the above provisions apply if notice is not given within 15 consecutive days after the day when the goods were handed over to the consignee.[9]

If the state of the goods at the time they were handed over to the consignee has been the subject of a joint survey or inspection by the parties, notice in writing need not be given of loss or damage ascertained during such survey or inspection.[10]

---

3   Annex I, Art 12.
4   Annex I, Art 13(1).
5   Annex I, Art 14(1).
6   Annex I, Art 15(1).
7   Annex I, Art 15(3).
8   Annex I, Art 19(1).
9   Annex I, Art 19(2).
10   Annex I, Art 19(3).

No compensation is payable for loss resulting from delay or delivery unless a notice has been given in writing to the carrier within 60 consecutive days after the day when the goods were handed over to the consignee.[11]

(7) LIMITATION OF ACTION

Any action is time-barred if judicial or arbitral proceedings have not been instituted within a period of 2 years.[12]

(8) LIMITATION OF LIABILITY

The liability of the carrier for loss resulting from loss of or damage to goods is limited to an amount equivalent to 835 units of account per package or other shipping unit or 2·5 units of account per kilogramme of gross weight of the goods lost or damaged, whichever is the higher.[13]

Where a container or similar article of transport is used to consolidate goods, the package or other shipping units enumerated in the bill of lading as packed in such article of transport are deemed packages or shipping units.[14] Except as aforesaid the goods in such article of transport are deemed one shipping unit.[15]

The liability of the carrier for delay in delivery is limited to an amount equivalent to $2\frac{1}{2}$ times the freight payable for goods delayed but not exceeding the total freight payable under the contract.[16]

The carrier is not entitled to limit his liability if it is proved that the loss, damage or delay in delivery resulted from an act or omission of the carrier done with intent to cause such loss, damage or delay or recklessly and with knowledge that such loss, damage or delay would probably result.[17]

---

11 Annex I, Art 19(5).
12 Annex I, Art 19(1). As to the time from which the limitation period commences, see Annex I, Art 19(2), (3), (4).
13 Annex I, Art 6(1)(a). The 'unit of account' is the Special Drawing Right as defined in the International Monetary Fund: Annex I, Art 26(1).
14 Annex I, Art 6(2)(a).
15 Annex I, Art 6(2)(a).
16 Annex I, Art 6(1)(b).
17 Annex I, Art 8(1). Where he is guilty of similar conduct, a servant or agent of the carrier cannot limit his liability: Annex I, Art 8(2).

SOME USUAL CLAUSES OF BILLS OF LADING

The actual terms[18] of bills of lading vary from company to company. But usually there are provisions in them setting out:

(1) the name of the vessel, port of shipment, port of delivery, and the person to whom delivery is to be made;

(2) the number of the goods shipped, their apparent condition, and leading marks;[19]

(3) a clause incorporating the Hague-Visby Rules;[20]

(4) a list of 'excepted' perils;[21]

(5) a 'deviation' clause;[1]

(6) the amount of the freight to be paid;[2]

(7) the extent of the shipowner's lien over the goods carried;[3]

(8) how delivery is to be made;[4]

(9) a clause incorporating the York–Antwerp Rules 1974 in relation to general average;[5]

(10) a 'Both-to-Blame' Collision Clause;[6]

(11) what law is to govern the contract;[7]

(12) an arbitration clause.[8]

IMPLIED UNDERTAKINGS IN BILLS OF LADING

Various undertakings are implied in bills of lading by Common Law or imposed by statute.

---

18 For a case where it was alleged that the terms and conditions printed on the back of a bill of lading were in a type so small and faint as to be illegible, see *PS Chellaram & Co Ltd v China Ocean Shipping Co* [1989] 1 Lloyd's Rep 413, Supreme Ct of New South Wales (Admiralty Division), where, however, the shipowners were held to be entitled to rely on them since the bill of lading was in their standard form, and a legible copy would be readily available. (See the judgment of Carruthers J, ibid at 428.)

19 See pp 90–91, ante. On the effect of 'weight and condition unknown' clauses, see p 86, ante.

20 Even when the Hague Rules do not apply to the bill of lading *proprio vigore*, the parties are entitled to incorporate them into the contract.

21 See pp 181–189, post   **1** See p 22, ante.

2 See pp 257–267, post.   **3** See pp 275–277, post.

4 See pp 165–166, post.   **5** See pp 220–221, post.

6 See pp 186–187, post.   **7** See pp 137–139, post.

8 See eg *Denny, Mott and Dickson Ltd v Lynn Shipping Co Ltd* [1963] 1 Lloyd's Rep 339, where the bill of lading incorporated a clause in a charter-party, which stated: 'All claims must be made in writing and the Claimant's Arbitrator must be appointed within twelve months of final discharge, otherwise the claim shall be deemed waived and absolutely barred.' See further as to this case, p 172, post.

(a) On the part of the shipowner

The shipowner undertakes:

(1) that his ship is seaworthy;
(2) that she shall proceed with reasonable despatch; and
(3) that she shall proceed without unjustifiable deviation.

(1) SEAWORTHINESS

(a) At Common Law

As we have seen, the duty of a shipowner under a voyage charter-party is to supply a ship which is seaworthy in fact.[9] The same rule applies in the case of a bill of lading. Similarly, seaworthiness includes cargo-worthiness.

Thus, in *Cargo per Maori King v Hughes*[10]

Where the contract was to carry frozen meat, the ship was *held* to be unseaworthy unless provided with suitable refrigerating machinery.

The shipowner cannot protect himself by ambiguous and general words.[11]

Thus, in *Ingram & Royle Ltd v Services Maritime du Treport*[12]

A stipulation was inserted in the bill of lading absolving the shipowners from every duty, warranty, or obligation, provided they exercised reasonable care in connection with the upkeep of the ship.
Held, that this was too ambiguous to exempt the shipowners from the obligation to provide a seaworthy ship.

Further, in *Nelson Line (Liverpool) Ltd v James Nelson & Sons Ltd*[13]

Frozen meat had been shipped under an agreement which stated that the shipowner would not be liable for any damage 'which is capable of being covered by insurance'. The meat arrived in a damaged condition on account of the unseaworthiness of the vessel.
Held, that the clause was not sufficiently clear to exempt the shipowners from being liable to supply a seaworthy ship.

---

 9 See pp 14–16, ante.
10 [1895] 2 QB 550.
11 *Elderslie SS Co v Borthwick* [1905] AC 93.
12 [1914] 1 KB 541.
13 [1908] AC 16, HL. See also *The Rossetti* [1972] 2 Lloyd's Rep 116, QBD (Admiralty Court), where there was a conflict between the provisions on unseaworthiness in two of the clauses of the bill of lading, and it was held that there was no clear exception of liability for unseaworthiness. (See the judgment of Brandon J, ibid, at 116.)

Again, limitation of liability to a specified sum,[14] or a clause totally exempting the shipowner from liability if the claim is not made within a given time,[15] cannot avail the shipowner where the loss is due to unseaworthiness unless clear and express words are used to indicate it.

Thus, in *Tattersall v National SS Co*[16]

Cattle were shipped under a bill of lading which provided that the shipowners were not to be responsible for disease or mortality, and that in no circumstances should they be held liable for more than £5 for each of the animals. The ship had not been properly disinfected before the cattle were received on board, with the result that they contracted foot-and-mouth disease.

Held, that the omission to disinfect the ship constituted a breach of the undertaking of cargoworthiness, and so the shipowners were prevented from relying on the clause in the bill of lading limiting liability to £5 for each of the cattle.

(b) By statute

Where the Carriage of Goods by Sea Act 1971 applies,[17] no absolute undertaking as to seaworthiness is implied.[18] The carrier has, however, before and at the beginning of the voyage to exercise due diligence (i) to make the ship seaworthy; (ii) to properly man, equip and supply her; and (iii) to make the holds, refrigerating and cool chambers, and all other parts of the ship in which goods are carried fit and safe for their reception,[19] carriage and preservation.[20]

Further, the vessel must be seaworthy in the sense of being fit to discharge the goods and deliver them at the specified port of destination.[1]

'Seaworthiness' is used in its ordinary meaning and not in any extended or unnatural meaning. It means that the vessel with her master and crew is herself fit to encounter the perils of the voyage

---

14   *Tattersall v National SS Co* (1884) 12 QBD 297.
15   *Atlantic Shipping and Trading Co Ltd v Louis Dreyfus & Co* [1922] 2 AC 250.
16   Supra.
17   See pp 95–98, ante.
18   Carriage of Goods by Sea Act 1971, s 2.
19   In *The Fehmarn* [1964] 1 Lloyd's Rep 355, the bill of lading was not governed by the Hague Rules, but contained a clause in substantially the same terms as those of Art III, r 1, and it was held that the carriers were in breach because they had not properly cleaned the vessel's tanks for the reception of the cargo of turpentine, which arrived at the port of discharge in a contaminated condition.
20   Carriage of Goods by Sea Act 1971, Sch, Art III, r 1.
 1   *Empresa Cubana Importada de Alimentos Alimport v Ismos Shipping Co SA, The Good Friend* [1984] 2 Lloyd's Rep 586, QBD (Commercial Court) at 592 (per Staughton J).

and also that she is fit to carry the cargo safely on that voyage.[2] Thus, a vessel is still fit to do so even though she has to be lightened to pass through the Panama Canal.[3]

The words 'before and at the beginning of the voyage' mean the period from at least the beginning of the loading until the vessel starts on her voyage.[4]

The word 'voyage' means the contractual voyage from the port of loading to the port of discharge as declared in the bill of lading.[5] Where the voyage is divided into 'stages' eg as regards bunkering, the carrier's obligation is to exercise due diligence before and at the beginning of the voyage to have the vessel adequately bunkered for the first stage, and to arrange for adequate bunkers of the proper kind at intermediate ports so that the contractual voyage may be performed.[6]

Whether due diligence has been exercised is a matter of fact in each case. Cases on this point have related to a failure to provide sufficient bunker fuel,[7] a failure in the ship's steering gear,[8] the blowing out of a boiler tube,[9] a fault in a vessel's design,[10] a failure to see that a valve was properly tightened,[11] thawing out frozen scupper pipes by the use of an acetylene torch,[12] a failure in a vessel's reduction gear,[13] a failure to equip a tramp vessel with radar and loran,[14] a failure to instruct engineers in the operation of an oil fuel

---

2   *Actis Co Ltd v The Sanko SS Co Ltd, The Aquacharm* [1982] 1 Lloyd's Rep 7 at 11, CA (per Lord Denning MR).
3   Ibid.
4   *Maxine Footwear Co Ltd v Canadian Government Merchant Marine Ltd* [1959] AC 589, [1959] 2 All ER 740, PC; *Western Canada SS Co Ltd v Canadian Commercial Corpn* [1960] 2 Lloyd's Rep 313 at 319 (Supreme Court of Canada).
5   *The Makedonia, Owners of Cargo Laden on Makedonia v Makedonia Owners* [1962] P 190, [1962] 2 All ER 614.
6   Ibid.
7   *Northumbrian Shipping Co Ltd v Timm & Son Ltd* [1939] AC 397, [1939] 2 All ER 648, HL. *The Makedonia, Owners of Cargo Laden on Makedonia v Makedonia Owners*, supra.
8   *The Assunzione* [1956] 2 Lloyd's Rep 468.
9   *Goulandris Bros Ltd v B Goldman & Sons Ltd* [1958] 1 QB 74, [1957] 3 All ER 100.
10 *Riverstone Meat Co Pty Ltd v Lancashire Shipping Co Ltd* [1959] 1 QB 74, [1958] 3 All ER 261 (at first instance).
11 *Riverstone Meat Co Pty Ltd v Lancashire Shipping Co Ltd* [1961] AC 807, [1961] 1 All ER 495, HL.
12 *Maxine Footwear Co Ltd v Canadian Government Merchant Marine Ltd*, supra.
13 *Union of India v Reederij Amsterdam NV* [1963] 2 Lloyd's Rep 223, HL.
14 *President of India v West Coast SS Co, The Portland Trader* [1964] 2 Lloyd's Rep 443, US Court of Appeals, where it was held that the employment of radar and loran in the navigation of tramp vessels was not so essential that their absence

system,[15] the engagement of an incompetent engineer,[16] a failure to provide a plan of the piping in a vessel's engine room,[17] a failure to check a valve in the forward hold suction line and thus causing a hold to be unsafe for the carriage of the cargo,[18] a failure to notice that the coamings of a deep tank hatch were defective,[19] a failure to see that a vessel's sanitary water system was in order,[20] a failure to have on board the latest Admiralty List of Radio Signals,[1] permitting a faulty container, which was part of a ship's equipment and liable to break loose, to remain on board,[2] a failure to examine the shell plating of a vessel,[3] a failure to lash a deck cargo with the result that it could shift substantially and to ensure a vessel's stability,[4] a failure to check cracks and other defects in a cast iron water box on the inlet side of a vessel's main condenser,[5] a failure to discover that the steelwork of a vessel was corroded,[6] a failure to see that the trunking

would give rise to a finding of unseaworthiness; *American Smelting and Refining Co v SS Irish Spruce and Irish Shipping Ltd, The Irish Spruce* [1976] 1 Lloyd's Rep 63, District Court, Southern District of New York.

15   *The Makedonia, Owners of Cargo Laden on Makedonia v Makedonia Owners* [1962] P 190, [1962] 2 All ER 614.

16   *Robin Hood Flour Mills Ltd v N M Paterson & Sons Ltd, The Farrandoc* [1967] 2 Lloyd's Rep 276, Exchequer Court of Canada. As to this aspect of the case, see the judgment of Thurlow J, ibid, at 281–2; that of Noel J, ibid, at 286–7; and that of Gibson J, ibid, at 289.

17   Ibid. As to this aspect of the case, see the judgment of Thurlow J, ibid, at 280, that of Noel J, ibid, at 286, and that of Gibson J, ibid, at 289.

18   *Fisons Fertilizers Ltd and Fisons Ltd v Thomas Watson (Shipping) Ltd* [1971] 1 Lloyd's Rep 141, Mayor's and City of London Court. For the evidence as to when the defect occurred, see ibid, at 142–143.

19   *Sears Roebuck & Co v American President Lines Ltd, The President Monroe* [1972] 1 Lloyd's Rep 385, District Court, Northern District of California.

20   *International Produce Inc and Greenwich Mills Co v SS Frances Salman, Swedish Gulf Line AB and Companhia de Navegacao Maritima Netumar, The Frances Salman* [1975] 2 Lloyd's Rep 355, District Court, Southern District of New York.

 1   *American Smelting and Refining Co v SS Irish Spruce and Irish Shipping Ltd. The Irish Spruce,* supra.

 2   *Houlden & Co v SS Red Jacket and American Export Lines Ltd, The Red Jacket* [1978] 1 Lloyd's Rep 300, District Court, Southern District of New York.

 3   *The Hellenic Dolphin* [1978] 2 Lloyd's Rep 336, QBD (Admiralty Court).

 4   *The Friso* [1980] 1 Lloyd's Rep 469, QBD (Admiralty Court). (See the judgment of Sheen J, ibid, at 475.)

 5   *Metals and Ores Pte Ltd v Compania de Vapores Stelvi SA, The Tolmidis* [1983] 1 Lloyd's Rep 530, QBD (Commercial Court). (See the judgment of Neill J, ibid at 538.)

 6   *Aktieselskabet de Danske Sukkerfabriker v Bajamar Compania Naviera SA, The Torenia* [1983] 2 Lloyd's Rep 210, QBD (Commercial Court). (See the judgment of Hobhouse J, ibid, at 230).

of the vessel was not infested with insects,[7] and whether the fittings of the vessel were adequate for the carriage of deck cargo.[8]

The negligence of his servants or agents will be sufficient to affect him with liability; but he will not be responsible for negligence on the part of the shipbuilders in constructing the ship, unless he himself or someone for whose default he is responsible was in some way at fault, as, for example, by negligently passing bad work.[9]

However, he will be liable for negligence on the part of ship repairers to whom the vessel has been sent for repairs.

Thus, in *Riverstone Meat Co Pty Ltd v Lancashire Shipping Co Ltd*[10]

A fitter employed by ship repairers negligently refixed some inspection covers on some storm valves. Water entered the valves during the voyage and damaged the cargo.
Held, the negligence of the fitter was a lack of due diligence for which the carrier was responsible.

He will also be liable for the failure of a compass adjuster to exercise due diligence.[11]

The certificate of a Lloyd's surveyor is likely to be accepted by the Court as conclusive to show that the carrier has exercised due diligence when it relates to a case in which he has built or bought a ship in the first instance.[12] To go behind it 'would involve a retrogression beyond the point to which a reasonable (shipowner) can be expected to go'.[13] But it is not so likely to be accepted where it relates to his duty as to the day-to-day maintenance and upkeep of his ship.[14]

A clause stating that a survey certificate shall be 'conclusive evidence of due diligence' to make the ship seaworthy is void under Article III, r 8 of the Act.[15]

---

7   *Empresa Cubana Importada de Alimentos Alimport v Tasmos Shipping Co SA, The Good Friend* [1984] 2 Lloyd's Rep 586, QBD (Commercial Court).
8   *The Tilia Gorthon* [1985] 1 Lloyd's Rep 552, QBD (Admiralty Court).
9   *W Angliss & Co (Australia) Proprietary Ltd v P & O Steam Navigation Co* [1927] 2 KB 456.
10 [1961] AC 807, [1961] 1 All ER 495, HL.
11 *Paterson SS Ltd v Robin Hood Mills Ltd* (1937) 58 Ll L Rep 33, PC.
12 *W Angliss v P & O Co*, supra; *Waddle v Wallsend Shipping Co, The Thordoc* [1952] 2 Lloyd's Rep 105; *Riverstone Meat Co Pty Ltd v Lancashire Shipping Co Ltd* [1959] 1 QB 74, [1958] 3 All ER 261 (at first instance).
13 *Waddle v Wallsend Shipping Co Ltd, The Thordoc* [1952] 2 Lloyd's Rep 105 at 130.
14 *Cranfield Bros Ltd v Tatem Steam Navigation Co Ltd* (1939) 64 Ll L Rep 264 at 267; *The Assunzione*, supra.
15 *The Australia Star* (1940) 67 Ll L Rep 110 at 116.

Under the Act, it has been held that the onus of proving unseaworthiness is upon those who allege it; it is then for the carrier to show, if he can, that in fact he did exercise due diligence.[16]

Thus if the cargo is not delivered:

(i) the cargo owners must prove non-delivery in accordance with the terms of the bill of lading;

(ii) the shipowners may then show that they are protected by one of the exceptions in Article IV, r 2;[17]

(iii) the burden of proof is then on the cargo owners to prove that the loss was caused by unseaworthiness;

(iv) if the cargo owners prove unseaworthiness, the shipowners are liable (since the exceptions in Article IV, r 2 are subject to the obligation as to seaworthiness in Article III, r 1)[18] unless they can show that they exercised due diligence to make the ship seaworthy before and at the beginning of the voyage.[19]

(3) REASONABLE DESPATCH

As in the case of a voyage charter-party,[20] it is implied in bills of lading that the voyage must be prosecuted with reasonable despatch.

The Carriage of Goods by Sea Act 1971 makes no reference to the implied undertaking as to reasonable despatch. It seems, therefore that that undertaking forms part of the contract even though the Act applies. The omission to mention the point in the Rules seems to have been due to an oversight, as it was clearly intended that no term other than those laid down by the Act should be implied in a contract governed by it.

---

16 Carriage of Goods by Sea Act 1971, Sch, Art IV, r 1; *W Angliss and Co v P & O Co*, supra; *Charles Goodfellow Lumber Sales Ltd v Verreault Hovington and Verreault Navigation Inc* [1971] 1 Lloyd's Rep 185, Supreme Court of Canada, where it was held that the production of a certificate of seaworthiness signed by an inspector appointed by the Department of Transport was not sufficient to discharge the burden of proof that due diligence had been exercised by the shipowner's. See the judgment of Ritchie J, ibid, at 194; *Empresa Cubana Importado de Alimentos Alimport v Iasmos Shipping Co SA, The Good Friend* [1984] 2 Lloyd's Rep 586, QBD (Commercial Court) at 588 (per Staughton J).

17 See p 200, post.

18 See pp 194–200, post.

19 *Empresa Cubana Importado de Alimentos Alimport v Iasmos Shipping Co SA, The Good Friend*, supra, at 588 (per Staughton J).

20 See pp 19–20, post.

(3) NO DEVIATION

The general rule

(a) At Common Law. As in the case of a voyage charter-party,[1] it is implied in all bills of lading that no deviation will be made from the contractual route, unless such deviation is justified, ie where it is made for purposes necessary for the prosecution of the voyage or for the safety of the adventure, or to save human life.

(b) By statute. The most important alteration of the law with regard to deviation effected by the Carriage of Goods by Sea Act 1971 is that, in cases to which the Act applies,[2] deviation for the purpose of saving property at sea is justified and therefore not deemed to be a breach of the contract.[3]

The Act also provides that 'any reasonable deviation' is not to be considered a breach of the contract.[4] Whether or not a particular deviation is reasonable is a question of fact in each case.[5]

Thus, in *Stag Line Ltd v Foscolo, Mango & Co Ltd*[6]

In the course of a voyage from Swansea to Constantinople a vessel deviated from the contractual route in order to land at St Ives some engineers who has been testing her fuel-saving apparatus. After leaving St Ives she struck a rock and was lost.
Held, not a reasonable deviation.

In that case Lord Atkin said:[7]

'A deviation may, and often will, be caused by fortuitous circumstances never contemplated by the original parties to the contract, and may be reasonable though it is made solely in the interests of the ship or solely in the interests of the cargo or indeed in the direct interest of neither; as for instance where the presence of a passenger or of a member of the ship or crew was urgently required after the voyage had begun on a matter of national importance; or where some person on board was a fugitive from justice, and there were urgent reasons for his immediate appearance. The true test seems to be what departure from the contract voyage might a prudent

---

1 See pp 21–22, ante.
2 See pp 95–98, ante.
3 Carriage of Goods by Sea Act 1971, Sch, Art IV, r 4.
4 Ibid.
5 *Stag Line Ltd v Foscolo Mango & Co Ltd* [1932] AC 328, [1931] All ER Rep 666, HL; *Accinanto Ltd v J Ludwig Mowinckels A/S, The Ocean Liberty* [1953] 1 Lloyd's Rep 38, CA; *Thiess Bros (Queensland) Pty Ltd v Australian Steamships Pty Ltd* [1955] 1 Lloyd's Rep 459; *Georgia-Pacific Corpn v Marilyn L, Elvapores Inc, Evans Products Co and Retla SS Co, The Marilyn L* [1972] 1 Lloyd's Rep 418, District Court for the Eastern District of Virginia, Norfolk Division, where the master had not followed the route suggested by the Pacific Weather Analysis.
6 Supra.
7 [1932] AC at 343.

person controlling the voyage at the time make and maintain having in mind all the relevant circumstances existing at the time including the terms of the contract and the interest of all parties concerned, but without obligation to consider the interests of any one as conclusive.'

Again, in *Thiess Bros (Queensland) Pty Ltd v Australian Steamships Pty Ltd*[8] A vessel was required by the terms of a bill of lading to deliver a cargo at Melbourne. She deviated to Newcastle (NSW) only 4 miles off her course to take on bunkers for her next voyage.
Held, not a reasonable deviation.

But in *Danae Shipping Corpn v TPAO and Guven Turkish Insurance Co Ltd, The Daffodil B*[9]

Whilst on a voyage from Milazzo, Sicily, to Tutunciftlik, Turkey, the vessel deviated to Lavrion, Greece, a small port on the east coast of Greece to get a generator repaired, instead of going to Piraeus.
Held, the deviation was a reasonable one, for Lavrion was just as safe as Piraeus if not safer in that if the vessel had become disabled in a crowded seaway while approaching Piraeus, the danger of collision with other vessels would have been at least as great if not greater than if she had become disabled on entering Lavrion.[10]

Where goods are packed in containers and stowed on the deck of a container ship built for the purpose of carrying deck cargo, such shipment does not constitute an unreasonable deviation.[11]

Express clauses permitting deviation. As in the case of voyage charter-parties,[12] bills of lading often contain a clause which gives the shipowner the right to call at ports off the ordinary trade route.
Thus, in *Leduc & Co v Ward*[13]

Where the bill of lading gave 'liberty to call at any ports in any order and to deviate for the purpose of saving life or property,' the voyage being from Fiume to Dunkirk, the ship was taken out of her course to Glasgow on the shipowner's private business. She was lost in a storm in the Clyde.
Held, the above clause merely gave a right to call at any ports in the ordinary course of the voyage. The shipowner was therefore liable.

In construing all such clauses as the above, the Court will apply

---

8   [1955] 1 Lloyd's Rep 459, Supreme Court of New South Wales.
9   [1983] 1 Lloyd's Rep 498, QBD (Commercial Court).
10 See the judgment of Lloyd J, ibid, at 502.
11 *Du Pont de Nemours International SA and E I Du Pont de Nemours & Co Inc v SS Mormacvega etc and Moore-McCormack Lines Inc, The Mormacvega* [1974] 1 Lloyd's Rep 296, US Court of Appeals, Second Circuit. (See the judgment of Timbers Ct J, ibid, at 300.)
12 See p 22, ante.
13 (1888) 20 QBD 475.

the general principle that the main object of the contract must not be defeated. So, even where the deviation clause gives liberty to call at ports *outside* the direct geographical voyage in express terms, such liberty will be limited, by inclusion in the contract of a special description of the voyage undertaken (eg 'Malaga to Liverpool'), to permission to call at ports on the course of that voyage.[14]

On the other hand, a very comprehensive deviation clause protected the shipowner in *Connolly Shaw Ltd v Nordenfjeldske SS Co*[15]

Lemons were shipped from Palermo to London under a bill of lading which provided: '. . . the ship is to be at liberty, either before or after proceeding towards the port of delivery of the said goods, to proceed to or return to and stay at any ports or places whatsoever (although in a contrary direction to or out of or beyond the route of the said port of delivery) once or oftener in any order backwards or forwards for loading or discharging cargo passengers coals or stores or for any purpose whatsoever . . . and also such ports places and sailing shall be deemed included within the intended voyage of the said goods.' Before proceeding to London the ship deviated to Hull. In spite of the delay, the lemons arrived in London in good condition, but in the interval the price of lemons had fallen.
Held, that the indorsee of the bills of lading could not recover damages against the shipowners, for the deviation to Hull was covered by the clause.

(B) On the part of the shipper

A shipper impliedly undertakes that the goods which he ships are not dangerous when carried in the ordinary way, unless

(1) he expressly notifies the shipowner to the contrary,
or (2) the shipowner knows, or ought to know, that they are dangerous.[16]

Thus, in *Brass v Maitland*[17]

Bleaching powder containing chloride of lime was shipped and damaged other goods on board. The shipowner, having been made liable for the damage, sued the shipper. It was proved that the shipper knew of the character of the goods he had shipped.
Held, that as the master ought to have known that the powder contained chloride of lime, the shipper was not liable.[18]

---

14 *Glynn v Margetson & Co* [1893] AC 351; *G H Renton & Co Ltd v Palmyra Trading Corpn of Panama* [1957] AC 149, [1956] 3 All ER 957, HL.
15 (1934) 50 TLR 418.
16 *Bamfield v Goole and Sheffield Transport Co Ltd* [1910] 2 KB 94.
17 (1856) 6 E & B 470.
18 See also *Sebastian SS Owners v De Vizcaya* [1920] 1 KB 332; *The Domald* [1920]

It seems that the true nature of this implied undertaking is not that of an *absolute* guarantee of the harmlessness of the goods, but only a guarantee that the goods are not dangerous to the knowledge of the shipper, and that he has taken reasonable care to assure himself of that fact.[19]

Where the nature of the goods shipped is liable to cause the forfeiture or detention of the ship, the goods are 'dangerous' with the meaning of this principle,[20] subject, of course, to the limitations (1) and (2) set out above.[21]

But the shipper does not impliedly undertake that the cargo can be expeditiously unloaded.

Thus, in *Transoceanica Societa Italiana de Navigazione v H S Shipton & Sons*[22]

A cargo of barley contained some sand and stones. The suction pump employed in the discharge of the vessel became choked in consequence, and she was delayed.
Held, the shipper was not liable for the delay.

The statutes mentioned in the previous chapter relating to the carriage of dangerous goods apply also where they are carried under bills of lading.[1] In addition, where the Carriage of Goods by Sea Act 1971 applies,[2] the carrier or the master is entitled to destroy or render innocuous dangerous goods without being liable to pay compensation.[3]

TRANSFER OF RIGHTS AND LIABILITIES UNDER A BILL OF LADING

At Common Law contracts were not assignable. Hence a transfer of a bill of lading with the intention of passing the property in the

 P 56; *Heath Steele Mines Ltd v The Erwin Schroeder* [1969] 1 Lloyd's Rep 370, Exchequer Court of Canada, Nova Scotia Admiralty District, where it was held that the master could not have known the danger in carrying a cargo of copper concentrate and what precautions should have been taken. See the judgment of Pottier J, ibid, at 374.

19 Per Atkin J, in *Mitchell, Cotts & Co v Steel Bros & Co* [1916] 2 KB 610 at 614; see also Lord Ellenborough's dictum in *Williams v East India Co Ltd* (1802) 3 East 192 at 200.

20 *Mitchell, Cotts & Co v Steel Bros & Co*, supra.

21 See per Sir Henry Duke P, in *The Lisa* [1921] P at 46–47. The decision was reversed on other grounds: (1924) 40 TLR 252.

22 [1923] 1 KB 31.

 1 See pp 24–25, ante.

 2 See pp 95–98, ante.

 3 Carriage of Goods by Sea Act 1971, Sch, Art IV, r 6 (see Appendix E).

goods did not transfer the rights and liabilities under the contract of carriage; it merely passed the property in the goods.

But a great change was made by the Bills of Lading Act 1855.[4] Section 1 provides that:

'Every consignee of goods named in a bill of lading,[5] and every endorsee[6] of a bill of lading, to whom the property in the goods therein mentioned shall pass upon or by reason of such consignment or endorsement, shall have transferred to and vested in him all rights of suit, and be subject to the same liabilities in respect of such goods as if the contract contained in the bill of lading had been made with himself.'

It is not certain whether there can be only one consignee named in a bill of lading. The Act seems to contemplate the possibility of more than one consignee being named.[7]

Under s 1 of the Act, when property in the goods passes upon or by reason of an endorsement, contractual rights of suit and contractual liabilities are transferred to the endorsee.[8] When property does not so pass, there is no such transfer.[9]

Another view is that the property need only pass from the shipper to the consignee or indorsee under a contract in pursuance of which the goods are consigned to him under the bill of lading, or in pursuance of which the bill of lading is indorsed in his favour.[10] It has also been said, however, that the view that if the property in the

---

4 See Appendix C, post.

5 See e g *Seateam & Co K/S A/S v Iraq National Oil Co, The Sevonia Team* [1983] 2 Lloyd's Rep 640, QBD (Commercial Court), where the property in some crude oil was held to have passed to the consignee on its consignment. (See the judgment of Lloyd J, ibid, at 644.)

6 See e g *The Berkshire* [1974] 1 Lloyd's Rep 185, QBD (Admiralty Court), where the bill of lading was endorsed by the shippers in blank and transferred by them to the receivers; *Pacific Molasses Co and United Trading Co Ltd v Entre Rios Compania Naviera SA, The San Nicholas* [1976] 1 Lloyd's Rep 8, CA, where it was held that there was at least a prima facie case that the property passed by indorsement; *The Aramis* [1989] 1 Lloyd's Rep 213, CA, where no property in the goods passed because they formed part of a single undivided bulk cargo. (See the judgment of Bingham LJ, ibid, at 218.)

7 *Seateam & Co K/S A/S v Iraq National Oil Co, The Sevonia Team*, supra, at 643 (per Lloyd J).

8 *The Aramis*, supra, at 218 (per Bingham LJ).

9 Ibid, at 218 (per Binham LJ).

10 *Pacific Molasses Co and United Trading Co Ltd v Entre Rios Compania Naviera SA, The San Nicholas*, supra, at 13 (per Roskill LJ); *Karlshamns Olje Fabriker v Eastport Navigation Corpn, The Elafi* [1981] 2 Lloyd's Rep 679, QBD (Commercial Court), at 687 (per Mustill J); *Seateam & Co K/S A/S v Iraq National Oil Co, The Sevonia Team*, supra, at 643 (per Lloyd J). In *The Aramis*, supra, the Court of Appeal expressed no opinion as to the correctness of the first two cases mentioned in this footnote. (See the Judgment of Bingham LJ: [1989] 1 Lloyd's Rep at 218.)

goods passes otherwise than on or by reason of the consignment or indorsement, the rights of suit do not pass to the receiver cannot be supported.[11]

Merely being the holder of a bill of lading does not give a title to a person to sue the shipowner in contract.[12]

The contract transferred

The contract transferred is that embodied in the bill of lading including, of course, such terms as are implied by law in all contracts of carriage by sea, eg not to deviate. If the bill of lading does not contain some term of the original agreement, that term will not be binding as between shipowner and indorsee of the bill of lading.

Thus, in *Leduc v Ward*[13]

A ship deviated to Glasgow and was lost. The indorsee of the bill of lading sued for non-delivery of the goods.
Held, that evidence to show that, before the goods were put on board, the shippers had agreed to the deviation to Glasgow was not, as between the shipowner and the indorsee of the bill of lading, admissible to vary the contract contained in it.

Where goods are shipped under a bill of lading and the charterer of the vessel is named as consignee, the charterer, if he indorses the bill of lading to a third party, has no claim for substantial damages against the shipowners in respect of the loss of the goods for he has no proprietary interest in them.

Thus, in *The Albazero*[14]

Crude oil was shipped at La Salina, Venezuela, on board a vessel for carriage to Antwerp under a bill of lading naming the charterers of the vessel as consignees. The bill of lading was subsequently indorsed by them to a third party. Later the vessel and her cargo were lost. The charterers claimed substantial damages from the shipowners contending that the shipowners were in breach of the terms of the charter-party and that the loss had been caused thereby.
Held, the action failed because the charterers had no proprietary interest in the goods at the time of the loss, and had suffered no loss.

---

11 *Seateam & Co K/S A/S v Iraq National Oil Co, The Sevonia Team*, supra, at 643 (per Lloyd J).
12 *Mitsui & Co Ltd v Flota Mercante Grancolombiana SA, The Ciudad de Pasto and Ciudad de Neiva* [1987] 2 Lloyd's Rep 392, QBD (Commercial Court) at 400 (per Hobhouse J).
13 (1888) 20 QBD 475.
14 [1976] 2 Lloyd's Rep 467, HL. (See the judgment of Lord Diplock, ibid, at 472.)

Passing of the property in the goods

The Common Law gave effect to the mercantile usage[15] whereby indorsement and delivery of a bill of lading during the transit gave to the indorsee such property in the goods as it was the intention of the parties to transfer.

In order that the property in the goods may pass by assignment of the bill of lading, the following conditions must be complied with:

(1) *The bill of lading must be transferable on the face of it.*

(2) *The goods must be in transit.*
They need not be at sea, but they must have been handed over to the shipowner or forwarding agent for carriage and not yet delivered to any person having a right to claim them under a bill of lading.[16]

(3) *The bill of lading must have been put in circulation by a person who had a good title to the goods.*
(In this respect bills of lading differ from negotiable instruments, for a bona fide holder for value of such instruments gets a good title irrespective of prior equities.)

(4) *There must have been an intention to transfer the property.*
The indorsement and delivery of a bill of lading passes only such property in the goods as the parties intended to pass. Hence, it may:

(a) Pass no property at all.
It is common for an unpaid seller to reserve the right of disposing of the goods by taking the bills of lading in his own or his agent's name as consignee. The bill is sent to the agent in order to prevent the buyer obtaining delivery of the goods before payment of the price. Clearly no property in the goods is intended to pass to the agent in such a case.
Other instances of no property passing are where the

15 See *Lickbarrow v Mason* (1794) 1 Sm LC 13th edn, p 703; Chorley and Tucker's *Leading Cases* (4th edn 1962), p 293.
16 See the dictum of Willes J, quoted with approval in *Barber v Meyerstein* (1870) 39 LJCP 187 at 191. See also *Barclays Bank Ltd v Customs and Excise Comrs* [1963] 1 Lloyd's Rep 81, QBD, where Diplock LJ, said (at 88): 'So long as the contract is not discharged [ie by surrendering possession of the goods to the person entitled to them], the bill of lading ... remains a document of title by indorsement and delivery of which the rights of property in the goods can be transferred.'

indorser has no property to pass, or where the goods have already been delivered by the shipowner to a third party. *or*

(b) Pass the property subject to a condition.

The unpaid seller may ensure payment by a conditional indorsement of the bill of lading. This may be effected by forwarding to the buyer one of the bills of lading together with a bill of exchange for the price of the goods. In this connection the Sale of Goods Act 1979, s 19(3) provides that:

> 'Where the seller of goods draws on the buyer for the price, and transmits the bill of exchange and bill of lading to the buyer together, to secure acceptance or payment of the bill of exchange, the buyer is bound to return the bill of lading if he does not honour the bill of exchange, and if he wrongfully retains the bill of lading, the property in the goods does not pass to him.'

It should be observed, however, that the buyer in this case is a person in possession of a document of title to goods with the consent of the seller. Consequently, if he transfers it to a bona fide purchaser for value, the latter gets a valid title to the goods under the Factors Act 1889,[17] even though the original buyer has not accepted the bill of exchange.[18] *or*

(c) Pass the property absolutely. *or*

(d) Merely effect a mortgage or pledge of the goods as security for money lent.

An instance of this is where a shipper lodges an indorsed bill of lading with a bank, which discounts for him the draft attached to it with a view to providing fresh trading capital at once.

Thus, in *Sewell v Burdick*[19]

> Machinery was consigned to Poti deliverable to shipper or assigns on payment of freight. The shipper pledged the bills of lading with bankers as security for a loan. The shipper having failed to claim the goods, they were sold by the Russian customs authorities, but did not realise more than the amount of the customs duty and charges. The shipowner sought to recover the freight from the bank as holder of the bills of lading.
>
> *Held*, the mere indorsement and delivery of a bill of lading by way of pledge did not pass the property in the goods to an indorsee so as to make him liable on the contract in the bill of lading.

17 Section 9. See also Sale of Goods Act 1979, s 25(1).
18 *Cahn and Mayer v Pocketts Bristol Channel Steam Packet Co* [1899] 1 QB 643; Chorley and Tucker's *Leading Cases* (4th edn 1962), P 194.
19 (1884) 10 App Cas 74.

Lord Selborne's speech in this case make it clear that the question is one of the intention of the parties. He said:[20]

'One test is whether the shipper retains any such proprietary right in the goods as to make it just that he should also retain rights of suit against the shipowner under the contract in the bill of lading. If he does, the [Bills of Lading Act 1855] can hardly be intended to take those rights from him and transfer them to the endorsee. If they are not transferred, neither are the liabilities.'

But the Bills of Lading Act 1855 is not restricted to cases of out-and-out-sale. It would probably apply to an indorsee of a bill of lading by way of security 'who converts his symbolical into real possession by obtaining delivery of the goods'.[1]

Further, it should be observed that the mere fact that an indorsee of the bill of lading has not thereby acquired the general property in the goods does not necessarily mean that he has no remedy against the shipowner.

So, in *Brandt v Liverpool, Brazil and River Plate Steam Navigation Co Ltd*[2]

A bill of lading was indorsed to pledgees. On the faith thereof they made an advance to the shipper and obtained the goods on presenting the bill of lading and paying the freight.

Held, that, although they could not invoke the Bills of Lading Act 1855, yet a contract to deliver and accept the goods in accordance with the terms of the bill of lading ought to be inferred from the fact that, on the bill of lading being presented and the freight paid, the goods had been delivered and accepted.

Preservation of shipowner's right to freight

The Bills of lading Act 1855, s 2 preserves the right of the shipowner to claim freight from the original shipper although the bill of lading may have been assigned by him.

Preservation of shipper's right of stoppage in transit

The Bills of Lading Act 1855, s 2, preserves the right of the original shipper to stop the goods in transit.

20   Ibid, at p 84.
1   Ibid, at p 86.
2   [1924] 1 KB 575. See also *Peter Cremer, Westfaelische Central Genossenschaft GmbH and Intergraan NV v General Carriers SA, The Dona Mari* [1973] 2 Lloyd's Rep 366, QBD (Commercial Court).

Besides the right of conditional indorsement and of reserving the right of disposal, the unpaid seller can resume possession of the goods by exercising the right of stoppage in transit. This is defined by the Sale of Goods Act 1979, s 44, as follows:

'Subject to this Act, when the buyer of goods becomes insolvent, the unpaid seller who has parted with the possession of the goods has the right of stopping them in transit, that is to say, he may resume possession of the goods as long as they are in course of transit, and may retain them until payment or tender of the price.'

There are four points to be noted in connection with this right, namely:

(1) The buyer must be insolvent. He need not be bankrupt. It is sufficient if he cannot pay his debts as they fall due.[3]

(2) The right can be exercised only while the goods are in transit.[4] The question of the duration of the transit is primarily one of the intention of the parties. Ordinarily the transit begins when the goods leave the seller's possession, and ends when they get into the possession of the buyer. Delivery to the buyer's agent for the purpose of forwarding puts an end to the transit if the further destination has not been notified to the seller; otherwise it does not.[5]

Delivery to carriers does not end the transit even though they are employed by the buyer, unless the intention of the parties is clearly to the contrary. Thus, if the buyer charters a ship and sends for the goods, the transit is not terminated by shipment of the goods, although the seller does not know where the goods are being taken.[6] But, where the charter-party amounts to a demise so that the buyer has complete control of the ship, an unconditional delivery to the master puts an end to the transit.[7] Further, where the buyer actually owns the vessel, the presumption is even stronger that an unconditional delivery, negativing the right of stoppage in transit, is

---

3 Sale of Goods Act 1979, s 62(4), which states that: 'A person is deemed to be insolvent within the meaning of this Act if he has either ceased to pay his debts in the ordinary course of business, or cannot pay his debts in the ordinary course of business, or cannot pay his debts as they become due, whether he has committed an act of bankruptcy or not.'
4 *Lickbarrow v Mason* (1794) 1 Sm L C (13th edn), p 703; Chorley and Tucker's *Leading Cases* (4th edn 1962), p 293.
5 *Re Isaacs, ex p Miles* (1885) 15 QBD 39.
6 *Re Cock, ex p Rosevear China Clay Co* (1879) 11 ChD 560.
7 *Fowler v M'Taggart* (1801) cited at 1 East 522.

intended.[8] Again, where the carrier agrees to hold the goods for the consignee, eg to warehouse them for him, the transit will be considered at an end.[9]

(3) Its exercise does not rescind the contract of sale, but merely restores possession of the goods to the seller.[10] Thus, s 48(1) of the Sale of Goods Act 1979 states:

'Subject to this section, a contract of sale is not rescinded by the mere exercise by an unpaid seller of his right of . . . stoppage in transit.'

(4) It is defeated by a bona fide transfer of the bill of lading for value.[11] Generally the right of stoppage in transit exists against the buyer and all who claim under him. It is available against a purchaser from him.

Thus, s 47(1) of the Sale of Goods Act 1979 states:

'Subject to this Act, the unpaid seller's right of . . . stoppage in transit is not affected by any sale or other disposition of the goods which the buyer may have made, unless the seller has assented to it.'

But where such a purchaser takes a bill of lading or other document of title bona fide and for value, the right of stoppage in transit is lost, for s 47(2) of the Act of 1979 goes on to state:

'Where a document of title to goods has been lawfully transferred to any person as buyer or owner of the goods, and that person transfers the document to a person who takes it in good faith and for valuable consideration, then—
  (a) if the last-mentioned transfer was by way of sale the unpaid seller's right of lien or retention or stoppage in transit is defeated; and
  (b) if the last-mentioned transfer was made by way of pledge or other disposition for value, the unpaid seller's right of lien or retention or stoppage in transit can only be exercised subject to the rights of the transferee.'

The indorsee of a bill of lading is thus in a better position than the original consignee, for the latter's title to the goods is subject to the seller's right of stoppage in transit.

Thus, in *Lickbarrow v Mason*[12]

T shipped goods under a bill of lading (in four parts) made out to 'T or order or assigns'. Two of the bills of lading were indorsed in blank and sent to Freeman, the

---

8   *Merchant Banking Co of London v Phoenix Bessemer Steel Co* (1877) 5 ChD 205.
9   *Foster v Frampton* (1826) 6 B & C 107.
10 *Kemp v Falk* (1882) 7 App Cas 573.
11 *Lickbarrow v Mason* (1794) 1 Sm L C (13th edn), p 703; Chorley and Tucker's *Leading Cases* (4th edn 1962), p 293.
12 Supra.

buyer of the goods. Freeman sold the goods and transferred the two bills of lading to Lickbarrow, a bona fide purchaser for value. Freeman became bankrupt. T tried to stop the goods in transit, and sent one bill of lading to Mason, who obtained possession of the goods.

Held, that T's right to stop the goods had been defeated by the assignment to Lickbarrow, who was therefore entitled to recover the goods.

Effect of subsequent re-indorsement

If the indorsee of a bill of lading sells the goods and re-indorses the bill of lading, he ceases to be responsible for liabilities under the contract; but if he retains the bill of lading, a mere re-sale will not free him.[13] Re-indorsement must take place while the goods are in transit and before delivery.

THE UNFAIR CONTRACT TERMS ACT 1977

By the Unfair Contract Terms Act 1977, s 2(1), which is expressly extended to cover any contract for the carriage of goods by ship,[14] a person cannot by reference to any contract term or to a notice given to persons generally or to particular persons exclude or restrict his liability for death or personal injury resulting from negligence.[15]

Subject to this sections 2,[16] 3,[17] 4[18] and 7[19] do not extend to such contracts except in favour of a person dealing as consumer.[20]

COMPARISON OF BILL OF LADING WITH MATE'S RECEIPT

By way of contrast, the effect of the mate's receipt as conferring rights upon its holder is much more limited. Lord Wright has stated that a mate's receipt

---

13 *Fowler v Knoop* (1878) 4 QBD 299.
14 Unfair Contract Terms Act 1977, Sch 1. A detailed discussion of the provisions of this Act is outside the scope of this book.
15 For the meaning of negligence, see Unfair Contract Terms Act 1977, s 1.
16 Which relates to 'negligence liability'.
17 Which relates to 'liability arising in contract'.
18 Which relates to 'unreasonable indemnity clauses'.
19 Which relates to 'miscellaneous contracts under which goods pass'.
20 Unfair Contract Terms Act 1977, Sch 1. As to the meaning of dealing as consumer, see ibid, s 12.

'is not a document of title to the goods shipped. Its transfer does not pass property in the goods, nor is its possession equivalent to possession of the goods. It is not conclusive, and its statements do not bind the shipowner as do the statements in a bill of lading signed within the master's authority. It is, however, prima facie evidence of the quantity and condition of the goods received, and prima facie it is the recipient or possessor [of the mate's receipt] who is entitled to have the bill of lading issued to him. But if the mate's receipt acknowledges receipt from a shipper other than the person who actually receives the mate's receipt, and, in particular, if the property is in that shipper, and the shipper has contracted for the freight, the shipowner will prima facie be entitled, and indeed bound, to deliver the bill of lading to that [shipper].'[1]

A trade custom, however, has been proved to the effect that in trade between Sarawak and Singapore mate's receipts are universally adopted as documents of title in the same way as bills of lading.[2]

1   *Nippon Yusen Kaisha v Ramjiban Serowgee* [1938] AC 429 at 445–6.
2   *Kum v Wah Tat Bank Ltd* [1971] 1 Lloyd's Rep 439, PC. But the custom was held to be inconsistent with the words 'not negotiable' in the mate's receipt concerned. (See the judgment of Lord Devlin, ibid, at 444–445.) As to proof of trade custom, see pp 136–137, post.

Chapter 4

The construction of charter-parties and bills of lading

There are well established rules which guide the Courts in the interpretation of charter-parties and bills of lading. But only certain evidence is admissible. Sometimes the particular system of law which governs the contract has to be ascertained. This is a matter of 'The Conflict of Laws'.

SOME RULES OF CONSTRUCTION

'Questions of construction are very often questions of first impression. They depend immensely upon the circumstances of each individual case and the precise words used in the contracts to be construed. The Court guides itself, of course, by such canons of construction as are available and relevant to the problem in hand.'[1]

Further, it must be noted that 'the interpretation of a charter-party cannot be conducted solely on the basis of the ordinary English meaning of the words which the parties have used in their contract. Regard must be had to what the same or similar words have been held to mean in the past.'[2]

The following are some of the rules which must be kept in mind:
(1) The primary consideration in construing any contract is the intention of the contracting parties.

Thus, a charter-party or a bill of lading must be construed in the light of the particular undertaking with which it is concerned.[3]

---

1 *Marifortuna Naviera SA v Government of Ceylon* [1970] 1 Lloyd's Rep 247 at 256, QBD (Commercial Court) (Mocatta J).
2 *Marc Rich & Co Ltd v Tourloti Compania Naviera SA, The Kalliopi A* [1988] 2 Lloyd's Rep 101, CA, at 105 (per Staughton LJ).
3 *Glynn v Margetson & Co* [1893] AC 351; *Australian Oil Refining Pty Ltd v R W Miller & Co Ltd* [1968] 1 Lloyd's Rep 448, High Court of Australia, where Barwick CJ, said (ibid, at 452): 'Thus, although the contract which the parties made was called a charter-party and contained many provisions commonly found in contracts relating merely to the carriage of goods, that contract must, in my

(2) Where there is a conflict between the printed and written[4] parts
of the contract owing to an error or to inadvertence, the intention
expressed by the written part should, as a general rule, be preferred
to that expressed by the printed part.[5]

It is therefore unnecessary, and indeed often impossible, to give
full effect to every printed clause.[6]

(3) Any ambiguous term of the contract is to be construed most
strongly against the party for whose benefit it is intended, i e usually,
in the case of a bill of lading, against the shipowner.[7]

opinion, be construed having regard to the whole relationship in which the
parties stood and to all the rights and obligations they sought to create or to
accept.'; *Segovia Compagnia Naviera SA v R Pagnan and Fratelli, The Aragon*
[1975] 2 Lloyd's Rep 216, QBD (Commercial Court), where Donaldson J, said
(ibid. at 221): 'Charter-parties are like any other contract and must be construed
as such. Their true construction is a matter of law not fact. The duty of the Court
is to ascertain the presumed common intention of the parties, to be deduced from
the words used and the background to the transaction. Their actual, but
uncommunicated, intentions are irrelevant.'; *Sarma Navigation SA v Sidermar
SpA, The Sea Pioneer* [1982] 1 Lloyd's Rep 13, CA, where the two charter-parties
were not to be treated separately, and were complementary to each other (see the
judgment of Lord Denning MR, ibid, at 16); *Transamerican SS Corpn v Tradax
Export SA, The Oriental Envoy* [1982] 2 Lloyd's Rep 266, QBD (Commercial
Court), where it was held that the two charter-parties were to be treated separately
and that demurrage under both of them was payable (see the judgment of
Parker J, ibid, at 272); *President of India v Olympia Sauna Shipping Co SA, The
Ypatia Halcoussi* [1984] 2 Lloyd's Rep 455, QBD (Commercial Court), where it
was held to be inconceivable that the parties intended 3 separate loading places
on the River Columbia, which between them were over 60 miles apart, to be one
single port. (See the judgment of Hirst J, ibid, at 458.)

4 Or typed.
5 *Hadjipateras v Weigall & Co* (1918) 34 TLR 360; *Gesellschaft Burgerlichin Rechts
v Stockholms Rederiaktiebolag Svea, The Brabant* [1965] 2 Lloyd's Rep 546, QBD
(Commercial Court). (See the judgment of McNair J, ibid, at 553.); *Ismail v
Polish Ocean Lines, The Ciechocinek* [1975] 2 Lloyd's Rep 170, QBD (Commercial
Court). (See the judgment of Kerr J, ibid, at 186.); *revsd* on other grounds; [1976]
1 Lloyd's Rep 489, CA; *Bravo Maritime (Chartering) Est v Alsayed Abdullah
Mohamed Baroom, The Athinoula* [1980] 2 Lloyd's Rep 481 at 487, QBD
(Commercial Court) (per Mocatta J); *Navrom v Callitsis Ship Management SA,
The Radauti* [1988] 2 Lloyd's Rep 416, CA.
6 *Gray v Carr* (1871) LR 6 QB 522.
7 *Burton v English* (1883) 12 QBD 218; *Diana Maritime Corpn of Monrovia v
Southerns Ltd* [1967] 1 Lloyd's Rep 114, QBD (Commercial Court), at 123 (per
Megaw J); *Encyclopaedia Britannica Inc v Hong Kong Producer and Universal
Marine Corpn* [1969] 2 Lloyd's Rep 536, US Ct of Appeals, Second Circuit, at 542
(per Anderson Ct J). For a case where a time bar clause relating to demurrage
had been prepared by the charterers and was construed against them, see *Pera
Shipping Corpn v Petroship SA, The Pera* [1985] 2 Lloyd's Rep 103, CA.

This is known as the 'contra proferentem' rule.

(4) The rule of interpretation known as the 'ejusdem generis' rule is often applied. That is to say, general words which are tacked on to specific words are to be construed as referring only to things or circumstances of the same kind as those described by the specific words.

Thus, in *Tillmans & Co SS v Knutsford Ltd*[8]

The words 'war, disturbance or any other cause' were *held* not to cover ice, despite the universality of the general words 'any other'.

In some cases, however, the general words are the governing words, and the specific words are subordinate.

Thus, in *Ambatielos v Anton Jurgens Margarine Works*[9]

A clause ran '. . . vessel detained by causes over which the charterers have no control, viz quarantine, ice, hurricanes . . . etc.; no demurrage payable.'

Held, that the general words were the governing words and that a strike was therefore within the exception. It should be observed that the specific words were, in this case, tacked on to the general words, and not vice versa.

But doubt has been expressed as to whether the ejusdem generis rule or the discussion of it in relation to different words is really of much assistance where the clause to be construed contains the words 'such as'.[10]

Thus, in *Diana Maritime Corpn of Monrovia v Southerns Ltd*[11]

A bill of lading stated that if a vessel was prevented from entering the port of discharge or was likely to be delayed there for an unreasonable time 'owing to causes beyond the carrier's control such as blockade, interdict, war, strikes, lockouts, disturbances, ice, storms or the consequences thereof', the carrier was entitled to proceed to a convenient port to discharge. The vessel discharged at a convenient port because of delay being anticipated at the contractual port of discharge. The cargo owners brought an action against the carrier for breach of contract, claiming damages for the forwarding expenses which they had paid to get the cargo to the contractual port of discharge.

Held, the carrier was liable. The parties never intended to include all causes beyond

8   [1908] AC 406.
9   [1923] AC 175.
10 *Diana Maritime Corpn of Monrovia v Southerns Ltd* [1967] 1 Lloyd's Rep 114, QBD (Commercial Court), at 122 (per Megaw J).
11 [1967] 1 Lloyd's Rep 114, QBD (Commercial Court). See the judgment of Megaw J, ibid, at 123. Cf *Micada Compania Naviera SA v Texim* [1968] 2 Lloyd's Rep 57, QBD (Commercial Court), where a clause in a time charter-party stated that 'no live stock nor injurious inflammable or dangerous goods (such as acids, explosives, calcium carbide, ferro silicon, naphtha, motor spirit, tar, or any of their products) to be shipped', and it was held that the proper construction of the words in brackets was that they were merely intended by way of exemplification and were not intended by way of restriction. (See the judgment of Donaldson J, ibid, at 61.)

the carrier's control, but only such causes beyond his control as those specified. Accordingly, the vessel should not have discharged at a port other than the contractual port.

The ejusdem generis rule may be excluded by apt words in the document.

Thus, in *Sidermar SpA v Apollo Corpn, The Apollo*[12]

A clause in a time charter-party stated that hire would cease to be payable 'in the event of loss of time from deficiency and/or default of men, or deficiency of stores, fire, breakdown or damage to hull, machinery or equipment, grounding, detention by average accidents to ship or cargo, drydocking for the purpose of examination or painting bottom or by any other cause whatsoever preventing the full working of the vessel'.

Held, that the use of the word 'whatsoever' coming after the words 'or by any other cause' excluded the application of the ejusdem generis rule, and hire ceased when the vessel was unable to load due to the port authorities not granting free pratique until she had been inspected after two members of her crew were discharged at a previous port of call suffering from suspected typhus.

Similarly, in *Belcore Maritime Corpn v Flli. Moretti Cereali SpA, The Mastro Giorgis*[13]

A time charter-party stated: 'In the event of the loss of time from default and/or . . . by any other cause whatsoever preventing the full working of the vessel the payment of hire shall cease for the time thereby lost . . .'

Held, that the use of the word 'whatsoever' excluded the ejusdem generis rule, and hire was not payable for the period during which the vessel was under arrest.[14]

(5) It is not settled whether the Court is entitled to refer to a clause which has been deleted from the document.[15]

(6) The whole of the document must be looked at.[16]

---

12 [1978] 1 Lloyd's Rep 200, QBD (Commercial Court). (See the judgment of Mocatta J, ibid, at 204.)

13 [1983] 2 Lloyd's Rep 66, QBD (Commercial Court).

14 See the judgment of Lloyd J, ibid, at 66. For the 'off-hire' clause, see pp 47–51, ante.

15 Cases where it was held that it was *not* legitimate to refer to a deleted clause include: *Ambatielos v Anton Jurgens Margarine Works* [1923] AC 175 at 185, HL (per Viscount Finlay); *M A Sassoon & Sons Ltd v International Banking Corpn* [1927] AC 711 at 721, PC (per Viscount Sumner); *Firzel, Berry & Co v Eastcheap Dried Fruit Co* [1962] 1 Lloyd's Rep 370 at 375 (per McNair J), affd [1962] 2 Lloyd's Rep 11; *Compania Naviera Termar SA v Tradax Export SA* [1965] 1 Lloyd's Rep 198 at 204 (per Mocatta J); *Hang Fung Shipping and Trading Co Ltd v Mullion & Co Ltd* [1967] 1 Lloyd's Rep 511 at 526 (per McNair J). Cases where it was held that it was legitimate to refer to a deleted clause include: *Baumwoll Manufactur Von Scheibler v Gilchrest & Co* [1892] 1 QB 253 at 256 (per Lord Esher MR); *Anastasia SS (Owners) v Ugleexport Charkow* (1933) 46 Ll L Rep 1 at 6 (per Scrutton LJ); *Louis Dreyfus et Cie v Parnaso Cia Naviera SA, The Dominator* [1959] 1 QB 498 at 513 (per Diplock J).

16 *Nereide SpA di Navigazione v Bulk Oil International Ltd, The Laura Prima* [1982] 1 Lloyd's Rep 1 at 6, HL (per Lord Roskill).

Thus, in *Nereide SpA di Navigazione v Bulk Oil International Ltd, The Laura Prima*[17]

Cl 6 of a voyage charter-party that on arrival at the customary anchorage the master was to give notice of readiness to load,[18] berth or no berth and that lay time[19] should begin on the expiration of 6 hours after such notice or on the vessel's arrival in berth, but that where delay was caused to the vessel getting into berth after giving notice of readiness to load over which the charterer had no control, such delay should not count as lay time. Cl 9 stated that the vessel was to load at 'any safe place reachable on arrival which should be designated and procured by the charterer'. The charterer contended that the word 'berth' in cl 6 meant 'any berth'.

Held, by the House of Lords, that the charter-party must be read as a whole, and the word 'berth' in cl 6 meant the designated and procured berth referred to in cl 9.[20]

(7) The grammatical construction should be adopted except where there is a clear intention to the contrary.

(8) The words must be construed in their ordinary meaning.

Thus, the word 'reachable' in the phrase 'reachable on her arrival' means 'able to be reached.[1] It is not limited to a case where a failure of a vessel to reach the place concerned is due to physical causes.[2]

So, in *Arnt J Moerland v Kuwait Petroleum Corpn, The Fjordaas*[3]

A charter-party stated that the vessel should discharge at any safe place reachable on her arrival to be designated by the charterers. They designated a berth which could not be reached because of prohibition of night navigation and the absence of tugs.

Held, that the berth was not reachable on arrival for that expression was not confined to cases where there was delay due to physical causes.

But technical words must be given their technical meaning.[4]

---

17   [1982] 1 Lloyd's Rep 1, HL.
18   See pp 245–246, post.
19   See pp 237–238, post.
20   See the judgment of Lord Roskill: [1982] 1 Lloyd's Rep at 6. See also *Sametiet Johs Stove v Istanbul Petrol Rafinerisi A/S, The Johs Stove* [1984] 1 Lloyd's Rep 38 at 40 (per Lloyd J); *Palm Shipping Inc v Kuwait Petroleum Corpn, The Sea Queen* [1988] 1 Lloyd's Rep 500, QBD (Commercial Court) at 502 (per Saville J).
 1   *The President Brand* [1967] 2 Lloyd's Rep 338, QBD (Commercial Court); *Nereide SpA di Navigazione v Bulk Oil International Ltd, The Laura Prima* [1982] 1 Lloyd's Rep 1, HL; *K/S Arnt J Moerland v Kuwait Petroleum Corpn, The Fjordaas* [1988] 1 Lloyd's Rep 336, QBD (Commercial Court).
 2   *K/S Arnt J Moerland v Kuwait Petroleum Corpn, The Fjordaas*, supra.
 3   [1988] 1 Lloyd's Rep 336, QBD (Commercial Court).
 4   See e g *Tropwood AG of Zug v Jade Enterprises Ltd, The Tropwind* [1982] 1 Lloyd's Rep 232, CA, where the meaning of the words 'on her voyage' in a shipping context was to be found by reference to the meaning to be attached to them by persons in the shipping trade. (See the judgment of Lord Denning MR, ibid, at 236.)

(9) The meaning must be limited by the context in which the words are used.[5]

(10) The words of the document must, if possible, be construed liberally, so as to give effect to the intention of the parties.

(11) Where the words are capable of two constructions, the reasonable construction is to be preferred as representing the presumed intention of the parties.

(12) An express term in a document overrides any implied term which is inconsistent with it.[6]

(13) The same words or phrases in a document should where possible be given the same meaning but this rule must always yield to the particular context.[7]

THE EVIDENCE WHICH IS ADMISSIBLE

Where a contract has been reduced to writing, the general rule is that oral evidence is inadmissible to add to, vary or contradict the written instrument.[8]

There is, however, a presumption that the parties to a commercial contract entered into it with reference to the customs prevailing in the particular trade or locality to which the contract relates, provided such customs are reasonable, certain and notorious.[9]

---

5 See eg *Bulk Transport Group Shipping Co Ltd v Seacrystal Shipping Ltd, The Kyzikos* [1989] 1 Lloyd's Rep 1, HL, where the context in which the acronym 'wibon' (ie 'whether in berth or not') was to be found in the charter-party was considered.

6 See eg *Islamic Republic of Iran Shipping Lines v Royal Bank of Scotland plc, The Anna Ch* [1987] 1 Lloyd's Rep 266, QBD (Commercial Court), where a term that the charterers were obliged to order the vessel to discharge at a safe port in the vicinity of Bandar Khomeini could not be implied because such term was in conflict with the express option given to the charterers to nominate another port.

7 *Tor Line AB (Renamed Investment AB Torman) v Alltrans Group of Canada Ltd, The TFL Prosperity* [1984] 1 Lloyd's Rep 123 at 128, HL (per Lord Roskill).

8 *Goss v Lord Nugent* (1833) 5 B & Ad 58 at 64; *Jacobs v Batavia and General Plantations Trust Ltd* [1924] 1 Ch 287 at 295; *Northern Sales Ltd v The Giancarlo Zeta, The Giancarlo Zeta* [1966] 2 Lloyd's Rep 317 (Exchequer Court, British Columbia Admiralty District), where the Court refused to admit evidence to show that a broker had informed the plaintiff that the plaintiff had an option to load 11,000 tons, although the freight contract stated that the cargo was to consist of '10,000 tons, 10 per cent. more or less quantity at owners' option', for such evidence attempted to add, vary or contradict the terms of the contract. (See the judgment of Norris J, at 326–7.)

9 As in *Kum v Wah Tat Bank Ltd* [1971] 1 Lloyd's Rep 439, PC, where a trade custom to the effect that in trade between Sarawak and Singapore mate's receipts were universally adopted as documents of title in the same way as bills of lading

This presumption can be rebutted only by showing that the parties intended to exclude the custom, and the most effective way of doing this is by showing that the express terms of the contract are inconsistent with the usage which it is sought to incorporate.[10] 'Any custom of the port to the contrary notwithstanding' is a good example of such an express term.[11]

Thus, in *A/S Sameiling v Grain Importers (Eire) Ltd*[12]

A charter-party provided that shipowners' stevedores were to be employed in discharging grain cargo. At the discharging port of Cork there was a custom that the receivers of the cargo had the right to fill the grain into bags or buckets *before* discharge and to debit the shipowners with half the cost.

Held, that this custom was not inconsistent with the express term of the charter-party, and so was effective.

'To fall within the exception of repugnancy the [usage] must be such as if expressed in the written contract would make it insensible or inconsistent'.[13] Therefore, while the usage may regulate the mode of performance, it must not be such as to change the intrinsic character of the contract.[14] In the case of a bill of lading, evidence

was established, but was held not to be applicable because the mate's receipt contained the words 'not negotiable'. (See the judgment of Lord Devlin, ibid, at 444–445.) As to mate's receipts, see pp 128–129, ante. In *Encyclopaedia Britannica Inc v The Hong Kong Producer and Universal Marine Corpn* [1969] 2 Lloyd's Rep 536, US Ct of Appeals, Second Circuit, an alleged custom in the shipping industry of carrying containerised cargo on deck, regardless of the provisions of the bill of lading, was not established. See the judgment of Anderson Ct J, ibid, at 544. In *Du Pont de Nemours International SA and E I Du Pont de Nemours & Co Inc v SS Mormacvega etc and Moore-McCormack Lines Inc, The Mormacvega* [1973] 1 Lloyd's Rep 267, District Court, Southern District of New York, it was held that an alleged practice to ship containers on deck was not sufficiently old to make it a trade custom. (See the judgment of Brieant DJ, ibid, at 270.) (The decision was subsequently affirmed on a different point: [1974] 1 Lloyd's Rep 296, US Court of Appeals, Second Circuit.) In *Nissan Automobile Co (Canada) Ltd v Owners of Vessel Continental Shipper, The Continental Shipper* [1976] 2 Lloyd's Rep 234, Federal Court of Appeal of Canada, it was proved that it was the practice of the trade for cars to be shipped uncrated.

10   See, eg *Kum v Wah Tat Bank Ltd*, supra; *President of India v Olympia Sauna Shipping Co SA, The Ypatia Halcoussi* [1984] 2 Lloyd's Rep 455, QBD (Commercial Court), where it was held that a document relating to the 'customs of the port— Columbia River District' should not be taken into account since the construction was clear and there was no evidence that either the shipowners or the charterers had any knowledge of the document. (See the judgment of Hirst J, ibid, at 459).

11   *Brenda Co v Green* [1900] 1 QB 518.

12   [1952] 2 All ER 315. See also *Akt Helios v Ekman & Co* [1897] 2 QB 83.

13   Per Lord Campbell CJ, in *Dale v Humfrey* (1857) 7 E & B at 275.

14   *Les Affréteurs Réunis Société Anonyme v Leopold Walford (London) Ltd* [1919] AC 801.

of usage will be more readily admitted than in the case of a charter-party; whereas the charter-party is the contract, the bill of lading is merely a memorandum of the contract.

If a contract contains words which, in their context, are fairly capable of bearing more than one meaning, and if it is alleged that the parties have in effect negotiated on an agreed basis that the words bore only one of the two possible meanings, it is permissible for the Court to examine the extrinsic evidence relied on to see whether the parties have, in fact, used the words in question in one sense only, so that they have in effect given their own dictionary meaning to the words as the result of their common intention.[15]

Thus, in *Partenreederei MS Karen Oltmann v Scarsdale Shipping Co Ltd, The Karen Oltmann*[16]

A vessel was chartered under a time charter-party for '2 years, 14 days more or less'. A clause stated: 'Charterers to have the option to redeliver the vessel after 12 months' trading subject to giving 3 months' notice'. The owners contended that the words 'after 12 months' trading' meant 'on the expiry of 12 months' trading'. The charterers maintained that they meant 'at any time after the expiry of 12 months' trading'.
Held, pre-contractual telex exchanges could be referred to in support of the owners' contentions.

THE CONFLICT OF LAWS[17]

The parties to a bill of lading or a charter-party are often resident in different countries, and the place or places where the contract is to be performed are often different from the place where the contract was made. Hence it is important to find out which system of law is applicable to any particular contract. This is called the 'governing' or 'proper' law of the contract. Lord Atkin explained the rules determining the proper law of a contract thus:[18]

'The legal principles which are to guide an English Court on the question of the proper law of a contract are now well settled. It is the law which the parties intended to apply. Their intention will be ascertained by the intention expressed in the contract,

15 *Partenreederei MS Karen Oltmann v Scarsdale Shipping Co Ltd, The Karen Oltmann* [1976] 2 Lloyd's Rep 708 at 712 (per Kerr J).
16 [1976] 2 Lloyd's Rep 708.
17 See generally Cheshire and North, *Private International Law* (11th edn 1987), pp 447ff; Dicey and Morris, *Conflict of Laws* (11th edn 1987).
18 *R v International Trustee for the Protection of Bondholders Aktiengesellschaft* [1937] AC 500 at 529, [1937] 2 All ER 164 at 166, applied in *The Metamorphosis* [1953] 1 All ER 723 at 726 in relation to a bill of lading as evidence of a contract of carriage; and in *The Assunzione* [1954] P 150, [1954] 1 All ER 278, CA.

if any, which will be conclusive. If no intention be expressed, the intention will be presumed by the Court from the terms of the contract and the relevant surrounding circumstances. In coming to its conclusion, the Court will be guided by rules which indicate that particular facts or conditions lead to a prima facie inference, in some cases an almost conclusive inference, as to the intention of the parties to apply a particular law, eg the country where the contract is made, the country where the contract is to be performed, if the contract relates to immovables the country where they are situated, the country under whose flag the ship sails in which goods are contracted to be carried. But all these rules only serve to give prima facie indications of intention: they are all capable of being overcome by counter indications, however, difficult it may be in some cases to find such.'

Further, in a case decided by the House of Lords, it was stated that the proper law of the contract was the system of law by reference to which the contract was made or that with which the transaction had its closest and most real connection.[19]

In another leading case Lord Wright, when delivering the judgment of the Privy Council, again stressed the fact that the proper law of the contract depends on the intention of the parties 'to be ascertained in each case on a consideration of the terms of the contract, the situation of the parties, and generally on all the surrounding facts'.[20]

It will have been noticed that in the case of contracts of carriage by sea Lord Atkin referred to the prima facie rule that the law of the ship's flag applies. There are many illustrations of this rule.

Thus, in *Lloyd v Guibert*:[1]

A French ship was chartered by a British subject in the Danish West Indies for a voyage from Haiti to Liverpool. She put into a Portuguese port for repairs, and the master was obliged to borrow money on a bottomry bond to pay for the repairs. As the value of the ship and freight proved insufficient to repay the loan, the cargo had to contribute. The plaintiff, as owner of the cargo, claimed an indemnity from the shipowner. To this he was entitled by Danish, Portuguese, and English law, but not by French law.

Held, that the master's authority was limited by the law of the ship's flag, and consequently the cargo-owner was not entitled to an indemnity.

---

19   Re *United Rlys of Havana and Regla Warehouses Ltd* [1960] 2 All ER 332 at 364 (per Lord Morris). See also *Rossano v Manufacturers Life Insurance Co Ltd* [1963] 2 QB 352, [1962] 2 All ER 214, [1962] 1 Lloyd's Rep 187, QBD (Commercial Court) (life insurance); *Bonython v Commonwealth of Australia* [1951] AC 201, PC; *Compagnie d'Armement Maritime SA v Compagnie Tunisienne de Navigation SA* [1971] AC 572, [1970] 3 All ER 71, HL.

20   *Mount Albert Borough Council v Australasian Temperance and General Mutual Life Assurance Society Ltd* [1938] AC 224 at 240, [1937] 4 All ER 206 at 214.

 1   (1865) LR 1 QB 115; *Coast Lines Ltd v Hudig and Veder Chartering NV* [1972] 1 Lloyd's Rep 53, CA, where it was *held* that if, in the determination of the proper law of the contract, the scales were evenly balanced, the law of the flag could be taken as a last resort. (See the judgment of Lord Denning MR, ibid, at 57.)

However, the prima facie rule that the law of the flag governs contracts of carriage by sea is subject to the paramount rule of the intention of the parties, which may be express, or implied from the circumstances of the case.

Thus, in *The Industrie*[2]

London merchants negotiated a charter-party in London with English brokers for the carriage of rice from India to England in a ship belonging to a German owner and flying the German flag. The contract was made on an ordinary English charter-party form, which contained phrases peculiar to English law and stipulated that freight should be payable in sterling.

Held, the deliberate choice of English legal expressions, together with the fact that the contract was made in London between two English firms, indicated a clear intention to make an English contract.

There appears to be some doubt as to the law governing a contract for through carriage partly by land and partly by sea. Probably the best view is that as regards the land journey the law of that country applies, while the law of the flag governs the sea transit, unless a contrary intention is expressed in, or can be implied from, the contract[3].

Where there is an express statement by the parties of their intention to select the law of the contract, it is difficult to see what qualifications are possible, provided that the intention expressed is bona fide and legal[4], and provided there is no reason for avoiding the choice on the ground of public policy.[5]

2 [1894] P 58. See also *The Adriatic* [1931] P 241; *The Njegos* [136] P 90; *The Assunzione* [1954] P 150, [1954] 1 All ER 278, CA.
3 See *Moore v Harris* (1876) 1 App Cas 318; *The Patria* (1871) 41 LJ Adm 23.
4 See eg *Furness Withy (Australia Pty) Ltd v Metal Distributors (UK) Ltd, The Amazonia* [1989] 1 Lloyd's Rep 403, QBD (Commercial Court), where an arbitration clause stated that the charter-party was to be governed by English law, but was held to be void under the (Australian) Sea-Carriage of Goods Act 1924, s 9. (See the judgment of Gatehouse J, ibid at 405.)
5 *Vita Food Products Inc v Unus Shipping Co Ltd* [1939] AC 277 at 290, [1939] 1 All ER 513, at 521 (per Lord Wright), PC; *P S Chellaram & Co Ltd v China Ocean Shipping Co* [1989] 1 Lloyd's Rep 413, Supreme Ct of New South Wales (Admiralty Division), where there were no grounds of public policy militating against the intention expressed in the bill of lading that it should be governed by Chinese law. (See the judgment of Carruthers J, ibid, at 424.)

Chapter 5

The preliminary voyage

The undertaking to proceed to the port of loading

The undertaking of the shipowner that the ship will proceed to the port of loading affords a good example of a clause which the Court may, according to the particular surrounding circumstances of each case, find to be a condition or merely a warranty.[1] For it will be *either*:

(1) An absolute undertaking to sail for, or arrive at, such port by a fixed date; *or*
(2) an undertaking merely to use reasonable diligence, eg 'proceed with all convenient despatch'.

In the former case, it is a condition precedent to the charterer's liability to load that the ship shall sail or arrive by the date named.

Thus, in *Glaholm v Hays*[2]

A charter-party provided that the vessel was to sail from England for the port of loading on or before 4 February. She did not sail until 22 February.
Held, the charterer was not bound to load.

Where a charter-party specifies the estimated time of arrival of a vessel at the port of loading, there is an absolute obligation on the shipowners to sail to there on the date on which when proceeding with all convenient speed it would normally be necessary to sail in order to reach the port on or about the estimated date of arrival.[3]

Thus, in *Mitsui OSK Lines v Garnar Grain Co Inc: The 'Myrtos'*[4]

A charter-party stated 'vessel to be nominated 20 days prior to vessel's ETA'. On 11

1 For an example, see the 'Gencon' charter-party, clause 1, line 8 (Appendix B).
2 (1841) 2 Man & G 257.
3 *Mitsui OSK Lines Ltd v Garnac Grain Co Inc, The Myrtos* [1984] 2 Lloyd's Rep 449, QBD (Commercial Court). (See the judgment of Leggatt J, ibid, at 454).
4 [1984] 2 Lloyd's Rep 449, QBD (Commercial Court).

140

June 1980 the shipowners nominated the *Myrtos*, and on 27 June the charterers nominated Houston as the loading port. She did not arrive there until 15 July. The charterers claimed damages on the ground that the shipowners were in breach of the clause because she ought to have arrived by 1 July.

Held, by the Queen's Bench Division (Commercial Court), that the clause was a condition, and the charterers were entitled to damages.

If the charterer loads the cargo on a vessel which does not sail for the loading port on the date named and arrives there late, he is entitled to claim damages for the delay.[5]

But where no definite time is fixed, the undertaking is to proceed in a reasonable time. In that case (if the delay does not defeat the charterer's object in engaging the ship) he must load, and seek his remedy for any loss caused by the delay in an action for damages.[6] If, however, the undertaking to use diligence is broken in such a way as to frustrate the object of the adventure, the charterer will be entitled to refuse to load.

Thus, in *Freeman v Taylor*[7]

The ship was to go to Cape Town and then proceed with all convenient speed to Bombay. By reasonable diligence she might have arrived at Bombay six weeks earlier than she did arive.

Held, the charterer was justified in refusing to load.[8]

Cancelling clauses

There may be a cancelling clause in the charter-party, in which case the charterer has the option, under the terms of the contract, of repudiating, in certain stipulated circumstances.[9]

The fixing of a cancelling date in a charter-party merely gives warning to the shipowner that non-arrival by the cancelling date

---

5 *Transworld Oil Ltd v North Bay Shipping Corpn, The Rio Claro* [1987] 2 Lloyd's Rep 173, QBD (Commercial Court), where, however, the claim failed because the loss was too remote.

6 *Forest Oak Steam Shipping Co Ltd v Richard & Co* (1899) 5 Com Cas 100.

7 (1831) 1 LJCP 26.

8 See also *Jackson v Union Marine Insurance Co* (1874) LR 10 CP 125.

9 For examples of cancelling clauses, see the 'Gencon' charter-party, clause 10 (Appendix B) and the 'Baltime 1939' charter-party, clause 22 (Appendix B). See also *Johs Thode v Vda De Gimeno y Cia SL, The Steendiek* [1961] 2 Lloyd's Rep 138, CA. For a case where the charterers were held not to be entitled to cancel the charter-party because they were in breach in ordering the vessel to the port of delivery as and when they did, see *Shipping Corpn of India Ltd v Naviera Letasa SA* [1976] 1 Lloyd's Rep 132, QBD (Com Ct).

may go to the root of the contract so as to entitle the charterer to rescind. It does not relieve the shipowner of his primary obligation to proceed with all convenient speed to the port of loading, or of his secondary obligation, in the event of non-performance of that primary obligation, to reimburse the charterer for any loss sustained by him as a result of such non-performance.[10]

A cancelling clause is a forfeiture clause and 'so not to be applied lightly'.[11]

A cancelling clause may even be so strict as not to give the charterer any choice.[12]

The shipowner is under a duty to send the vessel to the port of loading even though it is impossible for her to get there by the cancelling date. If he does not do so, the charterer can sue for any damage which may have resulted.[13]

If the vessel does not arrive by the cancelling date, and the charterer incurs expenses eg by having to make alternative arrangements for the shipment of cargo on a vessel other than on the chartered vessel, these expenses can be claimed by him from the shipowner where they are in the reasonable contemplation of the parties.[14]

Where the charterer is late in exercising his option to cancel, the shipowner can still accept a notice of cancellation, and waive any rights he may have in respect of the delay.[15]

There is no *contractual* right to rescind a charter-party unless and until the date specified in the clause has been reached.[16]

Thus, in *Cheikh Boutros Selim El-Khoury v Ceylon Shipping Lines Ltd, The Madeleine*[17]

10   *C Czarnikow Ltd v Koufos, The Heron 11* [1966] 1 Lloyd's Rep 595 at 610, CA (per Diplock LJ).
11   *Noemijulia SS Co Ltd v Minister of Food* [1951] 1 KB 223 at 228 (per Devlin J). See further, *Cheikh Boutros Selim El-Khoung v Ceylon Shipping Lines Ltd, The Madeleine* [1967] 2 Lloyd's Rep 224 at 237, QBD (Commercial Court) (per Roskill J).
12   See *Adamson v Newcastle SS Freight Insurance Association* (1879) 4 QBD 462.
13   *Moel Tryvan Ship Co Ltd v Andrew Weir & Co* [1910] 2 KB 844, CA; *Bucknall Bros v Tatem & Co* (1900) 83 LT 121, CA.
14   *Blackgold Trading Ltd of Monrovia v Almare SpA di Navigazione of Genoa, The Almare Seconda and Almare Quinta* [1981] 2 Lloyd's Rep 433, QBD (Commercial Court). See the judgment of Robert Goff J, ibid, at 436.
15   *Den Norske Afrika Og Australie Line v Port Said Salt Association Ltd* (1924) 20 Ll L Rep 184, CA.
16   *Cheikh Boutros Selim El-Khoury v Ceylon Shipping Lines Ltd, The Madeleine* [1967] 2 Lloyd's Rep 224, QBD (Commercial Court), at 245 (per Roskill J).
17   [1967] 2 Lloyd's Rep 224, QBD (Commercial Court).

A vessel was chartered under a time charter-party, which stated that she was to be delivered to the charterers at Calcutta. A cancelling clause provided that: 'Should the vessel not be delivered by 6 pm on 10 May, 1957, the charterers to have the option of cancelling.' On 9 May the shipowners informed the charterers that she would be delivered on the morning of 10 May. But she was inspected by a port health authority inspector, who ordered that she should be fumigated. Fumigation could not be completed before midnight 10/11 May. So at 8 am on 10 May the charterers purported to cancel the charter-party.

Held, (obiter) that the purported cancellation under the cancelling clause was of no effect because the time (ie 6 pm on 10 May) had not been reached.

But where the charterer seeks to say that the contract has been frustrated or that there has been an anticipatory breach which entitles him to rescind, then he has such rights as are given him at *Common Law*.[18]

In such a case all the attendant uncertainties as to the right to claim rescission, whether the right is said to arise from alleged frustration or alleged anticipatory breach, will no doubt arise, and the commercial certainty accorded by a cancelling clause will not exist.[19]

The application and scope of exception clauses

The exception clauses in a charter-party may apply to the preliminary voyage to the port of loading.

Hence if a chartered ship is prevented from, or delayed in, getting to the loading port by a peril excepted 'during the voyage', the exception applies.[20] This, however, is the case only when the preliminary voyage is clearly incidental to, and therefore is considered as part of, the charter voyage. If the ship is disabled by excepted perils while completing a voyage on which she was engaged at the time of chartering, the shipowner will not be excused.[1]

Where the exceptions relate to the whole of the charter-party, the fact that the delay was caused by an excepted peril is a good defence

---

18 *Cheikh Boutros Selim El-Khoury v Ceylon Shipping Lines Ltd, The Madeleine*, supra, at 245 (per Roskill J).

19 Ibid, at 245–6 (per Roskill J). His Lordship suggested that if it was desired to introduce certainty into these matters, it would be necessary to alter the clause ('Baltime 1939' charter-party, clause 22), though it appeared to have existed in very much its present form for many years: ibid, at 245.

20 *Harrison v Garthorne* (1872) 26 LT 508.

1 *Monroe Bros Ltd v Ryan* [1935] 2 KB 28; *Evera SA Comercial v North Shipping Co Ltd* [1956] 2 Lloyd's Rep 367.

by a shipowner to an action for damages for failure to start for the loading port by an agreed date; but this will not affect the charterer's right to rescind the contract if the ship does not sail or arrive by the agreed date. The latter right is an absolute one and is not subject to the exceptions.[2] In other words, the excepted perils only operate to relieve from liability; they do not enable the shipowner to plead that he has performed an obligation which he has not performed.

Thus, in *Smith v Dart & Son*[3]

A charter-party contained an exception clause stating that 'dangers and accidents of the seas . . . of what nature and kind soever' were mutually excepted. The vessel was to arrive at the first loading port free of pratique by 15 December. By another clause, if she did not get there by that date, the charterer could cancel the charter-party. She arrived by 13 December, but was not free of pratique until after 15 December, so the charterers cancelled the charter-party on 16 December.

Held, they were entitled to do so and the shipowners could not plead that the vessel had not reached the loading port by reason of the excepted perils.

Frustration of the preliminary voyage

Either party may be discharged on the ground of impossibility of performance or on the ground of delay, *where no breach of contract by either party has taken place.*[4]

2   *Harrison v Garthorne*, supra; *Smith v Dart & Son* (1884) 14 QBD 105.
3   (1884) 14 QBD 105; *Transworld Oil Ltd v North Bay Shipping Corpn, The Rio Claro* [1987] 2 Lloyd's Rep 173, QBD (Commercial Court), where it was held (obiter) that the shipowners could not rely on an exceptions clause to excuse them from sailing to the port of loading on a specified date.
4   For 'frustration', see pp 70–78, ante.

Chapter 6

Loading, discharge and delivery

LOADING

The duties of the shipowner

It is the shipowner's duty to send the ship to the agreed,[1] or, in the absence of special agreement, to the usual place of loading. He must then give notice to the charterer that the ship is ready to load.[2] If he fails to do so, and delay in commencing to load is thereby caused, the charterer will not be responsible, as he is not bound to look out for the ship.[3] If the place named for loading is simply a port or dock, notice may be given as soon as the ship arrives in the port or dock although she is not in the particular spot where the loading is to take place; but this cannot be done when the place is more particularly indicated.[4]

Where a charter-party states that the charterer must nominate the port of loading eg before the vessel leaves her previous port of call

---

1 Once the selection of a berth in a port charter-party has been notified to the shipowner, it cannot be changed unilaterally by the charterer: *Venizelos ANE of Athens v Société Commerciale de Cereales et Financière SA of Zurich, The Prometheus* [1974] 1 Lloyd's Rep 350, QBD (Commercial Court). (See the judgment of Mocatta J, ibid, at 355.) The shipowner will have to pay the expense of hiring tugboats to keep the vessel at the nominated berth where this is necessary by reason of the weather conditions: *Cosmar Compania Naviera SA v Total Transport Corpn, The Isabelle* [1984] 1 Lloyd's Rep 366, CA. (See the judgment of Sir Donaldson MR, ibid, at 368.)
2 For a case where the charter-party stated that the shipowner was to be responsible for all expenses incurred by the charterer if the vessel was not ready in accordance with the notice of readiness to load which had been given, see *Marifortuna Naviera SA v Government of Ceylon* [1970] 1 Lloyd's Rep 247, QBD (Commercial Court).
3 *Stanton v Austin* (1872) LR 7 CP 651.
4 *Nelson v Dahl* (1879), 12 ChD at 581.

or on the signing of the charter-party if she has already sailed, and he fails to do so, he renders himself liable to the shipowner for any loss incurred[4a].

The duties of the shipowner, charterer and master as regards loading were explained by Lord Wright as follows:[5]

'Apart from special provisions or circumstances, it is part of the ship's duty to stow the goods properly . . . In modern times, the work of stowage is generally deputed to stevedores, but that does not generally relieve the shipowners of their duty, even though the stevedores are, under the charter-party, to be appointed by the charterers, unless there are special provisions which either expressly or inferentially have that effect.'

Lord Wright then referred to the terms of the charter-party before the Court. It contained a clause, which is often employed, that the charterers were to load, stow and trim the cargo at their expense.[6] His Lordship continued:

'I think that these words necessarily import that the charterers take into their hands the business of loading and stowing the cargo. It must follow that they not only relieve the ship of the duty of loading and stowing, but, as between themselves and the shipowners, relieve them of liability for bad stowage, except as qualified by the words "under the supervision of the captain" . . . These words expressly give the master a right which I think he must in any case have—namely, a right to supervise the operations of the charterers in loading and stowing. . . . To the extent that the master exercises supervision, and limits the charterers' control of the stowage, the charterers' liability will be limited in a corresponding degree.'

It has also been held in one case that, in the absence of any provision in a charter-party making the charterers responsible for

---

4a   *SIB International SRL v Metallgesellschaft Corpn, The Noel Bay* [1989] 1 Lloyd's Rep 361, CA, where the shipowners concluded a substitute charter-party.

5   *Canadian Transport Co Ltd v Court Line Ltd* [1940] AC 934 at 943–4, [1940] 3 All ER 112 at 118–9. See further *Mannix Ltd v N M Paterson & Sons Ltd* [1966] 1 Lloyd's Rep 139 at 142–3 (Supreme Court of Canada), (per Ritchie J).

6   See eg *C H Z Rolimpex v Eftavrysses Compania Naviera SA, The Panaghia Tinnou* [1986] 2 Lloyd's Rep 586, QBD (Commercial Court). In *Blandy Bros & Co Lda v Nello Simoni Ltd* [1963] 2 Lloyd's Rep 393, CA, the charterers failed to prove a custom of the fruit and vegetable trade that the shipper was responsible for loading and stowing charges. The shipowners failed to prove a custom of the port of Funchal that the shipper paid for bringing the cargo alongside, and that the ship paid for the labour employed on board, ie in loading and stowing. In *Agro Co of Canada Ltd v Parnassos Shipping Corpn, The Marylisa* [1982] 2 Lloyd's Rep 290, QBD (Commercial Court) the charterers failed to show that the cost of loading and discharging a cargo of grain from the wing tanks of a vessel, which was more expensive than the cost of loading and discharging from the main cargo holds, was for the shipowners' account. (See the judgment of Robert Goff J, ibid, at 294–295.)

the stowage of a mechanical shovel, the inspection made by the ship's officers of the way in which the shovel was placed and secured on deck and their approval of it was evidence negativing any implied agreement to relieve the shipowner of the obligation implied by law 'to receive the goods and carefully arrange and stow them in the ship.'[7]

In another case a clause stating 'dunnaging and stowage instructions given by the charterers to be carefully followed but to be executed under the supervision of the master and he is to remain responsible for proper stowage and dunnaging' was held not to relieve the shipowners from their duty to stow the cargo safely.[8]

Where a clause in a charter-party stated 'charterers to have full use of the ship's gear as on board', it was held that this did not imply that the charterers were to be responsible for stowage.[9]

Since prima facie the stowage of cargo is the ship's responsibility, it is within the authority of a ship's agent to arrange for and pay for the work of stowage.[10]

The shipowner must not stow goods on deck[11] unless

(i) there is a trade usage to that effect;[12] or
(ii) the charterer has given his express[13] or implied consent.[14]

The duties of the charterer

Various duties have to be performed by the charterer:

(1) He must procure a cargo.

---

7   *Mannix Ltd v N M Paterson & Sons Ltd* [1966] 1 Lloyd's Rep 139, Supreme Court of Canada.

8   *Ismail v Polish Ocean Lines, The Ciechocinek* [1975] 2 Lloyd's Rep 170, QBD (Commercial Court). (See the judgment of Kerr J, ibid, at 185); *rvsd* on other grounds: [1976] 1 Lloyd's Rep 489, CA. For a case where it was held that the sole responsibility for loading rested with the charterers without interference by the master except that he could have required them to alter the loading process for securing the seaworthiness, safe trim and stress of the vessel, see *Georgia-Pacific Corpn v Marilyn L, Elvapores Inc Evans Products Inc and Retla SS Co, The Marilyn L* [1972] 1 Lloyd's Rep 418, District Court for the Eastern District of Virginia, Norfolk Division.

9   Ibid.

10 *Blandy Bros & Co Lda v Nello Simoni Ltd* [1963] 2 Lloyd's Rep 393, CA.

11 *Gould v Oliver* (1840) 2 Man & G 208.   **12** Ibid.

13 *Burton v English* (1883) 12 QBD 218; *Wright v Marwood* (1881) 7 QB 62, CA, *Johnson v Chapman* (1865) 19 CBNS 563.

14 *Gould v Oliver,* supra; *Milward v Hibbert* (1842) 3 QB 120 at 136 (per Lord Denman).

(2) He must bring it alongside the vessel.
(3) He must load a full and complete cargo.
(4) He must load in the time stipulated.

(1) *Procuring the cargo*
The charter-party does not as a rule contain provisions as to how the cargo is to be procured. It presupposes that the charterer has the cargo in readiness on the quay.

The fact that it has become impossible to provide a cargo does not, as a rule, relieve the charterer of liability.

Where the shipowner himself undertakes to procure a cargo, he is under the same strict liability as usually falls on the charterer.

Thus, in *Hills v Sughrue*[15]

The shipowner agreed to proceed to Ichaboe and there find and load a full cargo of guano. There was no guano to be found there within a reasonable time after the ship's arrival.
Held, the shipowner was none the less liable to the charterer.

In some cases, however, the charterer will be excused from the liability to provide a cargo, or, if he has one, from the liability to load it:

(a) Where events have rendered performance of the contract illegal either by English law,[16] or by the law of the country in which performance was to have taken place.[17] Thus, in *Esposito v Bowden*[18]

A cargo of wheat was to be loaded at Odessa. Before the ship arrived there, war broke out between England and Russia.
Held, the charterer was relieved from liability to load a cargo, since performance of the contract would have been contrary to English law as to trading with an enemy.

(b) Where the shipowner has broken a condition precedent. For example, we have already seen that the undertaking as to the position of the ship at the date of the charter-party is a condition precedent.[19]

(c) Where there are express provisions in the contract which

---

15 (1846) 15 M & W 253.
16 *Esposito v Bowden* (1857) 27 LJQB 17.
17 *Ralli Bros v Compania Naviera Sota y Aznar* [1920] 2 KB 287.
18 Supra.
19 *Behn v Burness* (1863) 2 B & S 751; for the facts, see p 67, ante.

relieve the charterer. Thus, in *Gordon SS Co Ltd v Moxey Savon & Co Ltd*[20]

A ship was chartered to carry coal from Penarth to Buenos Aires. The charter-party provided that, in the event of a strike or lock-out causing a stoppage among coal workers, the charter was to be void if the stoppage lasted six running days from the time when the vessel was ready to load. On 4 April 1912, the ship was ready to load; but, owing to a coal strike, no coal arrived at Penarth for shipment until 11 April.

Held, although the strike itself ended on 9 April, the stoppage was due to it, and the charterers were entitled to cancel the charter-party.

(d) Where the whole adventure has been frustrated.

The doctrine of frustration has been explained in an earlier chapter.[1]

(e)   Where the failure to load a cargo is due to the shipowner's default[2] provided that he has no legal excuse for such default.[3]

In this case the charterer can recover from the shipowner any damages sustained as a direct result of the shipowner's default.

Where the shipowner has repudiated the contract, the charterer is not only discharged from his obligation to provide and load a cargo, but need not do so even if the shipowner subsequently declares his willingness to accept it.[4]

(2) *Bringing the cargo alongside*

Where the contract stipulates that the cargo is to be brought 'alongside' by the charterer, the expense and risk of doing so are transferred to him. He must actually bring the cargo to the ship's side, and, if necessary, bear the cost of lighterage.

Thus, a usual clause states:

'The cargo to be brought alongside in such a manner as to enable vessel to take the goods with her own tackle . . . Charterers to procure and pay the necessary men on shore or on board the lighters to do the work there, vessel only heaving the cargo on board.'[5]

---

20   (1913) 18 Com Cas 170.
 1   See pp 70–78, ante.
 2   *Seeger v Duthie* (1860) 8 CBNS 45.
 3   See *Phosphate Mining Co v Rankin, Gilmour & Co* (1916) 86 LJKB 358.
 4   *Danube and Black Sea Rly, and Kustenjie Harbour Co Ltd v Xenos* (1863) 13 CBNS 825.
 5   'Gencon' form, clause 5(a). See Appendix B. See eg *Skibs A/S Trolla and Skibs A/S Tautra v United Enterprises and Shipping (Pte) Ltd, The Tarva* [1973] 2 Lloyd's Rep 385, Singapore High Court, where, on the true construction of the charter-party, the responsibility for heaving the cargo on board was that of the charterers, but in that operation they were to have the free use of the vessel's derricks, winches, gins and falls. (See the judgment of Chua J, ibid, at 388.)

Where there is a custom as to loading at the port, it will bind even persons ignorant of it unless it is inconsistent with the written contract. Provided such a custom is reasonable, certain, and not contrary to law, there is a presumption that the parties contracted with reference to it. This can be rebutted only by the inconsistency of the custom with the express terms of the contract.[6]

Moreover, such matters as strikes, ice, and so on, though they may be individually named in the charter-party as exceptions, will afford no excuse to the charterer if he was prevented from, or delayed in, bringing the cargo down to the ship by one or more of them. He will only be protected if the actual loading is interfered with.[7] If loading was rendered *commercially* impossible by an excepted peril, the charterer will be excused, even though it was not *absolutely* impossible to load.[8] In *Grant & Co v Coverdale, Todd & Co*[9]

A ship was to proceed to Cardiff and load iron. The time for loading was to commence as soon as the vessel was ready to load except in cases of strikes, frosts, or other unavoidable accidents preventing loading. Owing to frost, delay occurred in bringing the cargo *to the dock.*
Held, the charterer was liable.

At some ports, however, there is no storage accommodation, and goods have to be brought from storing places at some distance from the actual place of loading. In such cases, the charterer will be entitled to the benefit of the excepted perils during the transit from the storing places, provided such transit substantially forms part of the operation of loading, for the parties are taken to have contracted with that reservation in mind.[10]

Sometimes the charter-party gives the charterer the right to shift to another berth.[11]

---

6   *The Nifa* [1892] P 411.
7   *Grant & Co v Coverdale, Todd & Co* (1884) 9 App Cas 470; see, however, Lord Selborne's remarks, ibid, at 477.
8   *Matheos SS v Louis Dreyfus & Co* [1925] AC 654.
9   (1884) 9 App Cas 470.
10 *Hudson v Ede* (1868) LR 3 QB 412; see *Grant v Coverdale*, supra, at 477.
11 *Cosmar Compania Naviera SA v Total Transport Corpn, The Isabelle* [1984] 1 Lloyd's Rep 366, CA, where a clause in a charter-party stated: 'Charterers shall have the right of requiring the vessel to shift at ports of loading . . . from a loading . . . berth or place and back to the same or to another such berth or place . . . on payment of all additional expenses incurred', and it was held that the shipowners were not entitled to additional expenses where the order to shift was given by the port authority and not by the charterers. (See the judgment of Sir John Donaldson MR, ibid, at 368.)

(3) *Loading a full and complete cargo*

Where the ship has been chartered, the charterer's undertaking is to load a full cargo, not one equal to the ship's burden as stated in the charter-party. Consequently, in *Hunter v Fry*[12]

The ship was described as 'of the burden of 261 tons or thereabouts', but could have carried 400 tons of the agreed cargo.

Held, the shipowners were entitled to damages for loss of freight arising from the fact that only 336 tons were shipped.

Similarly, in *Windle v Barker*[13]

The ship was described as 'of the measurement of 180 to 200 tons or thereabouts'.

Held, the charterer was not entitled to refuse to load her because in fact she measured 257 tons.

The obligation to load a full and complete cargo is subject to the operation of the de minimis rule. The test of performance of the obligation is whether the departure from the precise terms of the obligation was so trivial as to be negligible or whether it had some significance.[14]

Each case depends on its own facts. Thus, in one case, a cargo of 12,588 tons 4 cwt. was held not commercially equivalent to 12,600 tons and was not in a commercial sense a full and complete cargo, for the quantity was, on the facts, outside the limits of the de minimis rule.[15]

The reason for the obligation to load a full cargo is that otherwise the shipowner would lose freight on account of some part of the ship's carrying capacity not being utilised. Hence, if a full cargo is not loaded, the charterer must pay not only freight on the goods actually shipped but also dead freight,[16] and the obligation to pay it is sometimes transferred to holders of the bills of lading by means of a 'cesser' clause which gives a lien for dead freight on the goods shipped.[17]

Sometimes, however, the charter-party states that the amount of cargo to be loaded is to be decided by the shipowners, eg '10,000 tons of 2,240 lbs., 10% more or less at owners' option'.[18]

12 (1819) 2 B & Ald 421.
13 (1856) 25 LJQB 349.
14 *Margaronis Navigation Agency Ltd v Henry W Peabody & Co of London Ltd* [1964] 2 Lloyd's Rep 153, CA.
15 Ibid, Diplock LJ said (ibid, at 159) that the application of the de minimis rule was simple, though difficulties might arise in borderline cases on particular facts. He considered it to be a matter of mixed law and fact (ibid, at 160).
16 See p 267, post.
17 See pp 254–256, post.
18 *Northern Sales Ltd v The Giancarlo Zeta, The Giancarlo Zeta* [1966] 2 Lloyd's Rep 317, Exchequer Court, British Columbia Admiralty District.

Sometimes, however, it is expressly stated that a minimum cargo must be loaded.[19]

A charter-party often provides that only 'lawful merchandise' must be loaded. This term means such goods as are ordinarily shipped from the port of loading. Furthermore, it has been decided that to be 'lawful merchandise', goods loaded under the charter-party must not only be such as can be loaded without breach of the law in force at the port of loading, but must also be such as can lawfully be carried and discharged at the port of discharge.[20]

Sometimes the charter-party authorises the loading of several types of cargo. In this event the charterer may load a full cargo of any one or more of them, unless there is a contrary stipulation, although that cargo may not produce as much freight as the cargo anticipated.

Thus, in *Moorsom v Page*[1]

The charter-party provided for a cargo of 'copper, tallow, and hides or other goods'. Tallow and hides were tendered, but the shipowner demanded copper as well.
Held, the option was with the charterer even though ballast was required as a consequence of his selecting the lighter goods.

Where the charterer is under an obligation to load a full cargo and has the option of loading several kinds of goods, he cannot choose to load goods which leave broken stowage and no others; he is obliged to fill up the spaces.

Thus, in *Cole v Meek*[2]

Where the charterer was to provide 'a full and complete cargo of sugar or other lawful produce', he loaded mahogany logs, which were produce of the port of loading, but left spaces between the logs.
Held, he was bound to provide sugar or other produce of the port of loading to fill the spaces, and must pay damages for not doing so.

But the charterer may be excused from liability for broken stowage by a custom of the port of loading.

Thus, in *Cuthbert v Cumming*[3]

A charter-party provided for a 'full and complete cargo of sugar, molasses and/or other lawful produce'. It was customary at the port of loading to load sugar and

---

19   See eg *Total Transport Corpn v Amoco Trading Co, The Altus* [1985] 1 Lloyd's Rep 423, QBD (Commercial Court), where the charterers contracted to load a minimum of 40,000 tons of crude oil.
20   *Leolga Compania de Navigacion v John Glynn & Son Ltd* [1953] 2 QB 374, [1953] 2 All ER 327.
1   (1814) 4 Camp 103.
2   (1864) 33 LJCP 183.
3   (1855) 11 Exch 405.

molasses in hogsheads and puncheons. This was done; but spaces were left large enough to take small packages of sugar, cocoa, etc.

Held, it was sufficient for the charterer to load in the customary way.

So also, where the cargo to be carried can be loaded in two different ways, one of which is more economical of space than the other, but each of which is a usual method of loading cargo of the relevant type, the charterer can load in whichever of these ways he pleases, unless he is expressly forbidden so to do by the charter-party. The mere fact that he is under a duty to load a full and complete cargo will not suffice to deprive him of this choice, or to render him liable for dead freight as the result merely of adopting the less economical method.[4]

If the charter-party states that the charterer is entitled to load an alternative cargo, eg wheat and/or maize and/or rye, and after the loading of the wheat has commenced the export of wheat is prohibited, it is implied that he should be given a reasonable time to determine how to deal with the altered conditions and make arrangements to ship a cargo which can be loaded.[5] What is a reasonable time is a matter of fact.

If the prevention of loading arises from a strike, a similar rule will be applied.[6]

Sometimes there will be an *obligation* on the charterer to load an alternative cargo, but sometimes he has an unfettered *option* to do so. In each case it turns on the interpretation of the particular words used in the charter-party.[7]

Thus, in *Reardon Smith Line Ltd v Ministry of Agriculture, Fisheries and Food*[8]

A charter-party provided that the charterer was to load 'a full and complete cargo . . . of wheat in bulk . . . and/or barley in bulk and/or flour in sacks'. The charterer had the option 'of loading up to one-third cargo of barley and one-third cargo of flour' at an increased rate of freight. The charterer began to load wheat, but a strike occurred and further loading was delayed.

Held, the primary obligation under the charter-party was to load wheat, and the charterer was under no liability to load an alternative cargo of barley and flour which were not affected by the strike.

---

4 *Angfartygs v Price and Pierce Ltd A/B* [1939] 3 All ER 672.
5 *H A Brightman & Co v Bunge y Born, Limitada Sociedad Anonima Commercial Financiera y Industrial of Buenos Aires* [1924] 2 KB 619, CA.
6 *South African Despatch Line v Owners of the Panamanian SS Niki* [1960] 1 QB 518, [1960] 1 All ER 285.
7 *Reardon Smith Line Ltd v Ministry of Agriculture, Fisheries and Food* [1963] AC 691, [1963] 1 All ER 545, HL.
8 *Supra*.

(4) *Loading in the stipulated time*

The cargo must be loaded in the stipulated time. If it is not, the charterer will have to pay demurrage or damages for detention, as the case may be.[9]

Again, where a consecutive voyage charter-party is for a total of 'two years' consecutive voyages', each time the vessel is tendered for to the charterers for loading during that period they must load her within the laytime provisions.[10]

DISCHARGE

Naming the port of discharge

In the case of a general ship the port of discharge is stated in the bill of lading,[11] but where the ship is chartered, two cases arise which must be carefully distinguished:

(1) *Where the port is agreed on and named in the charter-party.* Here, unless limited by other clauses, the obligation to go to the port named is absolute.

(2) *Where the port is not named in the charter-party.* In this case the charterer must name a safe port, and the obligation is the same whether an express provision to that effect is inserted or not. If the charterer names a port which is not safe, the shipowner is discharged from liability to unload there; he can earn the freight by delivering at the nearest safe port.

But once the port has been named and accepted by, or on behalf of, the shipowner (eg by the master in signing bills of lading), he cannot afterwards refuse to go there on the ground that it is not safe. He can, however, claim damages for injury to the ship by reason of the port not being safe.[12]   If the ship is delayed by reason of the charterer's failure to name a port, the charterer will be liable in

---

9 Demurrage and damages for detention are considered in chapter 10, post.

10 *Suisse Atlantique Société d'Armement Maritime SA v Rotterdamsche Kolen Centrale NV* [1967] 1 AC 361, [1966] 2 All ER 61, [1966] 1 Lloyd's Rep 529, HL.

11 See e g *Heinrich Hanno & Co BV v Fairlight Shipping Co Ltd Hanse Schiffahrtskontor Gmbh v Andre SA, The Kostas K* [1985] 1 Lloyd's Rep 231, QBD (Commercial Court), where Lagos was nominated in the bill of lading as the discharging port, and the vessel went to Warri by mistake.

12 See p 160, post.

damages.[13] And if, by refusing to name a place of discharge, he prevents the shipowner from earning the freight, he will have to pay it as damages for breach of contract.[14]

Whether the instructions given to the master by the charterer do amount to an order to proceed to a named port of discharge depends on the circumstances.[15]

Where the charter-party provides that the ship is to proceed to a named port for orders, and that the charterer is to give such orders within a specified time after the master has given notice of the ship's arrival, the contract is construed as meaning that, even though the orders do not arrive within the time specified, the master must await their arrival for a reasonable time. He is not at liberty to leave the port of call as soon as the time specified has elapsed, though the charterer may, if the contract so provides, be liable to compensate the owners for the delay.[16]

Where the charterer is given an option as to the ports at which the vessel is to discharge, the Court may construe the clause as meaning that the ports must be taken in their geographical order.

Thus, in *Pilgrim Shipping Co Ltd v State Trading Corpn of India Ltd, The Hadjitsakos*[17]

A vessel was chartered for a voyage from British Columbia to 'one or two safe ports in India'. She proceeded via Singapore, and the charterers nominated Bombay and Calcutta as the discharging ports in that order.
Held, they were not entitled to do so for, on the true construction of the charter-party, the parties did not contemplate that the vessel would be asked to discharge, first, at a port on the west coast and, secondly, at an east coast port.

What constitutes a 'safe port'

The port specified by the charterer must be 'safe'. 'A "safe port" means a port to which a vessel can get laden as she is and at which

---

13 *Zim Israel Navigation Co Ltd v Tradax Export SA, The Timna* [1971] 2 Lloyd's Rep 91, CA, where the charterers were held liable in damages from the time when the order for the port of discharge should have been given to the time when it was in fact given.
14 *Stewart v Rogerson* (1871) LR 6 CP 424.
15 *Zim Israel Navigation Co Ltd v Tradax Export SA, The Timna*, supra, where the charterers sent a message to the master stating: 'The vessel allocated for discharging/lightering at Brake and we suggest tendering [the] notice of readiness anew upon vessel's arrival at Brake', and it was held that this message did not amount to an order to go to Brake. (See the judgment of Lord Denning MR, ibid, at 94, and that of Megaw LJ, ibid, at 95.)
16 *Procter Garrett Marston Ltd v Oakwin SS Co Ltd* [1926] 1 KB 244.
17 [1975] 1 Lloyd's Rep 356, CA. (See the judgment of Lord Denning MR, ibid, at 360 and that of Sir John Pennycuick, ibid, at 367.)

she can lay and discharge, always afloat'.[18] 'A port will not be safe unless, in the relevant period of time, the particular ship can reach it, use it, and return from it without, in the absence of some abnormal occurrence, being exposed to damage which cannot be avoided by good navigation and seamanship.'[19]

Thus, in *Leeds Shipping Co Ltd v Société Française Bunge*[20]

A charter-party stated that the vessel was to proceed to 'one or two safe ports in Morocco'. The charterer directed her to Mogador. In this port there was a lack of shelter and a liability to the sudden onset of a high wind which could not be predicted, and which might quickly cause an anchor to drag. The port was very near some rocks and the anchorage was very restricted.
Held, that the port was unsafe.

Moreover, it must be a port from which she can safely return.[1]

Thus, in *Islander Shipping Enterprises S A v Empresa Maritima del Estado S A, The Khian Sea*[2]

A vessel was ordered to a berth in Valparaiso. She tied up at Baron Wharf, which was exposed to a heavy swell during adverse weather conditions. Two other vessels anchored sufficiently close to the wharf to make it impossible for her to leave until they had been moved. She suffered ranging damage whilst they remained.
Held, the berth was unsafe for there was no evidence of any system to ensure that vessels using it would have adequate searoom if they had to leave in a hurry.

If a port is in fact unsafe, it is irrelevant that well-informed men might erroneously have pronounced it to be safe.[3]

The safety of the port should be viewed in respect of a vessel properly manned and equipped, and navigated and handled without negligence and in accordance with good seamanship.[4]

A port is not safe if more than ordinary prudence and skill is needed to avoid exposure to danger there.[5]

---

18   Per Sankey J, In *Hall Bros SS Co Ltd v Paul Ltd* (1914) 111 LT 811 at 812.
19   *Leeds Shipping Co Ltd v Société Française Bunge* [1958] 2 Lloyd's Rep 127, CA (per Sellers LJ).
20   [1958] 2 Lloyd's Rep 127, CA.
 1   *Limerick SS Co Ltd v WH Stott & Co Ltd* [1921] 1 KB 568; affd [1921] 2 KB 613.
 2   [1977] 2 Lloyd's Rep 439, QBD (Commercial Court). (See the judgment of Donaldson J, ibid, at 444.)
 3   *G W Grace & Co Ltd v General Steam Navigation Co Ltd* [1950] 2 KB 383, [1950] 1 All ER 201.
 4   *Leeds Shipping Co Ltd v Société Française Bunge*, supra, at 131 (per Sellers LJ).
 5   *Kristiandsands Tankrederi A/S v Standard Tankers (Bahamas) Ltd, The Polyglory* [1977] 2 Lloyd's Rep 353, QBD (Commercial Court).

Thus, in *Kristiandsands Tankrederi A/S v Standard Tankers (Bahamas) Ltd, The Polyglory*[6]

A vessel was ordered to proceed to Port la Nouvelle. Although she had loaded only 3,500 out of 7,000 tonnes of ballast, the master and the compulsory pilot decided that she should leave forthwith because the wind had reached Force 6 to 7. All the mooring lines and the port anchor were in. The starboard anchor dragged and damaged an underwater pipe line. Something more than ordinary prudence and skill was required to avoid exposure to danger.
Held, Port la Nouvelle was not a safe port.

The port must be safe for the particular vessel carrying the cargo she has on board. It must be politically as well as physically safe,[7] this being a question of fact in each case;[8] eg the shipowner is not bound to risk confiscation by entering a port which has been declared closed.[9] Again, if the named port is one at which no tugs are ever obtainable, and the chartered vessel cannot, by reason of her size, reach that port without the assistance of tugs, the port is not safe.[10]

Further, if there are insufficient tugs at the port of discharge for a vessel of the size concerned, the port is unsafe.[11]

Thus, in *Palm Shipping Inc v Vitol SA, The Universal Monarch*[12]

The charterers warranted that the port of discharge was safe. The vessel was ordered to Leixoes, Portugal. When she arrived there, there were only 3 tugs and she needed a total of 6 tugs because of her size. The shipowners met the costs of 3 extra tugs and she reached the port.
Held, the charterers were in breach of the safe port warranty, and must pay the shipowners for the costs of the extra tugs.

If the ship with all her cargo cannot safely get into the place named, the shipowner is entitled to unload at the nearest safe place. He is not bound by a custom to unload partly outside and partly inside the port.[13]

A temporary condition of danger, however, will not make the port unsafe, provided that such condition will not last an unreasonable

---

6 Ibid. (See the judgment of Parker J, ibid, at 366.)
7 *Kodros Shipping Corpn of Monrovia v Empresa Cubana de Fletes, The Evia (No 2)* [1982] 2 Lloyd's Rep 307 at 320, HL (per Lord Roskill).
8 See *Palace Shipping Co Ltd v Gans SS Line* [1916] 1 KB 138.
9 *Ogden v Graham* (1861) 31 LJQB 26.
10 *Axel Brostrom & Son v Dreyfus & Co* (1932) 38 Com Cas 79.
11 *Palm Shipping Inc v Vitol SA, The Universal Monarch* [1988] 2 Lloyd's Rep 483, QBD (Commercial Court).
12 [1988] 2 Lloyd's Rep 483, QBD (Commercial Court).
13 *The Alhambra* (1881) 6 PD 68.

time.[14] It has been said, however, that it does not follow 'that the converse is true, that any port which is safe at the moment, but which is liable to become dangerous at short notice, is necessarily a safe port within the meaning of a [particular] charter-party'.[15]

A port is unsafe if the delay in leaving it would be such as to frustrate the adventure.

Thus, in *Unitramp v Garnac Grain Co Inc, The Hermine*[16]

A vessel was prevented from leaving Destrehan, a port on the Mississippi, by a lowering of the draught in the river due to the continuing accretion of silt from floods originating upstream. There was a risk of delay of uncertain duration, and, in fact, she was delayed for 37 days.

Held, Destrehan was still a safe port, for the delay was not such as to frustrate the adventure.

It is not settled whether a voyage charterer[17] is under a duty to make a further nomination if the port which he has originally nominated becomes unsafe.[18]

Naming the berth of discharge

Where the charter-party states that the charterers are to nominate a safe berth, the only obligation at the time at which the order to proceed there is that the berth should be prospectively safe. The promise cannot be broken before the obligation to nominate the berth arises and does not cover the approach voyage.[19]

'Or so near thereto as she may safely get'

The clause 'Or so near thereto as she may safely get' is often added after the name of the port of discharge. Its effect is to limit what would otherwise be an absolute obligation on the shipowner to enter

---

14 See per Crompton J, in *Parker v Winlow* (1857) 27 LJQB 49 at 53; *Dahl v Nelson Donkin & Co* (1881) 6 App Cas 38.

15 Per Rowlatt J, in *Johnston Bros v Saxon Queen SS Co* (1913) 108 LT 564 at 565.

16 [1979] 1Lloyd's Rep 212, CA.

17 As to the obligation of a time charterer, see pp 33–34, ante.

18 *Kodros Shipping Corpn v Empresa Cubana de Fletes, The Evia (No 2) of Monrovia* [1982] 2 Lloyd's Rep 307, HL, at 310 (per Lord Diplock) and at 320 (per Lord Roskill).

19 *Atkins International HA v Islamic Republic of Iran Shipping Lines, The APJ Priti* [1987] 2 Lloyd's Rep 37, CA, where the vessel was damaged by a missile during the Iran/Iraq war while on her approach voyage to Bandar Khomeini.

the port named in spite of sand, bars, ice, blockade, etc. The clause is also used even where the port is not named in the charter-party.

The clause relates only to obstacles which are regarded as permanent, not to such as were contemplated as ordinary incidents of the voyage. A temporary obstacle, such as an unfavourable state of the tide or insufficient water to enable the ship to get into dock, will not make the place unsafe so as to discharge the shipowner from liability to unload there, unless the terms of the contract indicate otherwise;[20] and the mere presence of the clause under consideration is not sufficient to indicate otherwise.

The ship must wait until a temporary obstacle is removed; but the master, though bound to allow a reasonable time to elapse before having recourse to the clause,[1] is not bound to wait an unreasonable time.

Thus, in *Dahl v Nelson, Dolkin & Co*[2]

It was *held* that the voyage was not performed merely by bringing the goods to the entrance of the named dock, which was so crowded that the vessel could not get in for an indefinite period. Nevertheless, the charterer having refused to name another place of discharge, it was *held* that the shipowner was not bound to wait an unreasonable time in order to get into the dock.

In *Metcalfe v Britannia Ironworks Co*[3]

Delivery was to be made at Taganrog, on the Sea of Azof. The charter-party stipulated that the ship should go 'to Taganrog, or so near as she could safely get and deliver the cargo afloat'. In December, when the vessel arrived, the Sea of Azof was closed by ice and would not be open for five months.
Held, the shipowner was not entitled to freight by delivering as near as he could get. The question whether an obstacle was temporary or permanent was not so much one of length of time as of what might be regarded as contemplated incidents of the voyage. That the Sea of Azof should be frozen at that time of the year was regarded as reasonably within the contemplation of the parties.

Again, in *Athamas SS (Owners) v Dig Vijay Cement Co Ltd,*[4]

By the terms of a charter-party a vessel was to discharge her cargo at Pnom-Penh or 'so near thereto as she may safely get'. She could not get to Pnom-Penh, and had to discharge at Saigon, which was 250 miles away.
Held, that in the circumstances of the case the discharge at Saigon was sufficient compliance with the terms of the charter-party.

20 *Allen v Coltart* (1883) 11 QBD 782.
1 *The Varing* [1931] P 79 at 87, per Scrutton LJ.
2 Supra.
3 (1877) 2 QBD 423.
4 [1963] 1 Lloyd's Rep 287, CA.

Pearson LJ said[5] that the parties should be deemed to have general maritime knowledge and therefore to know that that part of the world was sparsely provided with ports, so that there might well be a long distance between the named port and any possible substitute. That differentiated the present case from one in which the named port was on the west coast of Europe or in the Mediterranean or in the Black Sea. The question was one of degree and to be decided on a basis of commercial knowledge and experience.

Frequently, the words 'always afloat' are incorporated in the clause. Many modern ships would be damaged by taking the ground, and these words serve to limit the shipowner's obligation. Thus, in *Treglia v Smith's Timber Co*[6]

The bill of lading contained these words and the ship could not discharge at the port named without taking the ground.
Held, the master was entitled to unload at the nearest safe place.

But this clause will not allow the shipowner to refuse to draw into a berth where the ship cannot lie continually afloat, if she can do so for a certain time.[7]

Waiting off port at charterer's request

Where a vessel waits off a port at the charterer's request, the shipowner is entitled to a reasonable remuneration for such a service.[8]

Damage caused by entering unsafe port

If the charterer nominates an unsafe port and the ship is damaged through going there, he will be liable for the damage, subject, of course, to possible questions of remoteness, or novus actus interveniens, eg if the master, knowing that the port is unsafe still

---

5   Ibid, at 302.
6   (1896) 1 Com Cas 360.
7   *Carlton SS Co v Castle Co* [1898] AC 486.
8   *Greenmast Shipping Co SA v Jean Lion et Cie SA, The Saronikos* [1986] 2 Lloyd's Rep 277, QBD (Commercial Court), where the vessel waited off Aqaba for about 9 days at the charterers' request.

insists on going there and the vessel suffers damage in consequence.[9] The test is: did the master act reasonably in going there? If he acted unreasonably, the charterer is not liable.

Thus, in *Reardon Smith Line Ltd v Australian Wheat Board*[10]

The charterer directed the vessel to a port in Western Australia. The vessel arrived at the port and while loading was being carried out, the wind freshened and soon increased to gale force, and she was severely damaged.

Held, the port was unsafe and that the master of the vessel had acted reasonably in going there. The damage to the vessel flowed from the breach of the charter-party, and consequently the charterer was liable.

Notice of readiness to discharge

When the ship has arrived at the place of discharge, the consignee or indorsee of the bill of lading must take steps to receive the goods. In the absence of a custom or special contract to the contrary, the shipowner is not bound to notify the consignees that he is ready to unload,[11] though, if he is intending to have recourse to the clause 'or so near thereto as she may safely get', he must inform them of the place to which he intends to proceed.[12]

In general, however, it is the duty of the holders of the bills of lading to look out for the arrival of the ship. The reason for this rule is that the bills of lading may have been assigned during the voyage, and the master may not know who is entitled to the goods.

But where the consignee's ignorance of the ship's arrival is due to some default on the part of the shipowner, eg entering the ship at the customs-house under a wrong or misleading name, he will not be liable for delay occasioned by it.[13] For it is the shipowner's duty to go through all the proper formalities on arrival, ie notification at the customs-house, delivery of papers, or whatever else local regulations may demand.

9 *Compania Naviera Maropan SA v Bowaters Pulp and Paper Mills Ltd* [1955] 2 QB 68, [1955] 2 All ER 241, CA; *Reardon Smith Line Ltd v Australian Wheat Board* [1956] AC 266, [1956] 1 All ER 456, PC; *Leeds Shipping Co Ltd v Société Française Bunge* [1958] 2 Lloyd's Rep 127, CA. The same rule is applied in the case of time charter-parties. See pp 32–33, ante.
10 [1956] AC 266, [1956] 1 All ER 456, PC.
11 *Harman v Mant* (1815) 4 Camp 161; *R Pagnan and Fratelli v Tradax Export SA* [1969] 2 Lloyd's Rep 150 at 154, QBD (Commercial Court) (per Donaldson J).
12 *The Varing*, supra.
13 *Bradley v Goddard* (1863) 3 F & F 638.

Discharging in the stipulated time

If the vessel is not discharged in the time stipulated, the charterer renders himself liable to pay demurrage or damages for detention, as the case may be.[14]

Again, where a consecutive voyage charter-party is for a total of 'two years' consecutive voyages', each time the vessel is tendered to the charterers for discharging during that period, they must discharge her within the laytime provisions.[15]

Cost of discharging

As to whether the shipowner or the charterer is to bear the cost of discharging will depend on the terms of the charter-party.

Thus, in *S G Embiricos Ltd v Tradax Internacional SA, The Azuero*[16]

A clause in a charter-party stated: 'Charterers' stevedores to be employed by vessel at discharge port and discharge to be free of expense to the vessel.' The stevedores at the port of discharge opened and closed the hatches during discharge. The shipowners alleged that the cost (other than the first opening and last closing) was part of the cost of discharging the vessel, whilst the charterers contended that the cost was part of the cost of the ship fulfilling her duty to take proper care of the cargo during discharge. *Held*, that the opening and closing of the hatches were part of the operation of discharge, and that therefore the charterers were liable.

A charter-party sometimes provides that the charterer is to have the option declarable on or before completion of loading free of expense to the vessel.[17]

'Seaworthy trim'

Where the vessel is to discharge at more than one port, the charter-party may provide that the vessel is 'to be left in seaworthy trim to shift between ports'.

The term 'seaworthy trim' means that she must be in trim to meet

14 Demurrage and damages for detention are considered in chapter 10, post.
15 *Suisse Atlantique Société d'Armement Maritime SA v Rottendamsche Kolen Centrale NV* [1967] 1 AC 361, [1966] 2 All ER 61, HL.
16 [1967] 1 Lloyd's Rep 464, QBD (Commercial Court).
17 *Belships Co Ltd Skibs A/S v President of India. The Belfri* [1972] 1 Lloyd's Rep 12, QBD (Commercial Court), where it was held that the option had been exercised in time. (See the judgment of Mocatta J, ibid, at 17.)

the perils of the passage by sea to the next port not only in the sense that she should be left with an adequate amount of cargo to keep her on an even keel, but also that where necessary part of her cargo should be bagged to stop it shifting while out at sea.[18]

DELIVERY

Unless he is protected by exception clauses in the charter-party or bill of lading[19], or by statute,[20] it is the duty of the shipowner to deliver the cargo. The remedy for breach of this duty is a right to claim damages for non-delivery[1] or short delivery[2], or damages for injury suffered by the cargo.[3]

Where delivery must be made

Unless otherwise agreed, the consignee must take the goods from alongside, though this obligation may be varied by a custom of the

18 *Britain SS Co Ltd v Louis Dreyfus & Co* (1935) 51 Ll L Rep 196 (per Mackinnon J): *J C Carras & Sons (Shipbrokers) Ltd v President of India. The Argabeam* [1970] 1 Lloyd's Rep 282 at 291, QBD (Commercial Court) (per Mocatta J).
19 See pp 180–189, post.
20 See pp 193–202, post.
1 See e g *Dhir and Jag Shakti* [1986] 1 Lloyd's Rep 1, PC; *The Aramis* [1989] 1 Lloyd's Rep 213, CA.
2 See e g *Rederiaktiebolaget Gustav Erikson v Ismail, The Herroe and Askoe* [1986] 2 Lloyd's Rep 281, QBD (Commercial Court); *Ben Shipping Co (Pte) Ltd v An-Board Bainne, The C Joyce* [1986] 2 Lloyd's Rep 285, QBD (Commercial Court); *Amoco Oil Co v Parpada Shipping Co Ltd, The George S* [1989] 1 Lloyd's Rep 369, CA, where there was a dispute concerning the method of measurement of an oil cargo; *Paros Shipping Corpn v Nafta (GB) Ltd, The Paros* [1987] 2 Lloyd's Rep 269, QBD (Commercial Court); *C Czarnikow v Partrenredeeri MS Juno, The Juno* [1986] 1 Lloyd's Rep 190, QBD (Commercial Court); *Indian Oil Corpn Ltd v Greenstone Shipping SA, The Ypatianna* [1987] 2 Lloyd's Rep 286, QBD (Commercial Court), where there was an admixture of a cargo of crude oil; *Ace Imports Pty Ltd v Companhia de Navegacio Lloyd Brasilero; The Esmeralda 1* [1988] 1 Lloyd's Rep 206, Supreme Court of New South Wales (Commercial Division); *BP Oil International Ltd, BP International Ltd and Société Francaise des Petroles BP v Surena Delmar Navegacion SA, The Irini M* [1988] 1 Lloyd's Rep 253, QBD (Commercial Court), where there was a dispute concerning the method of measurement of an oil cargo; *Navegazione Alta Italia SpA v Svenska Petroleum AB, The Nai Matteini* [1988] 1 Lloyd's Rep 452, QBD (Commercial Court).
3 See e g *Naviera Mogor SA v Société Metallurgique de Normandie, The Nogar Marin* [1988] 1 Lloyd's Rep 412, CA; *K Lokumal & Sons (London) Ltd v Lotte Shipping Co Pte Ltd, The August Leonhardt* [1985] 2 Lloyd's Rep 28, CA; *Société Francaise Bunge SA v Belcan NV, The Federal Huron* [1985] 2 Lloyd's Rep 189, QBD (Commercial Court).

port which is not inconsistent with the express terms of the contract. The general rule, however, is that the shipowner is only bound to deliver over the ship's side.

Thus, in *Petersen v Freebody & Co*[4]

A cargo of spars was to be discharged 'overside into lighters'. The consignee provided lighters at the ship's side, but did not employ sufficient men in the lighters to take delivery within the time fixed for unloading. The shipowner sued for damages in respect of the delay.

Held, the shipowner was not bound to put the spars on board the lighters. His duty was simply to put them over the rail of the ship and within reach of the men on board the lighters. Consequently the consignee was liable for the delay in unloading.

Production of bill of lading by consignee

The master is justified in delivering the goods to the consignee named in the bill of lading on production of it, or to the first person who presents a properly indorsed bill of lading, provided the master has no notice of dealings with other bills of the same set.

Thus, in *Glyn v East and West India Dock Co*[5]

Goods were deliverable 'to Cottom and Co, or assigns'. They deposited one bill of lading with the plaintiffs as security for a loan, and with a second bill they obtained delivery from the dock company. The plaintiffs sued the dock company for wrongful delivery.

Held, the action failed, for the company was entitled to deliver on presentation of a proper bill of lading.

If the master has notice of other claims to the goods, he delivers at his peril. His proper course is to interplead,[6] or deliver to one party on tender of an indemnity against the consequences should it turn out that another person was entitled to the goods.

---

4   [1895] 2 QB 294. For a case where the terms of the bill of lading were varied so as to authorise the shipowners to arrange lighterage of the cargo from the ship's side to a wharf, see *The Arawa* [1980] 2 Lloyd's Rep 135, CA.

5   (1882) 7 App Cas 591.

6   Interpleader is a process by which a person in possession of property claimed by two or more persons is able to be relieved from liability by compelling them to bring their claims before a Court at their own expense, thereby securing for himself the protection of the Court's order as to the disposal of the property. See Halsbury Laws of England (4th edn) Vol 25, paras 1001–1092.

Conversely, the master is not justified in delivering to any person who does not produce the bill of lading.[7]

Thus, in *The Stettin*[8]

Barrels of oil were shipped under bills of lading making them deliverable 'to Mendelsohn or assigns'. The shipper retained one bill of lading and sent the other to his agents to secure payment of the price. The master of the ship delivered the oil to Mendelsohn without production of the bill of lading.

Held, the shipowner was liable to the shipper for so delivering.

But it has been proved that up to 1978 it was common but not the universal practice in the carriage of oil cargoes for the master not to insist on the production of a bill of lading.[9]

Delivery to consignee personally

The goods must be handed over to the consignee or his agents.[10]

Thus, in *Bourne v Gatliff*[11]

Goods were consigned under a bill of lading to the plaintiff or his assigns. They were discharged at a wharf on the day after the ship's arrival. The consignees were not aware of the ship's arrival, and they were not at the wharf to take delivery. Within twenty-four hours of the discharge the goods were accidentally destroyed by fire. The jury found that delivery at the wharf did not constitute proper delivery by reason of any special custom of the port.

Held, the shipowner was liable for their value. A reasonable time must be allowed for claiming the goods, and, until that time had elapsed, the shipowner's liability as a

---

7 See e g *Mobil Shipping and Transportation Co v Shell Eastern Petroleum (Pte) Ltd, The Mobil Courage* [1987] 2 Lloyd's Rep 655, QBD (Commercial Court), where the shipowners refused to allow the discharge of the cargo without the production of the bill of lading or a letter of indemnity.

8 (1889) 14 PD 142. See also *Sze Hai Tong Bank Ltd v Rambler Cycle Co Ltd* [1959] AC 576, [1959] 3 All ER 182, PC; *Barclays Bank Ltd v Customs and Excise Comrs* [1963] 1 Lloyd's Rep 81 at 88, QBD (per Diplock LJ); *Rambler Cycle Co Ltd v Peninsular and Oriental Steam Navigation Co, Sze Hai Tong Bank Ltd (First Third Party), Southern Trading Co (Second Third Party)* [1968] 1 Lloyd's Rep 42 (Malaysia Federal Court).

9 *Hansen-Tangens Rederi III A/S v Total Transport Corpn, The Sagona* [1984] 1 Lloyd's Rep 194, QBD (Commercial Court). (See the judgment of Staughton J, ibid, at 203.)

10 For a case where the shipowners and the cargo owners entered into a compromise agreement for the delivery of the cargo in exchange for the cargo owners paying the port expenses, and it was held that the agreement was unenforceable because it was entered into under duress, see *Vantage Navigation Corpn v Suhail and Saud Bahwan Building Materials Inc, The Alev* [1989] 1 Lloyd's Rep 138, QBD (Commercial Court).

11 (1844) 7 M & G 850.

carrier continued. 'The contract was to deliver to the consignee in the port of London; instead of a delivery to the consignee, the goods were placed on Fenning's wharf'.[12]

But where the custom of the port of delivery recognises another mode of delivery, personal delivery is not necessary.[13] Thus, delivery to a dock company, where it is usual for the dock company to take cargo and store it until claimed, has been held sufficient.[14] Further, where the regulations of the port required the consignee to employ harbour porters to receive cargo, delivery to them was held sufficient to excuse the shipowner from liability for damage subsequently sustained by the goods.[15]

The shipowner may also be excused by statute or by express contract from his liability to make personal delivery.

Thus, in *Chartered Bank of India, Australia and China v British India Steam Navigation Co*[16]

Goods were shipped to Penang to be delivered there 'to order or assigns' under bills of lading which contained the condition that 'in all cases and under all circumstances liability of the Company shall absolutely cease when the goods are free of the ship's tackle, and thereupon the goods shall be at the risk for all purposes and in every respect of the shipper or consignee'. The landing agents appointed by the defendants fraudulently delivered the goods to persons other than the consignees.
Held, that, although there had been no delivery under the bill of lading, the above clause was operative and effectual to protect the shipowner.

Apportionment of cargo

Where goods have become mixed and unidentifiable on the voyage, two classes of cases must be distinguished:

(1) *Where this has resulted from excepted perils.* Here the consignees

12 Per Lord Lyndhurst in *Bourne v Gatliff*, supra, at 865.
13 *Petrocochino v Bott* (1874) LR 9 CP 355.
14 *Grange & Co v Taylor* (1904) 9 Com Cas 223.
15 *Knight SS Co v Fleming* (1898) 25 R 1070.
16 [1909] AC 369; *Pacific Milk Industries (M) Bhd v Koninklinjke (Royal Interocean Lines) and Federal Shipping and Forwarding Agency, The Straat Cumberland* [1973] 2 Lloyd's Rep 492, State of Selangor, Kuala Lumpur Sessions Court, where the clause in the bill of lading stated: 'wherever it is compulsory or customary at any port to deliver the cargo to the custom or port authorities, . . . delivery so made shall be considered as final delivery'. But see *Sze Hai Tong Bank Ltd v Rambler Cycle Co*, supra, where the action of the master in delivering the goods without production of the bill of lading was held to be a 'fundamental breach' of contract.

become tenants in common of the mixed goods in proportion to their respective interests, and the shipowner must deliver to them proportionately.[17] But the provisions of the bills of lading or a custom of the port of delivery may relieve him of this duty.[18]

(2) *Where the cause of the mishap was not an excepted peril.* Here the shipowner is liable to any particular bill of lading holder, and the mere delivery of a proportion of the mixed goods will not relieve him of it,[19] though, of course, a special provision in the bills of lading *might* do so if its terms were wide enough.

Thus, in *Sandeman and Sons v Tyzack etc Co*[20]

Bales of jute were consigned to various persons. The bills of lading provided that the number of packages signed for should be binding on the shipowner. The bales were specifically marked, but the shipowner was exempted from liability for obliteration or absence of marks. When the cargo was unloaded, fourteen bales were missing and eleven others could not be identified as belonging to any particular consignment. All but four of the consignees received the full number of bales, and the shipowner claimed to apportion the eleven bales among these four.

Held, as the shipowner had failed to deliver the full number of bales shipped, he was not entitled to claim the benefit of the exemption as to obliteration of marks; and he was liable for the full value of the missing bales and of those which could not be identified.

Where goods are shipped in bulk under different bills of lading covering undivided portions of the bulk, and the cargo is damaged on the voyage, the shipowner is under no obligation to apportion the loss, or the damaged goods, between the various holders. He is entitled to make complete delivery of sound goods to the first consignee to take delivery. This is so even where there is a special provision in the various bills of lading that each bill is to bear its proportion of shortage and damage; for this provision has been held merely to regulate the rights of the holders inter se.[1]

---

17 *Spence v Union Marine Insurance Co Ltd* (1868) LR 3 CP 427. See further, *Gill and Duffus (Liverpool) v Scruttons Ltd* [1953] 2 All ER 977, [1953] 1 WLR 1407. The position is the same where there is no fault on the part of the shipowner, and there is an admixture of part of the cargo belonging to him and of part of the cargo of another person: *Indian Oil Corpn Ltd v Greenstone Shipping SA Panama, The Ypatianna* [1987] 2 Lloyd's Rep 286, QBD (Commercial Court), where there was an admixture of a cargo of crude oil, and it was decided that it was not the sole property of the receivers, but was held in common between them and the shipowner, and that they were entitled to an amount equal to their contribution to the admixture.

18 *Grange v Taylor*, supra.

19 *Sandeman and Sons v Tyzack Co* [1913] AC 680.

20 Supra.

1 *Grange v Taylor*, supra.

Landing and warehousing unclaimed goods

At Common Law and under the powers given to him by the Merchant Shipping Act 1894, the master, as agent of the shipowner, has the right to land and warehouse unclaimed goods.[2]

The cessation of the shipowner's responsibility

The shipowner continues to be liable as a carrier until by the contract, or in the usual course of business, the transit is terminated and the goods have been warehoused for their owner until he is ready to receive them.[3] The mere fact that the goods have reached their destination is not enough to discharge the shipowner. The carrier may limit his liability to that of a bailee by giving notice that he has warehoused the goods and will no longer be responsible for their safe custody, provided the consignee accepts such notice.[4] The consignee's refusal to take delivery, or failure to do so within a reasonable time, also puts an end to the shipowner's liability as a carrier.

When the shipowner has warehoused the goods under s 493 of the Merchant Shipping Act 1894,[5] he is no longer responsible for their safety. The warehouseman is not an agent for the shipowner for the purpose of ensuring the safety of the goods. He is under an obligation 'to deliver the goods to the same person as the shipowner was by his contract bound to deliver them, and is justified or excused by the same circumstances as would justify or excuse the master'.[6]

The contract sometimes provides that the shipowner's liability ceases once the goods have been transhipped.[7]

---

2 See chapter 8, p 216, post.
3 See *Bourne v Gatliff* (1844) 7 Man & G 850.
4 *Mitchell v Lancashire and Yorkshire Rly Co* (1875) LR 10 QB 256.
5 See Appendix D, post.
6 Per Lord Blackburn in *Glyn v East and West India Dock Co* (1882) 7 App Cas 591 at 614. The dictum refers to the Merchant Shipping Act 1862, s 66, but applies to the later Act of 1894.
7 *The Berkshire* [1974] 1 Lloyd's Rep 185, QBD (Admiralty Court), where the clause in the bill of lading stated: 'Whenever the goods are consigned to a point where the ship does not expect to discharge the carrier or master may without notice forward . . . the goods . . . by any vessel . . . whether operated by the carrier or others . . . this carrier in making arrangements for any transhipment . . . shall be considered solely the forwarding agent of the shippers and without any responsibility whatsoever.'

The measure of damages

The rule as to the measure of damages laid down in a leading case is as follows:[8]

'Where two parties have made a contract which one of them has broken, the damages which the other party ought to receive in respect of such breach of contract should be, either such as may fairly and reasonably be considered arising naturally, i e according to the usual course of things, from such breach of contract itself, or such as may reasonably be supposed to have been in the contemplation of both parties at the time they made the contract, as the probable result of the breach of it'.

The problems which have arisen in applying these principles are very numerous, and they cannot be discussed in detail in an elementary work.[9] But the following illustrations will serve to show how the Courts have applied the general principles to the breach of contracts for carriage of goods by sea.

(1) *Where goods are lost or damaged.* Apart from special circumstances, the value of the goods for which compensation must be made, if they have been lost or damaged, is that which they would have had at the time and place at which they ought to have been delivered in proper condition.[10]

8   Per Alderson B, in *Hadley v Baxendale* (1854) 9 Exch 341. See also *Victoria Laundry (Windsor) Ltd v Newman Industries Ltd* [1949] 2 KB 528, [1949] 1 All ER 997.

9   For cases relating to the currency in which damages should be awarded, see *Société Française Bunge SA v Belcan NV, The Federal Huron* [1985] 2 Lloyd's Rep 189, QBD (Commercial Court), where judgment was given for the cargo receivers in US dollars and not in French francs; *Empresa Cubana Importadora de Alimentos v Octavia Shipping Co SA, The Kefalonia Wind* [1986] 1 Lloyd's Rep 273, QBD (Commercial Court), where damages in Cuban pesos were awarded.

10   *The Arpad* [1934] P 189. See also *Ceylon Government v Chandris* [1965] 2 Lloyd's Rep 204 at 216, QBD (Commercial Court) (per Mocatta J). See also *Club Coffee Co Ltd v Moore-McCormack Lines Inc Moore-McCormack Lines (Canada) Ltd, and Eastern Canada Stevedoring (1963) Ltd* [1968] 2 Lloyd's Rep 103, Exchequer Court of Canada, Ontario Admiralty District, where it was held that the measure of damages included Canadian customs duty which the holder of the bill of lading had had to pay on the undelivered goods. (See the judgment of Thurlow J, ibid, at 106); *Marubeni Corpn v Welsh Overseas Freighters Ltd, The Welsh Endeavour* [1984] 1 Lloyd's Rep 400, QBD (Commercial Court), where a shipment of rolls of paper was found to be damaged. (See the judgment of Neill J, ibid, at 404–405.); *Jag Dhir and Jag Shakti* [1986] 1 Lloyd's Rep 1, PC, where a cargo of salt was not delivered; *C Czarnikow Ltd v Partenredeeri MS Juno, The Juno* [1986] 1 Lloyd's Rep 190, QBD (Commercial Court), where there was a short delivery of a cargo of sugar; *The Aramis* [1989] 1 Lloyd's Rep 213, CA, where there was non-delivery of one part of a cargo of linseed expellers and short delivery of another part.

(2) *Where goods are delivered short of their destination.* The measure of damages was considered by the House of Lords in *Monarch SS Co Ltd v Karlshamns Oljefabriker AB* where Lord Porter said:[11]

'the direct and natural consequence is that the merchant should arrange for the carriage forward and charge the shipowner with the reasonable cost of doing so'.

In that case,

a British ship was chartered to carry soya beans from Manchuria in April 1939, and in June the charterers were given bills of lading in respect of them and nominated Karlshamn in Sweden as the port of discharge. Under the terms of the charter-party the owners were under a duty to supply a seaworthy ship. The ship was unseaworthy, and the voyage was thereby delayed. Soon after the outbreak of war in September 1939 the ship was ordered by the Admiralty to proceed to Glasgow, where the beans were discharged, They were then forwarded by the consignees (to whom the charterers had transferred the bills of lading which incorporated the terms of the charter-party) to Karlshamn in neutral ships at a cost of over £21,000.

Held, that the consignees were entitled to recover the cost of transhipment from the shipowners by way of damages.

Again, in *Ferruzzi France SA and Ferruzzi SpA v Oceania Maritime Inc, The Palmea*[12]

A vessel collided with a mooring buoy after leaving Rouen, and suffered damage. She was towed back to St. Wandrille on 25 September 1981. She lay there awaiting repairs until 26 November, when work commenced. On 2 December, the cargo was discharged to safeguard it against the risk of deterioration. On 5 January 1982 the charterers chartered another vessel to carry the cargo to the port of discharge. The delay in commencing repairs was due to the shipowners' fault.

Held, that the shipowners were liable for: (i) the cost of discharging the cargo; (ii) the inevitable cargo losses occurring in the course of discharge; (iii) the cost of storage before reshipment; and (iv) for any financial loss caused by delay in delivery.

(3) *Where there has been delay in carrying goods.* In this event, the measure of damages is generally the difference between the market value of the goods at the time when they ought to have been delivered and the time when they were in fact delivered.[13]

Thus, in *Ardennes SS (Owners of Cargo) v Ardennes SS (Owners)*[14]

Exporters of mandarin oranges shipped a cargo of them relying on an oral promise by the shipowners' agent that the ship would go straight from Cartagena to London. In fact she went first to Antwerp, with the result that when the cargo arrived in London,

---

11 [1949] 1 All ER 1 at 9.
12 [1988] 2 Lloyd's Rep 261, QBD (Commercial Court).
13 *Dunn v Bucknall Bros* [1902] 2 KB 614; *Koufos v C Czarnikow Ltd, The Heron II* [1969] 1 AC 350, [1967] 3 All ER 686, HL.
14 [1951] 1 KB 55, [1950] 2 All ER 517. See also *Heskell v Continental Express Ltd* [1950] 1 All ER 1033.

there had been an increase in the import duty on mandarins, and other cargoes of mandarins had arrived, causing a fall in price.

Held, that as the parties must have been aware that the earlier the goods arrived the better would be the price, the shipowners were liable in damages in respect of the increased import duty which the shippers had had to pay, and to the extent that the delayed arrival had caused them loss of market.

Again, in *Koufos v C Czarnikow Ltd, The Heron II*[15]

A vessel was chartered for a voyage from Constantza to Basrah for the carriage of sugar. She deviated to Berbera to load livestock for the shipowner. If she had not deviated, she would have arrived at Basrah 10 days earlier than she did in fact. The charterers claimed damages for the difference between the market value of the sugar at the due date of delivery and at the actual date of delivery.

Held, they were entitled to this sum.

In determining whether a particular type of loss or damage such as consequential loss of profit, is recoverable as damages for breach of a contract of carriage of goods by sea, the crucial question is whether, on the information available to the carrier when the contract was made, the loss or damage was sufficiently likely to result from the breach of contract to make it proper to hold that the loss or damage flowed naturally from the breach or that loss or damage of that kind should have been within his contemplation.[16]

Limitation of liability

As we shall see, the shipowner may be entitled to limit his liability for loss of or damage to the goods under the Merchant Shipping Act 1979, s 17, Sch 4.[17] Further, where the Carriage of Goods by Sea Act 1971 applies, he can limit his liability in accordance with Art IV, r 5 of the Schedule to that Act.[18]

---

15 [1969] 1 AC 350, [1967] 3 All ER 686, HL, not applying *The Parana* (1877) 2 PD 118.

16 *The Heron II, Koufos v C Czarnikow Ltd*, supra, at 691 (per Lord Reid). For a case where the receivers of the cargo claimed (i) loss of profits; (ii) loss brought about by the fact that due to the delay they had to buy 206 tonnes of chromite sand from their competitors; and (iii) loss of goodwill, see *Satef-Huttenes Albertus SpA v Paloma Tercera Shipping Co SA, The Pegase* [1981] 1 Lloyd's Rep 175, QBD (Commercial Court).

17 See pp 209–210, post.

18 See pp 205–209, post.

Time for bringing claims

(i) *Under the terms of contract*

If the goods are not delivered, or delivered in a damaged condition, a claim may be made within a period of six years[19] unless, as is common, there is a clause to the contrary in the charter-party or bill of lading. The time allowed is usually a short one, eg the arbitration clause in the 'Centrocon' charter-party states:

'All disputes from time to time arising out of this contract[20] shall . . . be referred to the final arbitrament of two arbitrators carrying on business in London. . . . Any claim must be made in writing and Claimants' Arbitrator appointed within 9 months of final discharge, and where this provision is not complied with the claim shall be deemed to be waived and absolutely barred. . . .'[1]

But where there is an arbitration clause in this form, and the goods are never 'discharged' because they have been totally lost when the vessel carrying them founders, the clause has no application and the period of six years applies. The word 'discharge' must not be read as referring to the date when the cargo 'should have been discharged in due performance of the contract'.

Thus, in *Denny Mott and Dickson Ltd v Lynn Shipping Co Ltd*[2]

Goods were shipped at Munksund, Sweden, on a vessel bound for London. The bill of lading incorporated clause 32 of the charter-party which contained an arbitration clause stating 'All claims must be made in writing and the claimant's arbitrator must be appointed within 12 months of the date of final discharge, otherwise the claim shall be deemed waived and absolutely barred'. The vessel carrying the goods was a total loss on 18 June 1959. The indorsees of the bill of lading brought an action against the shipowners on 17 June 1961. The shipowners contended that the claim was time-barred as the arbitrator was not appointed within 12 months of the date when the cargo should have been discharged.

Held, that the action was not time-barred, for clause 32 did not apply, for the cargo

---

19   Limitation Act 1980, s 5. See eg *Bosma v Larsen* [1966] 1 Lloyd's Rep 22, QBD (Commercial Court), where the claim was made nearly nine years after the discharge of the goods, and was held to be statute barred.

20   A claim for a general average contribution constitutes a 'dispute' for the purpose of the arbitration clause set out above: *Union of India v EB Aaby's Rederi A/S* [1974] 1 Lloyd's Rep 57, HL; *Alma Shipping Corpn v Union of India and the Chief Controller of Chartering, Ministry of Transport of India, The Astraea* [1971] 2 Lloyd's Rep 494, QBD (Commercial Court).

1   See eg *Liberian Shipping Corpn 'Pegasus' v A King & Sons Ltd* [1967] 2 QB 86, [1967] 1 All ER 934, CA; *Alma Shipping Corpn v Union of India and the Chief Controller of Chartering, Ministry of Transport of India, The Astraea*, supra; *Union of India v EB Aaby's Rederi A/S*, supra.

2   [1963] 1 Lloyd's Rep 339, QBD (Commercial Court). (See the judgment of Megaw J, ibid, at 345.)

had never been discharged as it had been totally lost. The words 'date of final discharge' did not mean the date when the cargo 'was discharged or should have been discharged'.

Where a consecutive voyage charter-party incorporates the 'Centrocon' arbitration clause, the words 'within 9 months of final discharge' mean within 9 months of final discharge under the voyage in respect of which a dispute arises, and do not mean within 9 months of completion of discharge of the last cargo carried under the charter-party.[3]

Where a charter-party states that a claim will be barred unless the claimant appoints an arbitrator within a specified period, the nominated arbitrator must be actually informed within that period that he has been appointed. Otherwise the claim will be barred.

Thus, in *Tradax Export SA v Volkswagenwerk AG*[4]

A charter-party contained an arbitration clause, which stated that if any dispute arose, each party should 'appoint an arbitrator within 3 months of final discharge'. Discharge of the cargo took place on 15 December 1963. A dispute had arisen between the parties and the charterers nominated their arbitrator on 27 January 1964, but did not inform him that they wished him to act as their arbitrator until 24 July. The shipowners, who had appointed their arbitrator on 17 February, contended that the charterers' claim was time-barred under the clause because the charterers had not effectively appointed their arbitrator in time.
Held, that the claim was barred. Appointment meant an effective appointment. A mere nomination unknown to the appointee was not an appointment of him.

The Court has power to extend the time for commencing arbitration proceedings if it is of the opinion that in the circumstances of the case undue hardship would otherwise be caused.[5]

(ii) *Under the Carriage of Goods by Sea Act 1971*
This Act provides that, where it applies,[6] unless notice of loss or damage and the general nature of such loss or damage is given in

3 *Agro Co of Canada Ltd v Richmond Shipping Ltd, The Simonburn* [1973] 1 Lloyd's Rep 392, CA. (See the judgment of Lord Denning MR, ibid, at 394.)
4 [1970] 1 Lloyd's Rep 62, CA. (See the judgment of Salmon LJ, ibid, at 65.)
5 Arbitration Act 1950, s 27.
6 See pp 95–98, ante. For a case where the charter-party purported to incorporate into its provisions the limitation period provided by the Carriage of Goods by Sea Act 1924, and it was held that, as a matter of construction, it did not do so, see *Overseas Tankship (UK) Ltd v BP Tanker Co Ltd* [1966] 2 Lloyd's Rep 386, QBD (Commercial Court). For cases where a charter-party effectively incorporated the limitation period stated in the Act of 1924, see *Henriksens Rederi A/S v T H Z Rolimpex, The Brede* [1973] 2 Lloyd's Rep 333, CA. (See the judgment of Lord Denning, MR, ibid, at 338.); *Nea Agrex SA v Baltic Shipping Co Ltd and Intershipping Charter Co, The Agios Lazaros* [1976] 2 Lloyd's Rep 47, CA; *Aries*

writing to the carrier or his agent at the port of discharge before or at the time of the removal of the goods into the custody of the person entitled to delivery thereof under the contract of carriage or if the loss or damage is not apparent, within 3 days, such removal is prima facie evidence of the delivery by the carrier of the goods as described in the bill of lading.[7]

The notice in writing need not be given if the state of the goods has, at the time of their receipt, been the subject of joint survey or inspection.[8]

The carrier and the ship are in any event discharged from all liability whatsoever unless suit is brought within 1 year of their delivery or of the date when they should have been delivered.[9] This period may however be extended if the parties so agree after the cause of action has arisen.[10]

Tanker Corpn v Total Transport Ltd, The Aries [1977] 1 Lloyd's Rep 334, HL; *Atlantic Shipping Co SA v Tradax Internacional SA, The Bratislava* [1977] 2 Lloyd's Rep 269, QBD (Commercial Court); *Consolidated Investment and Contracting Co v Saponaria Shipping Co Ltd, The Virgo* [1978] 2 Lloyd's Rep 167, CA.

7 Sch, Art III, r 6.

8 Ibid.

9 Ibid. In *Automatic Tube Co Pty Ltd and Email Ltd—Balfour Buzacott Division v Adelaide SS (Operations) Ltd, Adelaide SS Co Ltd and Adelaide SS Co Pty Ltd, The Beltana* [1967] 1 Lloyd's Rep 531 (Supreme Court of Western Australia) it was held that delivery was made for the purposes of Art III, r 6, either when the goods were landed on the wharf and freed from the ship's tackle, or at the latest, when they were placed in a warehouse and immediately became available to the consignee. (See the judgment of Neville J, ibid, at 540–1.) In *National Packaging Corpn v Nippon Yusen Kaisha (NYK Line)* [1973] 1 Lloyd's Rep 46, District Court, Northern District of California, it was held that the time-bar period started running after discharge plus notice to the consignee plus a reasonable opportunity to receive the goods. But in *American Hoesch Inc and Riblet Products Inc v SS Aubade and Maritime Commercial Corpn Inc* [1971] 2 Lloyd's Rep 423, District Ct of South Carolina (Charleston Division), it was held that 'delivery' was not synonymous with discharge and denoted a two-party transaction in which the consignee would have an opportunity to observe defects. See the judgment of Hemphill DJ, ibid, at 425; *Pacific Milk Industries (M) Bhd v Koninklinjke Jaya (Royal Interocean Lines) and Federal Shipping and Forwarding Agency, The Straat Cumberland* [1973] 2 Lloyd's Rep 492, State of Selangor, Kuala Lumpur Sessions Court. For a case where the shipowners were held to be estopped from relying on the time bar, see *Nippon Yusen Kaisha v Pacifica Navegacion SA, The Ion* [1980] 2 Lloyd's Rep 245, QBD (Commercial Court). For a case where the period of one year had expired and the cargo owner was allowed to amend the writ which had been issued and it was held that his right to sue the shipowner revived, see *Empresa Cubana Importadora de Alimentos v Octavia Shipping Co SA, The Kefalonia Wind* [1986] 1 Lloyd's Rep 273, QBD (Commercial Court).

10 Carriage of Goods by Sea Act 1971, Sch, Art III, r 6. See eg *Canadian Klockner*

The time bar of one year applies even where the shipowner is guilty of a fundamental breach of contract, eg in stowing the goods on deck.[11] But it does not apply where the shipowner has stolen the cargo.[11a]

In the case of any actual or apprehended loss or damage the carrier and the receiver must give all reasonable facilities to each other for inspecting and tallying the goods.[12]

The commencement of arbitration proceedings is 'suit brought' within the meaning of the above provisions.

Thus, in *The Merak*[13]

A cargo owned by the plaintiffs was shipped under a bill of lading subject to the Hague Rules, and was discharged on 21 November 1961, in a damaged condition. The bill of lading contained a clause stating that any dispute had to be referred to arbitration within 12 months of final discharge. The plaintiffs issued a writ on 15 November 1962, and the case came on for trial on 28 July 1964, when the trial Judge stayed the action on the ground that the parties had agreed to refer the dispute to arbitration. By 28 July 1964, the time limit under the arbitration clause had long since passed. The plaintiffs appealed, and claimed that the arbitration clause was void in that it conflicted with Art III, rr 6 and 8, of the Hague Rules, and that they were still entitled to bring an action within one year of final discharge, as they had done in fact. *Held*, that the action must be stayed. The arbitration clause was effective, and since the matter had not been referred to arbitration within 12 months, the plaintiffs were without a remedy. The word 'suit' in Art III, r 6, included the commencement of arbitration proceedings.

The words 'unless suit is brought within one year' mean 'unless the suit *before the Court* is brought within one year'. They do not mean 'unless suit brought *anywhere* within one year'.

Thus, in *Compania Colombiana de Seguros v Pacific Steam Navigation Co*:[14]

Ltd v Flint, Willy Kubon and Federal Commerce and Navigation Co Ltd D/S A/S, The Mica [1973] 2 Lloyd's Rep 478, Federal Court of Canada, Trial Division; for further proceedings in this case, see [1975] 2 Lloyd's Rep 371; *K Lokumal & Sons (London) Ltd v Lotte Shipping Co Pte Ltd, The August Leonhardt* [1985] 2 Lloyd's Rep 28, CA, where the shipowners were not estopped from denying that an extension had been granted.

11 *Kenya Railways v Antares Co Pte Ltd, The Antares (No 2)* [1987] 1 Lloyd's Rep 424, CA.

11a *Cia Portorafti Commerciale SA v Ultramar Panama Inc, The Captain Gregos* [1989] 2 All ER 54, QBD (Commercial Court). (See the judgment of Hirst J, ibid at 62.)

12 Carriage of Goods by Sea Act 1971, Sch, Art III, r 6.

13 [1965] P 223, [1965] 1 All ER 230, CA. not following the decision of the US Federal Court of Appeals in *Son Shipping Co Inc v De Fosse and Tanghe* [1952] AMC 1931. Davies LJ said ([1964] 2 Lloyd's Rep at 535) that is 'suit' excluded arbitration, then the Hague Rules would seem to discourage, if not actually prevent, the inclusion of an arbitration clause in a bill of lading.

14 [1963] 2 Lloyd's Rep 479, QBD (Commercial Court). (See especially the judgment of Roskill J, ibid, at 494–6.)

A cargo of electric cables loaded on the defendants' vessel was insured by the plaintiffs for a voyage from Buenaventura, Colombia, and was delivered in a damaged condition on 12 December 1954. The plaintiffs indemnified the cargo owners, who assigned to them their rights to sue the defendants. The plaintiffs brought an action in the Supreme Court of New York on 2 November 1955, against the defendants, but it was dismissed for lack of jurisdiction. The plaintiffs then brought the present action against the defendants on 7 January 1960, in the English Courts.
Held, that the action was statute-barred under Art III, r 6. The fact that the New York proceedings were brought within the period of one year was immaterial.

Further, the mere inclusion of an arbitration clause in a bill of lading to which the Hague Rules apply as a matter of contract does not deprive the carrier of the one-year limit.[15]

Where the 'Centrocon' arbitration clause is incorporated into a bill of lading to which the Act of 1971 applies, it is void in so far as it states that an arbitrator must be appointed within 9 months of final discharge.[16]

But where the loss or damage takes place after the goods are discharged, the one-year period of limitation does not operate, and the six year period applies because the Act of 1971 does not relate to anything happening to the goods after their discharge.[17]

The Court has power to extend the time for commencing arbitration proceedings if it is of the opinion that in the circumstances of the case undue hardship would otherwise be caused.[18]

But the Court has no such power in a case where the Carriage of Goods by Sea Act 1971 applies.[19]

An action for indemnity against a third person may be brought even after the expiration of the year if brought within the time allowed by the law of the Court seized of the case.[20] But the time

---

15   *Denny, Mott and Dickson Ltd v Lynn Shipping Co Ltd*, supra, at 344 (per Megaw J).
16   *Unicoopjapan and Marubeni-Iida Co Ltd v Ion Shipping Co, The Ion* [1971] 1 Lloyd's Rep 541, QBD (Commercial Court).
17   *Rambler Cycle Co Ltd v Peninsular and Oriental Steam Navigation Co, Sze Hai Tong Bank Ltd (First Third Party), Southern Trading Co (Second Third Party)* [1968] 1 Lloyd's Rep 42 (Malaysia Federal Court).
18   Arbitration Act 1950, s 27. See eg *Nea Agrex SA v Baltic Shipping Co Ltd and Intershipping Charter Co, The Agios Lazaros* [1976] 2 Lloyd's Rep 47, CA; *Atlantic Shipping Co SA v Tradax International SA, The Bratislava* [1977] 2 Lloyd's Rep 269, QBD (Commercial Court); *Consolidated Investment and Contracting Co v Saponaria Shipping Co Ltd, The Virgo* [1978] 2 Lloyd's Rep 167, CA.
19   *Kenya Railways v Antares Co Pte Ltd, The Antares* [1987] 1 Lloyd's Rep 424, CA. For cases where the Act of 1971 applies, see pp 95–98, ante.
20   Carriage of Goods by Sea Act 1971, Sch, Art III, r 6 bis. See eg *McCarren & Co*

allowed shall not be less than 3 months commencing from the day when the person bringing such action of indemnity has settled the claim or has been served with process in the action against himself.[1]

This rule (ie Article III, r 6 *bis*) creates a special exception to the generality of Article III, r 6. Rule 6 *bis*, in a case to which it applies, has a separate effect independently of r 6. The case to which r 6 *bis* applies is one where shipowner A, being under actual or potential liability to cargo-owner B, claims an indemnity by way of damages against ship or shipowner C. If the claim by shipowner A against ship or shipowner C is made under a contract of carriage to which the Hague-Visby Rules apply, then the time allowed for bringing it is that prescribed by r 6 *bis* and not that prescribed by r 6.[2]

There is no express requirement in r 6 *bis* that the liability to cargo-owner B in respect of which shipowner A claims an indemnity against ship or shipowner C must also arise under a contract to which the Hague-Visby Rules apply. There is no good reason why, when such a requirement is not expressed, it should be implied.[3]

(iii) *Under the British Maritime Law Association Agreement*

Where a shipowner is a member of the British Maritime Law Association, the period for bringing a claim is extended, for clause 4 of the Agreement provides as follows:

'The shipowners will, upon the request of any party representing the cargo (whether made before or after the expiry of the period of twelve months after the delivery of the goods or the date when the goods should have been delivered as laid down by the Hague Rules) extend the time for bringing suit for a further twelve months unless (A) notice of the claim with the best particulars available has not been given within the period of twelve months, or (B) there has been undue delay on the part of consignees, receivers or underwriters in obtaining the relevant information and formulating the claim.'[4]

Ltd v Humber International Transport Ltd and Truckline Ferries (Poole) Ltd, The Vechscroon [1982] 1 Lloyd's Rep 301, QBD (Commercial Court).

1   Carriage of Goods by Sea Act 1971, Sch, Art III, r 6 bis. The period of 3 months from the date stated is the minimum and not the maximum time allowed. The words used in both the English and French texts of the 1968 Protocol to the Convention are as clear as they could possibly be: *China Ocean Shipping Co v Owners of the Vessel Andros, The Xingcheng and Andros* [1987] 2 Lloyd's Rep 210, PC, at 214 (per Lord Brandon of Oakbrook).

2   *China Ocean Shipping Co v Owners of the Vessel Andros, The Xingcheng and Andros*, supra at 213 (per Lord Brandon of Oakbrook).

3   Ibid at 213 (per Lord Brandon of Oakbrook).

4   For a case where the shipowners' P & I club did not admit that the Agreement was applicable to the cargo owners' claim, see *K Lokumal & Sons (London) Ltd v Lotte Shipping Co Pte Ltd, The August Leonhardt* [1985] 2 Lloyd's Rep 28, CA.

Chapter 7

The exclusion and limitation of a shipowner's liability

Although goods have been lost or damaged whilst in the custody of the shipowner, he is not necessarily responsible, for his liability in respect of them may have been excluded by the rules of the Common Law or by the express terms of the contract or by statute. Further, even if he is liable, his liability may have been limited by a clause in the contract or by statute, so that the owner of the cargo will be unable to recover the full amount of his loss.

THE EXCLUSION OF LIABILITY

(A) At Common Law

The view usually accepted
It seems that, in spite of the disapproval of one eminent Judge,[1] the correct view of the law is

(1) that the liability of a shipowner at Common Law varies according as he is a common carrier[2] or not;[3]
(2) that a shipowner is deemed to be a common carrier only in respect of such ships (and, it is submitted, where a *portion* of a

---

1 Brett J (afterwards Lord Esher MR), in *Liver Alkali Co v Johnson* (1874) LR 9 Exch 338 at 344; and (as an obiter dictum) in *Nugent v Smith* (1875) 1 CPD 19 at 33.
2 *Fuji Electronics and Machinery Enterprise v New Necca Shipping Corpn, The Golden Lake* [1982] 2 Lloyd's Rep 632, Singapore High Court, where the shipowners were found not to be parties to the bills of lading, and were held to be common carriers. (See the judgment of Chua J, ibid, at 636.)
3 It may be that a shipowner who carries goods for another is never, strictly speaking, a common carrier, but only under a liability akin to that of a common carrier. This question is not one which can be discussed at length in a preliminary treatise.

ship is chartered, in respect of such *other portion* of that ship) as are employed as general ships;[4] and

(3) that the liability, at Common Law, of a shipowner is as follows:

> (A) *If he is a common carrier*, he is absolutely responsible to the owner of the goods carried for any loss or damage to them unless caused by:
>
> > (i) an act of God; *or*
> > (ii) an act of the Queen's enemies; *or*
> > (iii) inherent vice in the goods themselves; *or*
> > (iv) the negligence of the owner of the goods; *or*
> > (v) a general average sacrifice.

The severity of this rule of the Common Law is said to have had its origin in the danger of theft by the carrier's servants or collusion between them and thieves. To prevent this, the responsibility of an *insurer* for the safe delivery of the goods was imposed on the carrier in addition to his liability as a bailee for reward.[5]

> (B) *If he is not a common carrier*, his liability is only that of a bailee for reward; ie he need only exercise due care and diligence.[6]

It will thus be seen that the liability of a shipowner to a charterer of his ship is not the same as his liability to a shipper when the vessel is not under charter. For in the former case the ship is not a general ship; in the latter she is.

The alternative view

As has been indicated, however, the view of the law stated above is by no means universally accepted. The alternative view, which is preferred by many,[7] is to the effect that, at Common Law, the shipowner is *always* under a liability to deliver the goods received by him in the same condition as they were in when shipped, unless he has been prevented from so doing by one of the five causes mentioned

---

4 See *Scrutton on Charter-parties* (19th edn 1984), Article 103, p 201; and Halsbury's *Laws of England*, 4th edn, vol 43, para 447.
5 Per Lord Holt in *Coggs v Bernard* (1703) 2 Ld Raym 909 at 918.
6 Per Cockburn CJ, in *Nugent v Smith* (1876) 45 LJQB 697 at 700 et seq.
7 See eg Carver's *Carriage by Sea* (15th edn 1982), paras 4–7; and Halsbury's Laws of England (4th edn), vol 43, para 447.

above: in other words, that apart from special contract or statute every shipowner is under a liability akin to that of a common carrier, irrespective of whether the goods were shipped by a charterer or on a general ship.

The absence of a binding decision on the point is no doubt due, at least in part, to the fact that, in practice, goods are invariably shipped in pursuance of a contract the terms of which are set out in a bill of lading or in some other document. In such circumstances the position at Common Law is of no more than academic interest.

It has, however, been pointed out[8] that, in principle, there is no good reason for imposing upon the shipowner whose ship carries the goods of one person only a less strict liability with regard to those goods than he would have incurred had they been shipped by several persons; the reasoning applicable in the one case seems equally applicable in the other.

(B) By the express terms of the contract

In the case of charter-parties and those bills of lading to which the Carriage of Goods by Sea Act 1971 does not apply,[9] a shipowner is quite free to exclude his liability for loss or damage in any way that he thinks fit.

Thus, clause 13 of the 'Baltime 1939' charter-party states:

'Responsibility and Exemption
The Owners only to be responsible for delay in delivery of the Vessel or for delay during the currency of the Charter and for loss or damage to goods onboard if such delay or loss has been caused by want of due diligence on the part of the Owners or their Manager in making the Vessel seaworthy and fitted for the voyage or any other personal act or omission or default of the Owners or their Manager. The Owners not to be responsible in any other case nor for damage or delay whatsoever and howsoever caused even if caused by the neglect or default of their servants. The Owners not to be liable for loss or damage arising or resulting from strikes, lock-outs or stoppage or restraint of labour (including the Master, Officers or Crew) whether partial or general. The Charterers to be responsible for loss or damage caused to the Vessel or to the Owners by goods being loaded contrary to the terms of the Charter or by improper or careless bunkering or loading, stowing or discharging of goods or any other improper or negligent act on their part or that of their servants.'

Again, clause 2 of the 'Gencon' charter-party states:

8   Carver, op cit, para 5.
9   See pp 95–98, ante.

'Owners' Responsibility Clause
Owners are to be responsible for loss of or damage to the goods or for delay in delivery of the goods only in case the loss, damage or delay has been caused by the improper or negligent stowage of the goods (unless stowage performed by shippers/Charterers of their stevedores or servants) or by personal want of due diligence on the part of the Owners or their Manager to make the vessel in all respects seaworthy and to secure that she is properly manned, equipped and supplied or by the personal act or default of the Owners or their Manager.
And the Owners are responsible for no loss or damage or delay arising from any other cause whatsoever, even from the neglect or default of the Captain or crew or some other person employed by the Owners on board or ashore for whose acts they would, but for this clause, be responsible, or from unseaworthiness of the vessel on loading or commencement of the voyage or at any time whatsoever. Damage caused by contact with or leakage, smell or evaporation from other goods or by the inflammable or explosive nature or insufficient package of other goods not to be considered as caused by improper or negligent stowage, even if in fact so caused.'[10]

Whether an exclusion clause has been effectively incorporated into the contract so as to form part of it is in each case a matter of construction.[11]

SOME USUAL EXCEPTIONS

Most of the exceptions commonly met with have been the subject of judicial decisions delimiting their scope.

(1) *Act of God*

This exception, though one of the Common Law exceptions, is almost invariably inserted in a charter-party or a bill of lading. It covers any accident due to natural causes directly and exclusively, without human intervention, which no reasonable foresight could have avoided.[12] Damage caused by lightning, a storm, or even a

---

10 See *Ben Shipping Co (Pte) Ltd v An-Bord Bainne, The C-Joyce* [1986] 2 Lloyd's Rep 285, QBD (Commercial Court); *Rederiaktiebolaget Gustav Erikson v Ismail, The Herroe and Askoe* [1986] 2 Lloyd's Rep 281, QBD (Commercial Court), where it was held that the loss of some bags of potatoes had not been caused by any of the events for which the shipowners were liable.

11 *McCutcheon v David Macbrayne Ltd* [1964] 1 All ER 430, [1964] 1 Lloyd's Rep 16, HL, where it was held that the plea by the carriers that they were exempted from liability by their conditions of carriage failed, because, as a matter of construction, the conditions had not been effectively incorporated into the contract.

12 Per James LJ, in *Nugent v Smith* (1875) 45 LJQB 697 at 708; *Falconbridge Nickel Mines Ltd, Janin Construction Ltd and Hewitt Equipment Ltd v Chimo Shipping Ltd, Clarke SS Co Ltd and Munro Jorgensson Shipping Ltd* [1973] 2 Lloyd's Rep 469, Supreme Court of Canada, where the loss of the cargo could have been guarded against by the vessel's crew and the exercise of reasonable care and precautions. (See judgment of Ritchie J, ibid, at 474.)

sudden gust of wind, may be within this exception. But an accident arising from the navigation of a vessel in a fog would not be within the exception, because partly due to human intervention.[13]

(2) *The Queen's enemies*
This exception also is nearly always expressed in the contract. It does not cover acts done by robbers,[14] but only those done by public enemies. It is said[15] to have arisen from the fact that the bailee who had lost the goods had no remedy against public enemies because they were not within the jurisdiction of our courts. Probably the exception does not cover pirates.[16] It certainly covers enemies of the State to which the carrier belongs.[17] As to enemies of the State to which the shipper belongs, it does not appear that the carrier *requires* protection. If the goods are not contraband, they are not liable to seizure; if they are, this would amount to 'inherent vice' in them, and the carrier is not responsible.

It *seems* that if there is an express contract which does not stipulate for the Common Law exceptions of 'act of God' and 'the Queen's enemies', the shipowner will not be entitled to the benefit of them.[18] But he will not be liable for damage arising from inherent defects in the goods or from negligence of the shipper.[19]

(3) *Restraints of princes or rulers*
Besides the case falling within the previous exception, 'restraints of princes' includes any acts done, even in time of peace, by the sovereign power of the country where the ship may happen to be. It covers any restrictions imposed by order of an established government on importation or exportation, eg quarantine regulations, embargoes,[20] blockades or seizure of contraband goods.

It does not cover a seizure resulting from ordinary legal

---

13 *Liver Alkali Co v Johnson* (1874) LR 9 Exch 338.
14 *Mors v Slew (pr Sluce)* (1672) T Raym 220.
15 *Southcote's Case* (1601) Cro Eliz 815.
16 Per Byles J, in *Russell v Niemann* (1864) 34 LJCP 10 at 14.
17 *Russell v Niemann* (1864) 34 LJCP 10.
18 The question is discussed at length in Carver, op cit, para 131, but it is largely academic because the usual practice is expressly to insert these exceptions.
19 Per Willes J, in *Lloyd v Guibert* (1865) LR 1 QB 115 at 121. See also *Baxendale v Great Eastern Rly Co* (1869) LR 4 QB 244.
20 See eg *Seabridge Shipping Ltd v Antco Shipping Ltd, The Furness Bridge* [1977] 2 Lloyd's Rep 367, QBD (Commercial Court), where on the outbreak of the Arab-Israel war in 1973 Libya and other Arab countries imposed an embargo on shipments of oil to certain destinations.

proceedings,[1] nor acts done by a body of persons who are not authorised by an established government.

Whether a body of persons can be said to constitute an established government depends on the circumstances.

Thus, where a vessel was taken over by the FNLA during the civil war in Angola in 1975 and her master was ordered to carry a number of Portuguese refugees to Walvis Bay, the seizure was held to be a 'restraint of princes', for the leader of that body was to be regarded as a 'prince'.[2]

The exception excuses the shipowner from his obligation to deliver the cargo at the port of destination where to do so would expose the ship to real danger or seizure.

Thus, in *Nobel's Explosives Co v Jenkins & Co*[3]

Goods were shipped in England for Japan under a bill of lading excepting 'restraints of princes'. On the day the ship reached Hong Kong, war was declared between Japan and China. The master, therefore, landed at Hong Kong such part of the cargo as was contraband.
Held, the delivery of the contraband goods in Japan was prevented by the excepted peril.

Even where the restraint affects the person of the shipowner only and not the ship, the exceptions will protect him from liability.[4]

(4) *Seizure under legal process*
Though not, as has been seen, included under the previous exception, the benefit of this exception is often expressly provided by the terms of the contract.

(5) *Pirates or robbers by sea or land*
The word 'robbers' does not cover secret theft,[5] but only robbery by violence from outside the ship. Often the word "thieves' is added to this exception, but such word only covers thieves operating from outside the ship.[6]

---

1   *Crew, Widgery & Co v Great Western SS Co* [1887] WN 161.
2   *Silver Coast Shipping Co Ltd v Union Nationale des Co-operatives Agricoles des Céréales, The Silver Sky* [1981] 2 Lloyd's Rep 95, QBD (Commercial Court). (See the judgment of Parker J, ibid, at 98.)
3   [1896] 2 QB 326.
4   *Furness, Withy & Co v Rederiaktiebolaget Banco* [1917] 2 KB 873.
5   *Taylor v Liverpool and Great Western Steam Co* (1874) LR 9 QB 546.
6   Ibid.

(6) Strikes or lock-outs

This exception only covers stoppages arising out of trade disputes.[7] It has been held, for example, that a dismissal of labourers to save expense is not covered.[8]

In 1915 in one case it was held that the true definition of the word 'strike', though not an exhaustive one, was a general concerted refusal by workmen to work in consequence of an alleged grievance.[9]

But in a case[10] in 1966 it was pointed out[11] that the matter has not rested in that stable condition since then. It might be that since then one has had the great development of sympathetic strikes and the General Strike of 1926 when many of those out on strike had no grievance at all against an employer.

Thus, in *J Vermaas' Scheepvaartbedrijf NV v Association Technique de L'Importation Charbonnière, The Laga*[12]

A charter-party provided that 'any time lost through strikes' was not to count for the purpose of the lay days.[13] The chartered vessel was carrying coal and went to a French port for unloading. But the stevedores refused to unload her and all other ships carrying coal, thereby hoping to assist French miners who were on strike. The stevedores had no grievance against their employers, nor against the shipowners, the charterers or the receivers of coal cargoes.
Held, that the sympathetic strike of the stevedores was a 'strike' within the meaning

---

7   Sometimes the extent of a strike clause is limited to a strike by certain persons only. See e g *Caltex Oil (Australia) Pty Ltd v Howard Smith Industries Pty Ltd, The Howard Smith* [1973] 1 Lloyd's Rep 544, Supreme Court of New South Wales, Common Law Division, where the charter-party stated that the demurrage rate should be reduced for time lost 'through strike action by tugboat strike action by tugboat crews or pilots'.

8   *Re Richardsons and M Samuel & Co* [1898] 1 QB 261.

9   *Williams Bros (Hull) Ltd v Naamlooze Vennootschap W H Berghuys Kolenhandel* (1915) 21 Com Cas 253 at 257 (per Sankey J).

10   *J Vermaas Scheepvaarbedrijf NV v Association Technique de L'Importation Charbonniere, The Laga* [1966] 1 Lloyd's Rep 582, QBD (Commercial Court).

11   Ibid, at 590 (per McNair J).

12   [1966] 1 Lloyd's Rep 582, QBD (Commercial Court). (See especially the judgment of McNair J, ibid, at 590–1.) See also the judgment of Lord Denning MR in *Tramp Shipping Corpn v Greenwich Marine Inc, The New Horizon* [1975] 2 Lloyd's Rep 314, CA, where he said (ibid, at 317): 'I think a strike is a concerted stoppage of work by men done with a view to improving their wages or conditions, or giving vent to a grievance or making a protest about something or other, or supporting or sympathising with other workmen in such endeavour. It is distinct from a stoppage which is brought about by an external event such as a bomb scare or by apprehension of danger.'

13   I e the time allowed for loading or discharge, as the case may be. See pp 237–238 post.

of the charter-party, and the time during which it lasted did not count as part of the lay time.

A refusal to work part of the day only may be held to be a strike, even though such refusal is not in breach of contract.

Thus, in *Tramp Shipping Corpn v Greenwich Marine Inc, The New Horizon*[14]

A strike clause in a charter-party stated that time was not to count if the cargo could not be discharged by reason of a strike. The vessel arrived at St Nazaire where the crane and suction workers refused to work except on day work. There was a custom for them to work 24 hours if asked.

Held, by the Court of Appeal, that their refusal was a strike even though the form of abstention was limited to a portion of the day only, and even though they were not in breach of their contracts of employment in insisting on day work only. Accordingly, the time during which they refused to work did not count as lay time.

(7) *Barratry*

Every deliberate act of wrongdoing by the master or any of the crew against the ship or the cargo, without the authorisation or privity of the shipowner or his agent, is barratrous. It must be a wilful act deliberately done, and to the prejudice of the owners.[15] Thus, if the master scuttles the ship[16] or fraudulently sells the cargo,[17] or fraudulently deviates,[18] his act is barratrous. Where there is a charter-party by demise, the master is a servant of the charterer and not of the shipowner; so his acts may be barratrous as against the charterer, although done with the shipowner's consent.[19]

(8) *Jettison*

(9) *Collision*

It has been decided[20] that a collision due to any cause other than the negligence of the shipowner or his employees is a 'peril of the sea'. This exception appears, therefore, to have little or no value where the contract excepts 'perils of the sea'.

14   [1975] 2 Lloyd's Rep 314, CA.
15   *Compania Naviera Bachi v Henry Hosegood & Co Ltd* [1938] 2 All ER 189, where the refusal of the crew to discharge a vessel was held to be barratry.
16   *Ionides v Pender* (1873) 27 LT 244.
17   *Havelock v Hancill* (1789) 3 Term Rep 277.
18   *Mentz Decker & Co v Maritime Insurance Co* [1910] 1 KB 132.
19   *Soares v Thornton* (1817) 7 Taunt 627.
20   *The Xantho* (1887) 12 App Cas 503.

Where 'perils of the sea' are excepted, the shipper may have one of the following remedies for damage caused by collision:

(1) If the collision was due solely to the negligence of the carrying ship, he can sue on the bill of lading, for negligence defeats the exceptions.
(2) If another ship alone was in fault, he can sue its owner in tort.
(3) If both ships were to blame, he can recover a portion of the damage from each in proportion to the degree of blame attributable to each.[1]

A 'Both to Blame' collision clause is very frequently used, except in the Short Sea and Near Continental trades where goods are carried by shipowners who have no vessels which are likely to visit ports in the United States. Contrary to the practice in some European countries, an American shipowner whose ship is involved in a collision can attach in an American port *any* ship in the same ownership as the one with which he has collided, in spite of the fact that the collision may have occurred in some distant part of the world. The release of the attached ship can be secured only by provision of bail, usually a very large sum.

When the bail has been deposited by the owners of the attached ship, the American shipowner proceeds with the collision action in a court in the United States. By the law of that country, where cargo is lost or damaged in a collision for which both ships are to blame, the cargo-owner may recover in full against the non-carrying ship.[2] Then the non-carrying ship may claim one-half of this sum from the carrying ship.[3] This is an anomalous result because a shipowner is not directly responsible to cargo-owners for damage arising out of negligent navigation, provided that due diligence has been exercised to make the ship seaworthy.[4] Thus, if a shipowner is solely to blame for a collision, he is usually under no liability to cargo-owners. But if he is partly to blame, he will become indirectly liable to them, as explained above. Not unnaturally, shipowners felt aggrieved at this result, and in an endeavour to overcome the difficulty they adopted the 'both-to-blame collision clause'. A specimen clause is reproduced

---

1 Maritime Conventions Act 1911, s 1(1). The Law Reform (Contributory Negligence) Act 1945 by s 3 thereof, is expressly excluded from applying to any claim of which s 1 of the Maritime Conventions Act 1911 applies.
2 *The Beaconsfield* (1894) 158 US 303; *The Atlas* (1876) 93 US 302.
3 *The Chattahoochee* (1899) 173 US 540.
4 Harter Act 1893. s 3; (United States) Carriage of Goods by Sea Act 1936, s 4(2).

in Appendix B,[5] from which it will be seen that the object is to free the carrying ship from liability.

In 1952 the legality of the clause was tested in the United States in a case where a bill of lading, *not issued under a charter-party*, contained the clause. The Supreme Court decided that the clause was invalid as being a violation of the rule which, in general, forbids carriers from stipulating against the negligence of themselves or their employees.[6] But it may be that the decision would be different in the case of a charter-party with bills of lading thereunder, and for this reason the clause is still being used.

(10) *All the perils, dangers, and accidents of the sea*

This exception covers all occurrences which are peculiarly incident to a sea voyage and 'which could not be foreseen and guarded against by the shipowner or his servants as necessary or probable incidents of the adventure'.[7]

The occurrence need not be a rare nor an extraordinary one. Thus, it is not rare for rough seas to beat into a ship nor for a vessel to strand on rocks during fog; but both these would be within the exception, unless there was negligence on the part of those in charge of the ship. On the other hand, damage caused under ordinary climatic conditions by water entering the vessel, owing to the decayed state of her timbers, is not within the exception.[8]

But an incident which might equally well occur on land will not be covered, e g consumption of part of the cargo by vermin, or the bursting of boilers or steam-pipes.[9]

---

5 Post.
6 *United States of America v Atlantic Mutual Insurance Co* [1952] 1 TLR 1237. See also *Vendo International v Frances Hammer and Oxyness Shipping Co Inc, Simba and Det Ostasiatiske Kompagni A/S, The Frances Hammer* [1975] 1 Lloyd's Rep 305, District Court, Southern District of New York.
7 *Scrutton on Charter-parties* (19th edn 1984), Art 110, p 227; *Falconbridge Nickel Mines Ltd, Janin Construction Ltd and Hewitt Equipment Ltd v Chimo Shipping Ltd, Clarke SS Co Ltd and Munro Jorgensson Shipping Ltd* [1973] 2 Lloyd's Rep 469, Supreme Court of Canada; *Charles Goodfellow Lumber Sales Ltd v Verreault Hovington and Verreault Navigation Inc* [1971] 1 Lloyd's Rep 185, Supreme Court of Canada, where the authorities were reviewed by Ritchie J, ibid, at 187–190.
8 *Sassoon & Co v Western Assurance Co Ltd* [1912] AC 561.
9 *Thames and Mersey Marine Insurance Co Ltd v Hamilton Fraser & Co* (1887) 12 App Cas 484.

Thus, fire is not a peril of the sea,[10] nor does the term 'sea accident' include a fire at sea.[11]

In order to bring himself within this exception, it is not necessary for the shipowner to prove exactly how the loss was caused; it is sufficient if he shows that it was due to some unexpected occurrence of a kind to which a maritime adventure as such is subject.[12]

(11) *Loss or damage from any neglect of the carrier and/or his employees*

When this exception, commonly known as the 'negligence clause', is included in the contract, its effect is to protect the shipowner from liability even though he or his employees have been negligent.[13]

Whether liability for loss by negligence has been effectively excluded is a matter of construction in each case.[14]

Thus, where a charter-party stated that 'errors of navigation' were excluded, it was held that these words referred to non-negligent errors, and were not wide enough to embrace negligent errors.[15]

(12) *Insufficiency of packing*

It has been held that the carrier is protected by this exception[16] even when the loss is due to the insufficient packing of goods other than

10 *Hamilton, Fraser & Co v Pandorf & Co* (1887) 12 App Cas 518 at 523 (per Lord Bramwell).

11 *Oricon Waren-Handels gesellschaft mbH v Intergraan NV* [1967] 2 Lloyd's Rep 82, QBD (Commercial Court) (a case concerning a cif contract). (See especially the judgment of Roskill J, ibid, at 97–8.)

12 *The Stranna* [1938] P 69, [1938] 1 All ER 458.

13 See eg *Mineralimportexport v Eastern Mediterranean Maritime Ltd, The Golden Leader* [1980] 2 Lloyd's Rep 573, QBD (Commercial Court).

14 The general principles of construction of clauses relating to negligence are conveniently set out in *Lamport & Holt Lines Ltd v Coubro & Scrutton (M & I) Ltd and Coubrou and Scrutton (Riggers and Shipwrights) Ltd, The Raphael* [1982] 2 Lloyd's Rep 42, CA (a case concerning a shiprepairing contract). (See the judgment of Donaldson LJ, ibid, at 50.) See further, *Industrie Chimiche Italia Centrale SpA v Nea Ninemia Shipping Co SA, The Emmanuel C* [1983] 1 Lloyd's Rep 310, QBD (Commercial Court). (See the judgment of Bingham J, ibid, at 312.)

15 *Seven Seas Transportation Ltd v Pacifico Union Marina Corpn, The Satya Kailash and Oceanic Amity* [1984] 1 Lloyd's Rep 586, CA (see the judgment of Robert Goff LJ, ibid, at 597); *Industrie Chimiche Italia Centrale SpA v Nea Ninemia Shipping Co SA, The Emmanuel C,* supra, where there was a similar clause in the charter-party, and it was held that it did not exclude the shipowners' liability for grounding of the vessel due to their negligence. (See the judgment of Bingham J, ibid, at 314.)

16 See eg *Stelwyre Ltd v Kawasaki Kisen KK, The Masashima Maru* [1974] 2 Lloyd's

those actually damaged.[17] If, however, the insufficiency of the packing was apparent on reasonable inspection, the shipowner cannot rely on the exception;[18] presumably the same principle would apply where a carrier claimed the benefit of the exception 'insufficiency or inadequacy of marks'.

(13) *Act, neglect or default of the master, etc, in the navigation or management of the ship*

(14) *Fire*

The effect of negligence on the exceptions. If the shipowner has been guilty of negligence, he cannot rely on the 'excepted perils'.
   Thus, in *Siordet v Hall*[19]

Goods were shipped under a bill of lading excepting 'acts of God'. On the night before she was to sail the ship's boiler was filled, and, owing to frost, a pipe connected with the boiler burst, damaging the goods.
Held, although frost was 'an act of God', negligence in filling the boiler overnight excluded the exception.

   Again, where a clause in a charter-party stated that the liability of the shipowner 'for rot, decay or deterioration' was excluded, and a cargo of potatoes arrived in a deteriorated condition, it was held that the clause could not be relied on by the shipowner because he was guilty of negligence.[20]
   Negligence on the part of the shipowner or his agent defeats the exception of barratry, e g where the master could by reasonable care have prevented the crew from wrongfully damaging the cargo. But negligence itself is not barratry.[1]
   The exception of jettison does not cover cases where goods which were improperly stowed were afterwards jettisoned, for the improper stowage amounts to negligence.[2]
   Further, if the shipowner has negligently taken as part of the cargo goods which are likely to cause a seizure, he is liable to other

---

Rep 394, Ontario Supreme Court, where the shipowners failed to show that a cargo of galvanised wire which arrived in a damaged condition had been insufficiently wrapped.

17 *Goodwin, Ferreira & Co Ltd v Lamport and Holt Ltd* (1929) 141 LT 494.
18 *Silver and Layton v Ocean SS Co Ltd* [1930] 1 KB 416, [1929] All ER Rep 611.
19 (1828) 6 LJOS 137.
20 *Ismail v Polish Ocean Lines, The Ciechocinek* [1975] 2 Lloyd's Rep 170, QBD (Commercial Court); revsd on other grounds [1976] 1 Lloyd's Rep 489, CA.
 1 Per Channell J, in *Briscoe & Co v Powell & Co* (1905) 22 TLR 128 at 130.
 2 *Royal Exchange Shipping Co v Dixon* (1886) 12 App Cas 11.

shippers for delay arising from such a seizure, and cannot claim the benefit of the exception of 'restraints of princes'.[3]

The shipowner cannot plead that a loss has been caused by 'the Queen's enemies' unless he has used reasonable care, eg to avoid capture by ships. He is justified in deviating when there is reasonable danger of capture.[4]

But the shipowner can rely on the 'excepted perils' even if he has been negligent as long as 'negligence' itself is one of the 'excepted perils'.

Thus, in *Blackburn v Liverpool, Brazil and River Plate Steam Navigation Co*[5]

Sugar was stored in a tank at the bottom of the ship. The engineer negligently let salt water into the tank.
Held, the shipowner was not liable because the bill of lading contained an exception of 'perils of the sea whether arising from the negligence of the engineers or otherwise'.

But, of course, the negligence of a third party will not expose the shipowner to liability.

Thus, in *The Xantho*[6]

Salt water entered the ship and damaged the cargo owing to a collision caused solely by the negligence of *another* ship.
Held, the owner of the first vessel was not liable to the shipper.

The construction of the exceptions has sometimes been confused by placing on a wrong basis the distinction between their effect in a bill of lading and the operation of the same phrases (eg 'perils of the sea') in a contract of marine insurance.

On the part of the insurer, a contract of marine insurance is a positive undertaking to indemnify the shipowner in the event of the loss of his vessel from certain specified causes such as perils of the sea. Consequently, it is sufficient to entitle the shipowner to claim the indemnity that he should show that the vessel was lost by perils of the sea.

On the other hand, the exceptions in a bill of lading are merely limitations exempting the shipowner from the 'absolute liability of a common carrier'.[7] They relate to certain undertakings implied by law on the part of the shipowner, and, in the absence of express

---

3   *Dunn v Donald Currie & Co* [1902] 2 KB 614.
4   *The Teutonia* (1872) LR 4 PC 171.
5   [1902] 1 KB 290.
6   (1887) 12 App Cas 503.
7   Per Willes J, in *Notara v Henderson* (1872) LR 7 QB 225 at 235.

agreement to the contrary, he cannot claim the benefit of them if he has been guilty of negligence causing the loss complained of.[8]

The effect of an unjustifiable deviation on the exceptions. Unless the contract has been affirmed, a shipowner whose vessel has unjustifiably deviated cannot rely on the 'excepted perils'.[9]

The effect of unseaworthiness on the exceptions. Even if his vessel was unseaworthy, a shipowner can still rely on the 'excepted perils' if the loss has not been caused by unseaworthiness.[10]

Excepted perils and overcarrying. Sometimes the contract expressly gives to the carrier the right to carry the goods beyond their destination, provided that he tranships them and sends them back. In such case he will be entitled to the protection of the exceptions even after the transhipment.[11]

But, once again, negligence defeats the exceptions.

Thus, in *Searle v Lund*[12]

Owing to the negligence of the shipowner's employees, it was necessary to carry goods beyond their destination in order to avoid undue detention.

Held, although the bill of lading gave permission to overcarry to avoid undue delay, negligence prevented the shipowner from claiming the benefit of the exception.

THE BURDEN OF PROOF WHERE DAMAGE HAS BEEN CAUSED BY AN EXCEPTED PERIL

If the shipowner relies on an excepted peril, he must prove that the loss or damage was caused by it.[13] Thus, if it is clear that the damage must have arisen either from bad stowage or from 'perils of the sea', and the latter are excepted, in order to escape liability the shipowner must show that the damage arose from 'perils of the sea'.

If the shipowner proves that prima facie the cause of the damage was excepted, the burden shifts to the shipper, who must show that the real cause of the damage was something not excepted, eg negligence or unseaworthiness.

---

8   *The Xantho* (supra).
9   See p 23, ante.
10 See p 17, ante.
11 *Broken Hill Proprietary Co Ltd v Peninsular and Oriental Steam Navigation Co* [1917] 1 KB 688.
12 (1904) 20 TLR 390.
13 *The Xantho* (1887) 12 App Cas 503.

Thus, in *The Glendarroch*[14]

Cement was shipped under a bill of lading excepting 'perils of the sea'. This vessel went ashore, and there was no evidence indicating negligence on the part of the shipowner's employees.
Held, the burden of proving such negligence was on the cargo-owner.

Again, where such evidence of negligence on the part of the shipowner as the shipper has produced is not sufficient to turn the scale, but is sufficient to leave the matter in doubt, the burden is once more shifted back to the shipowner, who must prove absence of negligence.[15]

If the shipowner can only show that some part of the damage to the goods was due to a cause within the exception, he must also show how much of the damage is comprised in that part, otherwise he is liable for the whole.[16]

CAUSA PROXIMA NON REMOTA SPECTATUR

Where damage has been caused by several agencies, this rule must be observed in considering whether it was caused by an excepted peril.[17] The shipowner is not excused by the fact that a *remote* cause of the loss was an excepted peril. But it is clear that, even if the *proximate* cause was an excepted peril, the Court is not precluded from ascertaining whether this cause was brought into operation by the shipowner's default; if it was, he will be liable.

Thus, in *The Thrunscoe*[18]

The ventilators of the hold had to be kept closed owing to bad weather, and heat from the engines and boilers damaged the cargo.
Held, the severity of the weather was regarded as the direct cause of the damage, and this was a 'peril of the sea'.

Again, in *Standard Oil Co of New York v Clan Line Steamers Ltd*[19]

The master of a turret ship, not having been instructed by his owners as to the peculiarities of a turret ship, so handled her that she capsized. The loss was immediately due to perils of the sea which overwhelmed her when she capsized, liability for which was excepted.

---

14 [1894] P 226.
15 *Joseph Travers & Sons Ltd v Cooper* [1915] 1 KB 73, Cf *The Kite* [1933] P 154.
16 *Ceylon Government v Chandris* [1965] 2 Lloyd's Rep 204, QBD (Commercial Court) at 216 (per Mocatta J).
17 *The Xantho* (1887) 12 App Cas 503; *Hamilton, Fraser & Co v Pandorf & Co* (1887) 12 App Cas 518; Chorley and Tucker's *Leading Cases* (4th edn 1962), p 298.
18 *The Thrunscoe* [1897] P 301.
19 [1924] AC 100.

Held, the dominant cause was her unseaworthiness in that her master, though otherwise efficient, was inefficient in not being aware of the special danger.

(C) By statute

Certain statutory provisions exempt the shipowner from being liable. These are contained in:

(1) The Merchant Shipping Act 1894.[20]
(2) The Carriage of Goods by Sea Act 1971.[1]
(3) The Merchant Shipping Act 1979.[2]

(1) THE MERCHANT SHIPPING ACT 1894

Dangerous goods
If dangerous goods have been thrown overboard by the shipowner or the master, neither can be made liable for their loss.[3]

(2) THE CARRIAGE OF GOODS BY SEA ACT 1971

(a) *Dangerous goods*
The Act provides that, in cases to which it applies,[4] goods of an inflammable, explosive or dangerous nature to the shipment whereof the carrier, master or agent of the carrier, has not consented, with knowledge of their nature and character, may at any time before discharge be landed at any place or destroyed or rendered innocuous by the carrier without compensation.[5]

(b) *Loss or damage due to 'excepted perils'*
The Act provides that in cases to which it applies[6] neither the carrier nor the ship[7] shall be liable for loss or damage arising or resulting

20 See infra.
1 See p infra.
2 See p 201, post.
3 Merchant Shipping Act 1948, s 448(2). See generally pp 24–25, ante.
4 See pp 95–98, ante.
5 Carriage of Goods by Sea Act 1971, Sch Art IV, r 6.
6 See pp 95–98, ante.
7 A lash barge is not a 'ship': *Wirth Ltd v SS Acadia Forest and Lash Barge CG 204, The Acadia Forest* [1974] 2 Lloyd's Rep 563, District Court, Eastern District of Louisiana.

from certain causes.[8] These correspond, in general, to those considered above which are commonly excluded in charter-parties and those bills of lading to which the Act of 1971 does not apply.[9]

The defence that the peril is excepted applies in any action against the carrier in respect of loss or damage to the goods whether the action is founded in contract or in tort.[10]

If such action is brought against a servant or agent of the carrier (such servant or agent not being an independent contractor), such servant or agent is entitled to avail himself of the defences which the carrier is entitled to invoke under the Act.[11]

But the servant or agent is not entitled to do so if the damage resulted from an act or omission on his part done with intent to cause damage or recklessly and with knowledge that damage would probably result.[12]

The list of 'excepted perils'. The list of 'excepted perils' is as follows:

(i) *act, neglect or default of the master, mariner, pilot, or the servants of the carrier in the navigation or in the management of the ship;*

Thus, where a vessel grounded on a reef in the Sulu Sea, the carrier escaped liability because the loss of the cargo was due to the master's fault in navigation.[13] Similarly, a carrier was not liable for damage to the cargo caused by the vessel negligently striking a quay.[14] Again, when a vessel caused damage to another during a lightening operation, it was held that there was no liability for the damage because it was due to a fault in navigation.[15]

An 'act, neglect or default in the management of the ship' includes a failure to take soundings of the water level in the hold,[16] a failure

---

8 Carriage of Goods by Sea Act 1971, Sch Art IV, r 2.
9 See pp 95–98, ante.
10 Carriage of Goods by Sea Act 1971, Sch, Art IV bis, r 1.
11 Ibid, Sch, Art IV bis, r 2.
12 Ibid, Sch, Art IV bis, r 4.
13 *President of India v West Coast SS Co, The Portland Trader* [1964] 2 Lloyd's Rep 443, US Court of Appeals.
14 *Aliakmon Maritime Corpn v Iransocean Continental Shipping Ltd and Frank Truman Export Ltd, The Aliakmon Progress* [1978] 2 Lloyd's Rep 499, CA.
15 *Seven Seas Transportation Ltd v Pacifico Union Marina Corpn, The Satya Kailash and Oceanic Amity* [1984] 1 Lloyd's Rep 586, CA. (See the judgment of Robert Goff LJ, ibid, at 595).
16 *Riverstone Meat Co Pty Ltd v Lancashire Shipping Co Ltd* [1959] 1 QB 74 at 100, [1958] 3 All ER 261 at 272 (per McNair J).

to get rid of water in the hold after a collision,[17] a failure to use locking bars on the hatches at sea in heavy weather,[18] a failure to adjust the metacentric height of a vessel,[19] allowing a vessel to exceed her permitted draught,[20] and a failure to close the low sea inlet valves of a vessel and to close the overboard discharge valve from the main lubricating oil coolers.[1]

If the damage to the cargo results from some act relating to the ship herself and only incidentally damaging the cargo, the carrier can plead the exception of 'act, neglect or default in the management of the ship'. But he cannot do so if the act deals solely with the goods and not directly or indirectly with the ship herself.[2]

Thus, in *Gosse Millerd Ltd v Canadian Government Merchant Marine Ltd, The Canadian Highlander*[3]

A cargo of timplates was shipped in a vessel under a bill of lading incorporating the Hague Rules. During the voyage she had to go into dock for repairs. Whilst these were being executed, the hatches were left open so that the workmen could go in and out of the hold more easily. The hatches were not protected when rain was falling, and the tinplates were damaged in consequence.

Held, the shipowners were liable for they had failed properly and carefully to carry the goods as required by Art III, r 3. They could not rely on Art IV, r 2(a) for the term 'management of the ship' did not include negligence in the management of the hatches.

Similarly, it is not an 'act, neglect or fault in the management of the ship' where the loss is caused by the pilfering of the stevedores,[4] where the cargo is damaged owing to stevedores stealing a storm valve cover plate at a port of call,[5] where there has been a failure to secure the cargo on a barge to keep it from sliding and a failure to

---

17 *Leval & Co Inc v Colonial Steamships Ltd* [1961] 1 Lloyd's Rep 560, Supreme Court of Canada.
18 *International Packers London Ltd v Ocean SS Co Ltd* [1955] 1 Lloyd's Rep 218.
19 *Georgia-Pacific Corpn v Marilyn L, Elvapores Inc, Evans Products Co and Retla SS Co, The Marilyn L* [1972] 1 Lloyd's Rep 418, District Court for the Eastern District of Virginia, Norfolk Division.
20 *Actis Co Ltd v Sanko SS Co Ltd, The Aquacharm* [1982] 1 Lloyd's Rep 7, CA. (See the judgment of Lord Denning MR, ibid, at 9.)
1 *Metals and Ores Pte Ltd v Compania de Vapores Stelvi SA, The Tolmidis* [1983] 1 Lloyd's Rep 530, QBD (Commercial Court). (See the judgment of Neill J, ibid, at 539–540.)
2 *The Glenochil* [1896] P 10.
3 [1929] AC 223, [1928] All ER Rep 97, HL.
4 *Hourani v Harrison* (1927) 32 Com Cas 305, CA.
5 *Leesh River Tea Co Ltd v British India Steam Navigation Co Ltd, The Chyebassa* [1966] 2 Lloyd's Rep 193, CA.

tether the barge,[6] a failure to drain the fresh water system which might have caused the parting of a pipe,[7] a failure to alter course to get away from a storm centre,[8] and the surreptitious opening of a hatch by a member of the crew.[9]

(ii) *fire, unless caused by the actual fault or privity of the carrier;*

(iii) *perils, dangers and accidents of the sea or other navigable waters;*[10]

6 *Falconbridge Nickel Mines Ltd, Janin Construction Ltd and Hewitt Equipment Ltd v Chimo Shipping Ltd, Clarke SS Co Ltd and Munro Jorgensson Shipping Ltd* [1973] 2 Lloyd's Rep 469, Supreme Court of Canada.

7 *International Produce Inc and Greenwich Mills Co v SS Frances Salman, Swedish Gulf Line AB and Companhia de Navegacao Maritima Netumar, The Frances Salman* [1975] 2 Lloyd's Rep 355, District Court, Southern District of New York.

8 *The Washington* [1976] 2 Lloyd's Rep 453, Federal Court of Canada, Trial Division. (See the judgment of Heald, J, ibid, at 460.)

9 *The Bulknes* [1979] 2 Lloyd's Rep 39, QBD (Admiralty Court). (See the judgment of Sheen J, ibid, at 41.)

10 *Leesh River Tea Co Ltd v British India Steam Navigation Co Ltd, The Chyebassa,* supra, where it was held that the entry of sea water was a peril of the sea, but that this defence would fail if the cover plate had been removed in circumstances in which the shipowners were responsible for the stevedores' servants who removed it. (See the judgment of Sellers LJ, ibid, at 199–200, and that of Salmon LJ, ibid, at 202–3); *G E Crippen & Associates Ltd v Vancouver Tug Boat Co Ltd* [1971] 2 Lloyd's Rep 207, Exchequer Court, British Columbia Admiralty District, where a cargo of peat moss was found to be damaged, and it was held that the loss was not due to perils of the sea for the weather was normal for the time of year. (See the judgment of Walsh J, ibid, at 216); *United States of America v Eastmount Shipping Corpn, The Susquehanna* [1975] 1 Lloyd's Rep 216, District Court, Southern District of New York, where the weather was not so severe or unusual as to be classed as a 'peril of the sea'. (See the judgment of Frankel DJ, ibid, at 219); *Bruck Mills Ltd v Black Sea SS Co, The Grumant* [1973] 2 Lloyd's Rep 531, Federal Court of Canada, Trial Division, where the escape of apple concentrate in plastic containers was held not to be due to 'perils of the sea'; *William D Branson Ltd and Tomas Alcazar SA v Jadranska Slobodna Plovidba (Adriatic Tramp Shipping), The Split* [1973] 2 Lloyd's Rep 535, Federal Court of Canada, where the loss of a cargo of melons stowed in crates 17 high without air circulating in the hold was held not to have been caused by 'perils of the sea'; *Falconbridge Nickel Mines Ltd, Janin Construction Ltd and Hewitt Equipment Ltd v Chimo Shipping Ltd, Clarke SS Co Ltd and Munro Jorgensson Shipping Ltd* [1973] 2 Lloyd's Rep 469, Supreme Court of Canada, where the loss of a tractor and generating set was held not to due to 'perils of the sea', but to a failure to secure the cargo on a barge to keep it from sliding and a failure to tether the barge to the vessel; *International Produce Inc and Greenwich Mills Co v SS Frances Salman, Swedish Gulf Line AB and Companhia de Navegacao Maritima Netumar, The Frances Salman* [1975] 2 Lloyd's Rep 355, District Court, Southern District of New York, where the cargo was held to be damaged by bad stowage near a leaking sanitary water pipe and not by 'perils of the sea'; *The Washington* [1976] 2 Lloyd's Rep 453, Federal Court of Canada, Trial Division, where the defence

(iv) *act of God*;

(v) *act of war*;

(vi) *act of public enemies*;

(vii) *arrest or restraint of princes, rulers or people, or seizure under legal process*;

(viii) *quarantine restrictions*;[11]

(ix) *act or omission of the shipper or owner of the goods, his agent or representative*;[12]

(x) *strikes or lock-outs or stoppage or restraint of labour from whatever cause, whether partial or general*;

(ix) *riots and civil commotions*;

(xii) *saving or attempting to save life or property at sea*;

of perils of the seas failed because the carrier failed to establish that the weather encountered was the cause of the damage to the cargo of glass sheets and was of such a nature that the danger of damage to the cargo could not have been foreseen or guarded against as one of the incidents of the voyage. (See the judgment of Heald J, ibid at 459.); *The Tilia Gorthon* [1985] 1 Lloyd's Rep 552, QBD (Admiralty Court), where it was held that the loss was not due to 'perils of the sea' for the weather was by no means exceptional in the North Atlantic at that time of year.

11 *Empresa Cubana Importada de Alimentos Alimport v Iasmos Shipping Co SA, The Good Friend* [1984] 2 Lloyd's Rep 586, QBD (Commercial Court), where a cargo of soya bean meal was infested with two kinds of insect which were the subject of quarantine in Cuba, but, on the evidence, the loss was due to the shipowners failing to inspect the trunking of the vessel, and thus in breach of art III, r 1.

12 See e g *Ismail v Polish Ocean Lines, The Ciechocinek* [1976] 1 Lloyd's Rep 489, CA, where the shipper's agent assured the master that a cargo of potatoes was packed in suitable bags so that no dunnage was required, and it arrived in a damaged condition. (See the judgment of Lord Denning MR, ibid, at 495); *The Mekhanik Evgrafov and Ivan Derbenev* [1987] 2 Lloyd's Rep 634, QBD (Admiralty Court), where a cargo of newsprint was damaged, and the shipowners were held not to be able to rely on this exception because they had not proved that the loss occurred in this way.

(xiii) *wastage in bulk or weight or any other loss or damage arising from inherent defect, quality or vice of the goods;*[13]

(xiv) *insufficiency of packing;*[14]

---

13 *Easwest Produce Co v The Ship SS Nordnes* (1956) Ex CR 328 (onions); *Shaw, Savill and Albion Co Ltd v R Powley & Co Ltd* [1949] NZLR 668 (brandy); *Wm Fergus Harris & Son Ltd v China Mutual Steam Navigation Co Ltd* [1959] 2 Lloyd's Rep 500 (timber); *Albacora SRL v Westcott and Laurance Line Ltd* [1966] 2 Lloyd's Rep 53, HL (wet salted fish); *Jahn (Trading as C F Otto Weber) v Turnbull Scott Shipping Co Ltd and Nigerian National Line Ltd, The Flowergate* [1967] 1 Lloyd's Rep 1 (cocoa); *Chris Foodstuffs (1963) Ltd v Nigerian National Shipping Line Ltd* [1967] 1 Lloyd's Rep 293, CA (coco yams). But in *David McNair & Co Ltd and David Oppenheimer Ltd & Associates v The Santa Malta* [1967] 2 Lloyd's Rep 391 (Exchequer Court, British Columbia Admiralty District), where a cargo of melons, garlic and onions was stowed in the same hold as a cargo of fishmeal and became tainted thereby, it was held that the loss was due to bad stowage and lack of ventilation, and not due to inherent vice. In *G E Crippen and Associates Ltd v Vancouver Tug Boat Co Ltd,* supra, the damage to a cargo of peat moss was held not to be due to the inherent defect of uneven compression, for this defect would not by itself have caused the damage if the cargo had not been stowed four pallets high and if dunnage had not been used. (See the judgment of Walsh J, [1971] 2 Lloyd's Rep at 216). In *William D Branson Ltd and Tomas Alcazar SA v Jadranska Slobodna Plovidba (Adriatic Tramp Shipping), The Split* [1973] 2 Lloyd's Rep 535. Federal Court of Canada, Trial Division, the loss of a cargo of melons packed in crates 17 high without air circulating in the hold was held to be due not to 'inherent defect' but to improper stowage. In *Nissan Automobile Co (Canada) Ltd v Owners of Vessel Continental Shipper, The Continental Shipper,* [1976] 2 Lloyd's Rep 234, Federal Court of Canada, Trial Division, the damage to uncrated cars was found to be due to their being stowed too closely together and not to 'inherent vice'. In *Crelinsten Fruit Co and William D Branson Ltd v Maritime Fruit Carriers Co Ltd, The Lemoncore* [1975] 2 Lloyd's Rep 249, Federal Court of Canada, Trial Division, the loss of a cargo of apples and pears carried in a refrigerated vessel was held not to be due to 'inherent vice' but to bad stowage since it was a block stow without dunnage. In *Westcoast Food Brokers Ltd v The Ship Hoyanger and Westfal-Larsen & Co A/S, The Hoyanger* [1979] 2 Lloyd's Rep 79, Federal Court of Canada, Trial Division, apples were in an overripe condition when loaded, and their loss was held to be due to inherent vice. (See the judgment of Addy J, ibid, at 89.) In *Empresa Cubana Importada de Alimentos Alimport v Iasmos Shipping Co SA, The Good Friend,* supra, the defence of inherent vice in a cargo of soya bean meal failed because the shipowners had not inspected the vessel's trunking which was infested with insects; *The Mekhanik Evgrafov and Ivan Derbenev,* supra, where the damage to the cargo of newsprint was not the result of inherent vice but to improper ventilation, for which the shipowners were liable.

14 In *G E Crippen and Associates Ltd v Vancouver Tug Boat Co Ltd,* supra, the damage to the cargo of peat moss was held not to be due to insufficiency of packing. (See the judgment of Walsh J, [1971] 2 Lloyd's Rep at 216.) In *Nissan Automobile Co (Canada) Ltd v Owners of the Vessel Continental Shipper, The Continental Shipper,* supra, the damage to the cars was also held not to be due to

(xv) *insufficiency or inadequacy of marks*;[15]

(xvi) *latent defects not discoverable by due diligence*;[16]

(xvii) *any other cause arising without the actual fault or privity of the carrier, or*[17] *without the fault or neglect of the agents or servants of the carrier, but the burden of proof shall be on the person claiming the benefit of this exception to show that neither the actual fault or privity of the carrier nor the fault or neglect of the agents or servants of the carrier contributed to the loss or damage.*[18]

It must be borne in mind that, where the Act applies, no exception

'insufficiency of packing'. In *The Lucky Wave* [1985] 1 Lloyds' Rep 80, QBD (Admiralty Court) the damage to the cargo of galvanised steel was held not to be due to 'insufficiency of packing'.

15 See *British Imex Industries Ltd v Midland Bank Ltd* [1958] 1 QB 542, [1958] 1 All ER 264.

16 See eg *The Hellenic Dolphin* [1978] 2 Lloyd's Rep 336, QBD (Admiralty Court), where there was a latent defect in the shell plating of the vessel. (See the judgment of Lloyd J, ibid, at 343.); *The Bulknes* [1979] 2 Lloyd's Rep 39, QBD (Admiralty Court), where the vessel's hatch lid opened in a gale, and there was no evidence of a latent defect. (See the judgment of Sheen J, ibid, at 41.); *Empresa Cubana Importada de Alimentos Alimport v Iasmos Shipping Co SA, The Good Friend*, supra, where the shipowners pleaded the exception of a latent defect but did not succeed because they were in breach of art III, r 1 in not using due diligence to make the ship seaworthy.

17 The word 'or' here must be construed as meaning 'and': see *Brown & Co v Harrison* (1927) 43 TLR 633; *Paterson Steamships Ltd v Canadian Co-operative Wheat Producers Ltd* [1934] AC 538 at 549; *Leesh River Tea Co Ltd v British India Steam Navigation Co Ltd, The Chyebassa* [1966] 2 Lloyd's Rep 193 at 202, CA (per Salmon LJ).

18 See eg *Leesh River Tea Co Ltd v British India Steam Navigation Co Ltd, The Chyebassa*, supra, where the shipowners were held not to be liable for damage to the cargo owing to the stevedores stealing a storm valve cover plate at a port of call; *G E Crippen and Associates Ltd v Vancouver Tug Boat Co Ltd*, supra, where it was held that the damage to a cargo of peat moss had arisen without privity or fault on their part or fault or neglect of their agents or servants, for there was no negligence in stowing the cargo in the state of knowledge at the time with regard to the proper method of stowing that type of cargo. (See the judgment of Walsh J: [1971] 2 Lloyd's Rep at 217); *Jack L Israel Ltd v Ocean Dynamic Lines SA and Ocean Victory Ltd, The Ocean Dynamic* [1982] 2 Lloyd's Rep 88, QBD (Commercial Court), where a cargo of cherries was found to contain broken glass and the shipowners failed to prove that neither their actual fault or privity nor the fault of neglect of their agents or servants contributed to the loss (see the judgment of Robert Goff J, ibid, at 93); *The Mekhanik Evgrafov and Ivan Derbenev*, supra, where a cargo of newsprint was damaged and the shipowners were held not to be able to rely on this exception because they had not proved that the loss occurred in this way.

which does not appear in the foregoing list can be included, except where a special contract is permitted in the case of unusual shipments of particular goods;[19] for to incorporate some further exception would be to increase the carrier's immunity and diminish his responsibility.

Where the loss or damage is caused by the concurrent causative effects of an excepted and a non-excepted peril, the carrier remains liable but escapes liability only to the extent that he can prove that the loss or damage was caused by the excepted peril alone.[20]

Cases where the 'excepted perils' cannot apply
The shipowner cannot rely on the 'excepted perils' if he has not carried out his obligation under Art III, r 1 to exercise due diligence to make the ship seaworthy and its non-fulfilment causes the damage,[1] nor can he do so if the vessel makes a deviation not

---

19 See pp 104–105, ante.
20 *Aktieselskabet de Danske Sukkerfabrikker v Bajamer Compania Naviera SA, The Torenia* [1983] 2 Lloyd's Rep 210, QBD (Commercial Court). (See the judgment of Hobhouse J, ibid, at 219.)
 1 *Maxine Footwear Co Ltd v Canadian Government Merchant Marine Ltd* [1959] AC 589, [1959] 2 All ER 740, PC. See also Carriage of Goods by Sea Act 1971, Sch, Art IV, r 1 and *Robin Hood Flour Mills Ltd v N M Paterson & Sons Ltd, The Farrandoc* [1967] 2 Lloyd's Rep 276 at 283 (Exchequer Court of Canada) (per Noel J). *Fisons Fertilizers Ltd and Fisons Ltd v Thomas Watson (Shipping) Ltd* [1971] 1 Lloyd's Rep 141, Mayor's and City of London Court, where a cargo was damaged due to a valve in the forward hold suction line being jammed, and it was shown that the defect occurred before the beginning of the voyage; *Charles Goodfellow Lumber Sales Ltd v Verreault Hovington and Verreault Navigation Inc* [1971] 1 Lloyd's Rep 185, Supreme Court of Canada, where it was shown that the vessel's hull was not sufficiently strong to withstand the voyage, and the shipowners were held not to have discharged their duty under Art III, r 1, and accordingly could not plead that the loss was due to 'perils of the sea'. See the judgment of Ritchie J, ibid, at 188; *United States of America v Eastmount Shipping Corpn, The Susquehanna* [1975] 1 Lloyd's Rep 216, District Court, Southern District of New York, where the shipowners could not rely on the exception of 'perils of the seas' because the vessel had not sufficient bunkers on board at the beginning of the voyage. (See the judgment of Frankel DJ, ibid, at 219.); *American Smelting & Refining Co v SS Irish Spruce and Irish Shipping Ltd, The Irish Spruce* [1976] 1 Lloyd's Rep 63, District Court, Southern District of New York, where the shipowners could not rely on the exception of a fault in navigation because the vessel was unseaworthy as she did not have on board the latest Admiralty List of Radio Signals; *Empresa Cubana Importada de Alimentos Alimport v Iasmos Shipping Co SA, The Good Friend* [1984] 2 Lloyd's Rep 586, QBD (Commercial Court), where the shipowners could not rely on the exceptions of quarantine, latent defect and inherent vice because the vessel was unseaworthy in that there were insects in her trunking .

permitted by Art IV, r 4.[2]

Burden of proof of absence of negligence
The question as to the burden of proving the absence of negligence
is an unsettled one.

In a High Court decision it has been held that the shipowner will
be liable for the loss or damage to the goods even if this is due to
'excepted perils', unless he can prove that he has taken proper care
of them whilst they were in his custody,[3] ie has fulfilled his duties
under Art III, r 2.[4]

But in a case in the House of Lords, Lord Pearson stated that there
was no express provision, and in his opinion no implied provision,
in The Hague Rules that the shipowner was debarred from relying
on an exception unless he proved absence of negligence on his part.
But he did have to prove that the damage was caused by an excepted
peril or excepted cause, and in order to do that he might in a
particular case have to give evidence excluding causation by his
negligence.[5]

(c) *Loss or damage when value mis-stated*
Neither the carrier nor the ship is responsible in any event for loss
or damage to or in connection with the goods if their nature or value
has been knowingly mis-stated by the shipper in the bill of lading.[6]

(3) THE MERCHANT SHIPPING ACT 1979[7]

The owner[8] of a British ship is not liable for any loss or damage

---

2 *Stag Line Ltd v Foscolo, Mango & Co Ltd* [1932] AC 328, [1931] All ER Rep 666,
   HL, p 117–118, ante.
3 *Svenska Traktor Aktiebolaget v Maritime Agencies (Southampton) Ltd* 1953] 2 QB
   295, [1953] 2 All ER 570; *J Kaufman Ltd v Cunard SS Co Ltd* [1965] 2 Lloyd's
   Rep 564, Exchequer Court, Quebec Admiralty District (furs delivered in wet
   condition).
4 See pp 99–101, ante.
5 *Albacora SRL v Westcott and Laurance Line Ltd* [1966] 2 Lloyd's Rep 53 at 64,
   HL. See further the speech of Lord Pearce, ibid, at 61. In *Jahn (Trading as C F
   Otto Weber) v Turnbull Scott Shipping Co Ltd and Nigerian National Line Ltd, The
   Flowergate* [1967] 1 Lloyd's Rep 1, QBD (Commercial Court), Roskill J, said
   (ibid, at 8) that he proposed to follow Lord Pearson's view, leaving it open to the
   cargo owners, if they so desired, to argue to the contrary in a higher Court.
6 Carriage of Goods by Sea Act 1971, Sch, Art IV, r 5(h); *Frank Hammond Pty Ltd
   v Huddart Parker Ltd* [1956] VLR 496.
7 See Appendix D, pp 305–315, post.
8 'Owner' in relation to a ship, 'includes any part owner and any charterer, manager
   or operator of the ship': Merchant Shipping Act 1979, s 18(4).

(a) where any property on board the ship is lost or damaged by reason of fire on board the ship; or

(b) where any gold, silver, watches, jewels or precious stones on board the ship are lost or damaged by reason of theft, robbery or other dishonest conduct and their nature and value were not at the time of shipment declared by their owner or shipper to the owner or master of the ship in the bill of lading or otherwise in writing.[9]

But the owner is not entitled to exclude his liability if it is proved that the loss resulted from his personal act or omission, committed with intent to cause such loss, or recklessly and with knowledge that such loss would probably result.[10]

THE   LIMITATION OF LIABILITY

Although the shipowner may be responsible for the loss of or damage to the goods, his liability may be limited by

(A) the terms of the contract;
(B) statute.

(b) By the terms of the contract

In the case of a charter-party and of a bill of lading to which the Carriage of Goods by Sea Act 1971 does not apply,[11] a shipowner is entitled to limit his liability to any sum which he thinks fit. But in some cases he cannot rely on a limitation clause, eg where the loss was due to unseaworthiness, and liability for loss unseaworthiness was not excepted.[12]

Where the Carriage of Goods by Sea Act 1971 applies,[13] the shipowner cannot limit his liability to a sum less than 666·67 units of account per package or unit or 2 units of account per kilogramme of

9   Ibid, s 18(1). Similarly, the master or member of the crew can also exclude his liability where the loss or damage arises from anything done or omitted by him when acting in the capacity of master or member of the crew: ibid, s 18(2).
10   Ibid, s 18(3).
11   See pp 95–98, ante.
12   *Tattersall v National SS Co* (1884) 12 QBD 297 p 112, ante.
13   See pp 95–98, ante.

gross weight of the goods lost or damaged, whichever is the higher.[14]
Any clause purporting to do so will be void.[15]

Thus, in *The Morviken*[16]

The owners of an asphalt road-finishing machine shipped it at Leith, Scotland, on the
Dutch vessel 'Haico Holwerda' for carriage to Amsterdam and thence to Bonaire in
the Dutch Antilles under a bill of lading which by clause 2 stated that Dutch law
should apply and that all actions should be brought before the Court of Amsterdam.
At Amsterdam the machine was transhipped on to the Norwegian vessel 'Morviken'
for carriage to Bonaire. Whilst being discharged at Bonaire it was dropped on to the
quay and was damaged to the extent of £22,000. The owners of the machine claimed
damages, but the Dutch carriers applied for the action to be stayed in view of clause
2. By Dutch law the original Hague Rules, which entitled a carrier to limit his liability
to £250, applied whereas under Art IV, r 5(a) of the Hague–Visby Rules as set out in
the Carriage of Goods by Sea Act 1971 the sum would be far higher.
Held, by the House of Lords, that the action would not be stayed for the clause was
void under Act III, r 8 because it lessened the liability of the carrier.[17]

Again, a clause limiting a claim to the invoice value of the goods
has been held to be of no effect.[18]

Thus, in *Nabob Foods Ltd v Cape Corso (Owners)*[19]

A cargo of pepper was shipped from Liverpool to Vancouver. The bill of lading stated
that for the purpose of adjusting claims for which the shipowner was liable, the value
of the goods was to be deemed the invoice value plus freight and insurance if paid,
irrespective of whether any other value was greater or less.
Held, by the Exchequer Court of Canada, that this provision was repugnant to the
Hague Rules, Art III, r 8,[20] and therefore void.[1]

Further, a clause limiting the liability of the carrier of a number
of cartons of chicken portions to US $2 per kilo of the gross weight
of the goods lost or damaged was void, and could not be relied on by
the carrier.[2]

The general rule is that only the shipowner is entitled to limit his
liability, for any person who is not a party to the charter-party or bill
of lading has no rights under it.

---

14 Carriage of Goods by Sea Act 1971, Sch, Art IV, r 5(a). See pp 205–206, post.
15 Ibid, Sch, Art III, r 8.
16 [1983] 1 Lloyd's Rep 1, HL.
17 See the judgment of Lord Diplock, ibid, at 6.
18 *Nabob Foods Ltd v The Cape Corso* [1954] 2 Lloyd's Rep 40, Exchequer Court of
    Canada.
19 [1954] 2 Lloyd's Rep 40, Exchequer Court of Canada.
20 Which is the same as Art III, r 8 of the Hague-Visby Rules.
 1 See the judgment of Sidney Smith J : [1954] 2 Lloyd's Rep at 43.
 2 *Mayhew Foods Ltd v Overseas Containers Ltd* [1984] 1 Lloyd's Rep 317, QBD
    (Commercial Court).

Thus, in *Scruttons Ltd v Midland Silicones Ltd* [3]

Shipowners issued to the shippers of a drum containing chemicals a bill of lading, by the terms of which they were entitled to limit their liability if the goods were damaged through their negligence. The drum was damaged during its discharge by stevedores. The shippers sued the stevedores, who claimed to be entitled to limit their liability in accordance with the terms of the bill of lading.

Held, that they were not entitled to do so, because they were not parties to the bill of lading, and so were liable to pay in full for the damage which had been caused.

But if the carrier contracts as an agent for a third party, eg a stevedore, the third party can enforce the terms of the bill of lading against the shipper if

(i) the bill of lading makes it clear that the third party is intended to be protected by the provisions in it which limit liability;

(ii) the bill of lading makes it clear that the carrier, in addition to contracting for these provisions on his own behalf, is also contracting as agent for the third party that those provisions should apply to the third party;

(iii) the carrier has authority from the third party to do that (or perhaps later ratification by the third party would suffice); and

(iv) any difficulties about consideration moving from the third party would be overcome. [4]

Thus, in *New Zealand Shipping Co Ltd v A M Satterthwaite & Co Ltd, The Eurymedon* [5]

A bill of lading in respect of a drilling machine stated that the carrier acted as agent 'for all persons who are or might be his servants or agents from time to time', and that the limitation of liability provisions in the bill of lading were available to such servant or agent. The machine was damaged whilst being discharged by stevedores. The

---

3 [1962] AC 446, [1962] 1 All ER 1, HL. In the United States it has been held that the parties to a bill of lading may extend any contractual benefit to a third party by clearly expressing their intent to do so: *Carle and Montanari Inc v American Export Isbrandtsen Lines Inc and John W McGrath Corpn* [1968] 1 Lloyd's Rep 260, District Court, Southern District of New York, where a stevedore, although not a party to the bill of lading, was held to be entitled to the benefit of a provision in it enabling the carrier to limit his liability; *Cabot Corpn v The Mormascan, Moore-McCormack Lines Inc and John W McGrath Corpn* [1971] 2 Lloyd's Rep 351, US Ct of Appeals, Second Circuit; *Rupp v International Terminal Operating Co Inc, SS Mormacstar, Moore-McCormack Lines Inc and American Scantic Line, The Mormacstar* [1973] 2 Lloyd's Rep 485, US Court of Appeals, Second Circuit; *Tessler Bros (BC) Ltd v Italpacific Line and Matson Terminals Inc* [1975] 1 Lloyd's Rep 210, US Court of Appeals, Ninth Circuit.

4 *Scruttons Ltd v Midland Silicones Ltd* [1962] 1 All ER 1 at 10 (per Lord Reid).

5 [1974] 1 Lloyd's Rep 534, PC.

stevedores contended that they were entitled to limit their liability under the clause in the bill of lading.

Held, by the Judicial Committee of the Privy Council, that they were so entitled. The bill of lading brought into existence a unilateral bargain which became a full contract when the stevedores discharged the goods.[6] The discharge of the goods for the benefit of the shipper was the consideration for the agreement by the shipper that the stevedores should have the benefit of the limitation provisions in the bill of lading.[7] To give the stevedores the benefit of the limitation provisions was to give effect to the clear intentions of a commercial document.[8]

(B) By statute

The shipowner is entitled to limit his liability under:

    (1) The Carriage of Goods by Sea Act 1971.[9]

    (2) The Merchant Shipping Act 1979.[10]

(1) UNDER THE CARRIAGE OF GOODS BY SEA ACT 1971

In cases to which the Act of 1971 applies,[11] unless the nature and value of the goods have been declared by the shipper before shipment

---

6 Ibid, at 539 (per Lord Wilberforce).

7 Ibid, at 539 (per Lord Wilberforce).

8 Ibid, at 540 (per Lord Wilberforce). See further, *The Suleyman Stalksly* [1976] 2 Lloyd's Rep 609, Supreme Court of British Columbia, where an exemption clause in a bill of lading was held not to extend to stevedores for whom the shipowners had no authority to act as agents: *Salmond and Spraggon (Australia) Pty Ltd v Port Jackson Stevedoring Pty Ltd, The New York Star* [1980] 2 Lloyd's Rep 317, PC, where the stevedores could rely on the exception clauses in the bill of lading; *Eisen und Metall AG v Ceres Stevedoring Co Ltd and Canadian Overseas Shipping Ltd* [1977] 1 Lloyd's Rep 665, Court of Appeal, Province of Quebec, District of Montreal, where the terminal operators were held to be entitled to invoke the exception clause in the bill of lading for that was the clear intention of the parties to it; *Miles International Corpn v Federal Commerce and Navigation Co, Federal Stevedoring Ltd and Belcan NV, The Federal Schelde* [1978] 1 Lloyd's Rep 285, Superior Court of Quebec, where the stevedores could rely on the exception clause in the bill of lading for by the law of Quebec the clause constituted a valid stipulation pour autrui; *Lummus Co Ltd v East African Harbours Corpn* [1978] 1 Lloyd's Rep 317, High Court of Kenya, where a harbour authority could not rely on an exception clause in a bill of lading; *Raymond Burke Motors Ltd v Mersey Docks and Harbour Co* [1986] 1 Lloyd's Rep 155, QBD (Commercial Court), where a dock operator could not rely on an exception clause in a bill of lading which would have been issued (but was not, in fact, issued because the motor cycles were never shipped).

9 See infra.

10 See p 209, post.

11 See pp 95–98, ante.

and inserted in the bill of lading, neither the carrier nor the ship shall in any event be or become liable for any loss or damage to or in connection with the goods in an amount exceeding 666·67 units of account per package or unit or 2 units of account per kilogramme of gross weight of the goods lost or damaged, whichever is the higher.[12]

Actual insertion of the value in the bill of lading is necessary if the shipper wishes to obtain more than the maximum sum per package or unit laid down in the Act. The fact that the carrier knows the value is immaterial.[13]

Thus, in *Anticosti Shipping Co v Viateur St Amand*[14]

A truck valued at Can$4,222 was shipped at Port Menier for delivery at Rimouski. The shipper did not inform the carrier of its value, though the carrier knew that it was far in excess of Can $500 to which liability could be limited under the Hague Rules.

Held, by the Supreme Court of Canada, that the knowledge of the carrier was immaterial, and that the shipper had to make a declaration of its value under Art IV, r 5 if he wished to avoid the limitation provision.[15]

If the bill of lading does not contain a space in which the shipper can insert the declared value of the cargo, the shipowner is not entitled to limit his liability.[16]

Thus, in *General Electric Co v MV The Lady Sophie,*[17]

A quantity of component parts for gas turbine power plants was shipped on the mv 'Lady Sophie' for delivery in Saudi Arabia under a bill of lading in which there was no space for the shipper to insert the declared value of the cargo. The vessel encountered heavy seas off Rotterdam, and the parts were lost or damaged. The carriers sought to limit their liability under Art IV, r 5 to US$500 per package or unit.

Held, by the District Court for the Southern District of New York that they were not entitled to do so.[18]

The declaration made by the shipper, if embodied in the bill of

---

12 Carriage of Goods by Sea Act 1971, Sch, Art IV, r 5(a). This provision is modified in its application to hovercraft. See pp 280–281, post. The unit of account is the Special Drawing Right as defined by the International Monetary Fund: ibid, Sch, Art IV, r 5(d). The sums mentioned are to be converted into the national currency on the basis of the value of that currency on the date of judgment: ibid, Sch 4, Art IV, r 5(d); Merchant Shipping Act 1981, s 2(5). For the method of calculating the amount of the conversion, see ibid, s 3.

13 *Anticosti Shipping Co v Viateur St Amand* [1959] 1 Lloyd's Rep 352, Supreme Court of Canada.

14 [1959] 1 Lloyd's Rep 352, Supreme Court of Canada.

15 See the judgment of Rand J, ibid, at 357.

16 *General Electric Co v MV The Lady Sophie* [1979] 2 Lloyd's Rep 173, District Court for the Southern District of New York. See also *Sommer Corpn v Panama Canal Co* [1974] 1 Lloyd's Rep 287, US Court of Appeals, Fifth Circuit.

17 [1979] 2 Lloyd's Rep 173, District Court for the Southern District of New York.

18 See the judgment of Werker DJ, ibid, at 174.

lading, is prima facie evidence, but is not binding or conclusive on the carrier.[19]

Where a container, pallet or similar article of transport is used to consolidate goods, the number of packages or units enumerated in the bill of lading as packed in such article of transport is deemed to be the number of packages or units in calculating the amount beyond which the carrier or the ship is not liable. Where the number of packages or units is not enumerated in the bill of lading, the article of transport is considered to be the package or unit, and the amount is calculated accordingly.[20]

The word 'package' has been held to cover 6 cartons of 40 television tuners strapped to pallet boards,[1] a 42 ft cruiser carried in a cradle,[2] and a bundle containing 22 tin ingots.[3]

But where the shipowners chose to classify an uncrated yacht as 'unpacked', it could not be regarded as a 'package', and they could not limit their liability.[4]

An electrical transformer bolted to a skid,[5] and 'lift-on lift-off tanks' supplied by the shipowner for the carriage of liquid latex,[6] have been held not to be 'packages'.

---

19   Carriage of Goods by Sea Act 1971, Sch, Art IV, r 5(f).

20   Ibid, Sch, Art IV, r 4(c).

1   *Standard Electrica SA v Hamburg Sudamerikanische Dampfschiffahrts-Gesellschaft and Columbus Lines Inc* [1967] 2 Lloyd's Rep 193, US Court of Appeals, Second Circuit. Cf *International Factory Sales Service Ltd v Ship Aleksandr Serafimovich and Far Eastern SS Co, The Aleksandr Serafimovich* [1975] 2 Lloyd's Rep 346, Federal Court of Canada, Trial Division, where sewing machine heads were shipped in cartons fixed to pallets, and it was held that each carton was a package, for the description of the goods in the bill of lading, the numbering of the cartons and their visibility from outside the pallet showed that this was the intention of the parties. (See the judgment of Deputy Judge Smith, ibid, at 355.) As to the growing practice of carriers to receive cargo from shippers in a 'palletised' form or a 'containerised' form, see the judgment of Lumbard Ct J, in *Standard Electrica SA v Hamburg Sudamerikanische Dampfschiffahrts-Gesellschaft and Columbus Lines Inc*, supra, at 195.

2   *Island Yachts Inc v Federal Pacific Lakes Line* [1972] 1 Lloyd's Rep 426, District Court, Northern District of Illinois (Eastern District).

3   *Primary Industries Corpn v Barber Lines A/S and Skilos A/S Tropic, The Fernland* [1975] 1 Lloyd's Rep 461, Civil Court of City of New York.

4   *Van Breems v International Terminal Operating Co Inc and Holland America Line, The Prinses Margriet* [1974] 1 Lloyd's Rep 599, District Court, Southern District of New York.

5   *Hartford Fire Insurance Co v Pacific Far East Line Inc, The Pacific Bear* [1974] 1 Lloyd's Rep 359, US Court of Appeals, Ninth Circuit.

6   *Shinko Boeki Co Ltd v SS Pioneer Moon and United States Line Inc, The Pioneer Moon* [1975] 1 Lloyd's Rep 199, US Court of Appeals, Second Circuit.

Where a tractor and generating set were shipped on board a vessel and lost overboard whilst being discharged, each was held to be a 'unit'.[7]

The carrier is entitled to limit his liability to the stated sum per package or unit even if he has failed to exercise due diligence to make the vessel seaworthy,[8] but he cannot do so if he has loaded the cargo on deck for this constitutes a quasi-deviation.[9]

The total amount recoverable is fixed by reference to the value of the goods at the place and time at which they are discharged from the ship in accordance with the contract or should have been so discharged.[10]

The value is fixed according to the commodity exchange price, or, if there is no such commodity exchange price or current market price, by reference to the normal value of goods of the same kind and quality.[11]

By agreement between the carrier and the shipper a higher maximum may be fixed.[12] But the carrier cannot reduce the maximum laid down by the Act.[13]

If an action is brought against a servant or agent of the carrier (such servant or agent not being an independent contractor), the servant or agent is entitled to avail himself of the defences and limits of liability which the carrier is entitled to invoke under the Act.[14] But the aggregate of the amounts recoverable from the carrier and such servants and agents can in no case exceed the limit stated in the Act.[15] Further, a servant or agent of the carrier cannot limit his

---

7　*Falconbridge Nickel Mines Ltd, Janin Construction Ltd and Hewitt Equipment Ltd v Chimo Shipping Ltd, and Munro Jorgensson Shipping Ltd* [1973] 2 Lloyd's Rep 469, Supreme Court of Canada.

8　*Iligan Integrated Steel Mills Inc v SS John Weyerhauser, Weyerhauser Co and New York Navigation Co Inc, The John Weyerhauser* [1975] 2 Lloyd's Rep 439, US Court of Appeals, Second Circuit. (See the judgment of Friendly Ct J, ibid, at 442.)

9　*Jones v Flying Clipper* [1954] AMC 259.

10　Carriage of Goods by Sea Act 1971, Sch, Art IV, r 5(b). See e g *Mayhew Foods Ltd v Overseas Containers Ltd* [1984] 1 Lloyd's Rep 317, QBD (Commercial Court), where the shippers of a cargo of chicken and turkey portions failed to prove the value of the goods at the place of discharge, and were held to be entitled to recover no more than the cif invoice price. (See the judgment of Bingham J, ibid, at 321.)

11　Carriage of Goods by Sea Act 1971, Sch, Art IV, r 5(b).

12　Ibid, Sch, Art IV, r 5(g).

13　Ibid, Sch, Art IV, r 5(g).

14　Ibid, Sch, Art IV bis, r 2.

15　Ibid, Sch, Art IV, bis, r 3.

liability if it is proved that the damage resulted from an act or omission of the servant or agent done with intent to cause damage or recklessly and with knowledge that damage would probably result.[16]

(2) THE MERCHANT SHIPPING ACT 1979[17]

A shipowner[18] can limit his liability in respect of:

(i) claims in respect of loss of or damage to property occurring on board or in direct connection with the operation of the ship and consequential loss resulting from it; and

(ii) claims in respect of loss from delay in the carriage of cargo.[19]

A shipowner is not entitled to limit his liability if it is proved that the loss resulting from his personal act or omission, committed with intent to cause such loss or recklessly and with knowledge that such loss would probably result.[20]

The limit of liability in respect of claims in respect of loss of or damage to cargo or to claims in respect of delay is

(i) 167,000 units of account for a ship with a tonnage not exceeding 500 tons; and

(ii) for a ship with a tonnage in excess of 500 tons the following amount in addition

(a) for each ton from 501 to 30,000 tons, 167 units of account;

(b) for each ton from 30,001 to 70,000 tons, 125 units of account; and

(c) for each ton in excess of 70,000 tons, 83 units of account.[1]

The unit of account is the Special Drawing Right as defined by the

---

16 Ibid, Sch, Art IV, bis, r 4.
17 See Appendix D, post.
18 Merchant Shipping Act 1979, Sch 4, Part I, art 1, para 2. If any claim is made against any person for whose act, neglect or default the shipowner is responsible, that person is entitled to avail himself of the right to limit his liability: ibid, Sch 4, part I, para 4. The liability of a shipowner includes liability in an action brought against the vessel herself; ibid, Sch 4, Part I, art 1, para 5.
19 Ibid, Sch 4, Part I, art 2, para 1.
20 Ibid, Sch 4, Part I, art 4.
 1 Ibid, Sch 4, Part I, art 6(1). This provision is modified in relation to hovercraft. See pp 281–283, post. As to ships of less than 300 tons, see ibid, Sch 4, Part II, para 5(1). The tonnage is the ship's gross tonnage calculated in such manner as may be prescribed by an order made by the Secretary of State: ibid, Sch 4, Part II, para 5(2).

International Monetary Fund.[2] The sums mentioned are to be converted into the national currency of the State in which limitation is sought according to the date at which the limitation fund has been constituted payment is made or security is given which under the law of that State is equivalent to such payment.[3]

Any person alleged to be liable may constitute a limitation fund with the Court or other competent authority in any State which is a party to the Convention on Limitation of Liability for Maritime Claims 1976 and in which legal proceedings are instituted in respect of claims subject to limitation.[4]

The fund must be distributed among the claimants in proportion to their established claims against the fund.[5]

2   Ibid, Sch 4, Part I, art 8(1).
3   Ibid, Sch 4, Part I, art 8(1). As to the date for fixing the amount of the conversion, see ibid, Sch 4, Part II, para 7.
4   Ibid, Sch 4, Part I, art 10.
5   Ibid, Sch 4, Part I, art 12.

Chapter 8

The master

The master of a ship may be said to be regarded by the law as two persons rolled into one. He is the agent of the shipowner, and the agent of the owner or owners of the cargo. In each of these capacities he has certain duties and a certain authority.

THE DUTIES OF THE MASTER

The master has various duties at Common Law and by statute.

At Common Law

The duties of the master, which arise from his having charge of the ship and possession of the cargo, may be stated as follows:

(1) His first duty to the cargo-owners is to carry the cargo to its destination in the same ship.[1]

(2) He must take all reasonable care of the cargo, both during the ordinary course of the voyage and where some accident has exposed it to danger.[2] In doing so he must always act with a view to the benefit of the cargo-owners. If he acts reasonably, with that end in view, his conduct is justifiable, irrespective of the result.[3]

(3) In case of necessity, where extraordinary measures must be taken, eg a sale of part of the cargo, he must first communicate with the cargo-owners for instructions; where communication

---

1 *Notara v Henderson* (1872) LR 7 QB 225.
2 Ibid.
3 *Benson v Chapman* (1849) 2 HL Cas 696 at 720, and see per Sir Montague Smith in *Cargo ex Argos* (1873) 42 LJ Adm 1 at 56.

with them is impossible, he must take such extraordinary action as will be for their ultimate benefit.[4]

(4) He must collect general average contributions[5] for the benefit of those entitled to them, whether they are the cargo-owners or the shipowner, exercising the shipowner's lien[6] on the cargo, where necessary, until they are paid.[7]

(5) He must allow a reasonable time to the consignees of the cargo for taking delivery.[8]

(6) He must proceed on the voyage without unjustifiable deviation and with reasonable despatch.[9]

(7) He must do everything else which is necessary for the performance of the contract.[10]

By statute

Under the Carriage of Goods by Sea Act 1971, a shipper who furnishes the carrier with written information concerning

(a) the leading marks necessary for identification of the goods, and

(b) either the number of packages or pieces, or the quantity or weight, as the case may be,

has a right to insist on the master or other agent of the carrier issuing a bill of lading incorporating the information so furnished.[11]

It should, however, be observed that the master is not bound to show *both* the number of packages *and* the weight; if the number is stated, the phrase 'weight unknown' may properly be inserted, and will have full effect.[12]

Moreover, the master can refuse to incorporate in the bill the statements required by the Act if either he has reasonable grounds

---

4   See *The Hamburg* (1864) 2 Moo PCCNS 289 at 323.
5   As to general average contributions, see pp 221–227, post.
6   As to the shipowner's lien, see pp 273–274, post.
7   *Strang Steel & Co v Scott & Co* (1889) 14 App Cas 601.
8   *Bourne v Gatliff* (1844) 11 Cl & Fin 45 at 70. See p 165, ante.
9   See pp 19–24, ante.
10   *The Turgot* (1886) 11 PD 21.
11   Carriage of Goods by Sea Act 1971, Sch, Art III, r 3 (see Appendix E, post).
12   *Pendle and Rivett v Ellerman Lines Ltd* (1927) 33 Com Cas 70.

for suspecting that the information given by the shipper is inaccurate, or he has had no reasonable means of checking it.[13]

And, in the case of the leading marks, the master may refuse to show these in the bill of lading if the goods or their containers are not clearly marked 'in such a manner as should ordinarily remain legible until the end of the voyage'.[14]

Further, under the 1971 Act, any shipper can insist on the bill of lading incorporating a statement as to the 'apparent order and condition' of the goods.[15]

THE AUTHORITY OF THE MASTER

It is necessary to consider what are the limits set by the law to the ordinary authority of the master, as distinct from a consideration of what he may do in extraordinary circumstances, e g in time of grave peril.

His authority in ordinary circumstances

One broad principle must never be lost sight of: that is that, even in the absence of express instructions (by which, of course, he might be authorised to do anything), the authority of the master of a ship is very large and extends to all acts that are usual and necessary for the employment of the ship.[16]

He may make contracts for the hire of the ship, and enter into agreements to carry goods for freight.

Apart from notice to the contrary, persons dealing with the master may assume that he is a general agent having authority to bind the owners for the purposes and on the terms on which the vessel is usually employed.

The master has no power to carry goods freight-free[17] nor to sign bills of lading for a lower rate of freight than the owner has contracted for.[18]

He must not assume 'any other authority than the indispensable

---

13　Carriage of Goods by Sea Act 1971, Sch, Art III, r 3 (see Appendix E, post).
14　Ibid, Sch, Art III, r 3 (see Appendix E, post).
15　Ibid.
16　Per Jervis CJ, in *Grant v Norway* (1851) 20 LJCP 93 at 98.
17　Ibid.
18　*Pickernell v Jauberry* (1862) 3 F & F 217.

and necessary one of procuring a freight for the vessel according to the ordinary terms'.[19]

The authority of the master to bind his owners by charter-party only arises when he is in a foreign port and his owners are not there and there is difficulty in communicating with them.'[20] Further, the authority of a master of a foreign ship to contract on behalf of his owners is usually limited by the law of the ship's flag.[1]

The master has no authority to cancel or alter contracts already made by the owners.[2] Thus, he cannot alter the port of discharge or the amount of the freight.

But where the other party refuses to perform the original contract, the master may make the best arrangement possible for the employment of the ship.

Thus, in *Pearson v Goschen*[3]

The charterers became insolvent after part of the homeward cargo had been loaded. Their agents refused to load the rest of the cargo, and the master then agreed, under protest, to carry the whole homeward cargo at 30s per ton. The shipowners claimed freight at 90s per ton as originally agreed.
Held, as to the cargo shipped after the insolvency, the new agreement was valid; but as to that already on board, the original freight of 90s per ton was payable.

Where a master knew the load capacity of the ship's derrick, and that the shipper's cargo of machinery was too heavy for the derrick, but he still accepted the load, it was held that the action of the master was the effective cause of the damage to the derrick. The master's lack of authority to alter the terms of the contract of carriage did not transfer responsibility for that action from the shipowner to the shipper. Consequently the shipper was not to blame for the damage caused.[4]

The master is presumed to be the employee of the registered owner of the ship. On a change of ownership, the master's original authority and instructions are valid until he receives notice of the change; and, though the new owners may not be bound by his contracts, if they recognise his act in receiving goods on board, they must accept the terms on which he received them.[5]

---

19   Per Dr Lushington in *The Sir Henry Webb* (1849) 13 Jur 639.
20   Per Brett LJ, in *The Fanny* (1883) 48 LT 771 at 775.
 1   *Lloyd v Guibert* (1865) LR 1 QB 115.
 2   *Grant v Norway*, supra.
 3   (1864) 17 CBNS 352.
 4   *Brown and Root Ltd v Chimo Shipping Ltd* [1967] 2 Lloyd's Rep 398 (Supreme Court of Canada).
 5   Per Bramwell B, in *Mercantile Bank v Gladstone* (1868) 37 LJ Ex 130.

The master often signs bills of lading and charter-parties in his own name, without words showing that he is merely acting as agent for the owners. In such cases the other party can treat either the master or the shipowner as the person liable on the contract.

The master may himself sue on contracts made in his own name, but not where he acted merely as the employee of the owner.

Thus, in *Repetto v Millar's Karri and Jarrah Forests Ltd*[6]

The charter-party provided that the master should sign bills of lading and these incorporated the terms of the charter-party.
Held, that he could not sue the charterers for freight. His signature of the bills of lading was not a fresh contract, but merely a means of carrying out the charter-party.

The master may bind the shipowner or charterer by doing such things as are necessary on the part of the one or of the other to carry out the contract. Such necessaries for the voyage as the shipowner is bound by the contract to provide must, if purchased by the master on his behalf, be paid for by him, as also must such necessaries as were needed in order that the ship might sail, where it was in the shipowner's interest that the ship should sail;[7] and the charterer is similarly liable *mutatis mutandis*.[8]

But where the master has not disclosed to the suppliers of necessaries that under an existing time charter-party the charterer is liable for the particular disbursements in question, the shipowner will be liable to such suppliers to that extent.[9] The term 'necessaries' has a wide meaning, extending even to quay rent and the cost of destroying putrid cargo where the ship is liable for such charges, and could be prevented from sailing for their non-payment.[10]

In the tanker trade there is a general practice of masters being required to sign and signing documents relating to the use of jetties and berths, and having implied authority to bind the shipowners thereby to pay for any damage caused to the jetties or berths by the vessels using them.[11]

The mere presence of the owners' authorised agents, even where

---

6 [1901] 2 KB 306.
7 *The Turgot* (1886) 11 PD 21.
8 *The Beeswing* (1885) 53 LT 554.
9 *The Tolla* [1921] P 22.
10 *The Arzpeitia* (1921) 126 LT 29.
11 *Bahamas Oil Refining Co v Kristiansands Tankrederie A/S and Shell International Marine Ltd, The Polyduke* [1978] 1 Lloyd's Rep 211. (See the judgment of Kerr J, ibid, at 215.)

the owners are domiciled abroad and the agents are in England, does not oust the authority of the master to make disbursements.[12]

Again, the master may, if nobody presents a bill of lading or offers to give an indemnity in its place, land cargo on arrival, or, if prevented from so doing by the port authorities, may (and indeed it is his duty to[13]) deal with it as a reasonable man would, with a view to protecting the shipowner's interests by preserving the lien for freight, and in the best interest of the cargo-owner.[14]

His authority to bind the shipowner by admissions in the bill of lading has already been noted.[15]

The master has certain statutory powers of landing goods in the United Kingdom under the Merchant Shipping Act 1894.[16]

He is entitled to jettison dangerous goods or destroy them or render them innocuous.[17]

His authority in extraordinary circumstances

(a) THE PRINCIPLES INVOLVED

In cases of emergency the master may become the agent of the cargo-owners to take special measures to preserve the cargo or to minimise the loss arising from damage which has already been suffered. Such emergency only arises, however, when extraordinary action is necessary, and communication with his principals, whether they are the shipowners or the cargo-owners, is impracticable.

Here, again, the standard set up by the law is the same as holds good in other cases; ie action will be deemed to have been necessary when, in the interests of the whole of the adventure of the principals concerned, it would have appeared to a reasonable and prudent man to be so.[18]

The master's authority to act in the interests of the cargo-owner is part of his general authority as the employee of the shipowner, and

---

12 *The Equator* (1921) 152 LT Jo 259.
13 See p 266, post.
14 *Erichsen v Barkworth* (1858) 3 H & N 894; *Cargo ex Argos* (1873) 42 LJ Adm 1.
15 See pp 84–92, ante.
16 Sections 492–501 (see Appendix D, post).
17 Merchant Shipping Act 1894, ss 446–50 (see Appendix D, post): Carriage of Goods by Sea Act 1971, Sch, Art IV, r 6 (see Appendix E, post).
18 *Atlantic Mutual Insurance Co v Huth* (1880) 16 ChD 474.

therefore the shipowner will be liable if the master abuses his powers.

Thus, if the master improperly jettisons goods, the shipowner will be liable; for such an act is within the scope of his functions as the employee of the shipowner.[19]

But the master has no authority to take extraordinary measures for the cargo-owner if the latter or his representative can be communicated with.[20] If this can be done, he must obtain instructions from the owner of the goods and must obey them.[1] Where the charterer and the shipowner agreed on instructions which were ambiguous and were misinterpreted in good faith by the master, it was held that the charterer could not hold the shipowner liable.[2]

Further, supposing unforeseen circumstances to have arisen, if the master delays unreasonably before deciding on what action he must take, and the cargo suffers from such delay, the shipowner will be liable to the cargo-owners for the damage, for it is part of the *duty* of the master, as agent of the shipowner, to take all reasonable precautions to preserve the cargo.[3]

(b) EXAMPLES OF EXTRAORDINARY ACTION

Such extraordinary action as may be taken under this principle is as follows:

(1) *Action affecting the whole adventure:*

(i) Delay and/or deviation from proper route.[4]

(ii) Hypothecation of ship and cargo by giving a bottomry bond.[5]

The authority of the master to hypothecate the ship and cargo is a general rule of maritime law. Brett LJ explained it in this way:[6]

'It arises from the necessity of things; it arises from the obligation of the shipowner and the master to carry the goods from one country to another, and from it being

---

19 See e g *Federal Commerce and Navigation Co Ltd v Eisenerz GmbH, The Oak Hill* [1975] 1 Lloyd's Rep 105, Supreme Court of Canada, where the master in unloading the cargo after the vessel had stranded was held to be representing the shipowner but still to have an overriding duty to care for the cargo.
20 *Cargo ex Argos* (1873) 42 LJ Adm 1 at 56.
1 *Acatos v Burns* (1878) 47 LJ Ex 566.
2 *Miles v Haslehurst & Co* (1906) 12 Com Cas 83.
3 *Hansen v Dunn* (1906) 11 Com Cas 100.
4 See pp 21–24, ante.
5 *The Karnak* (1869) LR 2 PC 505. It is to be noticed, however, that at the present day bottomry bonds are virtually obsolete.
6 *The Gaetano and Maria* (1882) 7 PD 137 at 145.

inevitable from the nature of things that the ship and cargo may at some time or other be in a strange port where the captain may be without means, and where the shipowner may have no credit because he is not known there, that, for the safety of all concerned and for the carrying out of the ultimate object of the whole adventure, there must be a power in the master not only to hypothecate the ship but the cargo.'

The purpose of a bottomry bond is to enable the ship to complete the voyage. If she does not arrive at her destination, the lender loses his money. Consequently where several bonds have been given, a later bond takes priority over an earlier one. The later bond is given at a time of necessity when the earlier one would otherwise be frustrated, and the later bond is therefore entitled to be satisfied before the bond of earlier date.

A bottomry bond confers on the person advancing money under it a maritime lien on the ship, freight and cargo.[7]

The cargo cannot be resorted to in satisfaction of a bottomry bond unless the ship and freight are insufficient to satisfy the charge. If it was unnecessary to charge the cargo at all, the bottomry bond will be invalid as against the cargo-owner. Where expenditure is incurred for repairs to the ship of a more extensive character than were necessary, the bond will be valid against the cargo only to the extent to which such repairs were necessary for the purpose of the voyage.[8]

(iii) Conclusion of a salvage agreement.[9]

(iv) General average sacrifices and expenditure.[10]

(v) Sale of ship and cargo.[11]

(2) *Action affecting the cargo only*

(i) Sale of damaged goods at a port of call.[12]

Purchasers of a cargo from the master of a ship do not get a good title 'unless it is established that the master used all reasonable efforts to have the goods conveyed to their destination, and that he could not by any means available to him carry the goods, or procure the goods to be carried, to their destination as merchantable articles, or could not do so without an expenditure clearly exceeding their value after their arrival at their destination'.[13]

7   See chapter 12, post.
8   *The Onward* (1873) 42 LJ Adm 61 at 70.
9   *The Renpor* (1883) 8 PD 115.
10   See chapter 9.
11   But see *Cannan v Meaburn* (1823) 1 Bing 243.
12   *Australasian Steam Navigation Co v Morse* (1872) LR 4 PC 222.
13   Per Cotton LJ, in *Atlantic Mutual Insurance Co v Huth*, supra, at 481.

The fundamental rule that the master's authority to act for the cargo-owner arises from necessity, and cannot be exercised if the cargo-owner can be communicated with, is applied here with strictness.

Thus, in *Acatos v Burns*[14]

A cargo of maize which had become heated was sold at an intermediate port. The jury found that it was impossible to carry the cargo to its destination and that a sale was prudent under the circumstances, but that the necessity for a sale was not so urgent as to prevent communication with the cargo-owner.

Held, the shipowner was liable to the cargo-owner for selling without his consent. Baggallay LJ said: 'In order to justify the sale under the circumstances, there must be not only an absolute necessity but an inability to communicate with the owner of the cargo'.[15]

(ii) Transhipment of the cargo.[16]

(iii) Conclusion of a salvage agreement, where the ship herself is not in danger but only the cargo, or part of it.

(iv) General average sacrifices and expenditure, eg jettison.[17]

(v) Reconditioning of damaged goods, eg by landing them to dry them when one of the holds is flooded.

(vi) Hypothecation of the cargo by giving a respondentia bond.[18]

But the master has no authority to charge the cargo for such an advance unless the interests of the cargo-owner require it, and the ship and freight are an insufficient security for the sum required,[19] and he cannot obtain the necessary money in any other way.

The charge created by a respondentia bond becomes payable only in the event of the ship's safe arrival. If the ship is lost, the loan is not recoverable.

It is essential to the validity of a bottomry[20] or respondentia bond that a maritime risk should be involved, but the fact that the loan has been insured does not affect the character of the bond.[1]

A respondentia bond confers on the person advancing the money a maritime lien on the cargo only.[2]

14 (1878) 47 LJ Ex 566.
15 Ibid, at 568.
16 *The Soblomsten* (1866) LR 1 A & E 293.
17 As to general average sacrifice and general average expenditure, see pp 227–233, post.
18 *See Cargo ex Sultan* (1859) Sw 504.
19 *The Onward* (1873) 42 LJ Adm 61.
20 *The Indomitable* (1859) Sw 446.
1 See *The Dora Forster* [1900] P 241.
2 See chapter 12, pp 277–290, post.

Chapter 9

General average

It is necessary to distinguish between particular and general average. A person is entitled to a general average contribution if certain requirements are fulfilled. A general average loss consists of a general average sacrifice or a general average expenditure. Damage done to the property of third parties may be the subject of general average. When a claim for a general average contribution is made, it has to be adjusted.

PARTICULAR AND GENERAL AVERAGE

The invariable result of a particular average is that the loss falls on the owner of the particular property which has suffered the damage, whether that damage was due to a deliberate sacrifice or to an accident. Thus, if owing to heating, it becomes necessary to sell the cargo at an intermediate port, the cargo-owner will have to bear the loss arising from such a sale. The same principle applies to extraordinary expenditure during the voyage. If, owing to bad weather, the ship has to put in for repairs, the expense of such repairs must be borne by the shipowner.

But where the ship and cargo are exposed to a common danger and some part of the cargo or of the ship is intentionally sacrificed, or extra expenditure is incurred, to avert that danger, such loss or expenditure will be the subject of a general average contribution. It will be apportioned between ship and cargo in proportion to their salved values. This is a very ancient rule of maritime law. It found its way from the law of Rhodes into the Digest of Justinian, and through the usage of commerce it has become a part of the Common law of England.

Usually a clause is inserted in the contract of carriage incorporating the York–Antwerp Rules, which are a standard set of rules relating to general average. The name, 'York–Antwerp', is derived from the places where conferences were held which brought the Rules into existence. The title 'York–Antwerp' was first given to Rules formulated in 1877. They have been revised on several occasions, and the present ones are those of 1974.[1] But they do not constitute a complete or self-contained code and need to be supplemented by bringing into the gaps provisions of the general law which are applicable to the contract.[2]

The Carriage of Goods by Sea Act 1971 expressly provides that nothing therein 'shall be held to prevent the insertion in a bill of lading of any lawful provision regarding general average'.[3]

CONDITIONS FOR GENERAL AVERAGE CONTRIBUTION

For a sacrifice or expenditure to be the subject of general average contribution[4] the following conditions must obtain:

(1) THERE MUST BE A DANGER COMMON TO THE WHOLE ADVENTURE

The danger must be, in fact, a real one, not merely imagined to exist by the master, however reasonable such fear may be.[5]

Thus, in *Nesbitt v Lushington*[6]

A ship was stranded on the coast of Ireland during a period of great scarcity of food.

---

1 See Appendix G.
2 *Goulandris Bros Ltd v B Goldman & Sons Ltd* [1958] 1 QB 74, [1957] 3 All ER 100; *Federal Commerce and Navigation Co Ltd v Eisenerz GmbH, The Oak Hill* [1975] 1 Lloyd's Rep 105, Supreme Court of Canada, where Ritchie J, said (ibid, at 110): 'It would, in my opinion, be wrong to assume that . . . the York–Antwerp Rules are to be treated as a code governing the rights of the parties concerned to the exclusion of other rights and obligations created by the contract of carriage'.
3 Sch, Art V (see Appendix E, post).
4 A claim for a general average contribution is barred after 6 years from the date of the occurrence of the general average loss: *Chandris v Argo Insurance Co Ltd* [1963] 2 Lloyd's Rep 65, QBD (Commercial Court). The period of limitation does not run from the time when the general average statement is completed: ibid. See further, *Arthur L Liman as trustee in bankruptcy of A H Bull SS Co v India Supply Mission, The Beatrice* [1975] 1 Lloyd's Rep 220, District Court, Southern District of New York.
5 Per Brett LJ, in *Whitecross Wire Co Ltd v Savill* (1882) 8 QBD 653 at 662. See also *Watson & Sons Ltd v Firemen's Fund Insurance Co of San Francisco* [1922] 2 KB 355.
6 (1792) 4 Term Rep 783.

The inhabitants compelled the captain to sell wheat, which was on board, at less than its value. As they intended no injury to the vessel, there was no common danger.
Held, that this was not a general average loss.

But the fact that a part of the cargo has already been discharged will not preclude the owners of the rest, under all circumstances, from claiming a general average contribution from the shipowner.

Thus, in *Whitecross Wire Co Ltd v Savill*[7]

When most of the cargo had been discharged, a fire broke out on the ship, and the remainder of the cargo was damaged by water used in putting out the fire.
Held, that the shipowner must contribute in respect of the damage.

But under the York–Antwerp Rules 1974 it is sufficient if 'the extraordinary sacrifice or expenditure ... is ... reasonably made ...'.[8]

(2) THE SACRIFICE OR EXPENDITURE MUST BE REAL AND INTENTIONAL

Where the thing abandoned is already lost, there is no real sacrifice, and consequently no claim for contribution, e g cutting away a mast which is already virtually useless.[9]

But in *Johnson v Chapman*[10]

Deck cargo had broken loose in a storm so that it was a source of danger, and interfered with the working of the pumps.
Held, that the cargo was not virtually lost and its jettison amounted to a real sacrifice.

Under the York–Antwerp Rules 1974 the sacrifice or expenditure must be 'intentionally' made.[11] They also provide that 'loss or damage caused by cutting away wreck or parts of the ship which have been previously carried away or are effectively lost by accident shall not be made good as general average'.[12]

(3) THE SACRIFICE OR EXPENDITURE MUST BE NECESSARY

Generally the duty of deciding whether a sacrifice or expenditure is necessary rests with the master of the ship. But it is sufficient if the

---

7 Supra.
8 Rule A. See e g *Federal Commerce and Navigation Co Ltd v Eisenerz GmbH, The Oak Hill*, supra, where the master's decision to unload the cargo after the vessel had stranded was held to be reasonable and made for the benefit of the ship and cargo alike.
9 *Shepherd v Kottgen* (1877) 2 CPD 585.
10 (1865) 19 CBNS 563; Chorley and Tucker's *Leading Cases* (4th edn 1962), p 309.
11 Rule A.
12 Rule IV.

actual order is given by some other person, provided that the master sanctions it.

Thus, in *The Birkhall and Jeronica v Grampian SS Co Ltd*[13]

A fire broke out on board, and the master put into port. The fire increased, and the harbour master ordered that the ship should be scuttled. The master believed this course to be best in the interests of ship and cargo, so he raised no objection.

Held, that he had sanctioned the scuttling of the ship, and that the loss constituted a general average sacrifice.

(4) THE DANGER MUST NOT HAVE ARISEN THROUGH THE FAULT OF THE PERSON CLAIMING CONTRIBUTION, WHERE SUCH FAULT WOULD EXPOSE SUCH PERSON TO LEGAL LIABILITY FOR THE DAMAGE DONE

In order to prevent a person recovering a general average contribution on the ground that he was at fault, the fault must be something which constitutes an actionable wrong.

Accordingly, a shipowner cannot claim a general average contribution where he allowed a vessel to sail with smoke in her holds[14] or where she was unseaworthy on sailing[15] or the cargo had not been properly stowed.[16]   On the other hand, in *Greenshields, Cowie & Co v Stephens & Sons Ltd*[17]

During the voyage, a cargo of coal caught fire through spontaneous combustion.

Held, the shippers were entitled to a general average contribution from the shipowner in respect of damage to the coal in extinguishing the fire. There had been no negligence on the part of the shippers, and it was assumed that both parties were equally familiar with the liability of coal to spontaneous combustion in a climate like that of India.

13   (1896) 1 Com Cas 448.
14   *Gesellschaft fur Getreidchandel AG, Hugo Mathes and Schurr KG, Herman Schrader, E Kamffmeyer, Jurt A Becher, Getreide-Import Gesellschaft mbH v The Texas and Wilh Wilhemsen, The Texas* [1970] 1 Lloyd's Rep 175, District Court, Eastern District of New Orleans Division. (See the judgment of Cassibry DJ, ibid, at 176.)
15   *Diestelskamp v Baynes (Reading) Ltd, The Aga* [1968] 1 Lloyd's Rep 431, QBD (Commercial Court); *Wirth Ltd v SS Acadia Forest and Lash Barge CG 204, The Acadia Forest* [1974] 2 Lloyd's Rep 563, District Court, Eastern District of Louisiana; *United States of America v Eastmount Shipping Corpn, The Susquehanna* [1975] 1 Lloyd's Rep 216, District Court, Southern District of New York, where there were insufficient bunkers for the intended journey (see the judgment of Frankel DJ, ibid, at 219); *E B Aaby's Rederi A/S v Union of India, The Evje (No 2)* [1978] 1 Lloyd's Rep 351, CA, where the vessel had insufficient bunkers at the start of the voyage and broke down and had to be towed into port.
16   *Gemini Navigation Inc v Philipp Bros Division of Minerals and Chemicals, Philipp Corpn and Royal Insurance Co Ltd, The Ionic Bay* [1975] 1 Lloyd's Rep 287, US Court of Appeals, Second Circuit. (See the judgment of Waterman Ct J, ibid, at 294–295.)
17   [1908] AC 431.

Similarly, where the main engines of a vessel broke down due to the contamination of some lubricating oil, it was held that the shipowners were entitled to claim a general average contribution, for they had discharged the burden of proving due diligence by submitting oil samples for analysis and by receiving satisfactory reports on the oil.[18]

But where the contract of carriage makes certain exceptions to the liability which would otherwise fall on one of the parties, it prevents the grounds of such liability being imputed as a fault to the party in whose favour the exceptions are made.

Hence, if negligence of the shipowner is excepted in the contract, he can recover in respect of loss or expense incurred for the common safety even though his negligence made the loss or expense necessary.[19]

So also, where a general average sacrifice is incurred by reason of fire due to unseaworthiness, if the shipowner can invoke the Merchant Shipping Act 1979, s 18(1),[20] so as to avoid liability for the fire, he can recover a general average contribution.[1]

Again, a shipowner, who has deviated[2] from the contractual route, can still claim a general average contribution from the holder of a bill of lading which is subject to the Hague Rules[3] if the deviation is a 'reasonable' one within the meaning of Art IV, r 4[4] of the Rules.[5]

The 'amended Jason clause' should be inserted in all bills of lading for voyages to and from the United States. The necessity for it arises because of an important difference between American law and English law.

Briefly, the history of the subject in the United States is as follows. The Harter Act 1893, s 3, provides that if a shipowner exercises due care to make his vessel seaworthy, neither he, the vessel, her agent,

---

18 *Jugoslavenska Oceanska Plovidba v American Smelting and Refining Co, The Admiral Zmajevic* [1983] 2 Lloyd's Rep 86, QBD (Commercial Court). (See the judgment of Lloyd J, ibid, at 90.)
19 *The Carron Park* (1890) 15 PD 203; *Milburn v Jamaica Fruit Co* [1900] 2 QB 540; *Federal Commerce and Navigation Co Ltd v Eisenerz GmbH, The Oak Hill* [1975] 1 Lloyd's Rep 105, Supreme Court of Canada, where the charter-party exempted the shipowners from liability for loss caused by negligent navigation.
20 See p 201, ante, and Appendix D, post.
1 *Louis Dreyfus & Co v Tempus Shipping Co* [1931] AC 726.
2 As to deviation, see pp 21–24, ante.
3 See pp 95–98, ante.
4 See pp 117–118, ante.
5 *Danae Shipping Corpn v TPAO and Guven Turkish Insurance Co, The Daffodil B* [1983] 1 Lloyd's Rep 498, QBD (Commercial Court).

nor her charterer is liable for damage or loss arising from (inter alia) faults or errors in navigation, or in the management of the vessel. After this Act was passed, it was assumed that since it exempted a shipowner from liability for losses arising from negligent navigation, he was entitled to recover in general average for the ship's sacrifices which had minimised the greater loss for which he was now relieved from liability.[6]

Nevertheless, the Supreme Court of the United States held in *The Irrawaddy*[7] that the exemption in the Act did *not* entitle a shipowner to claim a contribution for a general average loss due to the negligence of his servants.

In English law there is not, and never has been, any rule corresponding with that laid down in *The Irrawaddy*. To overcome the difficulty, it became usual to insert a clause in bills of lading for vessels trading to and from the United States, expressly declaring that the shipowner could recover in general average in the event of negligence, provided that due diligence had been exercised to make the ship in all respects seaworthy. The legality of the clause was questioned, and it was eventually decided by the Supreme Court of the United States in *The Jason*[8] that the clause was valid.

Thereafter it became known as the 'Jason clause'. Subsequent decisions[9] necessitated certain changes in the drafting of the clause. The one now in use is generally called the 'amended Jason clause' and states as follows:

'In the event of accident, danger, damage or disaster before or after commencement of the voyage resulting from any cause whatsoever, whether due to negligence or not,

6 Lowndes and Rudolf's *Law of General Average and the York–Antwerp Rules* (10th edn 1975), para 84.
7 (1897) 171 US 187.
8 (1912) 225 US 32.
9 For details, see Lowndes and Rudolf, op cit, para 84, footnote 29. See also *Drew Brown Ltd v Orient Trader and Owners, The Orient Trader* [1973] 2 Lloyd's Rep 174, Supreme Court of Canada; *Gemini Navigation Inc v Philipp Bros Division of Minerals and Chemicals, Philipp Corpn and Royal Insurance Co Ltd, The Ionic Bay* [1975] 1 Lloyd's Rep 287, United States Court of Appeals, Second Circuit, where it was held the shipowners were not entitled to a general average contribution in respect of the expenses of the restowage of a cargo which they had stowed improperly; *E B Aaby's Rederi A/S v Union of India, The Evje (No 2)* [1978] 1 Lloyd's Rep 351, CA, where the vessel was unseaworthy by reason of insufficient bunkers at the beginning of the voyage; *The Hellenic Glory* [1979] 1 Lloyd's Rep 424, District Court for the Southern District of New York, where the vessel sustained engine failure caused by the negligence of the crew, and the shipowners were held to have failed to make her seaworthy before the commencement of the voyage.

for which or the consequence of which the Carrier is not responsible by statute, contract or otherwise, the cargo, shippers, consignees or owners of the cargo shall contribute with the Carrier in General Average to the payment of any sacrifices, losses or expenses of a General Average nature that may be made or incurred, and shall pay salvage and special charges incurred in respect of the cargo. If a salving ship is owned or operated by the Carrier, salvage shall be paid for as fully as if the salving ship or ships belong to strangers.'

But suppose goods have been jettisoned to avert a common danger caused by negligent navigation: can the owners of those goods claim against the owners of the rest of the cargo? It has been decided that they can.[10] The owners of the jettisoned goods 'were not privy to the master's fault and were under no duty, legal or moral, to make a gratuitous sacrifice of their goods for the sake of others to avert the consequences of his fault'.[11]   The York–Antwerp Rules 1974 provide that,

'Rights to contribution in general average shall not be affected though the event which gave rise to the sacrifice or expenditure may have been due to the fault of one of the parties to the adventure; but this shall not prejudice any remedies or defences which may be open against or to that party in respect of such fault.'[12]

The effect of the first part of the Rule is that the average adjustment is compiled on the assumption that the casualty has not been caused by anybody's fault.[13] The second part operates as a proviso qualifying the first part. The rights may be nullified or defeated or diminished or otherwise affected by the remedies.[14] For this purpose a 'fault' is a legal wrong which is actionable as between the parties at the time when the general average sacrifice or expenditure is made.[15]

(5) THE PROPERTY WHICH WAS IN DANGER MUST HAVE BEEN ACTUALLY BENEFITED BY THE SACRIFICE[16]

(6) ONLY DIRECT LOSSES ARE RECOVERABLE

The York–Antwerp Rules 1974 provide that:[17]

10   *Strang, Steel & Co v Scott & Co* (1889) 14 App Cas 601.
11   Per Lord Watson, ibid, at 609.
12   Rule D. *Westfal-Larsen & Co A/S v Colonial Sugar Refining Co Ltd* [1960] 2 Lloyd's Rep 206 (Supreme Court of New South Wales).
13   *Goulandris Bros Ltd v B Goldman & Sons Ltd* [1958] 1 QB 74, [1957] 3 All ER 100; *Federal Commerce and Navigation Co Ltd v Eisenerz GmbH, The Oak Hill* [1975] 1 Lloyd's Rep 105, Supreme Court of Canada.
14   *Goulandris Bros Ltd v B Goldman & Sons Ltd*, supra, at 106 and 93.
15   Ibid, at 114 and 104.
16   *Pirie & Co v Middle Dock Co* (1881) 44 LT 426. See also *Chellew v Royal Commission on the Sugar Supply* [1922] 1 KB 12.
17   Rule C. See p 233, post.

'Only such losses, damages or expenses which are the direct consequence of the general average act shall be allowed as general average.

Loss or damage sustained by the ship or cargo through delay, whether on the voyage or subsequently, such as demurrage,[18] and any indirect loss whatsoever, such as loss of market, shall not be admitted as general average.'

GENERAL AVERAGE SACRIFICE

There are three interests involved in a maritime venture—the cargo, the ship, and the freight. Consequently, a general average sacrifice may arise from:

(1) *Sacrifice of cargo*

The commonest instance of a general average sacrifice is jettison. The mere washing overboard of part of the cargo will not give rise to a general average contribution: nor will the throwing overboard of cargo by the crew or passengers out of private malice.

To give rise to a general average contribution, the cargo jettisoned must have been stowed in a proper place. Generally it is not proper to stow cargo on deck; and, in the absence of a special custom or the consent of the other interests in the adventure, the owner of deck cargo has no claim for a general average contribution if it is jettisoned.[19]

If the shipowner has agreed to receive deck cargo, the ship and freight must contribute to the loss, provided the owner of the jettisoned goods is the sole cargo-owner. But where there are other cargo-owners who have not consented to the stowing on deck, no contribution can be obtained from them or from the shipowner.[20]

But where goods are stowed on deck without the shipper's consent, the shipowner is alone responsible for their loss by jettison, because he has placed them in a dangerous position in breach of his undertaking to carry them safely.[1]

Again, cargo may sometimes have to be used as fuel to keep the engines and pumps going, where the ship has been delayed by a hurricane; or damage may be done to the cargo by pouring water on to it to extinguish a fire. In both cases the damage is a general average sacrifice.

---

18 As to demurrage, see chapter 10.
19 *Strang v Scott* (1889) 14 App Cas 601 at 608.
20 *Wright v Marwood* (1881) 7 QBD 62.
1 *Royal Exchange Shipping Co v Dixon* (1886) 12 App Cas 11.

The York–Antwerp Rules 1974 provide that

'No jettison of cargo shall be made good as general average unless such cargo is carried in accordance with the recognised custom of the trade.'[2]

'Damage done to a ship and cargo, or either of them, by or in consequence of a sacrifice made for the common safety, and by water which goes down a ship's hatches opened or other opening made for the purpose of making a jettison for the common safety, shall be made good as general average.'[3]

'Damage done to a ship and cargo, or either of them, by water or otherwise, including damage by beaching or scuttling a burning ship, in extinguishing a fire on board the ship, shall be made good as general average; except that no compensation shall be made for damage by smoke or heat however caused.'[4]

(2) *Sacrifice of ship or tackle*

Where any sacrifice of the ship, her stores or tackle is necessary to avert a common danger, it will be the subject of a general average contribution, unless it was incurred in fulfilling the shipowner's original contract to carry the goods safely to their destination.

All *ordinary* losses sustained by the ship must be borne by the shipowner. But sacrifices to meet the particular emergency, such as loss of the ship's tackle through using it for unusual purposes in order to secure her safety in specially difficult circumstances, will be the subject of a general average contribution.[5]

Similarly, where spare parts were cut up for fuel to keep a pump going, their value was held to be the subject of contribution, because this was not the use they were intended for and the ship would have gone down if the pumping had not been maintained.[6]

But where the tackle is insufficient for the ordinary needs of the ship, the shipowner cannot claim in respect of things destroyed to make up the deficiency.

If the ship is in danger of sinking, and the master deliberately runs her ashore for the purpose of saving the cargo and possibly also the ship, the loss of or damage to the ship is probably a general average sacrifice. The difficulty lies in the fact that, if the ship is practically certain to go down, there is no real sacrifice in stranding her.[7]

Still, the policy of the Courts is to encourage the master to act

2   Rule I.
3   Rule II.
4   Rule III.
5   See *Birkley v Presgrave* (1801) 1 East 220.
6   *Harrison v Bank of Australasia* (1872) LR 7 Exch 39.
7   See *Shepherd v Kottgen* (1877) 2 CPD 585.

impartially in the interest of *all* concerned, and to hold otherwise would be to encourage him to hazard the ship and the cargo in preference to incurring certain damage to the ship by stranding her to save the cargo. 'It would defeat the main utility of general average if at a moment of emergency the captain's mind were to hesitate as to saving the adventure through fear of casting a burden on his owners.'[8]

The York–Antwerp Rules 1974 provide that,

'When a ship is intentionally run on shore for the common safety, whether or not she might have been driven on shore, the consequent loss or damage shall be allowed in general average.'[9]

'Damage caused to any machinery and boilers of a ship which is ashore and in a position of peril, in endeavouring to refloat, shall be allowed in general average when shown to have arisen from an actual intention to float the ship for the common safety at the risk of such damage; but where a ship is afloat no loss or damage caused by working the propelling machinery and boilers shall in any circumstances be made good as general average.'[10]

'When a ship is ashore and cargo and ship's fuel and stores or any of them are discharged as a general average act, the extra cost of lightening, lighter hire and reshipping if incurred and the loss or damage sustained thereby, shall be admitted as general average.'[11]

'Ship's materials and stores, or any of them, necessarily burnt for fuel for the common safety at a time of peril shall be admitted as general average, when and only when an ample supply of fuel had been provided; but the estimated quantity of fuel that would have been consumed calculated at the price current at the ship's last port of departure at the date of her leaving, shall be credited to the general average.'[12]

(3) *Sacrifice of freight*

Where freight is payable on delivery, a jettison of the goods involves not only sacrifice of the goods themselves but also a loss of the freight on them. Accordingly, the person to whom the freight would have been payable, whether charterer or shipowner, is entitled to claim a contribution from the owners of the interests saved.

Thus, in *Pirie & Co v Middle Dock Co*[13]

Cargo damaged by a general average sacrifice had to be discharged at an intermediate port.

8   Per Grove J, in *Shepherd v Kottgen*, supra, at 69.
9   Rule V.
10   Rule VII.
11   Rule VIII.
12   Rule IX.
13   (1881) 44 LT 426.

Held, that a general average contribution was due from the cargo-owner in respect of the freight thus lost.

But where freight is payable in advance, it does not depend on the safe arrival of the goods, and a claim to a general average contribution in respect of freight cannot arise.

The York–Antwerp Rules 1974 provide that,

'Loss of freight arising from damage to or loss of cargo shall be made good as general average, either when caused by a general average act, or when the damage to or loss of cargo is made good. Deduction shall be made from the amount of gross freight lost of the charges which the owner thereof would have incurred to earn such freight, but has, in consequence of the sacrifice, not incurred.'[14]

GENERAL AVERAGE EXPENDITURE

Where extraordinary expenditure is incurred for the purpose of avoiding a common danger which threatens the ship and the cargo, such expenditure is the subject of a general average contribution in the same way as a loss voluntarily incurred by a sacrifice of the ship, cargo, or freight.

At the same time, it must be borne in mind that the shipowner is under an obligation to defray such expenditure as may be necessary to complete the voyage. It is sometimes difficult to determine whether expenditure is the subject of a general average contribution or has been incurred merely in fulfilment of the contractual obligation of the shipowner.

Payments for salvage services may or may not be general average expenditure. The liability to pay salvage attaches to the property saved in proportion to its value in the same way as general average claims attach. Where expenditure is incurred in saving both ship and cargo, eg in refloating a ship which has sunk or gone aground with her cargo, this is treated as a general average expenditure.[15]

But where the cargo has been safely discharged and further operations are directed to getting the ship afloat and towing her into a port for repairs, the further expenditure thus incurred will fall on the shipowner alone.[16]

The York–Antwerp Rules 1974 state that

14 Rule XV.
15 *Kemp v Halliday* (1865) 34 LJQB 233.
16 *Job v Langton* (1856) 26 LJQB 97.

'Expenditure incurred by the parties to the adventure on account of salvage, whether under contract or otherwise, shall be allowed in general average to the extent that the salvage operations were undertaken for the purpose of preserving from peril the property involved in the common maritime adventure.'[17]

When a ship puts into a port of refuge to repair damage done *by a general average sacrifice*, the cost of repairing the ship, together with other charges incidental thereto, is the subject of general average.[18] Such incidental charges would include the cost of reloading the cargo if it had to be unloaded in order to effect the repairs.

But this is not the case where the damage to be repaired arises in the ordinary course of the voyage.

Thus, in *Svendsen v Wallace Bros*[19]

A ship sprang a leak under no special stress of weather beyond the ordinary perils of the sea. Acting for the safety of the whole adventure, the master put into a port of refuge for repairs. It was necessary to unload the cargo in order to effect the repairs.
Held, the expenses of entering the port and of discharging the cargo were general average expenditure; but the warehousing charges, the expenses of the repairs, the cost of reloading the goods and the pilotage and harbour dues on leaving the port were not general average expenditure, because when they were incurred, the adventure was no longer in danger.[20]

Where by reason of an impending peril it has become unsafe for the ship and cargo to continue the voyage, deviation to a port of refuge is a general average act. But if the deviation was rendered necessary by the unseaworthiness of the ship, the shipowner cannot recover general average contributions in respect of the port of refuge expenses.[1]

Furthermore, it has been held that deviation ordered by the Admiralty for strategic reasons in wartime does not amount to a general average act, because the masters of the vessels obeying the order had no opportunity of exercising their own judgment or discretion.[2]

But unjustified deviation will debar the shipowner from claiming a general contribution, unless the cargo-owner has elected to affirm the contract.[3]

---

17 Rule VI.
18 *Atwood v Sellar & Co* (1880) 5 QBD 286.
19 (1885) 10 App Cas 404.
20 It is important to note that this Common Law rule does not apply in cases where the York–Antwerp Rules operate. See Rule X, p 232 and Appendix G, post.
1 *Schloss v Heriot* (1863) 14 CBNS 59.
2 *Athel Line Ltd v Liverpool and London War Risks Insurance Association Ltd* [1944] 1 KB 87, [1944] 1 All ER 46.
3 *Hain SS Co Ltd v Tate and Lyle Ltd* [1936] 2 All ER 597.

The master of a ship may incur general average expenditure as agent of the ship alone or as agent also of the cargo-owners.

Thus, in *Morrison SS Co Ltd v SS Greystoke Castle (Cargo Owners)*[4]

Two ships collided, one being one-fourth to blame and the other three-fourths. The latter had to put into port, and a general average expenditure was incurred. The owners of the cargo on that ship became liable to their shipowners for a general average contribution, and brought an action against the owners of the other ship, claiming (inter alia) one-fourth of this contribution.

Held, that the claim succeeded. The obligation of the cargo-owners to contribute to general average expenditure arose from the act of the master in incurring that expenditure on their behalf. If the cargo-owners had been merely liable to indemnify their shipowners, only the latter could have sued.

Under the York–Antwerp Rules 1974,

'When a ship shall have entered a port or place of refuge, or shall have returned to her port or place of loading in consequence of accident, sacrifice or other extraordinary circumstances which render that necessary for the common safety, the expenses of entering such port or place shall be admitted as general average; and when she shall have sailed thence with her original cargo, or part of it, the corresponding expenses of leaving such port or place consequent upon such entry or return shall likewise be admitted as general average.'[5]

Further, they state that,

'The cost of handling on board or discharging cargo, fuel or stores whether at a port or place of loading, call or refuge, shall be admitted as general average when the handling or discharge was necessary for the common safety or to enable damage to the ship caused by sacrifice or accident to be repaired, if the repairs were necessary for the safe prosecution of the voyage.'[6]

The wages and maintenance of the crew and other expenses incurred in entering the port of refuge and in staying there are also allowed as a general average expenditure under the Rules.[7]

Any extra expense incurred in place of another expense which would have been allowable as general average shall be deemed to be general average and so allowed without regard to the saving, if any, to other interests, but only up to the amount of the general expense avoided.[8]

The York–Antwerp Rules 1974 provide that,[9]

4   [1947] AC 265, [1946] 2 All ER 696.
5   Rule X(a).
6   Rule X(b).
7   Rule XI.
8   Rule F. See *Western Canada SS Co ltd v Canadian Commercial Corpn* [1960] 2 Lloyd's Rep 313 (Supreme Court of Canada) (replacement of broken tailshaft flown out by air as extra expense).
9   Rule C.

'Only such losses, damages or expenses which are the direct consequence of the general average act shall be allowed as general average.'

Thus, in *Australian Coastal Shipping Commission v Green*[10]

A vessel was in distress and a tug was employed to tow her to a port of safety. The towage contract included a clause whereby the owners of the vessel agreed to indemnify the tugowners for any loss of the tug. The tow rope parted and fouled the tug's propellers, and the tug became a total loss. The tugowners claimed damages from the owners of the vessel, who incurred expenses in defending the action.
Held, these expenses were general average expenditure, for the towage contract was a 'general average act' under Rule A of the York–Antwerp Rules 1950,[11] and the expenses were the direct consequence of such general average act.

DAMAGE DONE TO PROPERTY OF THIRD PARTIES

Damage done to the property of persons *not* concerned in the adventure can be the subject of general average.
Thus, in *Austin Friars SS Co Ltd v Spillers & Bakers Ltd*[12]

A ship had been stranded and was leaking badly. The master and pilot knew that in taking the ship into a dock they were liable to cause damage.
Held, that their action was reasonable and prudent in the interests of ship and cargo, and the damage done to the dock was the subject of general average.

---

10 [1971] QB 456, [1971] 1 All ER 353, CA. See the judgment of Lord Denning MR, ibid, at 358–359. See further, *Federal Commerce and Navigation Co Ltd v Eisenerz GmbH, The Oak Hill* [1975] 1 Lloyd's Rep 105, Supreme Court of Canada, where the expenses incurred in handling cargo which was unloaded after a vessel had stranded was held to be a 'direct consequence' of the general average act, but the negligence of the master and of the surveyors and of the stevedores who caused the damage to the cargo was not attributable to the general average act and was not the 'direct consequence' of it (see the judgment of Ritchie J, ibid, at 114); *Sea-Land Service Inc v Aetna Insurance Co, The Beauregard* [1977] 2 Lloyd's Rep 84, US Court of Appeals, Second Circuit, where a vessel, which was being towed off the rubble of a breakwater on which she had grounded, was pushed sideways by the wind, and suffered bottom damage, and the costs of towing were allowed as general average under Rule C, but not the bottom damage because it had not been shown that the shift of the vessel was the 'direct consequence' of the towing. (See the judgment of Mulligan Ct J, ibid, at 86.)
11 Now Rule A of the 1974 Rules.
12 [1915] 3 KB 586.

ADJUSTMENT OF GENERAL AVERAGE CONTRIBUTION

Unless it is specially agreed otherwise, the adjustment of the claims to contribution takes place after the conclusion of the voyage and is governed by the law of the place of delivery of the cargo.[13]

The shipowner cannot claim contribution from the cargo-owners if, after a general average expenditure has been incurred, the ship and cargo are lost before the conclusion of the voyage.[14]

The York–Antwerp Rules 1974 provide that,

'General average shall be adjusted as regards both loss and contribution upon the basis of values at the time and place when and where the adventure ends.'[15]

Further they state that,

'Repairs to be allowed in general average shall not be subject to deductions in respect of "new for old" where old material or parts are replaced by new unless the ship is over fifteen years old in which case there shall be a deduction of one-third. The deductions shall be regulated by the age of the ship from the 31st December of the year of completion of construction to the date of the general average act, except for insulation, life and similar boats, communications and navigational apparatus and equipment, machinery and boilers for which the deductions shall be regulated by the age of the particular parts to which they apply.

The deductions shall be made only from the cost of the new material or parts when finished and ready to be installed in the ship.

No deduction shall be made in respect of provisions, stores, anchors and chain cables.

Drydock and slipway dues and costs of shifting the ship shall be allowed in full.

The costs of cleaning, painting or coating of bottom shall not be allowed in general average unless the bottom has been painted or coated within the twelve months preceding the date of the general average act in which case one half of such costs shall be allowed.'[16]

They also provide that,

'The contribution to a general average shall be made upon the actual net value of the property at the termination of the adventure except that the value of cargo shall be the value at the time of discharge, ascertained from the commercial invoice rendered to the receiver or if there is no such invoice from the shipped value. The value of the cargo shall include the cost of insurance and freight unless and insofar as such freight is at the risk of interests other than the cargo, deducting therefrom any loss or damage suffered by the cargo prior to or at the time of discharge. The value of the ship shall

---

13 *Simonds v White* (1824) 2 B& C 805.
14 *Chellew v Royal Commission on the Sugar Supply* [1921] 2 KB 627; affd [1922] 1 KB 12.
15 Rule G.
16 Rule XIII.

be assessed without taking into account the beneficial or detrimental effect of any demise or time charterparty to which the ship may be committed.

To these values shall be added the amount made good as general average for property sacrificed, if not already included, deduction being made from the freight and passage money at risk of such charges and crew's wages as would not have been incurred in earning the freight had the ship and cargo been totally lost at the date of the general average act and have not been allowed as general average; deduction being also made from the value of the property of all extra charges incurred in respect thereof subsequently to the general average act, except such charges as are allowed in general average.

Where cargo is sold short of destination, however, it shall contribute upon the actual net proceeds of sale, with the addition of any amount made good as general average.

Passenger's luggage and personal effects not shipped under bill of lading shall not contribute in general average.'[17]

---

17   Rule XVII.

Chapter 10

Demurrage and despatch money

(A) DEMURRAGE

It is first necessary to define 'demurrage' and 'damages for detention' and to show the difference between them. A number of lay days are allowed to the charterer. It is important to notice when these commence, and to notice the effect of lay time being fixed. It is necessary to ascertain when loading is complete, what the rate of demurrage is, the persons by whom demurrage is payable and the accrual of the right of action for demurrage.

THE DIFFERENCE BETWEEN DEMURRAGE AND DAMAGES FOR DETENTION

A charter-party generally fixes a number of days called 'lay days' in which the ship is to be loaded or discharged, as the case may be.

'Demurrage' is a sum named in the charter-party to be paid by the charterer as *liquidated* damages for delay beyond the lay days.[1]

The shipowner is entitled to sue for 'damages for detention' if

  (i) the lay days have expired and demurrage has not been provided for; *or*

 (ii) the time for loading or discharge is not agreed, and a reasonable time for loading or discharge has expired; *or*

---

1 In the United States it has been held in *Randall v Sprague* (1896) 74 F 27 that demurrage is a form of liquidated damages payable whether or not the shipowner suffers actual damage. But later cases do not support this view: *The SS Hartismere* (1937) 18 F Supp 767; *D'Amico Mediterranean Pacific Line Inc v Proctor & Gamble Manufacturing Co, The Giovanni D'Amico* [1975] 1 Lloyd's Rep 202, District Court, Northern District of California.

(iii) demurrage is only to be paid for an agreed number of days and a further delay takes place.

In the case of a claim for 'damages for detention' the damages are *unliquidated*, i e for the Court to assess what loss has been suffered by the shipowner by his vessel being detained in port. As a general rule the measure of such damages is the rate agreed on for demurrage, if any.[2]

But where a breach of some other term of the contract, such as the obligation to load a full and complete cargo, is thereby caused, any additional damage referable to such breach may also be recovered, unless, on the true construction of the contract, the shipowner is precluded from claiming more than the agreed rate.[3]

THE NUMBER OF LAY DAYS

Where the charter-party names a number of 'days' or 'running days', these mean consecutive days including Sundays and holidays.[4] The word 'day' usually means a calendar day, and not a period of 24 hours calculated from the moment of the vessel's arrival.[5]

If the term 'working day' is used, this means the days on which work is normally done in the port,[6] and 'weather working days' are working days on which the weather allows work to be done.[7]

---

2 *Inverkip SS Co Ltd v Bunge & Co* [1917] 2 KB 193; *Suisse Atlantique Société D'Armement Maritime SA v Rotterdamsche Kolen Centrale NV* [1967] 1 AC 361, [1966] 2 All ER 61, HL.
3 *Reidar Aktieselskabet v Arcos Ltd* [1927] 1 KB 352; *Total Transport Corpn v Amoco Trading Co, The Altus* [1985] 1 Lloyd's Rep 423, QBD (Commercial Court).
4 *Nielsen v Wait* (1885) 16 QBD 67 at 72 (per Lord Esher MR).
5 *The Katy* [1895] P 56, CA.
6 *Westfal-Larsen & Co A/S v Russo-Norwegian Transport Co Ltd* (1931) 40 Ll L Rep 259; *Reardon Smith Line Ltd v Ministry of Agriculture, Fisheries and Food* [1963] AC 691, [1963] 1 All ER 545, HL; *Chief Controller of Chartering of the Government of India v Central Gulf SS Corpn* [1968] 2 Lloyd's Rep 173, QBD (Commercial Court), where it was held that Saturday in the port of Lake Charles, Louisiana, was a working although not a regular working day (see the judgment of Donaldson J, ibid, at 179); *Primula Compania Naviera SA v Finagrain Cie Commerciale Agricole et Financière SA, The Point Clear* [1975] 2 Lloyd's Rep 243, QBD (Commercial Court), where it was held that a Saturday in the port of Rotterdam counted as a lay day; *Tramp Shipping Corpn v Greenwich Marine Inc, The New Horizon* [1975] 2 Lloyd's Rep 314, CA, where it was the custom for crane and sucker drivers, if requested to do so by the stevedore companies, to work in shifts for 24 hours a day.
7 *Alvion SS Corpn of Panama v Galban Lobo Trading Co SA v Havana* [1955] 1 QB

Thus, in *Compania Naviera Azuero SA v British Oil and Cake Mills Ltd*[8]

A charter-party provided that a certain number of 'weather working days' should be allowed for discharge. There were several periods during which rain was heavy enough to stop or prevent discharge. In fact, however, no unloading was prevented, for the charterer had not planned to unload during these periods even if the weather had been fine.

Held, that in calculating the lay time deductions should be made in respect of the periods in which the rain fell, for a 'weather working day' was to be determined solely by the state of the weather on that day, although no plans had been made for working at the relevant time.[9]

A reasonable apportionment of the day must be made according to the incidence of the weather upon the length of day that the parties were working or might be expected to have been working at the time.[10] Such apportionment is entirely a question of fact.[11]

Sometimes the number of lay days allowed is not directly specified in the charter-party, but has to be calculated by reference to a daily rate of loading or discharge, eg 500 tons of the cargo per weather working day.[12]

430, [1954] 3 All ER 324; *Compania Naviera Azuero SA v British Oil and Cake Mills Ltd* [1957] 2 QB 293, [1957] 2 All ER 241; *Compania Crystal de Vapores of Panama v Herman and Mohatta (India) Ltd* [1958] 2 QB 196, [1958] 2 All ER 508; *Uglands Rederi A/S v The President of India, The Danita* [1976] 2 Lloyd's Rep 377, where it was held that the phraseology in one of the clauses in the charter-party was not such as to involve a departure from the usual meaning of 'weather working days'. (See the judgment of Mocatta J, ibid, at 381.)

8   Supra. The charter-party may provide that a certain number of weather working days are allowed but that time between 1700 hours on Friday and 0800 hours on the following Monday are not to count 'unless so used'. See *Sofial SA v Ove Skou Rederi, The Helle Skou* [1976] 2 Lloyd's Rep 205, QBD (Commercial Court).

9   But the words 'weather permitting working day' mean a working day which counts unless work is actually prevented by the weather: *Magnolia Shipping Co Ltd of Limassol v Joint Venture of the International Trading and Shipping Enterprises and Kinship Management Co Ltd of Brussels, The Camelia and Magnolia* [1978] 2 Lloyd's Rep 182, QBD (Commercial Court). (See the judgment of Brandon J, ibid, at 184.) The words '72 running hours weather permitting' mean '72 hours when the weather is of such a nature as to permit loading': *Dow Chemical (Nederland) BV v BP Tanker Co Ltd, The Vorras* [1983] 1 Lloyd's Rep 579, CA. (See the judgment of Sir John Donaldson MR, ibid, at 584.); *Gebr Broere BV v Saras Chimica SpA* [1982] 2 Lloyd's Rep 436, QBD (Commercial Court).

10   *Reardon Smith Line Ltd v Ministry of Agriculture, Fisheries and Food* [1963] AC 691, [1963] 1 All ER 545, HL.

11   Ibid.

12   See *Compania de Navigacion Zita SA v Louis Dreyfus et Compagnie* [1953] 2 All ER 1359, [1953] 1 WLR 1399, where the cargo was to be loaded 'at an average rate of not less than 150 tons per available working hatch per day'; *Lodza*

COMMENCEMENT OF THE LAY DAYS

Usually[13] the lay days commence when:

(1) the vessel is an 'arrived ship';
(2) she is ready to load or discharge; and
(3) the shipowner has given notice of readiness to load.[14]

But no notice of readiness to *discharge* is necessary,[15] unless there is an express provision to the contrary in the charter-party.

There is an implied term that the charterer must act with reasonable despatch and in accordance with the ordinary practice of the port in doing those acts which he must do to enable the vessel to become an 'arrived ship'.[16] The burden of proving breach of this term lies on the shipowners.[17]

> *Compania de Navigacione SA v Government of Ceylon, The Theraios* [1971] 1 Lloyd's Rep 209, CA, where the cargo was to be loaded 'at the average rate of 120 metric tons per hatch per weather working day'; *Clerco Compania Naviera SA v Food Corpn of India, The Savvas* [1982] 1 Lloyd's Rep 22, CA, where the cargo was to be discharged 'at the average rate of 1500 tons per weather working day of 24 consecutive hours', and the question was whether laytime commenced before the vessel lightened and whether laytime should be calculated on the basis of a full cargo before lightening took place; *Mosvolds Rederi A/S v Food Corpn of India, The King Theras* [1984] 1 Lloyd's Rep 1, CA, where the cargo was to be discharged from the vessel into lightening vessels 'at the rate of 1,000 tons . . . per weather working day of 24 consecutive hours, Saturday afternoon. Sundays and holidays excepted even if used', and a question arose as to the calculation of lay time when 4 lightening vessels were used. (See the judgment of Sir John Donaldson MR, ibid, at 4.); *President of India v Jebsens (UK) Ltd, The General Capinpin, Proteus, Free Wave and Dinara* [1989] 1 Lloyd's Rep 232, CA, where the vessels were to be discharged 'at the average rate of 1000 metric tonnes basis 5 or more available working hatches, pro rata if less number of hatches per weather working day.'

13 But sometimes the charter-party states that 'time lost in waiting for a berth is to count as loading time', ie even before the vessel is an 'arrived ship'. In the computation of time lost waiting for a berth there are to be excluded all periods which would have been left out in the computation of permitted laytime used up if the vessel had actually been in berth. Accordingly, in the case of an 'arrived ship' under a port charter-party there is no conflict between the laytime provisions and the 'time lost' provisions. The calculations under both provisions are the same; neither need prevail over the other: *Aldebaran Compania Maritima SA v Aussenhandel AG, The Darrah* [1976] 2 Lloyd's Rep 359 at 366, HL (per Lord Diplock). See further, *Nea Tyhi Maritime Co Ltd of Piraeus v Compagnie Grainière SA of Zurich, The Finix* [1978] 1 Lloyd's Rep 16, CA.
14 See p 145, ante.
15 See p 161, ante.
16 *Sunbeam Shipping Co Ltd v President of India, The Atlantic Sunbeam* [1973] 1 Lloyd's Rep 482 at 488, QBD (Commercial Court) (per Kerr J).
17 Ibid, at 488 (per Kerr J).

(1) An 'arrived ship'

Whether a ship is an 'arrived ship' will depend on whether the charter-party is:

(a) a port charter-party; or
(b) a berth charter-party.

(a) *Port charter-parties*

The rule is that where the charter-party names a *port* simply, without further particularity or qualification, the ship is an 'arrived ship' when, if she cannot proceed immediately to a berth, she has reached a position within the port where she is at the immediate and effective disposition of the charterer. If she is at the place where waiting ships usually lie, she is in such a position unless there are some extraordinary circumstances, proof of which lies on the charterer. If the vessel is waiting at some other place in the port, it is for the shipowner to prove that she is as fully at the disposition of the charterer as she would be if she were in the vicinity of the berth for loading or discharge.[18]

Thus, in *E L Oldendorff & Co GmbH v Tradax Export SA, The Johanna Oldendorff*[19]

A vessel carrying grain under a port charter-party anchored at the Bar anchorage at Liverpool. The anchorage was 17 miles from the usual discharging berth, but was the usual place where grain vessels lay whilst awaiting a berth.

Held, by the House of Lords that she was an 'arrived ship' when she reached the anchorage, for she was then at the immediate and effective disposition of the charterer.

Again, where a vessel reached the intersection anchorage at Buenos Aires, and was at a place where vessels customarily waited their turn for admission to a berth by the port authorities, she was held to be an 'arrived ship'.[20]

---

18 *E L Oldendorff & Co GmbH v Tradax Export SA, The Johanna Oldendorff* [1973] 2 Lloyd's Rep 285, HL. (See especially the judgment of Lord Reid, ibid, at 291, and that of Lord Dilhorne, ibid, at 299.)

19 [1973] 2 Lloyd's Rep 285, HL, overruling *Sociedad Financiera de Bienes Raices SA v Agrimpex Hungarian Trading Co for Agricultural Products* [1961] AC 135, [1960] 2 All ER 578, HL. All cases concerning an 'arrived ship' decided before 1973 must be read in the light of *E L Oldendorff & Co GmbH v Tradax Export SA, The Johanna Oldendorff*, supra.

20 *Venizelos ANE of Athens v Société Commerciale de Cereales et Financièrè SA of Zurich, The Prometheus* [1974] 1 Lloyd's Rep 350, QBD (Commercial Court). (See the judgment of Mocatta J, ibid, at 352.)

Where a vessel is directed to go to the port of Brake, she does not become an 'arrived ship' by anchoring at the Weser Lightship anchorage for that anchorage is outside the legal, fiscal and administrative limits of Brake, lying 25 miles from the mouth of the River Weser in an area where none of the port authorities of the Weser ports do any administrative acts or exercise any control over vessels waiting there. Charterers, shippers and shipowners who use the Weser ports do not regard the waiting area at the Lightship as forming part of any of the ports.[1]

If the voyage has not ended and the vessel is not waiting, she is not an 'arrived ship' even though she may be in a commercial and legal sense within the port when she is off a quay.

Thus, in *Federal Commerce and Navigation Co Ltd v Tradax Export SA, The Maratha Envoy*[2]

A vessel carrying grain anchored at the Weser Light vessel on 8 December 1970, while waiting for a berth at the port of Brake. On that day she made an excursion to Brake, turned there and went back to the Light vessel. On 12 December she made a similar excursion, turned at Brake and went back to the Light vessel.

Held, by the QBD (Commercial Court), that she was not an 'arrived ship' on 8 December or 12 December for the voyage had not ended nor was she waiting. She had merely been on a trip to Brake and back to the Light vessel, with no pause other than such as was inherent in the movement of turning. It was immaterial that she was in the port of Brake in a commercial and legal sense when she was off a quay.

If the charterers fail to nominate the port of discharge within the time limited by the charter-party, there is no implied term that the master may make the nomination himself, and thus cause the vessel to be an 'arrived ship'.

Thus, in *Zim Israel Navigation Co Ltd v Tradax Export SA, The Timna*[3]

The charterers were under a duty to nominate a port of discharge. On 31 December 1968 they told the master to 'proceed destination Weser'. On 2 January 1969, the

---

1 *Federal Commerce and Navigation Co Ltd v Tradax Export SA, The Maratha Envoy* [1977] 2 Lloyd's Rep 301, HL. (See the judgment of Lord Diplock, ibid, at 307.)

2 [1975] 2 Lloyd's Rep 233, QBD (Commercial Court). (See the judgment of Donaldson J, ibid, at 233.) The decision on this point was affirmed by the House of Lords, but the case was decided on other grounds: [1977] 2 Lloyd's Rep 301, HL. (See the judgment of Lord Diplock, ibid, at 309.)

3 *Zim Israel Navigation Co Ltd v Tradax Export SA, The Timna* [1970] 2 Lloyd's Rep 409, QBD (Commercial Court). (See the judgment of Donaldson J, ibid, at 413.) In the Court of Appeal this aspect of the case was not gone into, and the Court decided the case on other grounds: [1971] 2 Lloyd's Rep 91, CA. (See the judgment of Lord Denning MR, ibid, at 94.)

vessel reached the Weser Light vessel, which was about 25 miles off the mouth of the River Weser. No further orders were received, so the master moved her to Bremerhaven on 3 January and gave notice of readiness to discharge.

Held, the vessel was never an 'arrived ship' at Bremerhaven, and the notice of readiness to discharge was invalid.

(b) *Berth charter-parties*

But where the contract expressly reserves to the charterer the right to name a particular dock or berth, the lay days do not begin until the ship has arrived at that dock or berth.

Thus, in *Stag Line Ltd v Board of Trade*[4]

A charter-party required a vessel to proceed to 'one or two safe ports East Canada or Newfoundland, place or places as ordered by charterers and/or shippers'. She was ordered to the port of Miramichi, and on arrival there was told that she would be required to load at Millbank, a place within the port. As there was not then a berth for her, she had to wait for six days, in respect of which the shipowners claimed demurrage.

Held, that the charter-party gave the charterers an express right to nominate a 'place', meaning a berth within the port; therefore the vessel did not become an 'arrived ship' until arriving at the berth, and demurrage was not payable.

But sometimes a berth charter-party states that time is to count 'whether in berth or not'.

The phrase 'whether in berth or not' takes effect only when a berth is not available.[5] It does not apply where a berth is available but is unreachable because of bad weather.[6]

Thus, in *Seacrystal Shipping Ltd v Bulk Transport Group Shipping Co Ltd, The Kyzikos*[7]

A berth charter-party stated that discharging time was to commence at 1400 hours if notice was given before noon and that time was to count 'whether in berth or not'. The vessel arrived in the discharging port at 0645 hours on 17 December 1984. Notice of readiness was given before noon. The berth was available but she could not proceed there until 1450 hours on 20 December because of fog. The shipowners contended

---

4   [1950] 2 KB 194, [1950] 1 All ER 1105; *Cosmar Compania Naviera SA v Total Transport Corpn, The Isabelle* [1984] 1 Lloyd's Rep 366, CA.

5   *Seacrystal Shipping Ltd v Bulk Transport Group Shipping Co Ltd, The Kyzikos* [1989] 1 Lloyd's Rep 1, HL, at 8 (per Lord Brandon of Oakbrook).

6   Ibid, at 8 (per Lord Brandon of Oakbrook).

7   [1989] 1 Lloyd's Rep 1, HL.

that time commenced at 1400 hours on 17 December.

Held, by the House of Lords, that this contention failed and that time did not count during the period for which the vessel was prevented from proceeding to her berth by reason of fog. Notice of readiness could not be effectively given on 17 December at the time stated above, for the phrase 'whether in berth or not' did not apply where the berth was available but unreachable.

(2) Ready to load or discharge

It should be noted that lay days do not begin to run until the ship is, so far as she is concerned, ready to receive or discharge cargo, unless she would have been ready except for the charterer's default.[8]

Hence the charterer is not liable for delay where the ship, in common with all other vessels coming from a prescribed area, has to go into quarantine on her arrival at the port of loading or discharge.[9] But if at the port of discharge the ship comes within quarantine regulations on account of the cargo she is carrying, presumably the charterer is liable. At any rate he is liable for delay in obtaining the necessary customs-house papers for discharging, when the delay arises from the fact that special papers are required for the particular cargo carried.[10]

A vessel is not ready to load[11] or discharge[12] until she is ready in

---

8 *Vergottis v Wm Cory & Son Ltd* [1926] 2 KB 344.

9 *White v Winchester SS Co* 1886 23 SLR 342. Nor is he liable if the port which he nominates is strike-bound: *Reardon Smith Line Ltd v Ministry of Agriculture, Fisheries and Food* [1962] 1 QB 42, [1961] 2 All ER 577, CA.

10 *Hill v Idle* (1815) 4 Camp 327; *Sociedad Financiera de Bienes Raices SA v Agrimpex Hungarian Trading Co for Agricultural Products* [1961] AC 135, [1960] 2 All ER 578, HL (failure to obtain berthing permit); *Sunbeam Shipping Co Ltd v President of India, The Atlantic Sunbeam* [1973] 1 Lloyd's Rep 482, QBD (Commercial Court) (failure to obtain a document at Calcutta called a jetty challan).

11 *Armement Adolf Deppe v John Robinson & Co Ltd* [1917] 2 KB 204; *Bodewes Scheepswerven NV and Kuwa NV v Highways Construction Ltd, The Jan Herman* [1966] 1 Lloyd's Rep 402, Mayor's and City of London Court; *Compania de Naviera Nedelka SA v Tradax International SA, The Tres Flores* [1973] 2 Lloyd's Rep 247, CA, where the holds of the vessel were infested and required to be fumigated. For a case where the parties chose to advance the commencement of laytime and laytime commenced to count even though the ship had not reported nor was ready nor had received free pratique, see *Logs and Timber Products (Singapore) Pte Ltd v Keeley Granite (Pty) Ltd, The Freijo* [1978] 2 Lloyd's Rep 1, CA. For a case where the vessel had failed to obtain customs' clearance but had given notice of readiness to load under a clause in the charter-party entitling her to do so if she was unable to berth immediately on arrival, see *Compania Argentina de Navegacion de Ultramar v Tradax Export SA, The Puerto Rocca* [1978] 1 Lloyd's Rep 252.

12 *Government of Ceylon v Société Franco-Tunisienne d'Armement-Tunis* [1962] 2 QB

all her holds to give the charterer complete control of every part of her which is available for cargo.

The mere fact that free pratique has not been obtained does not mean that the ship is not ready to load, if, in fact, free pratique can be obtained at any time and without the possibility of delaying the loading.

Thus, in *Shipping Developments Corpn SA v Sojuzneftexport V/O, The Delian Spirit*[13]

A vessel reached the commercial area of Tuapse at 0100 hours on 19 February. Her master gave notice of readiness to load. She was directed to her berth on 24 February and arrived there at 1320 hours. Free pratique was granted at 1600 hours. Loading began at 2150 hours.

Held, the notice of readiness to load was valid because it could have been obtained at any time without the possibility of delaying the loading.

Sometimes, a charter-party may state that the vessel, in addition to being ready to load or discharge, must also be 'securely moored at the loading or discharging place'.[14] This expression means that she must be 'all fast at the spot where the actual process of loading or discharging is to occur'.[15]

(3) Notice of readiness

A clause[16] usually provides that the lay days are to commence after

416, [1960] 3 All ER 797 (charterer's cargo overstowed by other cargo loaded en route); *Agios Stylianos Compania Naviera SA v Maritime Associates International Ltd Lagos, The Agios Stylianos* [1975] 1 Lloyd's Rep 426, QBD (Commercial Court), where a cargo of cement was overstowed by a cargo of vehicles, and it was held that laytime did not begin to run until the cement was accessible; *Gerani Compania Naviera SA v General Organisation for Supply of Goods, The Demosthenes V* [1982] 1 Lloyd's Rep 275, QBD (Commercial Court), where the vessel was held to be ready to discharge even though some vacuators, which it was the duty of the shipowners to supply, were not on board. (See the judgment of Staughton J, ibid, at 278–279.); *Eurico SpA v Philipp Bros, The Epaphus* [1987] 2 Lloyd's Rep 215, CA, where the vessel was ready to discharge, but the cargo was not ready to be discharged because it had to be fumigated; *Transgrain Shipping BV v Global Transporte Oceanico SA, The Mexico I* [1988] 2 Lloyd's Rep 149, QBD (Commercial Court) (charterer's cargo overstowed by other cargo.).

13   [1971] 1 Lloyd's Rep 506, CA. (See the judgment of Lord Denning MR, ibid, at 510.)
14   *Plakoura Maritime Corpn v Shell International Petroleum Co Ltd* [1987] 2 Lloyd's Rep 258, QBD (Commercial Court).
15   Ibid at 262 (per Leggatt J).
16   See, e g 'Gencon' form, clause 6(c) (Appendix B).

the expiry of a specified time after the giving of the notice of readiness to load or discharge, eg

'Laytime for loading and discharging shall commence at 1 pm if notice of readiness is given before noon and at 6 am next working day if notice given during office hours after noon.[17]

Sometimes, the charter-party states that the time is to count 'from 24 hours after the receipt of the notice of readiness and vessel having also been entered at the Customs House'.[18] 'Entered' means 'entered on final entry'; the filing of a vessel's inward entry application is not sufficient.[19]

A notice of readiness is not valid unless it indicates that the vessel is ready to load or discharge, as the case may be, at the time at which it is given. It is insufficient if the notice merely indicates that she will be ready at a future time.

Thus, in *Christensen v Hindustan Steel Ltd*[20]

At 1900 hours on 28 October 1967 the master gave notice that the vessel would be ready to load on 29 October.

Held, that the notice was invalid even if the vessel was in fact ready at the time at

---

17 For a case where the lay days for loading and discharging had already expired before the vessel arrived at the discharging port, and it was held that the vessel was on demurrage immediately on her arrival there irrespective of the giving of notice of readiness to discharge, see *R Pagnan & Fratelli v Tradax Export SA* [1969] 2 Lloyd's Rep 150, QBD (Commercial Court). (See the judgment of Donaldson J, ibid, at 154.) For a case where notice of readiness to load was given on a public holiday, see *Pacific Carriers Corpn v Tradax Export SA, The North King* [1971] 2 Lloyd's Rep 460, QBD (Commercial Court). For a case where the notice of readiness to discharge was invalid because the vessel had not been entered at the Customs House, see *Venore Transportation Co v President of India, The Venore* [1973] 1 Lloyd's Rep 494, District Court, Southern District of New York.

18 See eg *Michalos NZ v Food Corpn of India, The Apollon* [1983] 1 Lloyd's Rep 409, QBD (Commercial Court); *Food Corpn of India v Carras Shipping Co Ltd, The Delian Leto* [1983] 2 Lloyd's Rep 496, QBD (Commercial Court); *President of India v Davenport Marine Panama SA, The Albion* [1987] 2 Lloyd's Rep 365, QBD (Commercial Court); *President of India v Diamantis Pateras (Hellas) Marine Enterprises Ltd, The Nestor* [1987] 2 Lloyd's Rep 649, QBD (Commercial Court).

19 *President of India v Davenport Marine Panama SA, The Albion*, supra; *President of India v Diamantis Pateras (Hellas) Marine Enterprises Ltd, The Nestor*, supra.

20 [1971] 1 Lloyd's Rep 395, QBD (Commercial Court).

which it was given. It was one of anticipated readiness and impliedly reported to the charterers that she was not yet ready.[1]

Whether a notice of readiness has been effectively given to the charterers or their agents is a question of fact in each case.[2]

The charterers may be estopped by their conduct from disputing the validity of a notice of readiness.[3] If a notice of readiness has been accepted, it can be rejected later only on the ground of fraud.[4]

EFFECT OF LAY TIME NOT BEING FIXED

The general principle is that where no definite period of lay days has been agreed on, the charterer is only bound to load and unload the ship within a reasonable time. This obligation is not very stringent, for it allows extraordinary circumstances to be taken into consideration. Thus, in *Hick v Raymond and Reid*[5]

No time was fixed for the unloading, and the unloading was delayed owing to a strike of dock labourers.
Held, that the shipowners were not entitled to damages for detention.

But a clause in a charter-party stating that the vessel is to be discharged 'with customary steamship dispatch' does not make the

---

1 See the judgment of Donaldson J, ibid, at 399–400. See further, *Compania de Naviera Nedelka SA v Tradax International SA, The Tres Flores* [1973] 2 Lloyd's Rep 247, CA, where the notice of readiness to load was invalid because it was given at a time when the holds of the vessel were infested and required to be fumigated. (See the judgment of Lord Denning MR, ibid, at 249.)

2 See eg *R Pagnan and Fratelli v Finagrain Compagnie Commerciale Agricole et Financière SA, The Adolf Leonhardt* [1986] 2 Lloyd's Rep 395, QBD (Commercial Court), where a notice of readiness to discharge initiated by radio but reaching the charterers' agents in written form qualified as written notice within cl 13 of the 'Centrocon' charter-party.

3 *Surrey Shipping Co Ltd v Compagnie Continentale (France) SA, The Shackleford* [1978] 2 Lloyd's Rep 154, CA, where the notices of readiness to discharge had been accepted by the receivers even though it was premature.

4 *Sofial SA v Ove Skou Rederi, The Helle Skou* [1976] 2 Lloyd's Rep 205, QBD (Commercial Court), where, however, fraud was not alleged.

5 [1893] AC 22. See further, *Hellenic Lines Ltd v Embassy of Pakistan* [1973] 1 Lloyd's Rep 363, US Court of Appeals, Second Circuit, where in a freight contract governed by English law it was held that where no time was fixed for the discharge of the cargo, a reasonable time was implied, and 'reasonable time' meant what was reasonable in the circumstances then existing. (See the judgment of Timbers CtJ, ibid, at 365.)

charter-party into a fixed lay time charter-party for the purpose of the principle set out above.[6]

EFFECT OF LAY TIME BEING FIXED

Where the time for loading or unloading is fixed by agreement, the only[7] cases in which the charterer is excused for his failure to load or discharge the ship within such time are:

(1) where the delay is due to the shipowner's fault, or that of his employees or agents acting within their authority;[8] *or*
(2) where the cause of the delay falls within an exceptions clause; *or*
(3) where loading or discharge is illegal.

(1) Fault of the shipowner

Where, owing to the voluntary act or negligence of the owner, the ship ceascs for a period to be ready to receive cargo, such period is excluded in calculating demurrage, eg if for his own convenience she leaves the berth for the purposes of bunkering,[9] or if she negligently grounds and so cannot get to her berth,[10] or if discharge is held up due to the cargo being contaminated due to his fault.[11]

Again, in *Gem Shipping Co of Monrovia v Babanaft (Lebanon) SARL, The Fontevivo*[12]

A vessel arrived at Lattakia, Syria. After her arrival there was aircraft activity near

6 *Hulthen v Stewart & Co* [1903] AC 389, HL.
7 See *Benson v Blunt* (1841) 1 QB 870.
8 But where there has been a deviation, unless the deviation has been waived, the shipowner cannot rely on a provision in a charter-party for loading or unloading in a fixed time: *United States Shipping Board v Bunge y Born Ltd Sociedad* (1925) 134 LT 303, HL. On the effect of deviation, see further *Hain SS Co Ltd v Tate and Lyle Ltd* [1936] 2 All ER 597. See pp 23–24, ante.
9 In *Re Ropner Shipping Co Ltd* [1927] 1 KB 879.
10 *Blue Anchor Line Ltd v Alfred C Toepfer International GmbH, The Union Amsterdam* [1982] 2 Lloyd's Rep 432.
11 *Associated Bulk Carriers Ltd v Shell International Petroleum Co Ltd, The Nordic Navigator* [1984] 2 Lloyd's Rep 182, QBD (Commercial Court), where the charterer alleged that there was a quantity of coal among an oil cargo due to the shipowner failing to clean the hold.
12 [1975] 1 Lloyd's Rep 339, QBD (Commercial Court). (See the judgment of Donaldson J, ibid, at 343.)

the port. Syrian anti-aircraft guns went into action. The incident did not exceed one hour. About 5 hours later the master yielded to pressure from the crew and decided to leave the port.

Held, by QBD (Commercial Court) that, on the evidence, the master's action was unjustified and that time did not run against laytime during the period of the vessel's absence from the port.

On the other hand, in *Houlder v Weir*[13]

During the course of unloading it was necessary to take in ballast to keep the ship upright. This caused the agreed time for discharge to be exceeded.

Held, that taking in ballast could not be regarded as a default on the part of the shipowner, and the charterers were therefore liable for the delay.

Sometimes the charter-party states that time shall not count against laytime when spent or lost as a result of a breach of its terms by the shipowner.[14]

(2) Exceptions clause in charterer's favour

Where the time for loading is fixed, and the lay days have once started to run, time will continue to run against the charterer, even though the ship is, by circumstances altogether beyond the control of either party, forced to leave port before loading is completed, unless the ship's departure was due to an exception of which the charterer can claim the benefit.[15]

Where a charter-party states that if delay is caused to a vessel getting into her berth after giving notice of readiness 'for any reason whatsoever over which the charterer has no control', the exception clause excuses the charterer in the case of delay by swell in getting to her berth.[16]

An exceptions clause protected the charterers in *Induna SS Co Ltd v British Phosphate Comrs, The Loch Dee*[17]

By the terms of a charter-party charterers undertook to discharge cargo at New

13   [1905] 2 KB 267.
14   *Mobil Shipping and Transportation Co v Shell Eastern Petroleum (Pte) Ltd, The Mobil Courage* [1987] 2 Lloyd's Rep 655, QBD (Commercial Court), where a triplicate bill of lading had been presented to the master for signature, and the shipowners were in breach of the charter-party because he had failed to sign.
15   *Cantiere Navale Triestina v Russian Soviet Naphtha Export Agency* [1925] 2 KB 172.
16   *Marocain de l'Industrie du Raffinage SA v Notos Maritime Corpn, The Notos* [1987] 1 Lloyd's Rep 503, HL.
17   [1949] 2 KB 430, [1949] 1 All ER 522.

Zealand ports at the rate of 1,500 tons per working day of twenty-four consecutive hours and to pay demurrage if the time allowed for discharge was exceeded. By an exception, demurrage was not to accrue in the event of delay by reason of, inter alia, 'intervention of constituted authorities or from any cause whatsoever beyond the control of the charterers'. At the time the charter-party was entered into, but unknown to either charterers or shipowners, an order was in force in New Zealand which made it illegal to work between 9 pm and 8 am, and thus rendered it impossible for the ship to discharge at the prescribed rate. Delay took place, and the shipowners claimed demurrage.

Held, that the shipowners' claim failed because the exception clause applied.

Again, in *The Amstelmolen*[18]

The charter-party provided that the charterer was not to be liable in the event of a delay caused by an 'obstruction'.

Held, that this exception covered a delay caused by other vessels occupying all available berths and so preventing the ship from loading.[19]

The word 'obstructions' is no less apt to cover ordinary congestion than extraordinary congestion.[20] There is no difference in principle whether there is one vessel or 100 causing the congestion, for the degree of congestion is irrelevant.[1] So also is the likelihood of congestion.[2]

If the charter-party states that time is not to count if the cargo cannot be loaded because of obstructions, and the charterer has made all arrangements to load at a customary berth but has not nominated such berth before the vessel is an 'arrived ship', he is entitled, on the berth of his choice being obstructed, to a reasonable time within which to make up his mind to load at an alternative berth if one is available and it is commercially practicable to use it.[3]

Sometimes the exception clause states that no deduction of time is

---

18 [1961] 2 Lloyd's Rep 1, CA.
19 In *Ionian Navigation Co Inc v Atlantic Shipping Co SA, The Loucas N* [1971] 1 Lloyd's Rep 215, CA, Lord Denning MR, said (ibid, at 218) that the decision was an unsatisfactory one 'which merchants and lawyers try to get out of'. But in *R Pagnan and Fratelli v Finagrain Compagnie Commerciale Agricole et Financière SA, The Adolf Leonhardt* [1986] 2 Lloyd's Rep 395, QBD (Commercial Court) Staughton J (ibid, at 401) said that this criticism was scarcely fair to the Judges in that case for they had followed, as they were bound to do, an earlier decision of the Court of Appeal.
20 *R Pagnan and Fratelli v Finagrain Compagnie Commerciale Agricole et Financière SA, The Adolf Leonhardt*, supra, at 401 (per Staughton J).
1 Ibid at 401 (per Staughton J).
2 *Navrom v Callitsis Ship Management SA, The Radauti* [1988] 2 Lloyd's Rep 416, CA, at 420 (per Lloyd LJ).
3 *Venizelos ANE of Athens v Société Commerciale de Cereales et Financière SA of Zurich, The Prometheus* [1974] 1 Lloyd's Rep 350, QBD (Commercial Court). (See the judgment of Mocatta J, ibid, at 356.)

to be allowed unless due notice, eg of a stoppage by an excepted cause, is given to the master.[4]

Once a vessel is on demurrage the exceptions clauses relieving a charterer from liability for delay caused, eg by a strike do not apply, unless there are clear words to that effect.[5]

Whether the words used in the charter-party have the effect of enabling the charterer to rely on the exceptions clauses even though the vessel is already on demurrage is a question of construction in each case.

Thus, in *Compania Naviera Aeolus SA v Union of India*[6]

A vessel had been chartered under a charter-party which contained a strike clause stating that the time for discharging should not count against the charterers during the continuance of a strike. The vessel began to discharge the cargo, but after the lay time had expired a strike took place which interrupted further unloading.

Held, that the charterers could not rely on the strike clause because it was not sufficiently clearly worded to have the effect of relieving them from the payment of demurrage. Consequently they had to pay demurrage for the whole period after the lay days had expired.

Again, in *Dias Compania Naviera SA v Louis Dreyfus Corpn, The Dias*[7]

---

4   *The Mozart* [1985] 1 Lloyd's Rep 239, QBD (Commercial Court), where the charterer failed to give notice of loss of time caused by the breakdown of a stacker-reclaimer for the carriage of coke between the ship and the store, and it was held that the charterer could rely on the exception clause because the master had all the information which would have been contained in the notice; *Valla Giovanni & C SpA v Gebr Van Weelde Scheepvaartkantoor BV, The Chanda* [1985] 1 Lloyd's Rep 563 (Commercial Court), where the stoppage of loading was due to floods, and the question was whether the notice given by the charterer's agents was valid.

5   *Compania Naviera Aeolus SA v Union of India* [1964] AC 868, [1962] 3 All ER 670, HL.

6   [1964] AC 868, [1962] 3 All ER 670, HL.

7   [1978] 1 Lloyd's Rep 325, HL. (See the judgment of Lord Diplock, ibid, at 329.) See also *Nippon Yusen Kaisha v Marocaine de l'Industrie du Raffinage SA, The Tsukuba Maru* [1979] 1 Lloyd's Rep 459, QBD (Commercial Court), where the laytime had expired and the tanker could not tie up at a sea line because of bad weather and it was held that the charterers could not rely on a clause stating that any delay due to inability of the vessel's facilities to load or discharge within the time allowed should not count as used laytime; *Sametiet M/T Johs Stove v Istanbul Petrol Rafinerisi A/S, The Johs Stove* [1984] 1 Lloyd's Rep 38, QBD (Commercial Court), where a clause stating that neither the shipowner nor the charterer was to be responsible 'for any delay arising or resulting from a strike' was held not to apply to the provisions in the charter-party relating to laytime and demurrage. (See the judgment of Lloyd J, ibid, at 41.); *Islamic Republic of Iran Shipping Lines v Royal Bank of Scotland plc, The Anna Ch* [1987] 1 Lloyd's Rep 266, QBD (Commercial Court), where the vessel was on demurrage and the charterers

A charter-party stated that 'at discharging the charterers have the option at any time to treat at their expense ship's cargo and time so used not to count'. The laytime expired on 26 October 1973. Between 9 and 25 November the receivers (for whom the charterers were responsible) had the cargo fumigated. Discharge was completed on 10 December. The owners claimed demurrage for the whole of the period after the laytime had expired.

Held, that the claim succeeded. The words 'time not to count' had no further application once laytime had expired.

Further, in *Food Corpn of India v Carras Shipping Co Ltd, The Delian Leto*[8]

A charter-party stated: 'Lightening, if any, at discharging ports to be at owners' risk and expense, and time used not to count as laytime'.

Held, once laytime had expired, the clause had no further application and the charterers were liable for the whole of the time used in lightening.[9]

(3) Illegality

The charterer will not be liable for delay if the loading or discharge becomes illegal.

THE COMPLETION OF THE LOADING

Where demurrage is claimed, it may become necessary to decide at what precise time loading was completed. The general rule has been stated as follows: 'In most cases, the mere reception or dumping down of the cargo on the ship does not involve completion of loading, because . . . the operation of loading involves all that is required to put the cargo in a condition in which it can be carried'.[10]

So, in *Argonaut Navigation Co Ltd v Ministry of Food, SS Argobee*[11]

It was necessary, both for the safety of the ship and also to comply with regulations in

could not rely on a clause which stated that steaming time from one port to another was not to count; *Superfos Chartering A/S v NBR (London) Ltd, The Saturnia* [1987] 2 Lloyd's Rep 43, CA, where the strike clause did not apply when the vessel was already on demurrage; *Marc Rich & Co Ltd v Tourloti Compania Naviera SA, The Kalliopi A* [1988] 2 Lloyd's Rep 101, CA, where the vessel was on demurrage and a clause containing an exception of 'restraint of princes' could not be relied on by the charterers.

8   [1983] 2 Lloyd's Rep 496, QBD (Commercial Court).
9   See the judgment of Lloyd J, ibid, at 499.
10 *Svenssons Travaruaktiebolog v Cliffe SS Co* [1932] 1 KB 490 at 494, per Wright J.
11 [1949] 1 KB 572, [1949] 1 All ER 160.

force at the loading port, for grain carried in the 'tween decks to be stowed in bags, and loose wheat was loaded for bagging on board.

Held, that loading was not completed until the grain had been bagged and stowed.

If the charterer has loaded the vessel before the lay days expire, he is not entitled to delay her sailing by failing to tender the bills of lading for signature, and will be liable in damages if he does so.

Thus, in *Nolisement (Owners) v Bunge and Born*[12]

A vessel was loaded 19 days before the expiration of the lay days. The charterers could not make up their minds as to what port of call to order her to. So they did not tender immediately the bills of lading for signature by the master, and they did not do so for another 3 days, by which time they had settled the name of the port of call. The vessel was accordingly delayed for these 3 days, and the shipowners sued the charterers for 2 days' delay (since the charterers were entitled by the terms of the charter-party to keep the vessel waiting for 24 hours after loading for the purpose of settling accounts).

Held, that the action succeeded, for once the vessel was loaded the charterers were under a duty to present the bills of lading for signature.

But the charterer is not obliged to load in a shorter time than the laytime, even if this is possible. Consequently, so long as loading has not been completed, the charterer is entitled to delay the vessel's sailing until the expiration of the laytime.[13]

Thus, in *Margaronis Navigation Agency Ltd v Henry W Peabody & Co of London Ltd*[14]

The charterer had loaded 12,588 tons, 4 cwt of a cargo by 29 December. Only 11 tons, 16 cwt remained to be loaded, and loading would only have taken another 40 minutes. The charterer completed loading on 2 January, which was within the period of laytime. The shipowner claimed damages for deliberately detaining the vessel, for she could have sailed earlier.

Held, that the shipowner's claim failed, for the charterer could keep the vessel in port for the whole of the laytime without incurring liability.

RATE OF DEMURRAGE

The rate of demurrage is expressly stated in the charter-party, e g

'Ten running days on demurrage at the rate of £2,000 per day or pro rata for any part

---

12 [1917] 1 KB 160.
13 *Margaronis Navigation Agency Ltd v Henry W Peabody & Co of London Ltd* [1965] 1 QB 300, [1964] 2 All ER 296, [1964] 1 Lloyd's Rep 173; affd [1965] 2 QB 430, [1964] 3 All ER 333, [1964] 2 Lloyd's Rep 153, CA. Another aspect of this case, viz whether the charterer had loaded a full and complete cargo subject to the limits of the de minimis rule is considered at p 151, ante.
14 Supra.

of a day, payable day by day, to be allowed Merchants altogether at ports of loading and discharge.'[15]

In certain circumstances only half demurrage may be payable, for the charter-party may provide, eg

'If there is a strike or lock-out affecting the cargo on or after vessel's arrival at port of discharge and same has not been settled within 48 hours, Receivers shall have the option of keeping vessel waiting until such strike or lock-out is at an end against paying half-demurrage after expiration of the time prescribed for discharging . . .'[16]

Where the shipowner claims demurrage, any payment made in respect of it in sterling must be converted into the foreign currency at the rate of exchange ruling at the date of payment and not that ruling when demurrage became due and payable,[17] unless there is a clause in the charter-party to the contrary, eg one stating that the exchange rate ruling on the bill of lading date is to apply.[18]

BY WHOM DEMURRAGE IS PAYABLE

Usually it will be the charterer[19] who will be liable for the payment of demurrage.[20] Sometimes the shipowner's right to claim demurrage is barred after a time specified in the charter-party.[1]

---

15 See 'Gencon' form, clause 7. (Appendix B, post.)
16 See 'Gencon' form, clause 15 (Appendix B, post). For examples, see *Salamis Shipping (Panama) SA v Edm Van Meerbeeck & Co SA The Onisilos* [1971] 2 All ER 497, CA, where it was held that half demurrage was payable from the end of a strike at the first of three discharging ports until discharge was completed at the third port. See the judgment of Lord Denning MR, ibid, at 501; *Superfos Chartering A/S v NBR (London) Ltd, The Saturnia* [1987] 2 Lloyd's Rep 43, CA, where the half rate provision had no application because the laytime had already expired before the discharge of the vessel was affected by the strike (see the judgment of Bingham J, ibid, at 371).
17 *George Veflings Rederi A/S v President of India, The Bellami* [1979] 1 Lloyd's Rep 123, CA; *Monrovia Tramp Shipping Co v President of India, The Pearl Merchant* [1978] 2 Lloyd's Rep 193, QBD (Commercial Court).
18 See eg *President of India v Lips Maritime Corpn, The Lips* [1987] 2 Lloyd's Rep 311, HL.
19 For a case where the charterers remained liable for the payment of demurrage by the receivers of the cargo even though there was a 'cesser clause' in the charter-party, see *Gerani Compania Naviera SA v Alfred C Toepfer, The Demosthenes V (No 2)* [1982] 1 Lloyd's Rep 282, QBD (Commercial Court). (See the judgment of Staughton J, ibid, at 284–285.) For 'cesser clauses', see p 254, post. For a case where the charterers contended that they had acted as agents for the receivers of the cargo, and that they incurred no personal liability to pay demurrage, see

A clause in the charter-party may state that the claim for demurrage must be supported by a copy of the notice of readiness, the statement of facts and the time sheets.[2]

If it is desired to make shippers or consignees other than persons who are parties to the charter-party liable for demurrage agreed on in the charter-party, there must be a clear stipulation to that effect in the bill of lading. The stipulation usually takes the form 'freight and all other conditions as per charter'.[3]

Even where the ship is not under charter, the bill of lading which is issued may make the shipper, consignee or holder of the bill of lading liable to pay demurrage.[4]

The charter-party or bill of lading often gives the shipowner a lien in respect of demurrage and damages for detention.[5]

The charter-party often contains a 'cesser clause'[6] which purports to relieve the charterer from paying demurrage, but in each case it is a question of construction whether it does relieve him in fact.[7]

Etablissement Biret et Cie SA v Yukiteru Kaiun KK and Nissui Shipping Corpn, The Sun Happiness [1984] 1 Lloyd's Rep 381, QBD (Commercial Court).

20 In the absence of agreement between the shipowner and the charterer regarding the payment of interest on unpaid demurrage, the shipowner has no remedy by way of a claim for general damages in respect of such interest if the amount due is paid late but before proceedings for its recovery have been commenced: *President of India v La Pintada Cia Navegacion SA* [1985] AC 104, [1984] 2 All ER 773, HL. But where the shipowner is able to prove that he has suffered special damage eg by himself having to pay interest on an overdraft as a result of the charterer's late payment of demurrage, the shipowner is entitled to claim such special damage even though the amount is paid before the commencement of proceedings for its recovery: ibid.

1 See eg *Pera Shipping Corpn v Petroship SA, The Pera* [1985] 2 Lloyd's Rep 103, CA, where, however, the shipowners' claim was not barred because the time bar clause was ambiguous; *Mariana Islands Steamship Corpn v Marimpex Mineraloel-Handelsgesellschaft mbH & Co KG, The Medusa* [1986] 2 Lloyd's Rep 328, CA.

2 See eg *Pera Shipping Corpn v Petroship SA, The Pera*, supra; *Mariana Islands Steamship Corpn v Marimpex Mineraloel-Handelsgesellschaft mbH & Co KG, The Medusa*, supra.

3 See *Porteus v Watney* (1878) 3 QBD 534.

4 Bills of Lading Act 1855, s 1. (See Appendix C.)

5 See chapter 12, post. For an example, see 'Gencon' charter-party, clause 8 (Appendix B).

6 See, further, on 'cesser clauses', pp 269–270, post.

7 See egg *Fidelitas Shipping Co Ltd v Exportchleb V/O* [1963] 2 Lloyd's Rep 113, CA, where it was held that by reason of the 'cesser clause' the charterers were not liable for demurrage at the port of loading; *Overseas Transportation Co v Mineralimportexport, The Sinoe* [1972] 1 Lloyd's Rep 201, CA, where the 'cesser clause' gave the shipowner a lien on the cargo for demurrage, but was held not to relieve the charterer from liability because, on the evidence, the lien was not an

The difficulty in construing 'cesser clauses' has arisen mainly on the question whether the charterer is to be relieved of liabilities accrued before completion of the loading, or whether the exemption applies only to liabilities arising after the goods have been shipped. Now, where it appears from the rest of the contract that another remedy is given to the shipowner for the liabilities already incurred by the charterer, he is held to be released from them.

It thus appears that the proper principle is that the exemption granted to the charterer is co-extensive with the lien given to the shipowner.[8]

Where no lien has been given in respect of a particular claim, the Courts will not enforce the exemption, unless there is a clear intention to free the charterer from liability in respect of that claim.[9]

It seems, further, that this principle, carried to its logical conclusion, involves the proposition that the charterer is still liable for damages for undue detention of the ship for the purpose of loading (ie beyond the period allowed for by the charter-party and covered by the demurrage clause) *despite* the 'cesser clause', for it has been decided that, where there is a demurrage clause in the charter-party, the lien for demurrage does not include a lien for damages for detention. Thus, in *Gray v Carr*[10]

The charter-party provided that the charterer's liability was to cease on shipment of

---

effective one. (See the judgment of Lord Denning MR, ibid, at 204.); *The Cunard Carrier, Elevanta and Martha* [1977] 2 Lloyd's Rep 261, QBD (Commercial Court), where no effective lien could be exercised at the ports of discharge (ie Basrah and Beirut) since at both ports the receivers were Government departments and also possibly because of the civil disorder in Beirut; *Granvias Oceanicas Armadora SA v Jibsen Trading Co, The Kavo Peiratis* [1977] 2 Lloyd's Rep 344, QBD (Commercial Court), where the question was whether it was possible for the shipowners to exercise a lien at the port of discharge; *Action SA v Britannic Shipping Corpn Ltd: The Aegis Britannic* [1987] 1 Lloyd's Rep 119, CA, where the question was whether there was a remedy against the receiver of the cargo.

8   See *Overseas Transportation Co v Mineralimportexport, The Sinoe* [1971] 1 Lloyd's Rep 514, QBD (Commercial Court), where Donaldson J, observed at 516: 'Cesser clauses are curious animals because it is now well established that they do not mean what they appear to say, namely that the charterers' liability shall cease as soon as the cargo is on board. Instead, in the absence of special wording . . . they mean that the charterers' liability shall cease if and to the extent that the owners shall have an alternative remedy by way of lien on the cargo.' The decision was subsequently affirmed by the Court of Appeal: [1972] 1 Lloyd's Rep 201.

9   See *Francesco v Massey* (1873) LR 8 Exch 101; *Dunlop & Sons v Balfour Williamson & Co* [1892] 1 QB 507.

10   (1871) LR 6 QB 522.

the cargo, allowed ten days' demurrage and gave a 'lien for demurrage'. The bill of lading provided for 'freight and all other conditions or demurrage as per charter'. The ship was detained at the port of loading beyond the ten days allowed on demurrage by the charter-party.

Held, that the shipowner had a lien against consignees under the bill of lading for the ten days' demurrage, but not for the detention beyond that time.

The charterer's conduct may show that he has waived his right to rely on a 'cesser clause'.[11]

ACCRUAL OF RIGHT OF ACTION FOR DEMURRAGE

A shipowner's cause of action for demurrage, being one for damages, accrues from the moment the vessel is detained beyond the lay days.[12] There is no such thing as a cause of action for late payment of damages.[13] The only remedy which the law affords for such delay is the discretionary award of interest pursuant to statute.[14]

(B) DESPATCH MONEY

If the charterer loads or discharges the vessel in a shorter time than is allowed to him by the lay days, he may be entitled to despatch money.[15] The amount of despatch money payable is often fixed at half the demurrage rate.[16]

11   *Marvigor Compania Naviera SA v Romanoexport State Co for Foreign Trade, The Corinthian Glory* [1977] 2 Lloyd's Rep 280, QBD (Commercial Court).

12   *President of India v Lips Maritime Corpn, The Lips* [1987] 2 Lloyd's Rep 311, HL.

13   Ibid.

14   Ibid.

15   *Tradax Internacional SA v Cerrahogullari TAS, The M Eregli* [1981] 2 Lloyd's Rep 169, QBD (Commercial Court), where the charterers were late in appointing an arbitrator in their claim for despatch money, but were granted an extension of the time limit under the Arbitration Act 1950, s 27; *Freedom Maritime Corp v International Bulk Carriers SA, The Khian Captain* [1985] 2 Lloyd's Rep 212, QBD (Commercial Court).

16   *Mosvolds Rederi A/S v Food Corpn of India, The King Theras* [1984] 1 Lloyd's Rep 1 at 2, CA (per Donaldson LJ). See e g *Fury Shipping Co Ltd v State Trading Corpn of India Ltd, The Atlantic Sun* [1972] 1 Lloyd's Rep 509, QBD (Commercial Court).

Chapter 11

Freight

Freight is the remuneration payable to the carrier for the carriage of goods by sea.[1] There are different types of freight. Freight can be claimed from certain persons, and it is to certain persons that it is payable.

THE DIFFERENT TYPES OF FREIGHT

When there is no provision to the contrary, freight is payable on the delivery of the goods,[2] and is calculated on the amount actually delivered.[3] Sometimes, however, the parties agree that a lump sum freight shall be paid irrespective of the amount of cargo carried. A frequent provision is that freight is to be paid in advance. In certain cases a pro rata freight is payable. If the consignee does not take delivery of the goods, the shipowner may be entitled to a back freight. If the charterer does not load a full cargo, damages for dead freight may be claimed.

(1) Freight payable on delivery

Payment of freight and delivery of the goods at the port of discharge are, unless otherwise agreed, concurrent conditions. The consignee

1   For a case where a tax on freight was payable to the Iraqi authorities at the ports of loading and discharge, see *Brovigtank A/S and I/S Brovig v Transcredit and Oil Tradeanstalt, The Gunda Brovig* [1982] 2 Lloyd's Rep 39, CA. (See the judgment of Lord Denning MR, ibid, at 40–41.)
2   *Krall v Burnett* (1877) 25 WR 305.
3   For a case concerning the rate of exchange applicable, see *Monrovia Tramp Shipping Co v President of India, The Pearl Merchant* [1978] 2 Lloyd's Rep 193, QBD (Commercial Court), where freight was payable 'on nett bill of lading weight at exchange rate ruling on bill of lading date'.

must, if required, pay the freight as the goods are delivered, and cannot withhold payment until delivery of the whole parcel.[4]

It is thus a condition precedent of the shipowner's right to recover freight that he should have delivered or been ready to deliver the goods. It was said by Willes CJ, that

'the true test of the right to freight, is the question whether the service in respect of which the freight was contracted to be paid has been substantially performed; and according to the law of England, as a rule, freight is earned by the carriage and arrival of the goods ready to be delivered to the merchant'.[5]

A charter-party sometimes provides that the charterer is entitled to deduct a specified amount from the freight for short delivery.[6]

Where a period is fixed during which freight is to be paid, the shipowner must be prepared to deliver the goods throughout the whole of that period if he wishes to claim payment.

So in *Duthie v Hilton*[7]

The bill of lading stipulated that 'freight [was] to be paid within 3 days after the arrival of ship before the delivery of any portion of the goods', and on the day after arrival an accidental fire necessitated the scuttling of the ship, whereby the cargo of cement was rendered commercially useless.
Held, that freight was not payable.

It is no defence to a claim for freight to show that the goods are damaged. The shipowner is entitled to full freight if he is ready to deliver at the port of destination the goods which were loaded. The charterer or consignee, as the case may be, cannot deduct from the

---

4   *Möller v Young* (1855) 24 LJQB 217 (revsd on another point, 25 LJQB 94). But if the charter-party states 'freight shall be payable immediately after completion of discharge', freight is not due bit by bit as each part of the cargo is discharged: *Canadian Pacific (Bermuda) Ltd v Lagon Maritime Overseas, The Fort Kipp* [1985] 2 Lloyd's Rep 168, QBD (Commercial Court).

5   Per Willes CJ in *Dakin v Oxley* (1864) 10 LT 268 at 270; *Aries Tanker Corpn v Total Transport Ltd, The Aries* [1977] 1 Lloyd's Rep 334. (See the judgment of Lord Wilberforce, ibid, at 337.); *Henriksens Rederi A/S v T H Z Rolimpex, The Brede* [1973] 2 Lloyd's Rep 333, CA; *Cleobulos Shipping Co Ltd v Intertanker Ltd, The Cleon* [1983] 1 Lloyd's Rep 586, CA. (See the judgment of Ackner LJ, ibid, at 590.)

6   See e g *Lakeport Navigation Co Panama SA v Anonima Petroli Italiana SpA, The Olympic Brilliance* [1982] 2 Lloyd's Rep 205, where a clause stated: 'If there is a difference of more than 0·50 per cent between bill of lading figures and delivered cargo as ascertained by Customs Authorities at discharging port, Charterers have the right to deduct from freight the cif value for the short delivered cargo', and it was held that the charterers had the right to make the deduction permanently, and not mrely to withhold the freight by way of security. (See the judgment of Kerr LJ, ibid, at 209.)

7   (1868) LR 4 CP 138.

freight the damage to the goods, but will have a separate cause of action for it, unless it was caused solely by excepted perils, whether excepted by express stipulation or by the operation of the Common Law.

Thus, in *Dakin v Oxley*[8]

Coal shipped under a charter-party had, through the negligence of the master, so deteriorated as not to be worth its freight. The charterer, therefore, abandoned it to the shipowner.

Held, he was nevertheless liable for freight, his remedy for damage to the coal being by cross-action.

Similarly, where the shipowner did not make available the full extent of the cargo spaces and was therefore in breach of contract, it was held that the charterer was not entitled to withhold part of the freight. He must enforce his right to claim damages for the breach by means of a cross-action.[9]

Again, a claim by the charterer for overtime cannot be set-off against the shipowner's claim for freight.[10]

But freight will not be payable unless the goods are delivered in such a condition that they are substantially and in a mercantile sense the same goods as those shipped.

Thus, in *Asfar v Blundell*[11]

A ship carrying dates was sunk in the Thames. The dates were recovered, but in a state which rendered them unfit for human consumption. They were sold for distilling purposes.

Held, no freight was payable because the goods delivered were, for business purposes, something different from those shipped.

Again, in *Montedison SpA v Icroma SpA, The Caspian Sea*[12]

The charterers loaded a cargo of 'Bachaquero Crude', which was a type of Venezuelan oil. When the cargo was delivered, it was found to contain paraffin. The charterers refused to pay the freight.

Held, by the Queen's Bench Division, that freight would be payable if what the shipowner had delivered could in commercial terms bear a subscription which sensibly and accurately included the words 'Bachaquero Crude'. The case would be remitted to the arbitrators to decide the point.[13]

---

8 (1864) 10 LT 268.
9 *Elena Shipping Ltd v Aidenfield Ltd, The Elena* [1986] 1 Lloyd's Rep 425, QBD (Commercial Court).
10 *Freedom Maritime Corpn v International Bulk Carriers SA and Mineral and Metals Trading Corpn of India Ltd, The Khian Captain (No 2)* [1986] 1 Lloyd's Rep 429, QBD (Commercial Court).
11 [1896] 1 QB 123. Chorley and Tucker's *Leading Cases* (4th edn 1962), p 307.
12 [1980] 1 Lloyd's Rep 91.
13 See the judgment of Donaldson J, ibid, at 181.

Unless the shipowner carries the goods to the destination agreed on, he is not entitled to any part of the freight. If the goods are lost on the way, *no matter how*, no freight is earned. The excepted perils afford the shipowner a good excuse for non-delivery of the goods, but he cannot earn freight by virtue of them. If the ship cannot finish the voyage, the shipowner must forward the goods by some other means or his claim to freight is lost.

Thus, in *Hunter v Prinsep*[14]

Where the voyage was from Honduras to London, freight was payable 'on a right and true delivery of the homeward bound cargo'. After being captured by the enemy, the vessel was recaptured and recommenced the voyage, but owing to bad weather she was driven ashore at St Kitts. The wreck and cargo were put up for sale without the consent of the cargo-owner. After paying claims for salvage, the master claimed to retain the balance of the proceeds of sale for freight.

Held, although the ship was prevented by excepted perils from completing the voyage, no freight was payable.

In that case[15] Lord Ellenborough stated the principles relating to the payment of freight as follows:

'The shipowners undertake that they will carry the goods to the place of destination, unless prevented by the dangers of the seas or other unavoidable casualties; and the freighter undertakes that if the goods be delivered at the place of their destination, he will pay the stipulated freight but it was only in that event, viz, of their delivery at the place of destination, that he, the freighter, engages to pay anything. If the ship be disabled from completing her voyage, the shipowner may still entitle himself to the whole freight, by forwarding the goods by some other means to the place of destination; but he has no right to any freight if they are not so forwarded, unless the forwarding of them be dispensed with, or unless there be some new bargain upon this subject. If the shipowner will not forward them, the freighter is entitled to them without paying anything.'

But where the shipowner is prevented solely by the act or default of the cargo-owner from carrying the goods to their destination, full freight is payable.

Thus, in *Cargo ex Galam*[16]

The ship was driven ashore at Scilly and the cargo had to be landed and stored there. The charterer wished to alter the port of destination and named Hamburg. But the holders of a respondentia bond on the cargo, payable at Falmouth, obtained an order from the Court for the removal of the cargo to London and its sale there.

Held, that as the shipowner had not abandoned his intention of completing the voyage, but had been prevented from doing so by the order of the Court, occasioned by the default of the cargo-owner, he was entitled to the freight.

14   (1808) 10 East 378.
15   Ibid, at 394.
16   (1863) 33 LJPM & A 97.

As long as delivery of the goods has been made, the shipowner is still entitled to claim freight even though the vessel has been overloaded in breach of the Merchant Shipping (Safety and Load Line Conventions) Act 1932.[17]

If the vessel unjustifiably deviates from the contractual route, the contractual rate of freight is not payable.[18] But if the goods are delivered safely, he will be entitled to a reasonable remuneration on a quantum meruit basis.[19]

Similarly, where a charter-party had been frustrated by the closure of the Suez Canal, a shipowner was entitled to a reasonable remuneration for bringing the goods safely to their destination via the Cape of Good Hope, but could not claim the contractual rate of freight.[20]

(2) Lump sum freight

To earn lump sum freight,[1] either the ship must complete the voyage, or else the cargo must be transhipped, or forwarded by some means other than the ship in which it was originally loaded, and delivered by the shipowner or his agents at its destination.[2]

Where the ship fails to complete the voyage and some portion of the cargo is lost, the question arises whether any deduction is to be made from the lump sum agreed on.

Thus, in *Thomas v Harrowing SS Co*[3]

Lump sum freight was payable on delivery of a cargo of props. The exception clause included 'perils of the sea'. Near the port of discharge, the vessel was driven ashore

17 *St John Shipping Corpn v Joseph Rank Ltd* [1957] 1 QB 267, [1956] 3 All ER 683.
18 *Joseph Thorley Ltd v Orchis SS Co Ltd* [1907] 1 KB 660, CA.
19 *Hain SS Co Ltd v Tate and Lyle Ltd* [1936] 2 All ER 597, HL.
20 *Société Franco Tunisienne d'Armement v Sidermar SpA, The Messalia* [1961] 2 QB 278, [1960] 2 All ER 529. This decision was overruled as to the question of frustration by *Ocean Tramp Tankers Corpn v Sofracht V/O, The Eugenia* [1964] 2 QB 226, [1964] 1 All ER 161, [1963] 2 Lloyd's Rep 381, CA, but not on the point considered above, so presumably on that point the decision at first instance still stands.
1 In *Shell International Petroleum Ltd v Seabridge Shipping Ltd, The Metula* [1978] 2 Lloyd's Rep 5, CA, although the freight was not a lump sum freight properly so called, it had the characteristics of a lump sum freight in that the freight was computed on the intaken quantity and was to be paid on that quantity even though there was a shortage. (See the judgment of Lord Denning MR, ibid, at 7.)
2 See per Lord Haldane LC, in *Thomas v Harrowing SS Co* [1915] AC 58 at 63; also per Tindal CJ, in *Mitchell v Darthez* (1836) 2 Bing NC 555 at 569 et seq.
3 [1915] AC 58.

by bad weather and became a total loss. Part of the cargo was washed ashore and was afterwards collected on the beach by the master's directions and deposited on the dock premises, the rest being lost by perils of the sea.

Held, the shipowners had performed their contract, which was to deliver the cargo so far as they were not prevented by 'perils of the sea'; and they were entitled to recover the whole lump sum freight, even though the charter-party stipulated that it should be payable 'on unloading *and right delivery* of the cargo'.

Where lump sum freight is payable on 'right and true delivery' of the cargo, these words do not mean right and true delivery of the whole of the cargo shipped, and accordingly freight becomes due when the cargo which has arrived at the port of discharge has been completely delivered.[4]

Further, it seems that where the ship arrives at her destination, the shipper must pay full lump sum freight even if some of the goods are lost through causes other than excepted perils.[5] Again, the cargo delivered need not be that which was agreed upon in the charter-party; for a different cargo may, in fact, have been loaded.[6]

Sometimes, however, the contract provides that the lump sum freight must be paid in advance and will not be returnable even if the vessel and/or her cargo are lost.[7]

Where a vessel is chartered for a lump sum freight, the charterers are not entitled to set off against the freight a claim for damages for an alleged failure to prosecute the voyage with reasonable dispatch.[8]

(3) Advance freight

Where advance freight is agreed upon, payment does not depend on delivery and must be made even though the ship is lost and the cargo never delivered.[9]

---

4   *Skibs A/S Trolla and Skibs A/S Tautra v United Enterprises and Shipping (Pte) Ltd, The Tarva* [1973] 2 Lloyd's Rep 385, Singapore High Ct. (See the judgment of Chua J, ibid, at 387.)

5   See per Sir E V Williams in *The Norway* (1865) 13 LT 50 at 52.

6   *Ritchie v Atkinson* (1808) 10 East 295.

7   E g in *Northern Sales Ltd v The Giancarlo Zeta, The Giancarlo Zeta* [1966] 2 Lloyd's Rep 317 (Exchequer Court, British Columbia Admiralty District), where the charter-party stated: 'Freight Rate: A lump sum $130,000 US currency fully prepared upon surrender of signed bills of lading, discountless and non-returnable vessel and/or cargo lost or not lost, freight deemed earned as cargo loaded on board.' As to advance freight, see infra.

8   *Gunnstein A/S & Co K/S v Jensen, Krebs and Nielsen, The Alfa Nord* [1977] 2 Lloyd's Rep 434, CA.

9   Freight clauses vary very greatly in their wording. In general, one case affords

Thus, in *De Silvale v Kendall*[10]

A vessel was chartered for a voyage from Liverpool to Maranham and back to Liverpool. She arrived at Maranham, and the shipper paid an advance freight of £192. She sailed on her homeward voyage, but was lost by capture.
Held, by the Court of King's Bench, that the shipper was not entitled to recover the advance freight.[11]

If after advance freight has been paid the voyage is abandoned, no part of the freight can be recovered.[12] Advance freight must be paid to the shipowner even if the goods are lost (by excepted perils) before payment, where they are lost after the due date of payment; nor is it recoverable if the goods are so lost after payment.

Where freight is made payable 'on final sailing', the ship must have left the port of departure, with no intention of returning.

Thus, in *Roelandts v Harrison*[13]

The ship was being towed out to sea when she ran aground in a ship-canal leading from the dock to the sea.
Held, freight payable 'on final sailing' was not due. The ship must have got clear of the port and be at sea, ready to proceed on the voyage.

As freight is prima facie payable on delivery of the goods, the burden of making out a case for advance freight is on the shipowner. Where freight was 'payable in London', it was held that the stipulation referred to the place and not to the time of payment. As the vessel was lost on the voyage, no freight became due.[14]

Sometimes there is a proviso that freight is to be paid 'ship lost or not lost'. This indicates an obligation to pay freight whether the ship is lost or not, provided that the loss is due to an excepted peril.[15]

Again, it is sometimes stipulated that freight shall be payable at a certain fixed time, or on the happening of a certain event, instead of merely 'in advance'.

little help in construing another: *Vagres Compania Maritima SA v Nissho-Iwai American Corpn, The Karin Vatis* [1988] 2 Lloyd's Rep 330 at 333 (per Lloyd LJ).
10 *De Silvale v Kendall* (1815) 4 M & S 37. For a case where advance freight was not due but was paid to the shipowners, who accepted it on the assumption that it was charter hire, and it was held that the freight was recoverable, see *Afro Produce (Supplies) Ltd v Metalfa Shipping Co Ltd, The Georgios* [1978] 2 Lloyd's Rep 197, QBD (Commercial Court). (See the judgment of Donaldson J, ibid, at 202.)
11 See the judgment of Bayley J: *De Silvale v Kendall*, supra, at 45.
12 *Civil Service Co-operative Society v General Steam Navigation Co* [1903] 2 KB 756.
13 (1854) 9 Exch 444.
14 *Krall v Burnett* (1877) 25 WR 305.
15 *Great Indian Peninsular Rly Co v Turnbull* (1885) 53 LT 325.

Thus, in *Oriental SS Co v Tylor*[16]

One-third of the freight was made payable 'on signing bills of lading'. The ship and cargo were lost before bills of lading had been signed, and the charterers refused to present them for signature, actually holding them back until the ship had sunk.
Held, the charterers must pay one-third of the freight charges as damages for breach of contract.

Where advance freight is to be paid 'within 5 days of the master signing bills of lading', and the charter-party is frustrated by the vessel and her cargo being lost before the end of the fifth day after the signing of the bills of lading, no advance freight is payable because there is no debt for which the shipowner could have sued in the normal course of events until after the expiry of the fifth day.[17]

Further, where a clause in a bill of lading stated that freight was to be 'completely earned on shipment', it was held that no freight was payable if the goods were never shipped on board.[18]

Where freight 'is deemed earned as cargo loaded', and payment of 95 per cent of the freight is to be paid within 3 days after completion of loading, ship lost or not lost, and the balance is to be paid in 20 days after completion of discharge, and the vessel is lost on her voyage, the balance must be paid within a reasonable time.[19] The completion of the discharge of the cargo was not a condition precedent to the shipowners' claim for the balance.[20]

But where the clause does not contain words to the effect that the freight 'is deemed earned as cargo loaded', and states that some of it must be paid on the signing of the bills of lading and the balance must be paid on completion of discharge, the shipowners have no cause of action for the balance.[1]

Once the right to advance freight has accrued, it must be paid in full and the charterer has no right to set-off against the shipowner

---

16 [1893] 2 QB 518.
17 *Compania Naviera General SA v Kerametal Ltd, The Lorna I* [1983] 1 Lloyd's Rep 373, CA. (See the judgment of Sir John Donaldson, ibid, at 375.)
18 *Seald-Sweet Sales Inc v Finnlines (Meriventi Oy), The Finn Forest* [1975] 2 Lloyd's Rep 92, District Court, Eastern District of New York.
19 *Vagres Compania Maritima SA v Nissho-Iwai American Corpn, The Karin Vatis* [1988] 2 Lloyd's Rep 330, CA.
20 Ibid. See the judgment of Lloyd LJ, ibid, at 332, and that of Slade LJ, ibid, at 336.
 1 *The Samos Glory* [1986] 2 Lloyd's Rep 603, QBD (Commercial Court), where there was a clause stating that the entire freight should remain at all times at owners' risk.

any claim which he himself has, eg in respect of the costs of the transhipment of the cargo.[2]

No set off is available to the charterer even if the shipowner wrongfully repudiates the charter-party after the freight has become due.[3]

Advance freight must be distinguished from advances of cash which it is often agreed shall be made by a charterer to meet the current expenses of the ship, and which are usually deducted from the freight if it becomes payable. The latter are simply a loan to the shipowner, and can be recovered in any case. An advance payment will be construed by the Court either as advance freight or as a loan according to the intention of the parties as expressed in the documents.[4]

If the charter-party shows that it was the intention of the parties that the charterer making the advances should insure them, that is almost conclusive that the advances are to be on account of freight.

Thus, in *Hicks v Shield*[5]

It was agreed that 'cash for ship's disbursements to be advanced to the extent of £300 free of interest, but subject to insurance, and £2 10s per cent commission'.

Held, the payment constituted advance freight, Lord Campbell said: 'This mention of insurance seems to me to stamp the transaction indelibly as a payment on account of freight, and not a mere loan; for if the advance was to be insured, it must be an advance of freight which is insurable whereas a loan is not.'

(4) Pro rata freight

Sometimes pro rata freight is payable, ie a payment proportionate to the part of the voyage accomplished or to the part of the cargo delivered.

Where the facts warrant an inference that delivery at an intermediate port is to be accepted as part performance of the contract, the law implies a promise to pay pro rata freight in proportion to the part of the voyage completed.[6]

To raise such an implied promise to pay pro rata freight the merchant must have the option of having his goods conveyed to the

---

2 *Bank of Boston Connecticut v European Grain and Shipping Ltd, The Dominique* [1989] 1 All ER 545, [1989] 2 WLR 440 HL.
3 Ibid.
4 *Allison v Bristol Marine Insurance Co* (1876) 1 App Cas 209 at 229.
5 (1857) 7 E & B 633.
6 *Hill v Wilson* (1879) 4 CPD 329.

port of destination. He must exercise a real choice. Thus, a promise to pay pro rata freight will not be implied merely from acceptance of the goods at an intermediate port where the master insisted on leaving them,[7] or from acceptance of the proceeds of sale where the master has exercised his discretion to sell the cargo in the interests of the cargo-owners.[8]

It follows that pro rata freight is payable only if the shipowner was able and willing to carry the cargo to its destination.

Thus, in *Vlierboom v Chapman*[9]

Rice was to be delivered at Rotterdam. During the voyage, some was jettisoned and the rest had to be sold at Mauritius.
Held, that as the shipowner could not have delivered at Rotterdam, no fresh agreement for the payment of pro rata freight could be inferred.

Again, in *St Enoch Shipping Co Ltd v Phosphate Mining Co*[10]

A vessel was on a voyage from Tampa to Hamburg. On 3 August 1914, she was warned by the Admiralty to go to an English port. Next day war broke out and it was impossible for her to go to Hamburg. She therefore discharged the cargo at Runcorn where the shipowners claimed pro rata freight.
Held, no freight was payable since the voyage had not been completed, and no new contract to take delivery at Runcorn instead of at Hamburg could be implied.

Sometime the cargo-owner expressly asks for delivery to be made at an intermediate port, and then freight is payable.

Thus, in *Christy v Row*[11]

Coal was shipped for Hamburg. Owing to the presence of a French army, it was dangerous to get to Hamburg and the cargo-owner asked for delivery at an intermediate port. Part of the cargo was delivered there, but the vessel was then ordered to leave the port. The cargo-owner refused to pay freight.
Held, there was an agreement to accept delivery at the intermediate port as a substituted performance of the contract, and full freight was payable on the goods delivered there.

(5) Back freight

Normal delivery at the port of destination may sometimes be prevented by some cause beyond the control of the master, eg a

---

7   *Metcalfe v Britannia Ironworks Co* (1877) 2 QBD 423.
8   *Hunter v Prinsep* (1808) 10 East 378.
9   (1844) 13 LJ Ex 384.
10   [1916] 2 KB 624.
11   (1808) 1 Taunt 300.

failure on the part of the cargo-owner to take delivery. In such cases the master may and must deal with the cargo for the benefit of its owners by landing it, carrying it on, or transhipping it, as may seem best. The shipowner may then charge the cargo-owners with 'back freight' to cover the expenses thus incurred in their interest.

Thus, in *Cargo ex Argos*[12]

A shipper had loaded a cargo of petroleum on board a vessel bound from London to Le Havre. When she reached Le Havre, the port authorities instructed the master to take her out of the harbour because there were large quantities of munitions there. The master tried to land the cargo at neighbouring ports, but eventually decided that it would be best to go back to London.
Held, the shipowner was entitled to back freight since, in all the circumstances, the master had dealt with the cargo for the benefit of the shipper as seemed best to him.

(6) Dead freight

Where a charterer has failed to fulfil his contract to provide a full cargo, the shipowner has a good cause of action against him for 'dead freight', i e damages.[13]

The claim for dead freight being a claim for damages for breach of contract, the shipowner is under a duty, where the charterer fails to load a full and complete cargo, to minimise the damage by obtaining other cargo, provided he acts reasonably in so doing. It follows that 'he must also have implied liberty to delay the charter voyage by the period of time reasonably and necessarily occupied in taking in that substituted cargo'.[14]

BY WHOM FREIGHT IS PAYABLE

The shipowner can claim freight from the following persons:

(1) the shipper of the goods;
(2) the consignee or indorsee of the bill of lading;

---

12 (1873) 42 LJ Adm 1.
13 See *McLean and Hope v Fleming* (1871) LR 2 Sc & Div 128. For a case where the charterers were held to be allowed to set off the amount of overpayment of dead freight against the shipowners' increased claim for demurrage, see *Bedford SS Co Ltd v Navico AG, The Ionian Skipper* [1977] 2 Lloyd's Rep 273, QBD (Commercial Court).
14 *Wallems Rederij A/S v W H Muller & Co, Batavia* [1927] 2 KB 99.

(3) a seller who stops the goods in transit;
(4) the charterer.

(1) The shipper of the goods

The liability to pay freight reserved in a bill of lading is primarily that of the shipper of the goods, unless he was merely acting as agent and made this clear at the time.

By shipping goods, the shipper impliedly agrees to pay the freight on them. He can be relieved of this obligation:

(1) by the shipowner giving credit to the consignee. Thus, if the master for his own convenience takes a bill of exchange from a consignee who was willing to pay cash, the shipper is discharged;[15] *or*
(2) by delivery of a bill of lading indorsed with a clause freeing the shipper from liability, the shipowner or his agent knowing, at the time, of the existence of such a clause.[16]

The Bills of Lading Act 1855, s 2, expressly preserves the shipowner's right to claim freight from the original shipper, so that the shipowner can elect to sue the holder of the bill of lading or the shipper.[17]

(2) The consignee or indorsee of the bill of lading

The bill of lading usually contains a clause making delivery conditional on the consignee or his assigns paying freight. The master of the ship is entitled to refuse delivery unless the freight is paid. The mere delivery of goods does not impose a legal liability to pay the freight on them,[18] but is evidence of an implied promise to do so.[19] A custom of the trade, and even earlier transactions between the same parties, are also admissible as evidence of an implied contract.

15 *Strong v Hart* (1827) 6 B & C 160.
16 See *Watkins v Rymill* (1883) 10 QBD 178.
17 See Appendix C, post.
18 *Sanders v Vanzeller* (1843) 4 QB 260.
19 *Cock v Taylor* (1811) 13 East 399; see also per Parke B, in *Möller v Young* (1855) 25 LJQB 94 at 96.

The Bills of Lading Act 1855, s 1,[20] imposes on all consignees or indorsees of a bill of lading, to whom the property in goods passes, the liability to pay freight.

Where the goods have been shipped on a chartered ship, the bills of lading often include a clause stating 'freight and all other conditions as per charter'. But this clause will not incorporate provisions which are inconsistent with the bill of lading or which do not affect the consignee's right to take delivery.[1] Thus, where the bill of lading specifies an amount to be paid as freight, this cannot be altered by a general reference to the charter-party such as in the clause set out above.

(3) A seller who stops the goods in transit

A seller who stops in transit[2] is liable to pay freight on the cargo being delivered to the buyer; if the seller refuses, he is liable in damages to the shipowner for the amount of the freight.[3] But he does not, by stopping in transit, become a party to the contract of affreightment.

(4) The charterer

In the case of a charter-party, the charterer is primarily liable for freight,[4] and the fact that he has sublet the services of the ship to persons who have put goods on board under bills of lading reserving the same freight does not release him. Even if the shipowner delivers goods to such shippers without insisting on the payment of freight, he can still recover it from the charterer.[5]

Where the charterer is merely an agent or broker to fill the ship with the goods of other persons, his liability is made to cease when

---

20 See Appendix C, post.
1 See *Hogarth Shipping Co Ltd v Blyth, Greene, Jourdain & Co Ltd* [1917] 2 KB 534.
2 See pp 125–127, ante.
3 *Booth SS Co Ltd v Cargo Fleet Iron Co Ltd* [1916] 2 KB 570.
4 For a case where the shipowners were unable to recover freight from the charterers and alleged that the brokers had negligently mis-stated the financial standing and reliability of the charterers and the shipowners claimed damages from the brokers, see *Markappa Inc v N W Spratt & Son Ltd, The Arta* [1985] 1 Lloyd's Rep 534, CA.
5 *Shepard v De Bernales* (1811) 13 East 565.

the goods are shipped. This is effected by means of a 'cesser clause' inserted in the charter-party and giving the shipowner a lien on the cargo for freight[6] and other claims under the charter-party.

It seems, however, that a 'cesser clause' in the charter-party will not free a charterer, who is also the shipper and is sued as such, from liability to pay freight arising on the bill of lading, and that this is so even though the bill of lading provides for freight 'as per charter-party', since the 'cesser clause' protects only charterers as such and not shippers as such.[7]

TO WHOM FREIGHT IS PAYABLE

To whom freight is payable depends upon the terms of the contract, subject to any subsequent dealings, eg the assignment of the freight or the mortgage of the ship.

Thus, freight may be payable to:

(1) THE SHIPOWNER

The shipowner is, in the case of a charter-party not by way of demise or bill of lading, prima facie entitled to the freight.

or

(2) THE MASTER

Even where the contract was not made between the master and the consignee, 'it has been held that [the master] may maintain an action against the consignee upon an implied promise to pay the freight, in consideration of his letting the goods out of his hands before payment'.[8] The master cannot, however, sue for freight where he signed the bill of lading merely as the shipowner's agent.[9]

or

(3) THE BROKER

or

---

6 See p 275, post.
7 *Rederi Aktiebolaget Transatlantic v Board of Trade* (1925) 30 Com Cas 117 at 125–6; *Hill SS Co v Hugo Stinnes Ltd* 1941 SC 324.
8 Per Lord Mansfield CJ, in *Brouncker v Scott* (1811) 4 Taunt 1 at 4.
9 *Repetto v Millar's Karri and Jarrah Forests Ltd* [1901] 2 KB 306.

(4) A THIRD PERSON

It may be that, under the contract, freight was made payable to a third person. Payment of freight to such a person will protect the shipper from an action for freight.

or

(5) THE CHARTERER

Where the charter-party is one of demise, the charterer can sue for freight, for the shipowner was not a party to the contract evidenced by the bill of lading. But it is otherwise if the charter-party is only one of hiring, and the bills of lading covering goods shipped by third persons are signed by the master.[10]

or

(6) AN ASSIGNEE OF THE FREIGHT OR THE SHIP

Where the owner of the freight has assigned it, it must be paid to the assignee when it falls due.[11]

The right to freight is incidental to the ownership of the ship which earns it, and therefore a transfer of a share in a ship passes the corresponding share in the freight, under an existing charter-party, without the mention of the word 'freight'.

or

(7) A MORTGAGEE OF THE SHIP

A mortgagee does not acquire a right to the freight unless he has taken actual or constructive possession of the ship. He then becomes entitled to all the freight which the ship is in the course of earning, and which she proceeds to earn after such possession comes into being.[12]

This position is to be contrasted with that resulting from the sale of the ship or a share in her; for 'the purchaser of a ship takes a right

---

10   *A Coker & Co Ltd v Limerick SS Co Ltd* (1918) 34 TLR 296.
11   See eg *Bank of Boston Connecticut v European Grain and Shipping Ltd, The Dominique* [1989] 1 All ER 545, [1989] 2 WLR 440, HL, where the shipowners assigned the advance freight to a bank.
12   See, however, *Shillito v Biggart* [1903] 1 KB 683.

to all accruing freight, to all profits of the ship, from the time of the assignment to him and the transfer of the ship to him'.[13]

If the shipowner subsequently mortgages the ship, and the mortgagee has no notice of a previous assignment, the mortgagee will have a better claim to the freight than the assignee.[14]

13   Per Mellish LJ, in *Keith v Burrows* (1877) 46 LJQB 452 at 457.
14   *Wilson v Wilson* (1872) LR 14 Eq 32.

Chapter 12

Liens

In general, there are two types of lien:

(A) possessory liens; and
(B) maritime liens.

(A) POSSESSORY LIENS

Possessory liens arise at Common Law and also by express agreement.

(I) AT COMMON LAW

The Common Law grants a lien to two persons:

(1) the shipowner;
(2) the broker or other agent who has arranged shipment of the cargo on behalf of the shipper.

(1) The shipowner's lien

At Common Law the shipowner has possessory liens on the cargo for freight (but not dead freight, nor advance freight, nor freight payable after delivery), for general average contributions,[1] and for money spent in protecting the cargo.[2]

The shipowner may do what is reasonable to maintain any of

---

1 *Marvigor Compania Naviera SA v Romanoexport State Co for Foreign Trade, The Corinthian Glory* [1972] 2 Lloyd's Rep 280, QBD (Commercial Court), where there was an express clause giving a lien in respect of general average.
2 See per Blackburn J, in *Hingston v Wendt* (1876) 1 QBD 367 at 373.

these liens in view of the fact that they are possessory liens, ie they can only be enforced by retaining actual or constructive (eg in a statutory warehouse) possession of the cargo. He may, of course, waive the lien for freight; on the other hand, it can be exercised against all goods consigned to the same person on the same voyage, even under different bills of lading, but not against goods on different voyages under different contracts.[3]

Further, the Common Law lien for freight is not displaced unless the terms of the contract are inconsistent with it.[4]

Where freight is made payable on delivery, there will be a lien for it whether given by the contract or not. But where freight is made payable otherwise than on delivery, there will be no lien unless it is expressly given.

Thus, in *Tamvaco v Simpson*[5]

Half the freight was made payable by a bill of exchange at three months from signing the bills of lading, and the bill of exchange had not become due when the ship reached the port of discharge.
Held, that there was no lien for this part of the freight, although the shipper had become insolvent.

At Common Law the lien for freight could be enforced only by retaining the goods. The shipowner had no power to sell them in order to pay the freight.

But by the Merchant Shipping Act 1894, s 497,[6] a power to sell the goods is conferred after they have been warehoused for ninety days and the freight and charges on them have not been tendered. In the case of perishable goods, the power of sale may be exercised earlier.

(2) The broker's lien

In addition to the shipowner's lien, there is at Common Law a broker's lien on the bill of lading for his charges in respect of goods he has shipped. If the lien is not satisfied before they have reached their destination, he may have the goods brought home in order to retain his lien on them, and is not liable to any action for so doing.[7]

---

3   *Bernal v Pim* (1835) 1 Gale 17.
4   *Chase v Westmore* (1816) 5 M & S 180.
5   (1866) LR 1 CP 363.
6   See Appendix D, post.
7   *Edwards v Southgate* (1862) 10 WR 528.

On the other hand, a broker who has negotiated a charter-party, as opposed to merely arranging for the shipment of goods under bills of lading, where his commission is due on the execution of the charter-party, has no lien and cannot enforce the payment of such commission by action on the charter-party, for he is not a party to the contract. The difficulty can, however, be overcome by the charterer suing the shipowner, the charterer acting as trustee for the broker.[8]

(II) BY EXPRESS AGREEMENT

Liens may be created by the contract, where they do not exist at Common Law, as, for example, for dead freight, demurrage,[9] damages for detention or even 'all charges whatsoever'.

A usual clause[10] in a voyage charter-party states

'Owners shall have a lien on the cargo for freight, dead-freight, demurrage and damages for detention. Charterers shall remain responsible for dead-freight and demurrage (including damages for detention) incurred at port of loading. Charterers shall also remain responsible for freight and demurrage (including damages for detention incurred at port of discharge, but only to such extent as the owners have been unable to obtain payment thereof by exercising the lien on the cargo.'

Where a charter-party gives the shipowner a lien on the cargo for the payment of the freight, and the freight is payable 'immediately after completion of discharge', the lien cannot be exercised until that time.[11]

As against an indorsee of the bill of lading, the word 'charges' does not include charges which are specifically mentioned in the charter-party.[12] It seems, however, that, as against the charterer, a lien in respect of expenses properly incurred by the shipowner in

---

8 *Robertson v Wait* (1853) 8 Exch 299; *Les Affréteurs Réunis SA v Leopold Walford (London) Ltd* [1919] AC 801; *Christie and Vesey v Maatschappij Tot Exploitatie van Schepen en Andere Zaken, The Helvetia NV* [1960] 1 Lloyd's Rep 540.

9 *Gray v Carr* (1871) LR 6 QB 522; *Gulf Steel Co Ltd v Al Khalifa Shipping Co Ltd, The Anwar Al Sabar* [1980] 2 Lloyd's Rep 261, QBD (Commercial Court); *Maritime Transport Operators GmbH v Louis Dreyfus & Cie, The Tropwave* [1981] 2 Lloyd's Rep 159, QBD (Commercial Court).

10 'Gencon' charter-party, cl 8 (Appendix B, post). For demurrage and damages for detention, see Chapter 10, ante.

11 *Canada Pacific (Bermuda) Ltd v Lagon Maritime Overseas, The Fort Kipp* [1985] 2 Lloyd's Rep 168, QBD (Commercial Court).

12 *Rederiaktieselskabet Superior v Dewar and Webb* [1909] 2 KB 998; *Gardner v Trechmann*, infra, was distinguished.

warehouseing the goods in order to avoid demurrage would be conferred by a clause granting a lien for 'freight, demurrage and all other charges whatsoever'.[13] But even a very widely worded clause giving a lien for any money due to the carrier from either shipper or consignee will not give a right of lien superior to the right of an unpaid seller who stops the goods in transit.[14]

The position of holders of a bill of lading, other than the charterer himself or his agent, where the bill of lading contains a lien clause, may be summarised by saying that

'unless the language used in the bill of lading is wide enough to extend the shipowner's rights, the holder of the bill of lading is entitled to have his goods delivered to him upon payment of the freight reserved by the bill of lading; as against him there is no lien for freight payable under the charter-party in respect of the same or other goods, or for the difference, if any, between the bill of lading freight and the [charter-party] freight,[15] or for dead freight, or for demurrage at the port of loading.[16]

To avoid the operation of this principle it must be made absolutely clear by the bill of lading that such was not the intention of the parties.[17] Mere notice of the charter-party is not sufficient to extend such liens, even where the holder of the bill of lading has himself prescribed, in his capacity as sub-charterer, the form of charter-party to be used.[18]

In *Gardner v Trechmann*[19]

The charter-party reserved freight at 31s 3d per ton. It contained a clause giving 'an absolute lien on the cargo for freight, dead freight, demurrage, lighterage at port of discharge, and average'. The master was given power to sign bills of lading at any rate of freight, and provision was made for him to demand payment in advance of the difference between charter-party and bill of lading freight. Bills of lading were signed reserving freight at 22s 6d per ton and containing a clause 'other conditions as per charter-party'.
Held, that the lien for charter-party freight was not preserved as against a consignee (other than the charterer) under the bill of lading. As to the clause 'other conditions as per charter-party', it was said: 'It brings in only those clauses of the charter-party which are applicable to the contract contained in the bill of lading; and those clauses of the charter-party cannot be brought in which would alter the express stipulations

---

13   *Harley v Gardner* (1932) 43 Ll L Rep 104.
14   *United States Steel Products Co v Great Western Rly Co* [1916] 1 AC 189.
15   *Gardner v Trechmann* (1884) 15 QBD 154.
16   Halsbury's Laws of England (4th edn), vol 43, para 692.
17   *Pearson v Goschen* (1864) 17 CBNS 352.
18   See *Turner v Haji Goolam Mahomed Azam* [1904] AC 826.
19   Supra.

in the bill of lading',[20] Again: 'It does not take in the clause of lien as to the charter-party freight'.[1]

Where, however, the consignee is also the charterer, the lien can be exercised for the full charter-party freight,[2] unless a new contract evidenced by the bill of lading shows a contrary intention.[3]

In the case of time charter-parties a usual clause[4] states:

'The owners to have a lien upon all cargoes and sub-freights belonging to the time charterers and any bill of lading freight for all claims under this charter, and the charterers to have a lien on the vessel for all moneys paid in advance and not earned.'[5]

Where the shipowner is a company the sub-freights are book debts, and the lien should be registered under the Companies Act 1985, s 395.[6] If it is not registered, it is void as against the liquidator.[7]

(B) MARITIME LIENS

Maritime liens are of a different nature from those noticed above, and they operate in a different way. A maritime lien is a privileged claim on a ship, or on her cargo, or on either both of these and the freight, in respect of service done to, or injury caused by, them.[8] A

---

20 Per Brett MR at 157.
1 Per Cotton LJ at 158.
2 *McLean and Hope v Fleming* (1871) LR 2 Sc & Div 128.
3 See per Willes J, in *Pearson v Goschen*, supra, at 374.
4 'Baltime 1939' form, cl 18.
5 See eg *Steelwood Carriers Inc of Monrovia Liberia v Evimeria Compania Naviera SA of Panama, The Agios Giorgis* [1976] 2 Lloyd's Rep 192, QBD (Commercial Court); *Aegnoussiotis Shipping Corpn of Monrovia v Kristian Jebsens Rederi of Bergen A/S, The Aegnoussiotis* [1977] 1 Lloyd's Rep 268, QBD (Commercial Court); *International Bulk Carriers (Beirut) SARL v Evlogia Shipping Co SA and Marathon Shipping Co Ltd, The Mihalios Xilas* [1978] 2 Lloyd's Rep 186, QBD (Commercial Court); *Re Welsh Irish Ferries Ltd, The Ugland Trailer* [1985] 2 Lloyd's Rep 372, Ch D; *Annagel Glory Compania Naviera SA v M Golodetz Ltd, Middle East Marketing Corpn (UK) Ltd, and Hammond, The Annangel Glory* [1988] 1 Lloyd's Rep 45, QBD (Commercial Court); *G & N Angelakis Shipping Co SA v Compagnie National Algerienne de Navigation, The Attika Hope* [1988] 1 Lloyd's Rep 439, QBD (Commercial Court). For a case where a charter-party stated that the shipowner had a lien on 'all sub-freights', and it was held that the lien extended to sub-sub-freights, see *Care Shipping Corpn v Latin American Shipping Corpn, The Cebu* [1983] 1 Lloyd's Rep 302, QBD (Commercial Court). (See the judgment of Lloyd J, ibid, at 306.)
6 *Re Welsh irish Ferries Ltd, The Ugland Trailer*, supra; *Annagel Glory Compania Naviera SA v M Golodetz Ltd, Middle East Marketing Corpn (UK) Ltd and Hammond*, supra.
7 Ibid.
8 *The Ripon City* [1897] P 226.

maritime lien cannot generally exist in respect of a foreign State-owned vessel or a vessel compulsorily requisitioned for public purposes by a sovereign State.[9] But where a vessel owned by a foreign State is engaged in ordinary trading, no immunity will be granted to her.[10]

Again, a maritime lien travels with the thing to which it attaches, into whosesoever hands that thing may pass; it is in no way dependent on possession, as are the other liens mentioned above. 'It is inchoate from the moment the claim or privilege attaches, and, when called into effect by the legal process of a proceeding in rem, relates back to the period when it first attached'.[11] Further, a maritime lien attaches and remains effective even if only pronounced by a foreign court.

The principal maritime liens recognised by English law are those in respect of disbursements of the master, salvage, wages,[12] and damage done by the ship to another ship or property resulting from want of skill or from negligent navigation.[13]

Maritime liens, if not properly discharged by the owner of the property affected, are enforced by proceedings in rem; if necessary, the Court will order the property charged to be sold.

Maritime liens which arise ex delicto (ie as a result of damage done by the thing affected), generally rank before those arising ex contractu (eg in respect of bottomry bonds or salvage), since an injured party has no option, whereas those who render services take the risk of subsequent claims attaching.[14] But the lien of *subsequent* salvors has priority over a damage lien of *earlier* date, because the salvors have preserved the property for the benefit of the earlier lienee.[15]

---

9   *The Parlement Belge* (1880) 5 PD 197; *The Porto Alexandre* [1920] P 30; *Compania Naviera Vascongada v SS Cristina* [1938] AC 485, [1938] 1 All ER 719.

10   *The Philippine Admiral* [1977] AC 373, [1976] 1 All ER 78, PC. The State Immunity Act 1978 provides that a State is not immune as respects an action in rem belonging to that State or an action in personam for enforcing a claim in connection with such a ship if, at the time when the cause of action arose, the ship was in use or intended for use for commercial purposes: s 10(2).

11   Halsbury's Laws of England (4th edn), vol 43, para 1131.

12   Including arrears of National Insurance contributions: *The Gee-Whiz* [1951] 1 All ER 876n; and contributions to a pension fund: *The Halcyon Skies, Powell v The Halcyon Skies* [1976] 1 Lloyd's Rep 461, QBD (Admiralty Court).

13   But see *The Rene* (1922) 38 TLR 790.

14   *The Veritas* [1901] P 304.

15   *The Inna* [1938] P 148; *The Lyrma (No 2)* [1978] 2 Lloyd's Rep 30, QBD (Admiralty Court). (See the judgment of Brandon J, ibid, at 33.)

Where there is more than one lien arising ex delicto, it seems that, if A obtains judgment before B institutes his action, A will have priority; but that, apart from such a case, the several claimants rank pari passu with each other.[16]

As between contractual lienees priority depends on a variety of factors which cannot here be examined in detail. One broad principle should, however, be noted: if, after a contractual lien has attached in favour of A, B preserves the security from destruction by rendering services (e g salvage) which confer on him a lien, B will have priority over A.[17] This principle applies to cases of salvage, to money advanced by mortgagees, and to the crew's lien for wages, all of which, both against other claims and inter se, rank in inverse order of attachment.[18]

In some cases there is a statutory right to arrest ship.[19] For example, where there is a claim for towage or salvage, or where goods or materials have been supplied to a ship for operation or maintenance,[20] or where there is a dispute as to the ownership of a ship, or where there is a claim by the master or seamen for wages earned, the Court may arrest the ship[1] or a ship in the same ownership[2] until the dispute is determined.

The object of arresting the ship is, of course, to secure her continued presence and to prevent her from slipping away. The right does not, strictly speaking, give rise to a lien, though it is sometimes so described. It should be noted that any maritime liens attaching to the ship at the time of her arrest have priority over the claim for which she was arrested.[3]

16 *The Stream Fisher* [1927] P 73.
17 *The Veritas*, supra.
18 *The Selina* (1842) 2 Notes of Cases 18; *The Hope* (1873) 1 Asp MLC 563; *The Veritas*, supra; *The Mons* [1932] P 109.
19 Supreme Court Act 1981, ss 20, 21.
20 *The Zafiro, John Carlbom & Co v Zafiro SS (Owners)* [1960] P 1, [1959] 2 All ER 537.
1 Supreme Court Act 1981, s 21(4)(a); *The Andrea Ursula, Medway Drydock and Engineering Co Ltd v Beneficial Owners of Ship Andrea Ursula* [1971] 1 All ER 821, [1971] 2 WLR 681.
2 Supreme Court Act 1981, s 21(4)(b); *The St Elefterio, Schwarz & Co (Grain) v St Elefterio ex Arion (Owners)* [1957] P 179, [1957] 2 All ER 374; *Monte Ulia (Owners) v The Banco (Owners)* [1971] 1 Lloyd's Rep 49, CA. A voyage charterer is not the 'beneficial owner' of a ship within the meaning of the Supreme Court Act 1981, s 21(4)(b); *Antaios Compania Naviera SA v Ledesma Overseas Shipping Corpn, The Ledesco Uno* [1978] 2 Lloyd's Rep 99, Hong Kong High Court (Admiralty Jurisdiction).
3 *Johnson v Black, The Two Ellens* (1872) LR 4 PC 161.

Chapter 13

Carriage of goods by hovercraft

The carriage of goods by hovercraft[1] is governed by the terms of the contract and by the Hovercraft Act 1968, and Orders made under it.[2]

The Act defines a 'hovercraft' as 'a vehicle which is designed to be supported when in motion wholly or partly be air expelled from the vehicle to form a cushion of which the boundaries include the ground, water or other surface beneath the vehicle'.[3]

The Hovercraft (Civil Liability) Order 1986,[4] applies with modifications

(1) the Carriage of Goods by Sea Act 1971, to the carriage of cargo by hovercraft;

(2) the Merchant Shipping Act 1979, in relation to the limitation of liability for damage caused by hovercraft;

(3) the Crown Proceedings Act 1947, to hovercraft owned by the Crown; and

(4) the Maritime Conventions Act 1911, as far as collisions are concerned.

(1) Application of the Carriage of Goods by Sea Act 1971

The Order[5] states that the Act is to apply in relation to the carriage

1 The Unfair Contract Terms Act 1977 applies to the charter-party of a hovercraft as it does to a charter-party of a ship. See p 79, ante. It applies to bills of lading in respect of goods shipped on a hovercraft as it does to goods shipped under bills of lading on a ship. See p 128, ante.

2 By virtue of s 1(1) of the Act.

3 Hovercraft Act 1968, s 4(1). But a 'hovercraft' is treated as a 'ship' for the purposes of the Harbours Act 1964, which by s 57(1) states '"ship", where used as a noun, includes every description of vessel used in navigation, seaplanes on the surface of the water and hover vehicles, that is to say, vehicles designed to be supported on a cushion of air.'

4 SI 1986/1305.

5 Hovercraft (Civil Liability) Order 1986, Art 4 and Sch 2.

of goods[6] by hovercraft (other than passengers' baggage)[7] as it applies to goods on board or carried by ship.

The Act, as modified by the Order, is set out in Sch 4.[8]

There are minor modifications, eg the word 'hovercraft' is substituted for 'ship' wherever that word occurs in the Act of 1971, and 'hoverport' is substituted for 'port'.[9] The words 'hovercraft fit for the voyage' are substituted for 'seaworthy ship'.[10]

The limit of liability is £494·06 per package or unit or £1·48 per kg of gross weight of the goods lost or damaged, whichever is the higher.[11]

(2) Application of the Merchant Shipping Act 1979

The Order states that the Act of 1979 shall apply, subject to certain modifications in relation to:

(a) loss of life or personal injury connected with a hovercraft which is caused to persons not carried by the hovercraft;

(b) loss or damage connected with a hovercraft which is caused to property; and

(c) infringements of rights through acts or omissions connected with a hovercraft.[12]

But the right to limit liability under the Act is available if and only if at the time of the incident causing the damage the hovercraft

(i) was on or over navigable water[13] or on or over the foreshore; or

(ii) was proceeding between navigable water and a hoverport; or

---

6   A vehicle and its contents are not treated as baggage, whereas any property of which the passenger takes charge himself is treated as baggage: ibid, Art 5.
7   Ibid, Sch 2.
8   See Appendix E, p 334, post.
9   Hovercraft (Civil Liability) Order 1986, Sch 2.
10   Ibid, Sch 2.
11   Ibid, Art 4 and Sch 2.
12   Ibid, Art 6 and Sch 3.
13   'Navigable water' means any water which is in fact navigable by ships or vessels, whether or not the tide ebbs and flows there, and whether or not there is a public right of navigation in that water: ibid, Art 2(1).

(iii) was on or over a hoverport either preparing for or after such transit.[14]

Further, the right to limit liability does not apply to claims in respect of

(i) loss or damage to passengers' baggage[15] carried by the hovercraft; or

(ii) loss of or damage to crew's[16] property carried by the hovercraft.[17]

The limits of liability for claims arising on any distinct occasion are calculated as follows:

(a) in respect of claims for loss of life or personal injury:

   (i) £142, 014 for a hovercraft with a maximum operational weight not exceeding 8,000 kg;

   (ii) £276,601 for a hovercraft with a maximum operational weight in excess of 8,000 kg, but not exceeding 13,000 kg;

   (iii) for a hovercraft with a maximum operational weight in excess of 13,000 kg the following amount in addition to that mentioned in (ii):

     —for each kg from 13,001 to 80,000 kg, £15·98

     —for each kg in excess of 80,000 kg, £10·64,

(b) in respect of any other claim:

   (i) £59,560 for a hovercraft with a maximum operational weight not exceeding 8,000 kg;

   (ii) £116,378 for a hovercraft with a maximum operational weight in excess of 8,000 kg, but not exceeding 13,000 kg;

   (iii) for a hovercraft with a maximum operational weight in excess of 13,000 kg, an amount in addition to that mentioned at (ii) which equals £4·48 for each additional kg.[18]

---

14 Ibid, Art 6(1).
15 As to the meaning of baggage, see footnote 6, supra. The liability in respect of passengers and baggage carried by hovercraft is governed by the Carriage by Air Act 1961 and the Carriage of Air (Supplementary Provisions) Act 1962, as modified by Sch 1 to the Order: ibid, Art 3 and Sch 1.
16 'Crew' means a person who is on board a hovercraft or employed in connection with that hovercraft or with salvage operations, if he was so on board or employed under a contract of service governed by the law of any part of the United Kingdom: ibid, Art 6(2). 'Salvage operations' are limited to salvage operations to or from a hovercraft and do not include any such operations to or from a ship: ibid, Art 6(2), Sch 4.
17 Ibid, Art 6(2), Sch 4.
18 Ibid, Art 6(1), Sch 4.

Where the amount calculated in respect of claims for loss of life or personal injury is insufficient to pay them in full, the amount calculated in respect of any other claim is available for payment of the unpaid balance. Such unpaid balance of claims for loss of life or personal injury ranks rateably with any other claim.[19]

The Act of 1979, as modified, is set out in Sch 4 to the Order.[20]

(3) Application of the Crown Proceedings Act 1947

The Order states that the provisions mentioned above with relation to the limitation of liability apply to Crown hovercraft as they apply in relation to other hovercraft.[1]

Further, the Crown Proceedings Act 1947, ss 6[2] and 30[3] are to apply in the case of hovercraft as they apply in the case of vessels.[4]

(4) Application of the Maritime Conventions Act 1911

The Order states that ss 1, 2, 3, 8 and 9(4) of the Maritime Conventions Act 1911, are to apply as if references therein to vessels included references to hovercraft.[5]

These sections concern

  (i) division of loss (ie the Court may apportion liability according to the degree in which each vessel was at fault);
 (ii) damages for personal injuries caused by the fault of two or more vessels;
(iii) the right of contribution (ie the right of an owner of a vessel, who has paid damages to a third party in excess of the proportion in which the vessel was at fault, to obtain a

---

19 Ibid, Art 6(1), Sch 4.
20 Ibid, Art 6(1), Sch 4. See Appendix D, p 315, post.
 1 Ibid, Art 8(1).
 2 Which concerns the application to Crown ships of rules as to division of loss etc.
 3 Which concerns limitation of action.
 4 Hovercraft (Civil Liability) Order 1986, Art 8(2).
 5 Ibid, Art 7.

contribution in respect of the amount of the excess from the owners of the other vessel at fault);

(iv) the period of limitation (which is generally 2 years from the date of the damages or loss or injury); and

(v) the application of the Act of 1911 to various parts of the Commonwealth.

Appendix A

Specimen bill of lading

NOTE

The form appearing opposite is reproduced by courtesy of the New Zealand Tonnage Committee.

Appendix B

Specimen charter-parties

NOTE

The forms commencing on the following page are reproduced by the courtesy of the Baltic and International maritime Conference.

Issued ¹/₁ 1909
Amended ¹/₁ 1911
Amended ¹/₁ 1912
Amended ¹/₁ 1920
Amended ¹/₁ 1939
Amended ¹/₁ 1950
Amended ¹/₁ 1974

Adopted by the Documentary Committee of the Chamber of Shipping of the United Kingdom and the Documentary Committee of The Japan Shipping Exchange, Inc.

Copyright, published by The Baltic and International Maritime Conference, Copenhagen.

1. Shipbroker	THE BALTIC AND INTERNATIONAL MARITIME CONFERENCE UNIFORM TIME-CHARTER (Box Layout 1974) CODE NAME: "BALTIME 1939"
	PART I
	2. Place and date
3. Owners/Place of business	4. Charterers/Place of business
5. Vessel's name	6. GRT/NRT
7. Class	8. Indicated horse power
9. Total tons d.w. (abt.) on Board of Trade summer freeboard	10. Cubic feet grain/bale capacity
11. Permanent bunkers (abt.)	
12. Speed capability in knots (abt.) on a consumption in tons (abt.) of	
13. Present position	
14. Period of hire (Cl. 1)	15. Port of delivery (Cl. 1)
	16. Time of delivery (Cl. 1)
17. (a) Trade limits (Cl. 2)	
(b) Cargo exclusions specially agreed	
18. Bunkers on re-delivery (state min. and max. quantity) (Cl. 5)	
19. Charter hire (Cl. 6)	20. Hire payment (state currency, method and place of payment; also beneficiary and bank account) (Cl. 6)
21. Place or range of re-delivery (Cl. 7)	22. War (only to be filled in if Section (C) agreed) (Cl. 21)
23. Cancelling date (Cl. 22)	24. Place of arbitration (only to be filled in if place other than London agreed) (Cl. 23)
25. Brokerage commission and to whom payable (Cl. 25)	
	26. Numbers of additional clauses covering special provisions, if agreed

It is mutually agreed that this Contract shall be performed subject to the conditions contained in this Charter which shall include Part I as well as Part II. In the event of a conflict of conditions, the provisions of Part I shall prevail over those of Part II to the extent of such conflict.

Signature (Owners)	Signature (Charterers)

Printed and sold by S. Straker & Sons Ltd., 49, Fenchurch Street, London EC3M 3JY by authority of The Baltic and International Maritime Conference, Copenhagen.

PART II

"BALTIME 1939" Uniform Time-Charter (Box Layout 1974)

It is agreed between the party mentioned in Box 3   1
as Owners of the Vessel named in Box 5 of the   2
grosstnet Register tonnage indicated in Box 6,   3
classed as stated in Box 7 and of indicated horse   4
power as stated in Box 8, carrying about the   5
number of tons deadweight indicated in Box 9 on   6
Board of Trade summer freeboard inclusive of bun-   7
kers stores, provisions and boiler water, having as   8
per builder's plan a cubic-feet grain bale capacity   9
as stated in Box 10, exclusive of permanent bun-   10
kers, which contain about the number of tons   11
stated in Box 11, and fully loaded capable of   12
steaming about the number of knots indicated in   13
Box 12 in good weather and smooth water on a   14
consumption of about the number of tons best   15
Welsh coal or oil-fuel stated in Box 12, now in   16
position as stated in Box 13 and the party men-   17
tioned as Charterers in Box 4, as follows   18

1.   Period/Port of Delivery/Time of Delivery   19
The Owners let, and the Charterers hire the Ves-   20
sel for a period of the number of calendar months   21
indicated in Box 14 from the time (not a Sunday   22
or a legal Holiday unless taken over) the Vessel   23
is delivered and placed at the disposal of the   24
Charterers between 9 a.m. and 6 p.m., or between   25
9 a.m. and 2 p.m. if on Saturday, at the port   26
stated in Box 15 in such available berth where   27
she can safely lie always afloat, as the Charterers   28
may direct, she being in every way fitted for or-   29
dinary cargo service.   30
The Vessel to be delivered at the time indicated   31
in Box 16.   32

2.   Trade   33
The Vessel to be employed in lawful trades for   34
the carriage of lawful merchandise only between   35
good and safe ports or places where she can   36
safely lie always afloat within the limits stated in   37
Box 17.   38
No live stock nor injurious, inflammable or dan-   39
gerous goods (such as acids, explosives, calcium   40
carbide, ferro silicon, naphtha, motor spirit, tar,   41
or any of their products) to be shipped.   42

3.   Owners to Provide   43
The Owners to provide and pay for all provisions   44
and wages, for insurance of the Vessel, for all   45
deck and engine-room stores and maintain her in   46
a thoroughly efficient state in hull and machinery   47
during service.   48
The Owners to provide one winchman per hatch.   49
If further winchmen are required, or if the steve-   50
dores refuse or are not permitted to work with   51
the Crew, the Charterers to provide and pay   52
qualified shore-winchmen.   53

4.   Charterers to Provide   54
The Charterers to provide and pay for all coals,   55
including galley coal, oil-fuel, water for boilers,   56
port charges, pilotages (whether compulsory or   57
not), canal steersmen, boatage, lights, tug-assist-   58
ance, consular charges (except those pertaining   59
to the Master, Officers and Crew), canal, dock and   60
other dues and charges, including any foreign   61
general municipality or state taxes, also all dock,   62
harbour and tonnage dues at the ports of de-   63
livery and re-delivery (unless incurred through   64
cargo carried before delivery or after re-delivery),   65
agencies, commissions, also to arrange and pay   66
for loading, trimming, stowing (including dunnage   67
and shifting boards, excepting any already on   68
board), unloading, weighing, tallying and delivery   69
of cargoes, surveys on hatches, meals supplied to   70
officials and men in their service and all other   71
charges and expenses whatsoever including de-   72
tention and expenses through quarantine (includ-   73
ing cost of fumigation and disinfection).   74
All ropes, slings and special runners actually   75
used for loading and discharging and any special   76
gear, including special ropes, hawsers and chains   77
required by the custom of the port for mooring   78
to be for the Charterers' account. The Vessel to   79
be fitted with winches, derricks, wheels and or-   80
dinary runners capable of handling lifts up to 2   81
tons.   82

5.   Bunkers   83
The Charterers at port of delivery and the Ow-   84
ners at port of re-delivery to take over and pay   85
for all coal or oil-fuel remaining in the Vessel's   86
bunkers at current price at the respective ports.   87
The Vessel to be re-delivered with not less than   88
the number of tons and not exceeding the num-   89
ber of tons of coal or oil-fuel in the Vessel's   90
bunkers stated in Box 18.   91

6.   Hire   92
The Charterers to pay as hire the rate stated in   93
Box 19 per 30 days, commencing in accordance   94
with Clause 1 until her re-delivery to the Owners.   95
Payment   96
Payment of hire to be made in cash, in the cur-   97
rency stated in Box 20, without discount, every   98
30 days, in advance, and in the manner prescribed   99
in Box 20.   100
In default of payment the Owners to have the   101
right of withdrawing the Vessel from the service   102
without, however, noting any protest and   103
without interference by any court or other   104
formality whatsoever and without prejudice to   105
any claim the Owners may otherwise have on the   106
Charterers under the Charter.   107

7.   Re-delivery   108
The Vessel to be re-delivered on the expiration   109
of the Charter in the same good order as when   110
delivered to the Charterers (fair wear and tear   111
excepted) at an ice-free port in the Charterers'   112
option at the place or within the range stated in   113
Box 21, between 9 a.m. and 6 p.m., and 9 a.m.   114
and 2 p.m. on Saturday, but the day of re-delivery   115
shall not be a Sunday or legal Holiday.   116
Notice   117
The Charterers to give the Owners not less than   118
ten days' notice at which port and on about   119
which day the Vessel will be re-delivered.   120
Should the Vessel be ordered on a voyage by   121
which the Charter period will be exceeded the   122
Charterers to have the use of the Vessel to   123
enable them to complete the voyage, provided it   124
could be reasonably calculated that the voyage   125
would allow re-delivery about the time fixed for   126
the termination of the Charter, but for any time   127
exceeding the termination date the Charterers to   128
pay the market rate if higher than the rate stipu-   129
lated herein.   130

8.   Cargo Space   131
The whole reach and burthen of the Vessel, in-   132
cluding lawful deck-capacity to be at the Char-   133
terers' disposal, reserving proper and sufficient   134
space for the Vessel's Master, Officers, Crew,   135
tackle, apparel, furniture, provisions and stores.   136

9.   Master   137
The Master to prosecute all voyages with the ut-   138
most dyspatch and to render customary assist-   139
ance with the Vessel's Crew. The Master to be   140
under the orders of the Charterers as regards   141
employment, agency, or other arrangements. The   142
Charterers to indemnify the Owners against all   143
consequences or liabilities arising from the Ma-   144
ster, Officers or Agents signing Bills of Lading   145
or other documents or otherwise complying with   146
such orders, as well as from any irregularity in   147
the Vessel's papers or for overcarrying goods.   148
The Owners not to be responsible for shortage,   149
mixture, marks, nor for number of pieces or   150
packages, nor for damage to or claims on cargo   151
caused by bad stowage or otherwise.   152
If the Charterers have reason to be dissatisfied   153
with the conduct of the Master, Officers, or En-   154
gineers, the Owners on receiving particulars of   155
the complaint, promptly to investigate the matter,   156
and, if necessary and practicable, to make a   157
change in the appointments   158

10.   Directions and Logs   159
The Charterers to furnish the Master with all in-   160
structions and sailing directions and the Master   161
and Engineer to keep full and correct logs ac-   162
cessible to the Charterers or their Agents.   163

11.   Suspension of Hire etc.   164
(A) In the event of drydocking or other necessary   165
measures to maintain the efficiency of the Ves-   166
sel, deficiency of men or Owners' stores, break-   167
down of machinery, damage to hull or other ac-   168
cident, either hindering or preventing the work-   169
ing of the Vessel and continuing for more than   170
twenty-four consecutive hours, no hire to be paid   171
in respect of any time lost thereby during the   172
period in which the Vessel is unable to perform   173
the service immediately required. Any hire paid   174
in advance to be adjusted accordingly.   175
(B) In the event of the Vessel being driven into   176
port or to anchorage through stress of weather,   177
trading to shallow harbours or to rivers or ports   178
with bars or suffering an accident to her cargo,   179
any detention of the Vessel and/or expenses re-   180
sulting from such detention to be for the Char-   181
terers' account even if such detention and/or ex-   182
penses, or the cause by reason of which either   183
is incurred, be due to, or be contributed to   184
by, the negligence of the Owners' servants.   185

12.   Cleaning Boilers   186
Cleaning of boilers whenever possible to be done   187
during service, but if impossible the Charterers   188
to give the Owners necessary time for cleaning.   189
Should the Vessel be detained beyond 48 hours   190
hire to cease until again ready.   191

13.   Responsibility and Exemption   192
The Owners only to be responsible for delay in   193
delivery of the Vessel or for delay during the   194
currency of the Charter and for loss or damage   195
to goods onboard, if such delay or loss has been   196
caused by want of due diligence on the part of   197
the Owners or their Manager in making the Ves-   198
sel seaworthy and fitted for the voyage or any   199
other personal act or omission or default of the   200
Owners or their Manager. The Owners not to be   201
responsible in any other case nor for damage or   202
delay whatsoever and howsoever caused even if   203
caused by the neglect or default of their ser-   204
vants. The Owners not to be liable for loss or   205
damage arising or resulting from strikes, lock-   206
outs or stoppage or restraint of labour (including   207
the Master, Officers or Crew) whether partial or   208
general.   209
The Charterers to be responsible for loss or dam-   210
age caused to the Vessel or to the Owners by   211
goods being loaded contrary to the terms of the   212
Charter or by improper or careless bunkering or   213
loading, stowing or discharging of goods or any   214
other improper or negligent act on their part or   215
that of their servants.   216

14.   Advances   217
The Charterers or their Agents to advance to the   218
Master, if required, necessary funds for ordinary   219
disbursements for the Vessel's account at any   220
port charging only interest at 6 per cent. p.a.,   221
such advances to be deducted from hire.   222

15.   Excluded Ports   223
The Vessel not to be ordered to nor bound to   224
enter: a) any place where fever or epidemics are   225
prevalent or to which the Master, Officers and   226
Crew by law are not bound to follow the Vessel   227
     228
b) any ice-bound place or any place where lights,   229
lightships, marks and buoys are or are likely to   230
be withdrawn by reason of ice on the Vessel's   231
arrival or where there is risk that ordinarily the   232
Vessel will not be able on account of ice to   233
reach the place or to get out after having com-   234
pleted loading or discharging. The Vessel not to   235
be obliged to force ice, if on account of ice the   236
Master considers it dangerous to remain at the   237
loading or discharging place for fear of the Ves-   238
sel being frozen in and/or damaged, he has   239
liberty to sail to a convenient open place and   240
await the Charterers' fresh instructions.   241
Unforeseen detention through any of above cau-   242
ses to be for the Charterers' account.   243

16.   Loss of Vessel   244
Should the Vessel be lost or missing, hire to   245
cease from the date when she was lost. If the   246
date of loss cannot be ascertained half hire to   247
be paid from the date the Vessel was last re-   248
ported until the calculated date of arrival at the   249
destination. Any hire paid in advance to be ad-   250
justed accordingly.   251

17.   Overtime   252
The Vessel to work day and night if required.   253
The Charterers to refund the Owners their out-   254
lays for all overtime paid to Officers and Crew   255
according to the hours and rates stated in the   256
Vessel's articles.   257

18.   Lien   258
The Owners to have a lien upon all cargoes and   259
sub-freights belonging to the Time-Charterers and   260
any Bill of Lading freight for all claims under   261
this Charter, and the Charterers to have a lien   262
on the Vessel for all moneys paid in advance   263
and not earned.   264

19.   Salvage   265
All salvage and assistance to other vessels to be   266
for the Owners and the Charterers' equal benefit   267
after deducting the Master's and Crew's propor-   268
tion and all legal and other expenses including   269
hire paid under the charter for time lost in the   270
salvage, also repairs of damage and coal or oil-   271
fuel consumed. The Charterers to be bound by   272
all measures taken by the Owners in order to   273
secure payment of salvage and to fix its amount.   274

20.   Sublet   275
The Charterers to have the option of subletting   276
the Vessel, giving due notice to the Owners, but   277
the original Charterers always to remain respon-   278
sible to the Owners for due performance of the   279
Charter.   280

21.   War   281
(A) The Vessel unless the consent of the Owners   282
be first obtained not to be ordered nor continue   283
to any place or on any voyage nor be used on   284
any service which will bring her within a zone   285
which is dangerous as the result of any actual   286
or threatened act of war, war hostilities, warlike   287
operations, acts of piracy or of hostility or ma-   288
licious damage against this or any other vessel   289
or its cargo by any person, body or State what-   290
soever, revolution, civil war, civil commotion or   291
the operation of international law, nor be ex-   292
posed in any way to any risks or penalties whatso-   293
ever consequent upon the imposition of Sanc-   294
tions, nor carry any goods that may in any way   295
expose her to any risks of seizure, capture, pe-   296
nalties or any other interference of any kind   297
whatsoever by the belligerent or fighting powers   298
or parties or by any Government or Ruler.   299
(B) Should the Vessel approach or be brought or   300
ordered within such zone, or be exposed in any   301
way to the said risks, (1) the Owners to be en-   302
titled from time to time to insure their interests   303
in the Vessel and/or hire against any of the risks   304
likely to be involved thereby on such terms as   305
they shall think fit, the Charterers to make a re-   306
fund to the Owners of the premium on demand,   307
and (2) notwithstanding the terms of Clause 11   308
hire to be paid for all time lost including any   309
lost owing to loss of or injury to the Master,   310
Officers, or Crew or to the action of the Crew in   311
refusing to proceed to such zone or to be ex-   312
posed to such risks.   313
(C) In the event of the wages of the Master, Of-   314
ficers and/or Crew or the cost of provisions and/   315
or stores for deck and/or engine room and or   316
insurance premiums being increased by reason   317
of or during the existence of any of the matters   318
mentioned in section (A) the amount of any in-   319
crease to be added to the hire and paid by the   320
Charterers on production of the Owners' account   321
therefor, such account being rendered monthly.   322
(D) The Vessel to have liberty to comply with   323
any orders or directions as to departure, arrival,   324
routes, ports of call, stoppages, destination, de-   325
livery or in any other wise whatsoever given by   326
the Government of the nation under whose flag   327
the Vessel sails or any other Government or any   328
person (or body) acting or purporting to act with   329
the authority of such Government or by any com-   330
mittee or person having under the terms of the   331
war risks insurance on the Vessel the right to   332
give any such orders or directions.   333
(E) In the event of the nation under whose flag   334
the Vessel sails becoming involved in war, hos-   335
tilities, warlike operations, revolution, or civil   336
commotion, both the Owners and the Charterers   337
may cancel the Charter and, unless otherwise   338
agreed, the Vessel to be re-delivered to the Ow-   339
ners at the port of destination or, if prevented   340
through the provisions of section (A) from reach-   341
ing or entering it, then at a near open and safe   342
port at the Owners' option, after discharge of any   343
cargo on board.   344
(F) If in compliance with the provisions of this   345
clause anything is done or is not done, such not   346
to be deemed a deviation.   347
Section (C) is optional and should be considered   348
deleted unless agreed according to Box 22.   349

22.   Cancelling   350
Should the Vessel not be delivered by the date   351
indicated in Box 23, the Charterers to have the   352
option of cancelling.   353
If the Vessel cannot be delivered by the cancel-   354
ling date, the Charterers, if required, to declare   355
within 48 hours after receiving notice thereof   356
whether they cancel or will take delivery of the   357
Vessel.   358

23.   Arbitration   359
Any dispute arising under the Charter to be re-   360
ferred to arbitration in London (or such other   361
place as may be agreed according to Box 24)   362
one Arbitrator to be nominated by the Owners   363
and the other by the Charterers, and in case the   364
Arbitrators shall not agree then to the decision   365
of an Umpire to be appointed by them, the award   366
of the Arbitrators or the Umpire to be final and   367
binding upon both parties.   368

24.   General Average   369
General Average to be settled according to York/   370
Antwerp Rules, 1974. Hire not to contribute to   371
General Average.   372

25.   Commission   373
The Owners to pay a commission at the rate   374
stated in Box 25 to the party mentioned in Box 375
25 on any hire paid under the Charter, but in no   376
case less than is necessary to cover the actual   377
expenses of the Brokers and a reasonable fee   378
for their work. If the full hire is not paid owing   379
to breach of Charter by either of the parties the   380
party liable therefor to indemnify the Brokers   381
against their loss of commission.   382
Should the parties agree to cancel the Charter,   383
the Owners to indemnify the Brokers against any   384
loss of commission but in such case the com-   385
mission not to exceed the brokerage on one   386
year's hire.   387

1. Shipbroker	RECOMMENDED THE BALTIC AND INTERNATIONAL MARITIME CONFERENCE UNIFORM GENERAL CHARTER (AS REVISED 1922 and 1976) INCLUDING "F.I.O." ALTERNATIVE, ETC. (To be used for trades for which no approved form is in force) CODE NAME: "GENCON" Part I
	2. Place and date
3. Owners/Place of business (Cl. 1)	4. Charterers/Place of business (Cl. 1)
5. Vessel's name (Cl. 1)	6. GRT/NRT (Cl. 1)
7. Deadweight cargo carrying capacity in tons (abt.) (Cl. 1)	8. Present position (Cl. 1)
9. Expected ready to load (abt.) (Cl. 1)	
10. Loading port or place (Cl. 1)	11. Discharging port or place (Cl. 1)
12. Cargo (also state quantity and margin in Owners' option, if agreed; if full and complete cargo not agreed state "part cargo") (Cl. 1)	
13. Freight rate (also state if payable on delivered or intaken quantity) (Cl. 1)	14. Freight payment (state currency and method of payment; also beneficiary and bank account) (Cl. 4)
15. Loading and discharging costs (state alternative (a) or (b) of Cl. 5; also indicate if vessel is gearless)	16. Laytime (if separate laytime for load. and disch. is agreed, fill in a) and b). If total laytime for load. and disch., fill in c) only) (Cl. 6)
	a) Laytime for loading
17. Shippers (state name and address) (Cl. 6)	b) Laytime for discharging
	c) Total laytime for loading and discharging
18. Demurrage rate (loading and discharging) (Cl. 7)	19. Cancelling date (Cl. 10)
20. Brokerage commission and to whom payable (Cl. 14)	
21. Additional clauses covering special provisions, if agreed.	

It is mutually agreed that this Contract shall be performed subject to the conditions contained in this Charter which shall include Part I as well as Part II. In the event of a conflict of conditions, the provisions of Part I shall prevail over those of Part II to the extent of such conflict.

Signature (Owners)	Signature (Charterers)

Printed and sold by S. Straker & Sons Ltd., 49 Fenchurch Street, London EC3M 3JY by authority of The Baltic and International Maritime Conference, (BIMCO) Copenhagen.

PART II

"Gencon" Charter (As Revised 1922 and 1976)

Including "F.I.O." Alternative, etc.

1. It is agreed between the party mentioned in Box 3 as Owners of the 1
steamer or motor-vessel named in Box 5, of the gross/nett Register 2
tons indicated in Box 6 and carrying about the number of tons of 3
deadweight cargo stated in Box 7, now in position as stated in Box 8 4
and expected ready to load under this Charter about the date in- 5
dicated in Box 9, and the party mentioned as Charterers in Box 4 6
that: 7
The said vessel shall proceed to the loading port or place stated 8
in Box 10 or so near thereto as she may safely get and lie always 9
afloat, and there load a full and complete cargo (if shipment of deck 10
cargo agreed same to be at Charterers' risk) as stated in Box 12 11
(Charterers to provide all mats and/or wood for dunnage and any 12
separations required, the Owners allowing the use of any dunnage 13
wood on board if required) which the Charterers bind themselves to 14
ship, and being so loaded the vessel shall proceed to the discharg- 15
ing port or place stated in Box 11 as ordered on signing Bills of 16
Lading or so near thereto as she may safely get and lie always 17
afloat and there deliver the cargo on being paid freight on delivered 18
or intaken quantity as indicated in Box 13 at the rate stated in 19
Box 13. 20

2. Owners' Responsibility Clause 21
Owners are to be responsible for loss of or damage to the goods 22
or for delay in delivery of the goods only in case the loss, damage 23
or delay has been caused by the improper or negligent stowage of 24
the goods (unless stowage performed by shippers/Charterers or their 25
stevedores or servants) or by personal want of due diligence on the 26
part of the Owners or their Manager to make the vessel in all respects 27
seaworthy and to secure that she is properly manned, equipped and 28
supplied or by the personal act or default of the Owners or their 29
Manager. 30
And the Owners are responsible for no loss or damage or delay 31
arising from any other cause whatsoever, even from the neglect or 32
default of the Captain or crew or some other person employed by the 33
Owners on board or ashore for whose acts they would, but for this 34
clause, be responsible, or from unseaworthiness of the vessel on 35
loading or commencement of the voyage or at any time whatsoever. 36
Damage caused by contact with or leakage, smell or evaporation 37
from other goods or by the inflammable or explosive nature or in- 38
sufficient package of other goods not to be considered as caused 39
by improper or negligent stowage, even if in fact so caused. 40

3. Deviation Clause 41
The vessel has liberty to call at any port or ports in any order, for 42
any purpose, to sail without pilots, to tow and/or assist vessels in 43
all situations, and also to deviate for the purpose of saving life and/ 44
or property. 45

4. Payment of Freight 46
The freight to be paid in the manner prescribed in Box 14 in cash 47
without discount on delivery of the cargo at mean rate of exchange 48
ruling on day or days of payment, the receivers of the cargo being 49
bound to pay freight on account during delivery, if required by Cap- 50
tain or Owners. 51
Cash for vessel's ordinary disbursements at port of loading to be 52
advanced by Charterers if required at highest current rate of ex- 53
change, subject to two per cent. to cover insurance and other ex- 54
penses. 55

5. Loading/Discharging Costs 56
* *(a) Gross Terms* 57
The cargo to be brought alongside in such a manner as to enable 58
vessel to take the goods with her own tackle. Charterers to procure 59
and pay the necessary men on shore or on board the lighters to do 60
the work there, vessel only heaving the cargo on board. 61
If the loading takes place by elevator, cargo to be put free in vessel's 62
holds, Owners only paying trimming expenses. 63
Any pieces and/or packages of cargo over two tons weight, shall be 64
loaded, stowed and discharged by Charterers at their risk and expense. 65
The cargo to be received by Merchants at their risk and expense 66
alongside the vessel not beyond the reach of her tackle. 67
* *(b) F.i.o. and free stowed /trimmed* 68
The cargo to be brought into the holds, loaded, stowed and/or trim- 69
med and taken from the holds and discharged by the Charterers or 70
their Agents, free of any risk, liability and expense whatsoever to the 71
Owners. 72
The Owners shall provide winches, motive power and winchmen from 73
the Crew if requested and permitted; if not, the Charterers shall 74
provide and pay for winchmen from shore and/or cranes, if any. (This 75
provision shall not apply if vessel is gearless and stated as such in 76
Box 15). 77
* *indicate alternative (a) or (b), as agreed, in Box 15.* 78

6. Laytime 79
* *(a) Separate laytime for loading and discharging* 80
The cargo shall be loaded within the number of running hours as 81
indicated in Box 16, weather permitting, Sundays and holidays ex- 82
cepted, unless used, in which event time actually used shall count. 83
The cargo shall be discharged within the number of running hours 84
as indicated in Box 16, weather permitting, Sundays and holidays ex- 85
cepted, unless used, in which event time actually used shall count. 86
* *(b) Total laytime for loading and discharging* 87
The cargo shall be loaded and discharged within the number of total 88
running hours as indicated in Box 16, weather permitting, Sundays and 89
holidays excepted, unless used, in which event time actually used 90
shall count. 91
(c) Commencement of laytime (loading and discharging) 92
Laytime for loading and discharging shall commence at 1 p.m. if 93
notice of readiness is given before noon, and at 6 a.m. next working 94
day if notice given during office hours after noon. Notice at loading 95
port to be given to the Shippers named in Box 17. 96
Time actually used before commencement of laytime shall count. 97
Time lost in waiting for berth to count as loading or discharging 98
time, as the case may be. 99
* *indicate alternative (a) or (b) as agreed, in Box 16.* 100

7. Demurrage 101
Ten running days on demurrage at the rate stated in Box 18 per 102
day or pro rata for any part of a day, payable day by day, to be 103
allowed Merchants altogether at ports of loading and discharging. 104

8. Lien Clause 105
Owners shall have a lien on the cargo for freight, dead-freight, 106
demurrage and damages for detention. Charterers shall remain re- 107
sponsible for dead-freight and demurrage (including damages for 108
detention), incurred at port of loading, Charterers shall also remain 109
responsible for freight and demurrage (including damages for deten- 110
tion) incurred at port of discharge, but only to such extent as the 111
Owners have been unable to obtain payment thereof by exercising 112
the lien on the cargo. 113

9. Bills of Lading 114
The Captain to sign Bills of Lading at such rate of freight as 115
presented without prejudice to this Charterparty, but should the 116
freight by Bills of Lading amount to less than the total chartered 117
freight the difference to be paid to the Captain in cash on signing 118
Bills of Lading. 119

10. Cancelling Clause 120
Should the vessel not be ready to load (whether in berth or not) on 121
or before the date indicated in Box 19, Charterers have the option 122
of cancelling this contract, such option to be declared, if demanded, 123
at least 48 hours before vessel's expected arrival at port of loading. 124
Should the vessel be delayed on account of average or otherwise, 125
Charterers to be informed as soon as possible, and if the vessel is 126
delayed for more than 10 days after the day she is stated to be 127
expected ready to load, Charterers have the option of cancelling this 128
contract, unless a cancelling date has been agreed upon. 129

11. General Average 130
General average to be settled according to York-Antwerp Rules, 131
1974. Proprietors of cargo to pay the cargo's share in the general 132
expenses even if same have been necessitated through neglect or 133
default of the Owners' servants (see clause 2). 134

12. Indemnity 135
Indemnity for non-performance of this Charterparty, proved damages, 136
not exceeding estimated amount of freight. 137

13. Agency 138
In every case the Owners shall appoint his own Broker or Agent both 139
at the port of loading and the port of discharge. 140

14. Brokerage 141
A brokerage commission at the rate stated in Box 20 on the freight 142
earned is due to the party mentioned in Box 20. 143
In case of non-execution at least 1/3 of the brokerage on the estimated 144
amount of freight and dead-freight to be paid by the Owners to the 145
Brokers as indemnity for the latter's expenses and work. In case of 146
more voyages the amount of indemnity to be mutually agreed. 147

15. GENERAL STRIKE CLAUSE 148
Neither Charterers nor Owners shall be responsible for the con- 149
sequences of any strikes or lock-outs preventing or delaying the 150
fulfilment of any obligations under this contract 151
If there is a strike or lock-out affecting the loading of the cargo, 152
or any part of it, when vessel is ready to proceed from her last port 153
or at any time during the voyage to the port or ports of loading or 154
after her arrival there, Captain or Owners may ask Charterers to 155
declare, that they agree to reckon the laydays as if there were no 156
strike or lock-out. Unless Charterers have given such declaration in 157
writing (by telegram, if necessary) within 24 hours, Owners shall 158
have the option of cancelling this contract. If part cargo has already 159
been loaded, Owners must proceed with same, (freight payable on 160
loaded quantity only) having liberty to complete with other cargo 161
on the way for their own account. 162
If there is a strike or lock-out affecting the discharge of the cargo 163
on or after vessel's arrival at or off port of discharge and same has 164
not been settled within 48 hours, Receivers shall have the option of 165
keeping vessel waiting until such strike or lock-out is at an end 166
against paying half demurrage after expiration of the time provided 167
for discharging, or of ordering the vessel to a safe port where she 168
can safely discharge without risk of being detained by strike or lock- 169
out. Such orders to be given within 48 hours after Captain or Owners 170
have given notice to Charterers of the strike or lock-out affecting 171
the discharge. On delivery of the cargo at such port, all conditions 172
of this Charterparty and of the Bill of Lading shall apply and vessel 173
shall receive the same freight as if she had discharged at the 174
original port of destination, except that if the distance of the sub- 175
stituted port exceeds 100 nautical miles, the freight on the cargo 176
delivered at the substituted port to be increased in proportion. 177

16. War Risks ("Voywar 1950") 178
(1) In these clauses "War Risks" shall include any blockade or any 179
action which is announced as a blockade by any Government or by any 180
belligerent or by any organized body, sabotage, piracy, and any hostile 181
or threatened war, hostilities, warlike operations, civil war, civil com- 182
motion, or revolution. 183
(2) If at any time before the Vessel commences loading, it appears that 184
performance of the contract will subject the Vessel or her Master and 185
crew or her cargo to war risks at any stage of the adventure, the Owners 186
shall be entitled by letter or telegram despatched to the Charterers, to 187
cancel this Charter 188
(3) The Master shall not be required to load cargo or to continue 189
loading or to proceed on or to sign Bill(s) of Lading for any adventure 190
on which or any port at which it appears that the Vessel, her Master 191
and crew or her cargo will be subjected to war risks. In the event of 192
the exercise by the Master of his right under this Clause after part or 193
full cargo has been loaded, the Master shall be at liberty either to 194
discharge such cargo at the loading port or to proceed therewith. 195
In the latter case the Vessel shall have liberty to carry other cargo 196
for Owners' benefit and accordingly to proceed to and load or 197
discharge such other cargo at any other port or ports whatsoever, 198
backwards or forwards, although in a contrary direction to or out of or 199
beyond the ordinary route. In the event of the Master electing to 200
proceed with part cargo under this Clause freight shall in any case 201
be payable on the quantity delivered. 202
(4) If at the time the Master elects to proceed with part or full cargo 203
under Clause 3. or after the Vessel has left the loading port, or the 204

PART II
"Gencon" Charter (As Revised 1922 and 1976)
Including "F.I.O." Alternative, etc.

last of the loading ports, if more than one, it appears that further 205
performance of the contract will subject the Vessel, her Master and 206
crew or her cargo, to war risks, the cargo shall be discharged, or if 207
the discharge has been commenced shall be completed, at any safe 208
port in vicinity of the port of discharge as may be ordered by the 209
Charterers. If no such orders shall be received from the Charterers 210
within 48 hours after the Owners have despatched a request by 211
telegram to the Charterers for the nomination of a substitute discharg- 212
ing port, the Owners shall be at liberty to discharge the cargo at 213
any safe port which they may, in their discretion, decide on and such 214
discharge shall be deemed to be due fulfilment of the contract of 215
affreightment. In the event of cargo being discharged at any such 216
other port, the Owners shall be entitled to freight as if the discharge 217
had been effected at the port or ports named in the Bill(s) of Lading 218
or to which the Vessel may have been ordered pursuant thereto. 219

(5) (a) The Vessel shall have liberty to comply with any directions 220
or recommendations as to loading, departure, arrival, routes, ports 221
of call, stoppages, destination, zones, waters, discharge, delivery or 222
in any other wise whatsoever (including any direction or recom- 223
mendation not to go to the port of destination or to delay proceeding 224
thereto or to proceed to some other port) given by any Government or 225
by any belligerent or by any organized body engaged in civil war, 226
hostilities or warlike operations or by any person or body acting or 227
purporting to act as or with the authority of any Government or 228
belligerent or of any such organized body or by any committee or 229
person having under the terms of the war risks insurance on the 230
Vessel, the right to give any such directions or recommendations. If 231
by reason of or in compliance with any such direction or recom- 232
mendation, anything is done or is not done, such shall not be deemed 233
a deviation. 234

(b) If, by reason of or in compliance with any such directions or re- 235
commendations, the Vessel does not proceed to the port or ports 236
named in the Bill(s) of Lading or to which she may have been 237
ordered pursuant thereto, the Vessel may proceed to any port as 238
directed or recommended or to any safe port which the Owners in 239
their discretion may decide on and there discharge the cargo. Such 240
discharge shall be deemed to be due fulfilment of the contract of 241
affreightment and the Owners shall be entitled to freight as if 242
discharge had been effected at the port or ports named in the Bill(s) 243
of Lading or to which the Vessel may have been ordered pursuant 244
thereto. 245

(6) All extra expenses (including insurance costs) involved in discharg- 246
ing cargo at the loading port or in reaching or discharging the cargo 247
at any port as provided in Clauses 4 and 5 (b) hereof shall be paid 248
by the Charterers and/or cargo owners, and the Owners shall have 249
a lien on the cargo for all moneys due under these Clauses. 250

17. GENERAL ICE CLAUSE 251
Port of loading 252

(a) In the event of the loading port being inaccessible by reason of 253
ice when vessel is ready to proceed from her last port or at any 254
time during the voyage or on vessel's arrival or in case frost sets in 255
after vessel's arrival, the Captain for fear of being frozen in is at 256
liberty to leave without cargo, and this Charter shall be null and 257
void. 258

(b) If during loading the Captain, for fear of vessel being frozen in, 259
deems it advisable to leave, he has liberty to do so with what cargo 260
he has on board and to proceed to any other port or ports with 261
option of completing cargo for Owners' benefit for any port or ports 262
including port of discharge. Any part cargo thus loaded under this 263
Charter to be forwarded to destination at vessel's expense but 264
against payment of freight, provided that no extra expenses be 265
thereby caused to the Receivers, freight being paid on quantity 266
delivered (in proportion if lumpsum), all other conditions as per 267
Charter. 268

(c) In case of more than one loading port, and if one or more of 269
the ports are closed by ice, the Captain or Owners to be at liberty 270
either to load the part cargo at the open port and fillup elsewhere 271
for their own account as under section (b) or to declare the Charter 272
null and void unless Charterers agree to load full cargo at the open 273
port. 274

(d) This Ice Clause not to apply in the Spring. 275

Port of discharge 276

(a) Should ice (except in the Spring) prevent vessel from reaching 277
port of discharge Receivers shall have the option of keeping vessel 278
waiting until the re-opening of navigation and paying demurrage, or 279
of ordering the vessel to a safe and immediately accessible port 280
where she can safely discharge without risk of detention by ice. 281
Such orders to be given within 48 hours after Captain or Owners 282
have given notice to Charterers of the impossibility of reaching port 283
of destination. 284

(b) If during discharging the Captain for fear of vessel being frozen 285
in deems it advisable to leave, he has liberty to do so with what 286
cargo he has on board and to proceed to the nearest accessible 287
port where she can safely discharge. 288

(c) On delivery of the cargo at such port, all conditions of the Bill 289
of Lading shall apply and vessel shall receive the same freight as 290
if she had discharged at the original port of destination, except that if 291
the distance of the substituted port exceeds 100 nautical miles, the 292
freight on the cargo delivered at the substituted port to be increased 293
in proportion. 294

Appendices C–H

SUMMARY

Appendix C

Bills of Lading Act 1855

(18 & 19 Vict c 111)

Whereas, by the custom of merchants, a bill of lading of goods being transferable by endorsement, the property in the goods may thereby pass to the endorsee, but nevertheless all rights in respect of the contract contained in the bill of lading continue in the original shipper or owner; and it is expedient that such rights should pass with the property: And whereas it frequently happens that the goods in respect of which bills of lading purport to be signed have not been laden on board, and it is proper that such bills of lading in the hands of a bona fide holder for value should not be questioned by the master or other persons signing the same on the ground of the goods not having been laden as aforesaid:

1. Consignees, and endorsees of bills of lading empowered to sue.—Every consignee of goods named in a bill of lading, and every endorsee of a bill of lading, to whom the property in the goods therein mentioned shall pass upon or by reason of such consignment or endorsement, shall have transferred to and vested in him all rights of suit, and be subject to the same liabilities in respect of such goods as if the contract contained in the bill of lading had been made with himself.

2. Saving as to stoppage in transitu, and claims for freight, etc.—Nothing herein contained shall prejudice or affect any right of stoppage *in transitu*, or any right to claim freight against the original shipper or owner, or any liability of the consignee or endorsee by reason or in consequence of his being such consignee or endorsee, or of his receipt of the goods by reason or in consequence of such consignment or endorsement.

3. Bill of lading in hands of consignee, etc., conclusive evidence of shipment as against master, etc.—Every bill of lading in the hands of a consignee or endorsee for valuable consideration, representing goods to have been shipped on board a vessel, shall be conclusive evidence of such shipment as against the master or other person signing the same, notwithstanding that such goods or some part thereof may not have been so shipped, unless such holder of the bill of lading shall have had actual notice at the time of receiving the same that the goods had not been in fact laden on board: Provided, that the master or other person so signing may exonerate himself in respect of such misrepresentation by showing that it was caused without any default on his part, and wholly by the fraud of the shipper, or of the holder, or some person under whom the holder claims.

Appendix D

Merchant Shipping Act 1894[1]

(57 & 58 Vict c 60)

PART V. SAFETY.

Dangerous Goods

446. Restrictions on carriage of dangerous goods.—(1) A person shall not send or attempt to send by any vessel, British or foreign, and a person not being the master or owner of the vessel, shall not carry or attempt to carry in any such vessel, any dangerous goods, without distinctly marking their nature on the outside of the package containing the same, and giving written notice of the nature of those goods and of the name and address of the sender or carrier thereof to the master or owner of the vessel at or before the time of sending the same to be shipped or taking the same on board the vessel.

(2) If any person fails without reasonable cause to comply with this section he shall for each offence be liable on conviction on indictment to a fine or on summary conviction to a fine not exceeding the statutory maximum; but it shall be a defence to show that the accused was merely an agent in the shipment of any such goods as aforesaid, and was not aware and did not suspect and had no reason to suspect that the goods shipped by him were of a dangerous nature. . . .

(3) For the purpose of this part of this Act the expression "dangerous goods" means aquafortis, vitriol, naphtha, benzine, gunpowder, lucifer matches, nitro-glycerine, petroleum, any explosives within the meaning of the Explosives Act 1875, and any other goods which are of a dangerous nature.

447. Penalty for misdescription of dangerous goods.—A person shall not knowingly send or attempt to send by, or carry or attempt to carry in, any vessel, British or foreign, any dangerous goods under a false description, and shall not falsely describe the sender or carrier thereof, and if he acts in contravention of this section he shall for each offence be liable on conviction

1 The Act is printed as amended.

on indictment to a fine or on summary conviction to a fine not exceeding the statutory maximum.

448. Power to deal with goods suspected of being dangerous.—(1) The master or owner of any vessel, British or foreign, may refuse to take on board any package or parcel which he suspects to contain any dangerous goods, and may require it to be opened to ascertain the fact.

(2) When any dangerous goods, or any goods, which in the judgment of the master or owner of the vessel, are dangerous goods, have been sent or brought aboard any vessel, British or foreign, without being marked as aforesaid, or without such notice having been given as aforesaid, the master or owner of the vessel may cause those goods to be thrown overboard, together with any package or receptacle in which they are contained; and neither the master nor the owner of the vessel shall be subject to any liability, civil or criminal, in any court for so throwing the goods overboard.

449. Forfeiture of dangerous goods improperly sent or carried.—(1) Where any dangerous goods have been sent or carried, or attempted to be sent or carried, on board any vessel, British or foreign, without being marked as aforesaid, or without such notice having been given as aforesaid, or under a false description, or with a false description of the sender or carrier thereof, any court having Admiralty jurisdiction may declare those goods and any package or receptacle in which they are contained, to be, and they shall thereupon be, forfeited, and when forfeited, shall be disposed of as the court direct.

(2) The court shall have, and may exercise, the aforesaid powers of forfeiture and disposal notwithstanding that the owner of the goods has not committed any offence under the provisions of this Act relating to dangerous goods, and is not before the court, and has not notice of the proceedings, and notwithstanding that there is no evidence to show to whom the goods belong; nevertheless the court may in their discretion, require such notice as they may direct to be given to the owner or shipper of the goods before they are forfeited.

450. Saving for other enactments relating to dangerous goods.—The provisions of this Part of this Act relating to the carriage of dangerous goods shall be deemed to be in addition to and not in substitution for, or in restraint of, any other enactment for the like object, so nevertheless that nothing in the said provisions shall be deemed to authorise any person to be sued or prosecuted twice in the same matter.

PART VII. DELIVERY OF GOODS

Delivery of goods and lien for freight.

492. Definitions under Part VII.—In this Part of this Act, unless the context otherwise requires:

The expression 'goods' includes every description of wares and merchandise:

The expression 'wharf' includes all wharves, quays, docks, and premises in or upon which any goods, when landed from ships, may be lawfully placed:

The expression 'warehouse' includes all warehouses, buildings, and premises in which goods, when landed from ships, may be lawfully placed:

The expression 'report' means the report required by the customs or excise laws to be made by the master of an importing ship:

The expression 'entry' means the entry required by the customs or excise laws to be made for the landing or discharge of goods from an importing ship:

The expression 'shipowner' includes the master of the ship and every other person authorised to act as agent for the owner or entitled to receive the freight, demurrage, or other charges payable in respect of the ship:

The expression 'owner' used in relation to goods means every person who is for the time entitled, either as owner or agent for the owner, to the possession of the goods, subject in the case of a lien (if any), to that lien:

The expression 'wharfinger' means the occupier of a wharf as herein-before defined:

The expression 'warehouseman' means the occupier of a warehouse as herein-before defined.

493. Power of a shipowner to enter and land goods on default by owner of goods.—(1) Where the owner of any goods imported in any ship from foreign parts into the United Kingdom fails to make entry thereof, or, having made entry thereof, to land the same or take delivery thereof, and to proceed therewith with all convenient speed, by the times severally herein-after mentioned, the shipowner may make entry of and land or unship the goods at the following times:

(a) If a time for the delivery of the goods is expressed in the charter-party, bill of lading, or agreement, then at any time after the time so expressed;

(b) If no time for the delivery of the goods is expressed in the charter-party, bill of lading, or agreement, then at any time after the expiration of seventy-two hours, exclusive of a Sunday or holiday, from the time of the report of the ship.

(2) Where a shipowner lands goods in pursuance of this section he shall place them, or cause them to be placed—

(a) if any wharf or warehouse is named in the charter-party, bill of lading, or agreement as the wharf or warehouse where the goods are to be placed and if they can be conveniently there received, on that wharf or in that warehouse; and

(b) in any other case on some wharf or in some warehouse on or in which goods of a like nature are usually placed; the wharf or warehouse being, if the goods are dutiable, a wharf or warehouse duly approved by the Commissioners of Customs and Excise for the landing of dutiable goods.

(3) If at any time before the goods are landed or unshipped the owner of the goods is ready and offers to land or take delivery of the same, he shall be allowed to do so, and his entry shall in that case be preferred to any entry which may have been made by the shipowner.

(4) If any goods are, for the purpose of convenience in assorting the same, landed at the wharf where the ship is discharged, and the owner of the goods at the time of that landing has made entry and is ready and offers to take delivery thereof, and to convey the same to some other wharf or warehouse, the goods shall be assorted at landing, and shall, if demanded, be delivered to the owner thereof within twenty-four hours after assortment; and the expense of and consequent on that landing and assortment shall be borne by the shipowner.

(5) If at any time before the goods are landed, or unshipped, the owner thereof has made entry for the landing and warehousing thereof at any particular wharf or warehouse other than that at which the ship is discharging, and has offered and been ready to take delivery thereof, and the shipowner has failed to make that delivery, and has also failed at the time of that offer to give the owner of the goods corrected information of the time at which the goods can be delivered, then the shipowner shall, before landing or unshipping the goods, in pursuance of this section, give to the owner of the goods or of such wharf or warehouse as last aforesaid twenty-four hours notice in writing of his readiness to deliver the goods, and shall, if he lands or unships the same without that notice, do so at his own risk and expense.

494. Lien for freight on landing goods.—If at the time when any goods are landed from any ship, and placed in the custody of any person as a wharfinger or warehouseman, the shipowner gives to the wharfinger or warehouseman notice in writing that the goods are to remain subject to a lien for freight or other charges payable to the shipowner to an amount mentioned in the notice, the goods so landed shall, in the hands of the wharfinger or warehouseman, continue subject to the same lien, if any, for such charges as they were subject to before the landing thereof; and the wharfinger or warehouseman receiving those goods shall retain them until the lien is discharged as herein-after mentioned, and shall, if he fails so to do, make good to the shipowner any loss thereby occasioned to him.

495. Discharge of lien.—The said lien for freight and other charges shall be discharged—

(1) upon the production to the wharfinger or warehouseman of a receipt for the amount claimed as due, and delivery to the wharfinger or warehouseman of a copy thereof or of a release of freight from the shipowner, and

(2) upon the deposit by the owner of the goods with the wharfinger or warehouseman of a sum of money equal in amount to the sum claimed as aforesaid by the shipowner;

but in the latter case the lien shall be discharged without prejudice to any other remedy which the shipowner may have for the recovery of the freight.

496. Provisions as to deposits by owners of goods.—(1) When a deposit as aforesaid is made with the wharfinger or warehouseman, the person making the same may, within fifteen days after making it, stating in the notice the sums, if any, which he admits to be payable to the shipowner, or, as the case may be, that he does not admit any sum to be so payable, but if no such notice is given, the wharfinger or warehouseman may, at the expiration of the fifteen days, pay the sum deposited over to the shipowner.

(2) If a notice is given as aforesaid the wharfinger or warehouseman shall immediately apprize the shipowner of it, and shall pay or tender to him out of the sum deposited the sum, if any, admitted by the notice to be payable, and shall retain the balance, or if no sum is admitted to be payable, the whole of the sum deposited, for thirty days from the date of the notice.

(3) At the expiration of those thirty days unless legal proceedings[2] have in the meantime been instituted by the shipowner against the owner of the goods to recover the said balance or sum, or otherwise for the settlement of any disputes which may have arisen between them concerning the freight or other charges as aforesaid, and notice in writing of those proceedings has been served on the wharfinger or warehouseman, the wharfinger or warehouseman shall pay the balance or sum to the owner of the goods.

(4) A wharfinger or warehouseman shall by any payment under this section be discharged from all liability in respect thereof.

497. Sale of goods by warehouseman.—(1) If the lien is not discharged, and no deposit is made as aforesaid, the wharfinger or warehouseman may, and, if required by the shipowner, shall, at the expiration of ninety days from the time when the goods were placed in his custody or, if the goods are of a perishable nature, at such earlier period as in his discretion he thinks fit, sell by public auction, either for home use or for exportation, the goods or so much thereof as may be necessary to satisfy the charges herein-after mentioned.

(2) Before making the sale the wharfinger or warehouseman shall give notice thereof by advertisement in two local newspapers circulating in the neighbourhood, or in one daily newspaper published in London, and in one local newspaper, and also, if the address of the owner of the goods has been stated on the manifest or the cargo, or on any of the documents which have come into the possession of the wharfinger or warehouseman, or is otherwise known to him, send notice of the sale to the owner of the goods by post.

(3) The title of a bona fide purchaser of the goods shall not be invalidated by reason of the omission to send the notice required by this section, nor shall any such purchaser be bound to inquire whether the notice has been sent.

---

2   An arbitration is a legal proceeding: see Arbitration Act 1950, s 29(1).

498. Application of proceeds of sale.—The proceeds of sale shall be applied by the wharfinger or warehouseman as follows, and in the following order:

(i) first, if the goods are sold for home use, in payment of any customs and excise duties owing in respect thereof; then

(ii) in payment of the expenses of the sale; then

(iii) in payment of the charges of the wharfinger or warehouseman and the shipowner according to such priority as may be determined by the terms of the agreement (if any) in that behalf between them; or, if there is no such agreement—

    (*a*) in payment of the rent, rates, and other charges due to the wharfinger or warehouseman in respect of the said goods; and then

    (*b*) in payment of the amount claimed by the shipowner as due for freight or other charges in respect of the said goods;

and the surplus, if any, shall be paid to the owner of the goods.

499. Warehouseman's rent and expenses.—Whenever any goods are placed in the custody of a wharfinger or warehouseman, under the authority of this Part of this Act, the wharfinger or warehouseman shall be entitled to rent in respect of the same, and shall also have power, at the expense of the owner of the goods, to do all such reasonable acts as in the judgment of the wharfinger or warehouseman are necessary for the proper custody and preservation of the goods, and shall have a lien on the goods for the rent and expenses.

500. Warehouseman's protection.—Nothing in this Part of this Act shall compel any wharfinger or warehouseman to take charge of any goods which he would not have been liable to take charge of if this Act had not been passed; nor shall he be bound to see the validity of any lien claimed by any shipowner under this Part of this Act.

501. Saving for powers under local Acts.—Nothing in this Part of this Act shall take away or abridge any powers given by any local Act to any harbour authority, body corporate, or persons, whereby they are enabled to expedite the discharge of ships or the landing or delivery of goods; nor shall anything in this Part of this Act take away or diminish any rights or remedies given to any shipowner or wharfinger or warehouseman by any local Act.

The Merchant Shipping (Liability of Shipowners and Others) Act 1900

(63 & 64 Vict c 32)

3. Limitation of liability where several claims arise on one occasion.—The limitation of liability under this Act shall relate to the whole of any losses and damages, which may arise upon any one distinct occasion, although such losses and damages may be sustained by more than one person, and shall apply whether the liability arises at common law or under any general or private Act of Parliament, and notwithstanding anything contained in such Act.

Merchant Shipping Act 1979

(1979 Chapter 39)

(a) IN RELATION TO VESSELS OTHER THAN HOVERCRAFT

Liability of shipowners and salvors

17. Limitation of liability.—(1) The provisions of the Convention on Limitation of Liability for Maritime Claims 1976 as set out in Part I of Schedule 4 to this Act (hereafter in this section and in Part II of that Schedule referred to as 'the Convention') shall have the force of law in the United Kingdom.

(2) The provisions of Part II of that Schedule shall have effect in connection with the Convention, and the preceding subsection shall have effect subject to the provisions of that Part.

18. Exclusion of liability.—(1) Subject to subsection (3) of this section, the owner of a British ship shall not be liable for any loss or damage in the following cases, namely—

(*a*) where any property on board the ship is lost or damaged by reason of fire on board the ship; or

(*b*) where any gold, silver, watches, jewels or precious stones on board the ship are lost or damaged by reason of theft, robbery or other dishonest conduct and their nature and value were not at the time of shipment declared by their owner or shipper to the owner or master of the ship in the bill of lading or otherwise in writing.

(2) Subject to subsection (3) of this section, where the loss or damage arises from anything done or omitted by any person in his capacity as master or member of the crew or (otherwise than in that capacity) in the course of his employment as a servant of the owner of the ship, the preceding subsection shall also exclude the liability of—

(*a*) the master, member of the crew or servant; and

(*b*) in a case where the master or member of the crew is the servant of a person whose liability would not be excluded by that subsection apart from this paragraph, the person whose servant he is.

(3) This section does not exclude the liability of any person for any loss or damage resulting from any such personal act or omission of his as is mentioned in article 4 of the Convention in Part I of Schedule 4 to this Act.

(4) In this section 'owner', in relation to a ship, includes any part owner and any charterer, manager or operator of the ship.

19. Provisions supplementary to ss 17 and 18.—(1) The enactments mentioned in Schedule 5 to this Act shall have effect with the amendments there specified (which are consequential on sections 17 and 18 of this Act).

(2) Her Majesty may by Order in Council provide that the said sections 17 and 18, the preceding subsection and Schedules 4 and 5 to this Act shall extend, with such modifications, if any, as are specified in the Order, to any of the following countries, namely—

(*a*) the Isle of Man;

(*b*) any of the Channel Islands;

(*c*) any colony;

(*d*) any country outside Her Majesty's dominions in which Her Majesty has jurisdiction in right of the government of the United Kingdom.

(3) Any statutory instrument made by virtue of the preceding subsection shall be subject to annulment in pursuance of a resolution of either House of Parliament.

(4) Nothing in the said sections 17 and 18 or the said Schedule 4 shall apply in relation to any liability arising out of an occurrence which took place before the coming into force of those sections, and subsection (1) of this section and Schedule 5 to this Act shall not affect the operation of any enactment in relation to such an occurrence.

SCHEDULE 4   Sections 17, 18, 19, 49, 51(2)

CONVENTION ON LIMITATION OF LIABILITY FOR MARITIME CLAIMS 1976

PART I

TEXT OF CONVENTION

CHAPTER I. THE RIGHT OF LIMITATION

ARTICLE 1

Persons entitled to limit liability

1. Shipowners and salvors, as hereinafter defined, may limit their liability in accordance with the rules of this Convention for claims set out in Article 2.

2. The term 'shipowner' shall mean the owner, charterer, manager or operator of a seagoing ship.

3. Salvor shall mean any person rendering services in direct connexion with salvage operations. Salvage operations shall also include operations referred to in Article 2, paragraph 1(d), (e) and (f).

4. If any claims set out in Article 2 are made against any person for whose act, neglect or default the shipowner or salvor is responsible, such person shall be entitled to avail himself of the limitation of liability provided for in this Convention.

5. In this Convention the liability of a shipowner shall include liability in an action brought against the vessel herself.

6. An insurer of liability for claims subject to limitation in accordance with the rules of this Convention shall be entitled to the benefits of this Convention to the same extent as the assured himself.

7. The act of invoking limitation of liability shall not constitute an admission of liability.

ARTICLE 2

Claims subject to limitation
1. Subject to Articles 3 and 4 the following claims, whatever the basis of liability may be, shall be subject to limitation of liability:
  (a) claims in respect of loss of life or personal injury or loss of or damage to property (including damage to harbour works, basins and waterways and aids to navigation), occurring on board or in direct connexion with the operation of the ship or with salvage operations, and consequential loss resulting therefrom;
  (b) claims in respect of loss resulting from delay in the carriage by sea of cargo, passengers or their luggage;
  (c) claims in respect of other loss resulting from infringement of rights other than contractual rights, occurring in direct connexion with the operation of the ship or salvage operations;
  (d) claims in respect of the raising, removal, destruction or the rendering harmless of a ship which is sunk, wrecked, stranded or abandoned, including anything that is or has been on board such ship;
  (e) claims in respect of the removal, destruction or the rendering harmless of the cargo of the ship;
  (f) claims of a person other than the person liable in respect of measures taken in order to avert or minimize loss for which the person liabile may limit his liability in accordance with this Convention, and further loss caused by such measures.
2. Claims set out in paragraph 1 shall be subject to limitation of liability even if brought by way of recourse or for indemnity under a contract or otherwise. However, claims set out under paragraph 1(d), (e) and (f) shall

not be subject to limitation of liability to the extent that they relate to remuneration under a contract with the person liable.

ARTICLE 3

Claims excepted from limitation
The rules of this Convention shall not apply to:
  (a) claims for salvage or contribution in general average;
  (b) claims for oil pollution damage within the meaning of the International Convention on Civil Liability for Oil Pollution Damage dated 29 November 1969 or of any amendment or Protocol thereto which is in force;
  (c) claims subject to any international convention or national legislation governing or prohibiting limitation of liability for nuclear damage;
  (d) claims against the shipowner of a nuclear ship for nuclear damage;
  (e) claims by servants of the shipowner or salvor whose duties are connected with the ship or the salvage operations, including claims of their heirs, dependants or other persons entitled to make such claims, if under the law governing the contract of service between the shipowner or salvor and such servants the shipowner or salvor is not entitled to limit his liability in respect of such claims, or if he is by such law only permitted to limit his liability to an amount greater than that provided for in Article 6.

ARTICLE 4

Conduct barring limitation
A person liable shall not be entitled to limit his liability if it is proved that the loss resulted from his personal act or omission, committed with the intent to cause such loss, or recklessly and with knowledge that such loss would probably result.

ARTICLE 5

Counterclaims
Where a person entitled to limitation under the rules of this Convention has a claim against the claimant arising out of the same occurrence, their respective claims shall be set off against each other and the provisions of this Convention shall only apply to the balance, if any.

CHAPTER II. LIMITS OF LIABILITY

ARTICLE 6

The general limits
1. The limits of liability for claims other than those mentioned in Article 7, arising on any distinct occasion, shall be calculated as follows:
   (*a*) in respect of claims for loss of life or personal injury,
         (i) 333,000 Units of Account for a ship with a tonnage not exceedings 500 tons,
         (ii) for a ship with a tonnage in excess thereof, the following amount in addition to that mentioned in (i):
         for each ton from 501 to 3,000 tons, 500 Units of Account;
         for each ton from 3,001 to 30,000 tons, 333 Units of Account;
         for each ton from 30,001 to 70,000 tons, 250 Units of Account, and
         for each ton in excess of 70,000 tons, 167 Units of Account,
   (*b*) in respect of any other claims,
         (i) 167,000 Units of Account for a ship with a tonnage not exceeding 500 tons,
         (ii) for a ship with a tonnage in excess thereof the following amount in addition to that mentioned in (i):
         for each ton from 501 to 30,000 tons, 167 Units of Account;
         for each ton from 30,301 to 70,000 tons, 125 Units of Account; and
         for each ton in excess of 70,000 tons, 83 Units of Account,
2. Where the amount calculated in accordance with paragraph 1(*a*) is insufficient to pay the claims mentioned therein in full, the amount calculated in accordance with paragraph 1(*b*) shall be available for payment of the unpaid balance of claims under paragraph 1(*a*) and such unpaid balance shall rank rateably with claims mentioned under paragraph 1(*b*).
4. The limits of liability for any salvor not operating from any ship or for any salvor operating solely on the ship to, or in respect of which he is rendering salvage services, shall be calculated according to a tonnage of 1,500 tons.

ARTICLE 7

The limit for passenger claims
1. In respect of claims arising on any distinct occasion for loss of life or personal injury to passengers of a ship, the limit of liability of the shipowner thereof shall be an amount of 46,666 Units of Account multiplied by the number of passengers which the ship is authorised to carry according to the ship's certificate, but not exceeding 25 million Units of Account.
2. For the purpose of this Article 'claims for loss of life or personal injury

to passengers of a ship' shall mean any such claims brought by or on behalf of any person carried in that ship:

    (*a*) under a contract of passenger carriage, or

    (*b*) who, with the consent of the carrier, is accompanying a vehicle or live animals which are covered by a contract for the carriage of goods.

ARTICLE 8

Unit of account

1. The Unit of Account referred to in Articles 6 and 7 is the Special Drawing Right as defined by the International Monetary Fund. The amounts mentioned in Articles 6 and 7 shall be converted into the national currency of the State in which limitation is sought, according to the value of that currency at the date the limitation fund shall have been constituted, payment is made, or security is given which under the law of that State is equivalent to such payment.

ARTICLE 9

Aggregation of claims

1. The limits of liability determined in accordance with Article 6 shall apply to the aggregate of all claims which arise on any distinct occasion:

    (*a*) against the person or persons mentioned in paragraph 2 of Article 1 and any person for whose act, neglect or default he or they are responsible; or

    (*b*) against the shipowner of a ship rendering salvage services from that ship and the salvor or salvors operating from such ship and any person for whose act, neglect or default he or they are responsible; or

    (*c*) against the salvor or salvors who are not operating from a ship or who are operating solely on the ship to, or in respect of which, the salvage services are rendered and any person for whose act, neglect or default he or they are responsible.

2. The limits of liability determined in accordance with Article 7 shall apply to the aggregate of all claims subject thereto which may arise on any distinct occasion against the person or persons mentioned in paragraph 2 of Article 1 in respect of the ship referred to in Article 7 and any person for whose act, neglect or default he or they are responsible.

ARTICLE 10

Limitation of liability without constitution of a limitation fund

1. Limitation of liability may be invoked notwithstanding that a limitation fund as mentioned in Article 11 has not been constituted.

2. If limitation of liability is invoked without the constitution of a limitation fund, the provisions of Article 12 shall apply correspondingly.

3. Questions of procedure arising under the rules of this Article shall be decided in accordance with the national law of the State Party in which action is brought.

CHAPTER III. THE LIMITATION FUND

ARTICLE 11

Constitution of the fund

1. Any person alleged to be liable may constitute a fund with the Court or other competent authority in any State Party in which legal proceedings are instituted in respect of claims subject to limitation. The fund shall be constituted in the sum of such of the amounts set out in Articles 6 and 7 as are applicable to claims for which that person may be liable, together with interest thereon from the date of the occurrence giving rise to the liability until the date of the constitution of the fund. Any fund thus constituted shall be available only for the payment of claims in respect of which limitation of liability can be invoked.

2. A fund may be constituted, either by depositing the sum, or by producing a guarantee acceptable under the legislation of the State Party where the fund is constituted and considered to be adequate by the Court or other competent authority.

3. A fund constituted by one of the persons mentioned in paragraph 1(*a*), (*b*) or (*c*) or paragraph 2 of Article 9 or his insurer shall be deemed constituted by all persons mentioned in paragraph 1(*a*), (*b*) or (*c*) or paragraph 2, respectively.

ARTICLE 12

Distribution of the fund

1. Subject to the provisions of paragraphs 1 and 2 of Article 6 and of Article 7, the fund shall be distributed among the claimants in proportion to their established claims against the fund.

2. If, before the fund is distributed, the person liable, or his insurer, has settled a claim against the fund such person shall, up to the amount he has paid, acquire by subrogation the rights which the person so compensated would have enjoyed under this Convention.

3. The right of subrogation provided for in paragraph 2 may also be exercised by persons other than those therein mentioned in respect of any amount of compensation which they may have paid, but only to the extent that such subrogation is permitted under the applicable national law.

4. Where the person liable or any other person establishes that he may be compelled to pay, at a later date, in whole or in part any such amount of compensation with regard to which such person would have enjoyed a right of subrogation pursuant to paragraphs 2 and 3 had the compensation been paid before the fund was distributed, the Court or other competent authority of the State where the fund has been constituted may order that a sufficient sum shall be provisionally set aside to enable such person at such later date to enforce his claim against the fund.

ARTICLE 13

Bar to other actions
1. Where a limitation fund has been constituted in accordance with Article 11, any person having made a claim against the fund shall be barred from exercising any right in respect of such a claim against any other assets of a person by or on behalf of whom the fund has been constituted.
2. After a limitation fund has been constituted in accordance with Article 11, any ship or other property, belonging to a person on behalf of whom the fund has been constituted, which has been arrested or attached within the jurisdiction of a State Party for a claim which may be raised against the fund, or any security given, may be released by order of the court or other competent authority of such State. However, such release shall always be ordered if the limitation fund has been constituted:
   (*a*) at the port where the occurrence took place, or, if it took place out of port, at the first port of call thereafter; or
   (*b*) at the port of disembarkation in respect of claims for loss of life or personal injury; or
   (*c*) at the port of discharge in respect of damage to cargo; or
   (*d*) in the State where the arrest is made.
3. The rules of paragraphs 1 and 22 shall apply only if the claimant may bring a claim against the limitation fund before the Court administering that fund and the fund is actually available and freely transferable in respect of that claim.

ARTICLE 14

Governing law
Subject to the provisions of this Chapter the rules relating to the constitution and distribution of a limitation fund, and all rules of procedure in connection therewith, shall be governed by the law of the State Party in which the fund is constituted.

CHAPTER IV. SCOPE OF APPLICATION

ARTICLE 15

This Convention shall apply whenever any person referred to in Article 1 seeks to limit his liability before the Court of a State Party or seeks to procure the release of a ship or other property or the discharge of any security given within the jurisdiction of any such State.

PART II

PROVISIONS HAVING EFFECT IN CONNECTION WITH CONVENTION

Interpretation
   1. In this Part of this Schedule any reference to a numbered article is a reference to the article of the Convention which is so numbered.

Right to limit liability
   2. The right to limit liability under the Convention shall apply in relation to any ship whether seagoing or not, and the definition of 'shipowner' in paragraph 2 of Article 1 shall be construed accordingly.

Claims subject to limitation
   3.—(1) Paragraph 1(*d*) of Article 2 shall not apply unless provision has been made by an order of the Secretary of State for the setting up and management of a fund to be used for the making to harbour or conservancy authorities of payments needed to compensate them for the reduction, in consequence of the said paragraph 1(*d*), of amounts recoverable by them in claims of the kind there mentioned, and to be maintained by contributions from such authorities raised and collected by them in respect of vessels in like manner as other sums so raised by them.
   (2) Any order under sub-paragraph (1) above may contain such incidental and supplemental provisions as appear to the Secretary of State to be necessary or expedient.
   (3) If immediately before the coming into force of section 17 of this Act an order is in force under section 2(6) of the Merchant Shipping (Liability of Shipowner and Others) Act 1958 (which contains provisions corresponding to those of this paragraph) that order shall have effect as if made under this paragraph.

Claims excluded from limitation
   4.—(1) The claims excluded from the Convention by paragraph (*b*) of Article 3 are claims in respect of any liability incurred under section 1 of the Merchant Shipping (Oil Pollution) Act 1971.

(2) The claims excluded from the Convention by paragraph (*c*) of Article 3 are claims made by virtue of any of sections 7 to 11 of the Nuclear Installations Act 1965.

The general limits

5.—(1) In the application of Article 6 to a ship with a tonnage less than 300 tons that article shall have effect as if—

(*a*) paragraph (*a*)(i) referred to 166,667 Units of Account; and

(*b*) paragraph (*b*)(i) referred to 83,333 Units of Account.

(2) For the purposes of Article 6 and this paragraph a ship's tonnage shall be its gross tonnage calculated in such manner as may be prescribed by an order made by the Secretary of State.

(3) Any order under this paragraph shall, so far as appears to the Secretary of State to be practicable, give effect to the regulations in Annex I of the International Convention on Tonnage Measurement of Ships 1969.

Limit for passenger claims

6.—(1) In the case of a passenger steamer within the meaning of Part III of the Merchant Shipping Act 1894 the ship's certificate mentioned in paragraph 1 of the Article 7 shall be the passenger steamer's certificate issued under section 274 of that Act.

(2) In paragraph 2 of Article 7 the reference to claims brought on behalf of a person includes a reference to any claim in respect of the death of a person under the Fatal Accidents Act 1976, the Fatal Accidents (Northern Ireland) Order 1977 or the Damages (Scotland) Act 1976.

Units of Account

7.—(1) For the purpose of converting the amounts mentioned in Articles 6 and 7 from special drawing rights into sterling one special drawing right shall be treated as equal to such a sum in sterling as the International Monetary Fund have fixed as being the equivalent of one special drawing right for—

(*a*) the relevant date under paragraph 1 of Article 8; or

(*b*) if no sum has been so fixed for that date, the last preceding date for which a sum has been so fixed.

(2) A certificate given by or on behalf of the Treasury stating—

(*a*) that a particular sum in sterling has been fixed as mentioned in the preceding sub-paragraph for a particular date; or

(*b*) that no sum has been so fixed for that date and that a particular sum in sterling has been so fixed for a date which is the last preceding date for which a sum has been so fixed.

shall be conclusive evidence of those matters for the purposes of those Articles; and a document purporting to be such a certificate shall, in any proceedings, be received in evidence and, unless the contrary is proved, be deemed to be such a certificate.

Constitution of fund

8.—(1) The Secretary of State may from time to time, with the concurrence of the Treasury, by order prescribe the rate of interest to be applied for the purposes of paragraph 1 of Article 11.

(2) Where a fund is constituted with the court in accordance with Article 11 for the payment of claims arising out of any occurrence, the court may stay any proceedings relating to any claim arising out of that occurrence which are pending against the person by whom the fund has been constituted.

Distribution of fund

9. No lien or other right in respect of any ship or property shall affect the proportions in which under Article 12 the fund is distributed among several claimants.

Bar to other actions

10. Where the release of a ship or other property is ordered under paragraph 2 of Article 13 the person on whose application it is ordered to be released shall be deemed to have submitted to (or, in Scotland, prorogated) the jurisdiction of the court to adjudicate on the claim for which the ship or property was arrested or attached.

Meaning of 'court'

11. References in the Convention and the preceding provisions of this Part of this Schedule to the court are—

(a) in relation to England and Wales, references to the High Court;
(b) in relation to Scotland, references to the Court of Session;
(c) in relation to Northern Ireland, references to the High Court of Justice in Northern Ireland.

Meaning of 'ship'

12. References in the Convention and in the preceding provisions of this Part of this Schedule to a ship include references to any structure (whether completed or in course of completion) launched and intended for use in navigation as a ship or part of a ship.

Meaning of 'State Party'

13. An Order in Council made for the purposes of this paragraph and declaring that any State specified in the Order is a party to the Convention shall, subject to the provisions of any subsequent Order made for those purposes, be conclusive evidence that the State is a party to the Convention.

(b) IN RELATION TO HOVERCRAFT

17. The Fourth Schedule to this Act shall have effect in relation to the limitation of liability for claims in respect of hovercraft.

18.—(1) Subject to subsection (3) of this section, the owner of a hovercraft registered in the United Kingdom shall not be liable for any loss or damage in the following cases, namely—

(*a*) where any property on board the hovercraft is lost or damaged by reason of fire on board the hovercraft; or

(*b*) where any gold, silver, watches, jewels or precious stones on board the hovercraft are lost or damaged by reason of theft, robbery or other dishonest conduct and their nature and value were not at the time of shipment declared by their owner or shipper to the owner or captain of the hovercraft in the bill of lading or otherwise in writing.

(2) Subject to subsection (3) of this section, where the loss or damage arises from anything done or omitted by any person in his capacity as captain or member of the crew or (otherwise than in that capacity) in the course of his employment as a servant of the owner of the hovercraft, the preceding subsection shall also exclude the liability of—

(*a*) the captain, member of the crew or servant; and

(*b*) in a case where the captain or member of the crew is the servant of a person whose liability would not be excluded by that subsection apart from this paragraph, the person whose servant he is.

(3) This section does not exclude the liability of any person for any loss or damage resulting from any such personal act or omission of his as is mentioned in article 4 of Part I of Schedule 4 to this Act.

(4) In this section 'owner', in relation to hovercraft, includes any part owner and any charterer, manager or operator of the hovercraft.

SCHEDULE 4

PART I

CHAPTER I. THE RIGHT OF LIMITATION

ARTICLE 1

Persons entitled to limit liability

1. Owners and salvors, as hereinafter defined, may limit their liability in accordance with the rules of this Part of this Schedule for claims set out in article 2.

2. The term 'owner' shall mean the owner, charterer, manager or operator of a hovercraft.

3. Salvor shall mean any person rendering services in direct connection with salvage operations. Salvage operations shall also include operations referred to in article 2, paragraph 1(*d*), (*e*) and (*f*). 'Salvage operations' are limited to salvage operations to or from a hovercraft, and do not include any such operations to or from a ship.

4. If any claims set out in article 2 are made against any person for whose

act, neglect or default the owner or salvor is responsible, such person shall be entitled to avail himself of the limitation of liability provided for in this Part of this Schedule.

5. In this Part of this Schedule the liability of an owner shall include liability in an action brought against the hovercraft herself.

6. An insurer of liability for claims subject to limitation in accordance with the rules of this Part of this Schedule shall be entitled to the benefits of this Part of this Schedule to the same extent as the assured himself.

7. The act of invoking limitation of liability shall not constitute an admission of liability.

ARTICLE 2

Claims subject to limitation
1. Subject to Articles 3 and 4 the following claims, whatever the basis of liability may be, shall be subject to limitation of liability:
   (*a*) claims in respect of loss of life or personal injury or loss of or damage to property (including damage to harbour works, basins and waterways and aids to navigation), occurring on board or in direct connection with the operation of the hovercraft or with salvage operations, and consequential loss resulting therefrom;
   (*b*) claims in respect of loss resulting from delay in the carriage of cargo;
   (*c*) claims in respect of other loss resulting from infringement of rights other than contractual rights, occurring in direct connection with the operation of the hovercraft or salvage operations;
   (*e*) claims in respect of the removal, destruction or the rendering harmless of the cargo of the hovercraft;
   (*f*) claims of a person other than the person liable in respect of measures taken in order to avert or minimize loss for which the person liable may limit his liability in accordance with this Part of this Schedule, and further loss caused by such measures.

2. Claims set out in paragraph 1 shall be subject to limitation of liability even if brought by way of recourse or for indemnity under a contract or otherwise. However, claims set out under paragraph 1(*e*) and (*f*) shall not be subject to limitation of liability to the extent that they relate to remuneration under a contract with the person liable.

ARTICLE 3

Claims excepted from limitation
The rules of this Part of this Schedule shall not apply to:
   (*a*) claims for salvage or contribution in general average;
   (*c*) claims subject to any international convention or national legislation governing or prohibiting limitation of liability for nuclear damage.

ARTICLE 4

Conduct barring limitation
A person liable shall not be entitled to limit his liability if it is proved that the loss resulted from his personal act or omission, committed with the intent to cause such loss, or recklessly and with knowledge that such loss would probably result.

ARTICLE 5

Counterclaims
Where a person entitled to limitation of liability under the rules of this Part of this Schedule has a claim against the claimant arising out of the same occurrence, their respective claims shall be set off against each other and the provisions of this Part of this Schedule shall only apply to the balance, if any.

ARTICLE 6

The limits
1. The limits of liability for claims arising on any distinct occasion shall be calculated as follows:
   (*a*) In respect of claims for loss of life or personal injury:
      (i) £142,014 for a hovercraft with a maximum operational weight not exceeding 8,000 kg,
      (ii) £276,601 for a hovercraft with a maximum operational weight in excess of 8,000 kg, but not exceeding 13,000 kg,
      (iii) for a hovercraft with a maximum operational weight in excess thereof the following amount in addition to that mentioned in (ii):
      —for each kg from 13,001 to 80,000 kg, £15·98.
      —for each kg in excess of 80,000 kg, £10·64.
   (*b*) In respect of any other claim,
      (i) £59,560 for a hovercraft with a maximum operational weight not exceeding 8,000 kg,
      (ii) £116,378 for a hovercraft with a maximum operational weight in excess of 8,000 kg, but not exceeding 13,000 kg,
      (iii) for a hovercraft with a maximum operational weight in excess thereof, an amount in addition to that mentioned at (ii) which equals £4·48 for each additional kg.
2. Where the amount calculated in accordance with paragraph 1(*a*) is insufficient to pay the claims mentioned therein in full, the amount calculated in accordance with paragraph 1(*b*) shall be available for payment of the

unpaid balance of claims under paragraph 1(*a*) and such unpaid balance shall rank rateably with claims mentioned under paragraph 1(*b*).

ARTICLE 9

Aggregation of claims
   1. The limits of liability determined in accordance with Article 6 shall apply to the aggregate of all claims which arise on any distinct occasion:
   (*a*) against the person or persons mentioned in paragraph 2 of Article 1 and any person for whose act, neglect or default he or they are responsible; or
   (*b*) against the owner of a hovercraft rendering salvage services from that hovercraft and the salvor or salvors operating from such hovercraft and any person for whose act, neglect or default he or they are responsible; or
   (*c*) against the salvor or salvors who are not operating from a hovercraft or whose are operating solely on the hovercraft to, or in respect of which, the salvage services are rendered and any person for whose act, neglect or default he or they are responsible.

ARTICLE 10

Limitation of liability without constitution of a limitation fund
   1. Limitation of liability may be invoked notwithstanding that a limitation fund as mentioned in Article 11 has not been constituted.
   2. If limitation of liability is invoked without the constitution of a limitation fund, the provisions of Article 12 shall apply correspondingly.

CHAPTER III. THE LIMITATION FUND

ARTICLE 11

Constitution of the fund
   1. Any person alleged to be liable may constitute a fund with the Court in respect of claims subject to limitation. The fund shall be constituted in the sum of such of the amounts set out in Article 6 as are applicable to claims for which that person may be liable, together with interest thereon from the date of the occurrence giving rise to the liability until the date of the constitution of the fund. Any fund thus constituted shall be available only for the payment of claims in respect of which limitation of liability can be invoked.

2. A fund may be constituted, either by depositing the sum, or by producing a guarantee considered to be adequate by the Court.

3. A fund constituted by one of the persons mentioned in paragraph 1(*a*), (*b*) or (*c*) of Article 9 or his insurer shall be deemed constituted by all persons mentioned in paragraph 1(*a*), (*b*) or (*c*), respectively.

ARTICLE 12

Distribution of the fund

1. Subject to the provisions of paragraphs 1 and 2 of Article 6, the fund shall be distributed among the claimants in proportion to their established claims against the fund.

2. If, before the fund is distributed, the person liable, or his insurer, has settled a claim against the fund such person shall, up to the amount he has paid, acquire by subrogation the rights which the person so compensated would have enjoyed under this Part of this Schedule.

3. The right of subrogation provided for in paragraph 2 may also be exercised by persons other than those therein mentioned in respect of any amount of compensation which they may have paid, but only to the extent that such subrogation is permitted under the applicable law.

4. Where the person liable or any other person establishes that he may be compelled to pay, at a later date, in whole or in part any such amount of compensation with regard to which such person would have enjoyed a right of subrogation pursuant to paragraphs 2 and 3 had the compensation been paid before the fund was distributed, the Court where the fund has been constituted may order that a sufficient sum shall be provisionally set aside to enable such person at such later date to enforce his claim against the fund.

ARTICLE 13

Bar to other actions

1. Where a limitation fund has been constituted in accordance with Article 11, any person having made a claim against the fund shall be barred from exercising any right in respect of such a claim against any other assets of a person by or on behalf of whom the fund has been constituted.

2. After a limitation fund has been constituted in accordance with Article 11, any hovercraft or other property, belonging to a person on behalf of whom the fund has been constituted, which has been arrested for a claim which may be raised against the fund, or any security given, shall be released by order of the Court.

Chapter IV. Scope of Application

Article 15

This part of this Schedule shall apply whenever any person referred to in Article 1 seeks to limit his liability before the Court or seeks to procure the release of a hovercraft or other property or the discharge of any security given within the jurisdiction of the Court.

Part II. Provisions having Effect in Connection with Part I of This Schedule

Interpretation
1. In this part of this Schedule any reference to a numbered article is a reference to the article of Part I of this Schedule which is so numbered.
8. The rate of interest to be applied for the purposes of paragraph 1 of Article 11 shall be the rate prescribed for the time being in any order made by the Secretary of State in exercise of his powers under paragraph 8 of Part II of Schedule 4 to the Merchant Shipping Act 1979 as it applies in connection with ships.

Distribution of fund
9. No lien or other right in respect of any hovercraft or property shall affect the proportions in which under Article 12 the fund is distributed among several claimants.

Bar to other actions
10. Where the release of a hovercraft or other property is ordered under paragraph 2 of Article 13 the person on whose application it is ordered to be released shall be deemed to have submitted to (or, in Scotland, prorogated) the jurisdiction of the Court to adjudicate on the claim for which the hovercraft or property was arrested or attached.

Meaning of 'Court'
11. References in Part 1 of this Schedule and the preceding provisions of this Part of this Schedule to the Court are—
 (a) in relation to England and Wales, references to the High Court;
 (b) in relation to Scotland, references to the Court of Session;
 (c) in relation to Northern Ireland, references to the High Court of Justice in Northern Ireland.

Merchant Shipping Act 1981

(1981 Chapter 10)

An Act to replace by amounts equivalent to special drawing rights of the International Monetary Fund the amounts in gold francs specified in certain provisions limiting the liability of shipowners and others.

[15 April 1981]

1. Substitution of special drawing rights in limitation provisions of Merchant Shipping Acts.—(1) Section 503 of the Merchant Shipping Act 1894, as amended by the Merchant Shipping (Liability of Shipowners and Others) Act 1958, shall have effect subject to the provisions of subsections (2) and (3) below, being provisions consequential on a Protocol signed on 21st December 1979 amending the International Convention of 1957 relating to the limitation of the liability of owners of sea-going ships.

(2) The amounts per ton to be taken into account under subsection (1)(i) and (ii) of the said section 503 shall, instead of being amounts respectively equivalent to 3,100 and 1,000 golds francs, be amounts respectively equivalent to 206·67 and 66·67 special drawing rights.

(3) The special drawing rights referred to above are the special drawing rights as defined by the International Monetary Fund, and their equivalent shall be determined on the basis of the value of sterling—

(a) if a limitation action is brought, on the date on which the limitation fund is constituted; and

(b) in any other case, on the date of the judgment in question.

(4) The amount per ton to be taken into account under section 2 of the Merchant Shipping (Liability of Shipowners and Others) Act 1900, as amended by the said Act of 1958, shall, instead of being an amount equivalent to 1,000 gold francs, be an amount equivalent to 66·67 special drawing rights and subsection (3) above shall apply also for the purposes of this subsection.

(5) In section 1(1) of the said Act of 1958 (which is in part superseded by the foregoing provisions)—

(a) the words 'or section two' to the end of paragraph (b) shall be omitted; and

(b) for the words 'and the number by which the amount substituted by paragraph (a) of this subsection is to be multiplied' there shall be substituted the words 'the number by which the amount equivalent to 206·67 special drawing rights is to be multiplied'.

(6) In section 5 of the said Act of 1958 (release of ship where guarantee given in Convention country) 'the Convention' shall mean the Convention there mentioned with or without the amendments made by the Protocol referred to in subsection (1) above and 'Convention country' shall be construed accordingly.

2. Substitution of special drawing rights in limitation provisions of Carriage of Goods by Sea Act 1971.—(1) In section 1 of the Carriage of Goods by Sea Act 1971 (which gives effect to the International Convention for the unification of certain rules of law relating to bills of lading signed at Brussels on 25 August 1924 as amended by the Protocol signed at Brussels on 23 February 1968) after the words in subsection (1) 'as amended by the Protocol signed at Brussels on 23 February 1968' there shall be inserted the words 'and by the Protocol signed at Brussels on 21 December 1979'.

(2) In consequence of the said Protocol of 1979 Article IV of the Rules set out in the Schedule to that Act shall be amended in accordance with the following provisions.

(3) In paragraph 5(*a*) of that Article—

(*a*) for the words 'the equivalent of 10,000 francs' there shall be substituted the words '666·67 units of account';

(*b*) for the words '30 francs per kilo' there shall be substituted the words '2 units of account per kilogramme'.

(4) For paragraph 5(*d*) of that Article there shall be substituted—

'(*d*) The unit of account mentioned in this Article is the special drawing right as defined by the International Monetary Fund. The amounts mentioned in sub-paragraph (*a*) of this paragraph shall be converted into national currency on the basis of the value of that currency on a date to be determined by the law of the Court seized of the case'.

(5) In its application by virtue of the said Act of 1971 paragraph 5(*d*) of the said Article IV shall have effect as if the date there mentioned were the date of the judgment in question.

(6) In its application by virtue of the said Act of 1971 Article X of the Rules set out in the Schedule to that Act shall have effect as if references to a contracting State included references to a State that is a contracting State in respect of the Rules without the amendments made by the said Protocol of 1979 as well as to one that is a contracting State in respect of the Rules as so amended, and section 2 of that Act (certification of contracting States) shall have effect accordingly.

3. Conversion of special drawing rights into sterling.—(1) For the purposes of section 1 above and of Article IV of the Rules set out in the Schedule to the Carriage of Goods by Sea Act 1971 as amended by section 2 above, the value on a particular day of one special drawing right shall be treated as equal to such a sum in sterling as the International Monetary Fund have fixed as being the equivalent of one special drawing right—

(*a*) for that day; or

(*b*) if no sum has been so fixed for that day, for the last day before that day for which a sum has been so fixed.

(2) A certificate given by or on behalf of the Treasury stating—

(*a*) that a particular sum in sterling has been fixed as aforesaid for a particular day; or

(*b*) that no sum has been so fixed for a particular day and that a particular sum in sterling has been so fixed for a day which is the last day for which a sum has been so fixed before the particular day,

shall be conclusive evidence of those matters for the purposes of subsection (1) above; and a document purporting to be such a certificate shall in any proceedings be received in evidence and, unless the contrary is proved, be deemed to be such a certificate.

(3) The Treasury may charge a reasonable fee for any certificate given in pursuance of subsection (2) above, and any fee received by the Treasury by virtue of this subsection shall be paid into the Consolidated Fund.

4. Extent.—(1) This Act extends to Northern Ireland.

(2) The provisions to which section 11 of the Merchant Shipping (Liability of Shipowners and Others) Act 1958 applies (extension to British possessions etc) shall include section 1 above and so much of the other provisions of this Act as relates to that section; and the provisions to which section 4 of the Carriage of Goods by Sea Act 1971 applies (extension to British possessions etc) shall include section 2 above and so much of the other provisions of this Act as relates to that section.

5. Short title, citation, repeals and commencement.—(1) This Act may be cited as the Merchant Shipping Act 1981.

(2) This Act, except so far as it relates to the Carriage of Goods by Sea Act 1971, shall be construed as one with the Merchant Shipping Acts 1894 to 1979 and may be cited with those Acts as the Merchant Shipping Acts 1894 to 1981.

(3) The enactments mentioned in the Schedule to this Act are hereby repealed to the extent specified in the third column of that Schedule.

(4) This Act shall come into force on such day as Her Majesty may by Order in Council appoint and different days may be appointed for different provisions or different purposes of the same provision.

(5) An Order under subsection (4) above may contain transitional provisions.

(6) Any judgment in respect of a liability limited by a provision amended by this Act shall, if given after the coming into force of the amendment, be given in accordance with the amended provision irrespective of when the liability arose.

SCHEDULE   Section 5(3)

REPEALS

Chapter	Short title	Extent of repeal
1958 c 62.	The Merchant Shipping (Liability of Shipowners and Others) Act 1958.	In section 1, in subsection (1) the words from 'or section two' to the end of paragraph (*b*) and subsections (2), (3) and (4).
1971 c 19.	The Carriage of Goods by Sea Act 1971.	Section 1(5).

Appendix E

Carriage of Goods by Sea Act 1971[1]

(1971 c 19)

(a) IN RELATION TO VESSELS OTHER THAN HOVERCRAFT

Be it enacted by the Queen's most Excellent Majesty, by and with the advice and consent of the Lords Spiritual and Temporal, and Commons, in this present Parliament assembled, and by the authority of the same, as follows:—

1. Application of Hague Rules as amended.—(1) In this Act, 'the Rules' means the International Convention for the unification of certain rules of law relating to bills of lading signed at Brussels on 25 August 1924, as amended by the Protocol signed at Brussels on 23 February 1968 and by the Protocol signed at Brussels on 21 December 1979.

(2) The provisions of the Rules, as set out in the Schedule to this Act, shall have the force of law.

(3) Without prejudice to subsection (2) above, the said provisions shall have effect (and have the force of law) in relation to and in connection with the carriage of goods by sea in ships where the port of shipment is a port in the United Kingdom, whether or not the carriage is between ports in two different States within the meaning of Article X of the Rules.

(4) Subject to subsection (6) below, nothing in this section shall be taken as applying anything in the Rules to any contract for the carriage of goods by sea, unless the contract expressly or by implication provides for the issue of a bill of lading or any similar document of title.

(5) [repealed].

(6) Without prejudice to Article X(c) of the Rules, the Rules shall have the force of law in relation to—

(a) any bill of lading if the contract contained in or evidenced by it expressly provides that the Rules shall govern the contract, and

(b) any receipt which is a non-negotiable document marked as such if the

---

1 The Act is printed as amended.

contract contained in or evidenced by it is a contract for the carriage
of goods by sea which expressly provides that the Rules are to govern
the contract as if the receipt were a bill of lading,
but subject, where paragraph (*b*) applies, to any necessary modifications and
in particular with the omission in Article III of the Rules of the second
sentence of paragraph 4 and of paragraph 7.

(7) If and so far as the contract contained in or evidenced by a bill of
lading or receipt within paragraph (*a*) or (*b*) of subsection (6) above applies
to deck cargo or live animals, the Rules as given the force of law by that
subsection shall have effect as if Article I(*c*) did not exclude deck cargo and
live animals.

In this subsection 'deck cargo' means cargo which by the contract of
carriage is stated as being carried on deck and is so carried.

2. Contracting States, etc—(1) If Her Majesty by Order in Council certifies
to the following effect, that is to say, that for the purposes of the Rules—

(*a*) a State specified in the Order is a contracting State, or is a contracting
State in respect of any place or territory so specified; or

(*b*) any place or territory specified in the Order forms part of a State so
specified (whether a contracting State or not),

the Order shall, except so far as it has been superseded by a subsequent
Order, be conclusive evidence of the matters so certified.

(2) An Order in Council under this section may be varied or revoked by
a subsequent Order in Council.

**3. Absolute warranty of seaworthiness not to be implied in contracts to
which Rules apply.**—There shall not be implied in any contract for the
carriage of goods by sea to which the Rules apply by virtue of this Act any
absolute undertaking by the carrier of the goods to provide a seaworthy
ship.

4. Application of Act to British possessions, etc—(1) Her Majesty may by
Order in Council direct that this Act shall extend, subject to such exceptions,
adaptations and modifications as may be specified in the Order, to all or any
of the following territories, that is—

(*a*) any colony (not being a colony for whose external relations a country
other than the United Kingdom is responsible),

(*b*) any country outside Her Majesty's dominions in which Her Majesty
has jurisdiction in right of Her Majesty's Government of the United
Kingdom.

(2) An Order in Council under this section may contain such transitional
and other consequential and incidental provisions as appear to Her Majesty
to be expedient, including provisions amending or repealing any legislation
about the carriage of goods by sea forming part of the law of any of the
territories mentioned in paragraphs (*a*) and (*b*) above.

(3) An Order in Council under this section may be varied or revoked by
a subsequent Order in Council.

5. Extension of application of Rules to carriage from ports in British possessions, etc—(1) Her Majesty may by Order in Council provide that section 1(3) of this Act shall have effect as if the reference therein to the United Kingdom included a reference to all or any of the following territories, that is—

(a) the Isle of Man;

(b) any of the Channel Islands specified in the Order;

(c) any colony specified in the Order (not being a colony for whose external relations a country other than the United Kingdom is responsible);

(d) any associated state (as defined by section 1(3) of the West Indies Act 1967) specified in the Order;

(e) any country specified in the Order, being a country outside Her Majesty's dominions in which Her Majesty has jurisdiction in right of Her Majesty's Government of the United Kingdom.

(2) An Order in Council under this section may be varied or revoked by a subsequent Order in Council.

6. Supplemental.—(1) This Act may be cited as the Carriage of Goods by Sea Act 1971.

(2) It is hereby declared that this Act extends to Northern Ireland.

(3) The following enactments shall be repealed, that is—

(a) the Carriage of Goods by Sea Act 1924,

(b) section 12(4)(a) of the Nuclear Installations Act 1965,

and without prejudice to section 38(1) of the Interpretation Act 1889, the reference to the said Act of 1924 in section 1(1)(i)(ii) of the Hovercraft Act 1968 shall include a reference to this Act.

(4) It is hereby declared that for the purposes of Article VIII of the Rules section 18 of the Merchant Shipping Act 1979 which entirely exempts shipowners and others in certain circumstances from liability for loss of, or damage to, goods) is a provision relating to limitation of liability.

(5) This Act shall come into force on such day as Her Majesty may by Order in Council appoint, and, for the purposes of the transition from the law in force immediately before the day appointed under this subsection to the provisions of this Act, the Order appointing the day may provide that those provisions shall have effect subject to such transitional provisions as may be contained in the Order.

SCHEDULE

THE HAGUE RULES AS AMENDED BY THE BRUSSELS PROTOCOL 1968

ARTICLE I.

In these Rules the following words are employed, with the meanings set out below:—

(*a*) 'Carrier' includes the owner or the charterer who enters into a contract of carriage with a shipper.

(*b*) 'Contract of carriage' applies only to contracts of carriage covered by a bill of lading or any similar document of title, in so far as such document relates to the carriage of goods by sea, including any bill of lading or any similar document as aforesaid issued under or pursuant to a charter-party from the moment at which such bill of lading or similar document of title regulates the relations between a carrier and a holder of the same.

(*c*) 'Goods' includes goods, wares, merchandise, and articles of every kind whatsoever except live animals and cargo which by the contract of carriage is stated as being carried on deck and is so carried.

(*d*) 'Ship' means any vessel used for the carriage of goods by sea.

(*e*) 'Carriage of goods' covers the period from the time when the goods are loaded on to the time they are discharged from the ship.

ARTICLE II.

Subject to the provisions of Article VI, under every contract of carriage of goods by sea the carrier, in relation to the loading, handling, stowage, carriage, custody, care and discharge of such goods, shall be subject to the responsibilities and liabilities, and entitled to the rights and immunities hereinafter set forth.

ARTICLE III.

1. The carrier shall be bound before and at the beginning of the voyage to exercise the due diligence to—

(*a*) Make the ship seaworthy.

(*b*) Properly man, equip and supply the ship.

(*c*) Make the holds, refrigerating and cool chambers, and all other parts of the ship in which goods are carried, fit and safe for their reception, carriage and preservation.

2. Subject to the provisions of Article IV, the carrier shall properly and carefully load, handle, stow, carry, keep, care for, and discharge the goods carried.

3. After receiving the goods into his charge the carrier or the master or agent of the carrier shall, on demand of the shipper, issue to the shipper a bill of lading showing among other things—

(*a*) The leading marks necessary for identification of the goods as the same are furnished in writing by the shipper before the loading of such goods starts, provided such marks are stamped or otherwise shown clearly upon the goods if uncovered, or on the cases or coverings in which such goods are contained, in such a manner as should ordinarily remain legible until the end of the voyage.

(*b*) Either the number of packages or pieces, or the quantity, or weight, as the case may be, as furnished in writing by the shipper.

(*c*) The apparent order and condition of the goods.

Provided that no carrier, master or agent of the carrier shall be bound to state or show in the bill of lading any marks, number, quantity or weight which he has reasonable ground for suspecting not accurately to represent the goods actually received, or which he has had no reasonable means of checking.

4. Such a bill of lading shall be prima facie evidence of the receipt by the carrier of the goods as therein described in accordance with paragraph 3(*a*), (*b*) and (*c*). However, proof to the contrary shall not be admissible when the bill of lading has been transferred to a third party acting in good faith.

5. The shipper shall be deemed to have guaranteed to the carrier the accuracy at the time of shipment of the marks, number, quantity and weight, as furnished by him, and the shipper shall indemnify the carrier against all loss, damages and expenses arising or resulting from inaccuracies in such particulars. The right of the carrier to such indemnity shall in no way limit his responsibility and liability under the contract of carriage to any person other than the shipper.

6. Unless notice of loss or damage and the general nature of such loss or damage be given in writing to the carrier or his agent at the port of discharge before or at the time of the removal of the goods into the custody of the person entitled to delivery thereof under the contract of carriage, or, if the loss or damage be not apparent, within three days, such removal shall be prima facie evidence of the delivery by the carrier of the goods as described in the bill of lading.

The notice in writing need not be given if the state of the goods has, at the time of their receipt, been the subject of joint survey or inspection.

Subject to paragraph 6 *bis* the carrier and the ship shall in any event be discharged from all liability whatsoever in respect of the goods, unless suit is brought within one year of their delivery or of the date when they should have been delivered. This period may, however, be extended if the parties so agree after the cause of action has arisen.

In the case of any actual or apprehended loss or damage the carrier and the receiver shall give all reasonable facilities to each other for inspecting and tallying the goods.

6 *bis*. An action for indemnity against a third person may be brought even after the expiration of the year provided for in the preceding paragraph if brought within the time allowed by the law of the Court seized of the case. However, the time allowed shall be not less than three months, commencing from the day when the person bringing such action for indemnity has settled the claim or has been served with process in the action against himself.

7. After the goods are loaded the bill of lading to be issued by the carrier, master, or agent of the carrier, to the shipper shall, if the shipper so demands, be a 'shipped' bill of lading, provided that if the shipper shall have previously

taken up any document of title such goods, he shall surrender the same as against the issue of the 'shipped' bill of lading, but at the option of the carrier such document of title may be noted at the port of shipment by the carrier, master, or agent with the name or names of the ship or ships upon which the goods have been shipped and the date or dates of shipment, and when so noted, if it shows the particulars mentioned in paragraph 3 of Article III, shall for the purpose of this article be deemed to constitute a 'shipped' bill of lading.

8. Any clause, covenant, or agreement in a contract of carriage relieving the carrier or the ship from liability for loss or damage to, or in connection with, goods arising from negligence, fault, or failure in the duties and obligations provided in this article or lessening such liability otherwise than as provided in these Rules, shall be null and void and of no effect. A benefit of insurance in favour of the carrier or similar clause shall be deemed to be a clause relieving the carrier from liability.

ARTICLE IV.

1. Neither the carrier nor the ship shall be liable for loss or damage arising or resulting from unseaworthiness unless caused by want of due diligence on the part of the carrier to make the ship seaworthy, and to secure that the ship is properly manned, equipped and supplied, and to make the holds, refrigerating and cool chambers and all other parts of the ship in which goods are carried fit and safe for their reception, carriage and preservation in accordance with the provisions of paragraph 1 of Article III. Whenever loss or damage has resulted from unseaworthiness the burden of proving the exercise of due diligence shall be on the carrier or other person claiming exemption under this article.

2. Neither the carrier nor the ship shall be responsible for loss or damage arising or resulting from—

(a) Act, neglect, or default of the master, mariner, pilot, or the servants of the carrier in the navigation or in the management of the ship.

(b) Fire, unless caused by the actual fault or privity of the carrier.

(c) Perils, dangers and accidents of the sea or other navigable waters.

(d) Act of God.

(e) Act of war.

(f) Act of public enemies.

(g) Arrest or restraint of princes, rulers or people, or seizure under legal process.

(h) Quarantine restrictions.

(i) Act or omission of the shipper or owner of the goods, his agent or representative.

(j) Strikes or lockouts or stoppage or restraint of labour from whatever cause, whether partial or general.

(*k*) Riots and civil commotions.

(*l*) Saving or attempting to save life or property at sea.

(*m*) Wastage in bulk or weight or any other loss or damage arising from inherent defect, quality or vice of the goods.

(*n*) Insufficiency of packing.

(*o*) Insufficiency or inadequacy of marks.

(*p*) Latent defects not discoverable by due diligence.

(*q*) Any other cause arising without the actual fault or privity of the carrier, or without the fault or neglect of the agents or servants of the carrier, but the burden of proof shall be on the person claiming the benefit of this exception to show that neither the actual fault or privity of the carrier nor the fault or neglect of the agents or servants of the carrier contributed to the loss or damage.

3. The shipper shall not be responsible for loss or damage sustained by the carrier or the ship arising or resulting from any cause without the act, fault or neglect of the shipper, his agents or his servants.

4. Any deviation in saving or attempting to save life or property at sea or any reasonable deviation shall not be deemed to be an infringement or breach of these Rules or of the contract of carriage, and the carrier shall not be liable for any loss or damage resulting therefrom.

5. (*a*) Unless the nature and value of such goods have been declared by the shipper before shipment and inserted in the bill of lading, neither the carrier nor the ship shall in any event be or become liable for any loss or damage to or in connection with the goods in an amount exceeding 666·67 units of account per package or unit or 2 units of account per kilogramme of gross weight of the goods lost or damaged, whichever is the higher.

(*b*) The total amount recoverable shall be calculated by reference to the value of such goods at the place and time at which the goods are discharged from the ship in accordance with the contract or should have been so discharged.

The value of the goods shall be fixed according to the commodity exchange price, or, if there be no such price, according to the current market price, or, if there be no commodity exchange price or current market price, by reference to the normal value of goods of the same kind and quality.

(*c*) Where a container, pallet or similar article of transport is used to consolidate goods, the number of packages or units enumerated in the bill of lading as packed in such article of transport shall be deemed the number of packages or units for the purpose of this paragraph as far as these packages or units are concerned. Except as aforesaid such article of transport shall be considered the package or unit.

(*d*) The unit of account mentioned in this Article is the special drawing right as defined by the International Monetary Fund. The amounts mentioned in sub-paragraph (*a*) of this paragraph shall be converted into national currency on the basis of the value of that currency on a date to be determined by the law of the Court seized of the case.

(*e*) Neither the carrier nor the ship shall be entitled to the benefit of the limitation of liability provided for in this paragraph if it is proved that the damage resulted from an act or omission of the carrier done with intent to cause damage, or recklessly and with knowledge that damage would probably result.

(*f*) The declaration mentioned in sub-paragraph (*a*) of this paragraph, if embodied in the bill of lading, shall be prima facie evidence, but shall not be binding or conclusive on the carrier.

(*g*) By agreement between the carrier, master or agent of the carrier and the shipper other maximum amounts than those mentioned in sub-paragraph (*a*) of this paragraph may be fixed, provided that no maximum amount so fixed shall be less than the appropriate maximum mentioned in that sub-paragraph.

(*h*) Neither the carrier nor the ship shall be responsible in any event for loss or damage to, or in connection with, goods if the nature or value thereof has been knowingly mis-stated by the shipper in the bill of lading.

6. Goods of an inflammable, explosive or dangerous nature to the shipment whereof the carrier, master or agent of the carrier has not consented with knowledge of their nature and character, may at any time before discharge be landed at any place, or destroyed or rendered innocuous by the carrier without compensation and the shipper of such goods shall be liable for all damages and expenses directly or indirectly arising out of or resulting from such shipment. If any such goods shipped with such knowledge and consent shall become a danger to the ship or cargo, they may in like manner be landed at any place, or destroyed or rendered innocuous by the carrier without liability on the part of the carrier except to general average, if any.

ARTICLE IV BIS.

1. The defences and limits of liability provided for in these Rules shall apply in any action against the carrier in respect of loss or damage to goods covered by a contract of carriage whether the action be founded in contract or in tort.

2. If such an action is brought against a servant or agent of the carrier (such servant or agent not being an independent contractor), such servant or agent shall be entitled to avail himself of the defences and limits of liability which the carrier is entitled to invoke under these Rules.

3. The aggregate of the amounts recoverable from the carrier, and such servants and agents, shall in no case exceed the limit provided for in these Rules.

4. Nevertheless, a servant or agent of the carrier shall not be entitled to avail himself of the provisions of this article, if it is proved that the damage resulted from an act or omission of the servant or agent done with intent to cause damage or recklessly and with knowledge that damage would probably result.

ARTICLE V.

A carrier shall be at liberty to surrender in whole or in part all or any of his rights and immunities or to increase any of his responsibilities and obligations under these Rules, provided such surrender or increase shall be embodied in the bill of lading issued to the shipper. The provisions of these Rules shall not be applicable to charter-parties, but if bills of lading are issued in the case of a ship under a charter-party they shall comply with the terms of these Rules. Nothing in these Rules shall be held to prevent the insertion in a bill of lading of any lawful provision regarding general average.

ARTICLE VI.

Notwithstanding the provisions of the preceding articles, a carrier, master or agent of the carrier and a shipper shall in regard to any particular goods be at liberty to enter into any agreement in any terms as to the responsibility and liability of the carrier for such goods, and as to the rights and immunities of the carrier in respect of such goods, or his obligation as to seaworthiness, so far as this stipulation is not contrary to public policy, or the care or diligence of his servants or agents in regard to the loading, handling, stowage, carriage, custody, care and discharge of the goods carried by sea, provided that in this case no bill of lading has been or shall be issued and that the terms agreed shall be embodied in a receipt which shall be a non-negotiable document and shall be marked as such.

Any agreement so entered into shall have full legal effect.

Provided that this article shall not apply to ordinary commercial shipments made in the ordinary course of trade, but only to other shipments where the character or condition of the property to be carried or the circumstances, terms and conditions under which the carriage is to be performed are such as reasonably to justify a special agreement.

ARTICLE VII.

Nothing herein contained shall prevent a carrier or a shipper from entering into any agreement, stipulation, condition, reservation or exemption as to the responsibility and liability of the carrier or the ship for the loss or damage to, or in connection with, the custody and care and handling of goods prior to the loading on, and subsequent to the discharge from, the ship on which the goods are carried by sea.

ARTICLE VIII.

The provisions of these Rules shall not affect the rights and obligations of the carrier under any statute for the time being in force relating to the limitation of the liability of owners of sea-going vessels.

ARTICLE IX.

These Rules shall not affect the provisions of any international Convention or national law governing liability for nuclear damage.

ARTICLE X.

The provisions of these Rules shall apply to every bill of lading relating to the carriage of goods between ports in two different States if:
  (a) the bill of lading is issued in a contracting State,
       or
  (b) the carriage is from a port in a contracting State,
       or
  (c) the contract contained in or evidenced by the bill of lading provides that these Rules or legislation of any State giving effect to them are to govern the contract,
whatever may be the nationality of the ship, the carrier, the shipper, the consignee, or any other interested person.

[*The last two paragraphs of this article are not reproduced. They require contracting States to apply the Rules to bills of lading mentioned in the article and authorise them to apply the Rules to other bills of lading.*]

[*Articles 11 to 16 of the International Convention for the unification of certain rules of law relating to bills of lading signed at Brussels on 25 August 1924 are not reproduced. They deal with the coming into force of the Convention, procedure for ratification, accession and denunciation, and the right to call for a fresh conference to consider amendments to the Rules contained in the Convention.*]

(b) IN RELATION TO HOVERCRAFT

1.—(1) In this Act, 'the Rules' means the International Convention for the unification of certain rules of law relating to bills of lading signed at Brussels on 25 August 1924, as amended by the Protocol signed at Brussels on 23 February 1968.

(2) The provisions of the Rules as set out in the Schedule to this Act, shall have the force of law.

(3) Without prejudice to subsection (2) above, the said provisions shall have effect (and have the force of law) in relation to and in connection with the carriage of goods in hovercraft where the hoverport of shipment is a hoverport in the United Kingdom, whether or not the carriage is between hoverports in two different States within the meaning of article X of the Rules.

(4) Subject to subsection (6) below, nothing in this section shall be taken

as applying anything in the Rules to any contract for the carriage of goods, unless the contract expressly or by implication provides for the issue of a bill of lading or any similar document of title.

(6) Without prejudice to article X(*c*) of the Rules, the Rules shall have the force of law in relation to—

(*a*) any bill of lading if the contract contained in or evidenced by it expressly provides that the Rules shall govern the contract, and

(*b*) any receipt which is a non-negotiable document marked as such if the contract contained in or evidenced by it is a contract for the carriage of goods which expressly provides that the Rules are to govern the contract as if the receipt were a bill of lading,

but subject, where paragraph (*b*) applies, to any necessary modifications and in particular with the omission in article III of the Rules of the second sentence of paragraph 4 and of paragraph 7.

(7) If and so far as the contract contained in or evidenced by a bill of lading or receipt within paragraph (*a*) or (*b*) of subsection (6) above applies to deck cargo or live animals, the Rules as given the force of law by that subsection shall have effect as if article I(*c*) did not exclude deck cargo and live animals.

In this subsection 'deck cargo' means cargo which by the contract of carriage is stated as being carried on deck and is so carried.

3. There shall not be implied in any contract for the carriage of goods to which the Rules apply by virtue of this Act any absolute undertaking by the carrier of the goods to provide a hovercraft fit for the voyage.

6.—(2) It is hereby declared that this Act extends to Northern Ireland.

(3) Without prejudice to section 16 of the Interpretation Act 1978, the reference to the Carriage of Goods by Sea Act 1924 in section 1(1)(*i*)(ii) of the Hovercraft Act 1968 shall include a reference to this Act.

SCHEDULE

ARTICLE I.

In these Rules the following words are employed, with the meanings set out below:—

(*a*) 'Carrier' includes the owner or the charterer who enters into a contract of carriage with a shipper.

(*b*) 'Contract of carriage' applies only to contracts of carriage covered by a bill of lading or any similar document of title, in so far as such document relates to the carriage of goods, including any bill of lading or any similar document as aforesaid issued under or pursuant to a charter party from the moment at which such bill of lading or similar document of title regulates the relations between a carrier and a holder of the same.

(*c*) 'Goods' includes goods, wares, merchandise, and articles of every kind whatsoever except live animals and cargo which by the contract of carriage is stated as being carried on deck and is so carried.

(e) 'Carriage of goods' covers the period from the time when the goods are loaded on, to the time they are discharged from the hovercraft.

ARTICLE II.

Subject to the provisions of article VI, under every contract of carriage of goods the carrier, in relation to the loading, handling, stowage, carriage, custody, care and discharge of such goods, shall be subject to the responsibilities and liabilities, and entitled to the rights and immunities hereinafter set forth.

ARTICLE III.

1. The carrier shall be bound before and at the beginning of the voyage to exercise due diligence to—
   (a) Make the hovercraft fit for the voyage.
   (b) Properly man, equip and supply the hovercraft.
   (c) Make the holds, refrigerating and cool chambers, and all other parts of the hovercraft in which goods are carried, fit and safe for their reception, carriage and preservation.

2. Subject to the provisions of article IV, the carrier shall properly and carefully load, handle, stow, carry, keep, care for, and discharge the goods carried.

3. After receiving the goods into his charge the carrier or the captain or agent of the carrier shall, on demand of the shipper, issue to the shipper a bill of lading showing among other things—
   (a) The leading marks necessary for identification of the goods as the same are furnished in writing by the shipper before the loading of such goods starts, provided such marks are stamped or otherwise shown clearly upon the goods if uncovered, or on the cases or coverings in which such goods are contained, in such manner as should ordinarily remain legible until the end of the voyage.
   (b) Either the number of packages or pieces, or the quantity, or weight, as the case may be, as furnished in writing by the shipper.
   (c) The apparent order and condition of the goods.
   Provided that no carrier, captain or agent of the carrier shall be bound to state or show in the bill of lading any marks, number, quantity, or weight which he has reasonable ground for suspecting not accurately to represent the goods actually received, or which he has had no reasonable means of checking.

4. Such a bill of lading shall be prima facie evidence of the receipt by the carrier of the goods as therein described in accordance with paragraph 3(a),

(*b*) and (*c*). However, proof to the contrary shall not be admissible when the bill of lading has been transferred to a third party acting in good faith.

5. The shipper shall be deemed to have guaranteed to the carrier the accuracy at the time of shipment of the marks, number, quantity and weight, as furnished by him, and the shipper shall indemnify the carrier against all loss, damages and expenses arising or resulting from inaccuracies in such particulars. The right of the carrier to such indemnity shall in no way limit his responsibility and liability under the contract of carriage to any other person other than the shipper.

6. Unless notice of loss or damage and the general nature of such loss or damage be given in writing to the carrier or his agent at the hoverport of discharge before or at the time of the removal of the goods into the custody of the person entitled to delivery thereof under the contract of carriage, or, if the loss or damage be not apparent, within three days, such removal shall be prima facie evidence of the delivery by the carrier of the goods as described in the bill of lading.

The notice in writing need not be given if the state of the goods has, at the time of their receipt, been the subject of joint survey or inspection.

Subject to paragraph 6 *bis* the carrier and the hovercraft shall in any event be discharged from all liability whatsoever in respect of the goods, unless suit is brought within one year of their delivery or of the date when they should have been delivered. This period may, however, be extended if the parties so agree after the cause of action has arisen.

In the case of any actual or apprehended loss or damage the carrier and the receiver shall give all reasonable facilities to each other for inspecting and tallying the goods.

6 *bis*. An action for indemnity against a third person may be brought even after the expiration of the year provided for in the preceding paragraph if brought within the time allowed by the law of the Court seized of the case. However, the time allowed shall be not less than three months, commencing from the day when the person bringing such action for indemnity has settled the claim or has been served with process in the action against himself.

7. After the goods are loaded, the bill of lading to be issued by the carrier, captain or agent of the carrier, to the shipper, shall, if the shipper so demands, be a 'shipped' bill of lading, provided that if the shipper shall have previously taken up any document of title to such goods, he shall surrender the same as against the issue of the 'shipped' bill of lading, but at the option of the carrier such document of title may be noted at the hoverport of shipment by the carrier, captain, or agent with the name or names of the hovercraft upon which the goods have been shipped and the date or dates of shipment, and when so noted, if it shows the particulars mentioned in paragraph 3 of article III, shall, for the purpose of this article, be deemed to constitute a 'shipped' bill of lading.

8. Any clause, covenant, or agreement in a contract of carriage relieving the carrier or the hovercraft from liability for loss or damage to, or in connection with, goods arising from negligence, fault, or failure in the duties and obligations provided in this article or lessening such liability otherwise

than as provided in these Rules, shall be null and void and of no effect. A benefit of insurance in favour of the carrier or similar clause shall be deemed to be a clause relieving the carrier from liability.

ARTICLE IV.

1. Neither the carrier nor the hovercraft shall be liable for loss or damage arising or resulting from unfitness for the voyage unless caused by want of due diligence on the part of the carrier to make the hovercraft fit for the voyage and to secure that the hovercraft is properly manned, equipped and supplied, and to make the holds, refrigerating and cool chambers and all other parts of the hovercraft in which goods are carried fit and safe for their reception, carriage and preservation in accordance with the provisions of paragraph 1 of article III. Whenever loss or damage has resulted from unfitness for the voyage the burden of proving the exercise of due diligence shall be on the carrier or other person claiming exemption under this article.

2. Neither the carrier nor the hovercraft shall be responsible for loss or damage arising or resulting from—

(a) Act, neglect, or default of the captain, member of the crew, pilot, or the servants of the carrier in the navigation or in the management of the hovercraft.

(b) Fire, unless caused by the actual fault or privity of the carrier.

(c) Perils, dangers and accidents of the sea or other navigable waters.

(d) Act of God.

(e) Act of war.

(f) Act of public enemies.

(g) Arrest or restraint of princes, rulers or people, or seizure under legal process.

(h) Quarantine restrictions.

(i) Act or omission of the shipper or owner of the goods, his agent or representative.

(j) Strikes or lockouts or stoppage or restraint of labour from whatever cause, whether partial or general.

(k) Riots and civil commotions.

(l) Saving or attempting to save life or property at sea.

(m) Wastage in bulk or weight or any other loss or damage arising from inherent defect, quality or vice of the goods.

(n) Insuffiency of packing.

(o) Insufficiency or inadequacy of marks.

(p) Latent defects not discoverable by due diligence.

(q) Any other cause arising without the actual fault or privity of the carrier, or without the fault or neglect of the agents or servants of the carrier, but the burden of proof shall be on the person claiming the benefit of this exception to show that neither the actual fault or privity of the carrier nor the fault or neglect of the agents or servants of the carrier contributed to the loss or damage.

3. The shipper shall not be responsible for loss or damage sustained by the carrier or the hovercraft arising or resulting from any cause without the act, fault or neglect of the shipper, his agents or his servants.

4. Any deviation in saving or attempting to save life or property at sea or any reasonable deviation shall not be deemed to be an infringement or breach of these Rules or of the contract of carriage, and the carrier shall not be liable for any loss or damage resulting therefrom.

5. (*a*) Unless the nature and value of such goods have been declared by the shipper before shipment and inserted in the bill of lading, neither the carrier nor the hovercraft shall in any event be or become liable for any loss or damage to or in connection with the goods in an amount exceeding £494·06 per package or unit or £1·48 per kilogramme of gross weight of the goods lost or damaged, whichever is the higher.

(*b*) The total amount recoverable shall be calculated by reference to the value of such goods at the place and time at which the goods are discharged from the hovercraft in accordance with the contract or should have been so discharged.

The value of the goods shall be fixed according to the commodity exchange price, or, if there be no such price, according to the current market price, or, if there be no commodity exchange price or current market price, by reference to the normal value of goods of the same kind and quality.

(*c*) Where a container, pallet or similar article of transport is used to consolidate goods, the number of packages or units enumerated in the bill of lading as packed in such article of transport shall be deemed the number of packages or units for the purpose of this paragraph as far as these packages or units are concerned. Except as aforesaid such article of transport shall be considered the package or unit.

(*e*) Neither the carrier nor the hovercraft shall be entitled to the benefit of the limitation of liability provided for in this paragraph if it is proved that the damage resulted from an act or omission of the carrier done with intent to cause damage, or recklessly and with knowledge that damage would probably result.

(*f*) The declaration mentioned in sub-paragraph (*a*) of this paragraph, if embodied in the bill of lading, shall be prima facie evidence, but shall not be binding or conclusive on the carrier.

(*g*) By agreement between the carrier, captain or agent of the carrier and the shipper other maximum amounts than those mentioned in sub-paragraph (*a*) of this paragraph may be fixed, provided that no maximum amount so fixed shall be less than the appropriate maximum mentioned in that sub-paragraph.

(*h*) Neither the carrier nor the hovercraft shall be responsible in any event for loss or damage to, or in connection with, goods if the nature or value thereof has been knowingly mis-stated by the shipper in the bill of lading.

6. Goods of an inflammable, explosive or dangerous nature to the

shipment whereof the carrier, captain or agent of the carrier has not consented with knowledge of their nature and character, may at any time before discharge be landed at any place, or destroyed or rendered innocuous by the carrier without compensation and the shipper of such goods shall be liable for all damages and expenses directly or indirectly arising out of or resulting from such shipment. If any such goods shipped with such knowledge and consent shall become a danger to the hovercraft or cargo, they may in like manner be landed at any place, or destroyed or rendered innocuous by the carrier without liability on the part of the carrier except to general average, if any.

ARTICLE IV BIS.

1. The defences and limits of liability provided for in these Rules shall apply in any action against the carrier in respect of loss or damage to goods covered by a contract of carriage whether the action be founded in contract or in tort.

2. If such an action is brought against a servant or agent of the carrier (such servant or agent not being an independent contractor), such servant or agent shall be entitled to avail himself of the defences and limits of liability which the carrier is entitled to invoke under these Rules.

3. The aggregate of the amounts recoverable from the carrier, and such servants and agents, shall in no case exceed the limit provided for in these Rules.

4. Nevertheless, a servant or agent of the carrier shall not be entitled to avail himself of the provisions of this article, if it is proved that the damage resulted from an act or omission of the servant or agent done with intent to cause damage or recklessly and with knowledge that damage would probably result.

ARTICLE V.

A carrier shall be at liberty to surrender in whole or in part all or any of his rights and immunities or to increase any of his responsibilities and obligations under these Rules, provided such surrender or increase shall be embodied in the bill of lading issued to the shipper. The provisions of these Rules shall not be applicable to charter parties, but if bills of lading are issued in the case of a hovercraft under a charter party they shall comply with the terms of these Rules. Nothing in these Rules shall be held to prevent the insertion in a bill of lading of any lawful provision regarding general average.

ARTICLE VI.

Notwithstanding the provisions of the preceding articles, a carrier, captain or agent of the carrier and a shipper shall in regard to any particular goods be at liberty to enter into any agreement in any terms as to the responsibility and liability of the carrier for such goods, and as to the rights and immunities of the carrier in respect of such goods, or his obligation as to fitness for the voyage, so far as this stipulation is not contrary to public policy, or the care or diligence of his servants or agents in regard to the loading, handling, stowage, carriage, custody, care and discharge of the goods carried, provided that in this case no bill of lading has been or shall be issued and that the terms agreed shall be embodied in a receipt which shall be a non-negotiable document and shall be marked as such.

Any agreement so entered into shall have full legal effect.

Provided that this article shall not apply to ordinary commercial shipments made in the ordinary course of trade, but only to other shipments where the character or condition of the property to be carried or the circumstances, terms and conditions under which the carriage is to be performed are such as reasonably to justify a special agreement.

ARTICLE VII.

Nothing herein contained shall prevent a carrier or a shipper from entering into any agreement, stipulation, condition, reservation or exemption as to the responsibility and liability of the carrier or the hovercraft for the loss or damage to, or in connection with, the custody and care and handling of goods prior to the loading on, and subsequent to the discharge from, the hovercraft on which the goods are carried.

ARTICLE IX.

These Rules shall not affect the provisions of any international Convention or national law governing liability for nuclear damage.

ARTICLE X.

The provisions of these Rules shall apply to every bill of lading relating to the carriage of goods between hoverports in two different States if:
   (*a*) the bill of lading is issued in the United Kingdom;
         or
   (*b*) the carriage is to or from a hoverport in the United Kingdom;
         or

(*c*) the contract contained in or evidenced by the bill of lading provides
that these Rules or legislation of any State giving effect to them are to
govern the contract,
whatever may be the nationality of the hovercraft, the carrier, the shipper,
the consignee or any other interested person.

Countries which are parties to the Hague Rules, as amended

The Carriage of Goods by Sea (Parties to Convention) Order 1985

(SI 1985 No 443)

1. This Order may be cited as the Carriage of Goods by Sea (Parties to Convention) Order 1985 and shall come into operation on 10 April 1985.

2. It is hereby certified that the contracting States to the International Convention for the Unification of Certain Rules of Law relating to Bills of Lading signed at Brussels on 25 August 1924, as amended by the Protocol signed at Brussels on 23 February 1968, and the territories in respect of which they are respectively contracting States are as listed in the Schedule to this Order.

3. The Carriage of Goods by Sea (Parties to Convention) Order 1982 is hereby revoked.

SCHEDULE   Article 2

Contracting States	Territories in respect of which they are respectively parties	Dates on which the Convention as amended came into force
The United Kingdom of Great Britain and Northern Ireland	Great Britain and Northern Ireland	23 June 1977
	The Isle of Man	23 June 1977
	Bermuda	1 February 1981
	British Antarctic Territory	20 January 1984
	British Virgin Islands	20 January 1984
	Cayman Islands	20 January 1984
	Falkland Islands	20 January 1984
	Falkland Islands Dependencies	20 January 1984

Contracting States	Territories in respect of which they are respectively parties	Dates on which the Convention as amended came into force
	Gibraltar	22 December 1977
	Hong Kong	1 February 1981
	Montserrat	20 January 1984
	Turks and Caicos Islands	20 January 1984
The Kingdom of Belgium	Belgium	6 December 1978
The Kingdom of Denmark	Denmark	23 June 1977
The Republic of Ecuador	Ecuador	23 June 1977
The Arab Republic of Egypt	Egypt	30 April 1983
The Republic of Finland	Finland	1 March 1985
The French Republic	France	23 June 1977
The German Democratic Republic	German Democratic Republic	14 May 1979
The Lebanese Republic	Lebanon	23 June 1977
The Kingdom of the Netherlands	The Kingdom of the Netherlands in Europe	26 July 1982
The Kingdom of Norway	Norway	23 June 1977
The Polish People's Republic	Poland	12 May 1980
The Republic of Singapore	Singapore	23 June 1977
Spain	Spain	14 February 1984
The Democratic Socialist Republic of Sri Lanka	Sri Lanka	21 January 1982
The Kingdom of Sweden	Sweden	23 June 1977
The Swiss Confederation	Switzerland	23 June 1977
The Syrian Arab Republic	Syria	23 June 1977
The Kingdom of Tonga	Tonga	13 September 1978

The York–Antwerp Rules 1974

Rule of interpretation.—In the adjustment of general average the following lettered and numbered Rules shall apply to the exclusion of any Law and Practice inconsistent therewith.

Except as provided by the numbered Rules, general average shall be adjusted according to the lettered Rules.

Rule A.—There is a general average act, when, and only when, any extraordinary sacrifice or expenditure is intentionally and reasonably made or incurred for the common safety for the purpose of preserving from peril the property involved in a common maritime adventure.

Rule B.—General average sacrifices and expenses shall be borne by the different contributing interests on the basis hereinafter provided.

Rule C.—Only such losses, damages or expenses which are the direct consequence of the general average act shall be allowed as general average.

Loss or damage sustained by the ship or cargo through delay, whether on the voyage or subsequently, such as demurrage, and any indirect loss whatsoever, such as loss of market, shall not be admitted as general average.

Rule D.—Rights to contribution in general average shall not be affected, though the event which gave rise to the sacrifice or expenditure may have been due to the fault of one of the parties to the adventure, but this shall not prejudice any remedies or defences which may be open against or to that party in respect of such fault.

Rule E.—The onus of proof is upon the party claiming in general average to show that the loss or expense claimed is properly allowable as general average.

Rule F.—Any extra expense incurred in place of another expense which would have been allowable as general average shall be deemed to be general average and so allowed without regard to the saving, if any, to other interests, but only up to the amount of the general average expense avoided.

Rule G.—General average shall be adjusted as regards both loss and contribution upon the basis of values at the time and place when and where the adventure ends.

This rule shall not affect the determination of the place at which the average statement is to be made up.

Rule I. Jettison of cargo.—No jettison of cargo shall be made good as general average unless such cargo is carried in accordance with the recognised custom of the trade.

Rule II. Damage by jettison and sacrifice for the common safety.—Damage done to a ship and cargo, or either of them, by or in consequence of a sacrifice made for the common safety, and by water which goes down a ship's hatches opened or other opening made for the purpose of making a jettison for the common safety, shall be made good as general average.

Rule III. Extinguishing fire on shipboard.—Damage done to a ship and cargo, or either of them, by water or otherwise, including damage by beaching or scuttling a burning ship, in extinguishing a fire on board the ship, shall be made good as general average; except that no compensation shall be made for damage by smoke or heat however caused.

Rule IV. Cutting away wreck.—Loss or damage sustained by cutting away wreck or parts of the ship which have been previously carried away or are effectively lost by accident shall not be made good as general average.

Rule V. Voluntary stranding.—When a ship is intentionally run on shore for the common safety, whether or not she might have been driven on shore, the consequent loss or damage shall be allowed in general average.

Rule VI. Salvage remuneration.—Expenditure incurred by the parties to the adventure on account of salvage, whether under contract or otherwise, shall be allowed in general average to the extent that the salvage operations were undertaken for the purpose of preserving from peril the property involved in the common maritime adventure.

Rule VII. Damage to machinery and boilers.—Damage caused to any machinery and boilers of a ship which is ashore and in a position of peril, in endeavouring to refloat, shall be allowed in general average when shown to have arisen from an actual intention to float the ship for the common safety at the risk of such damage; but where a ship is afloat no loss or damage caused by working the propelling machinery and boilers shall in any circumstances be made good as general average.

Rule VIII. Expenses lightening a ship when ashore, and consequent damage.— When a ship is ashore and cargo and ship's fuel and stores or any of them are discharged as a general average act, the extra cost of lightening, lighter hire and reshipping if incurred and the loss or damage sustained thereby, shall be admitted as general average.

Rule IX. Ship's material and stores burnt for fuel.—Ship's materials and stores, or any of them, necessarily burnt for fuel for the common safety at a time of peril, shall be admitted as general average, when and only when an ample supply of fuel had been provided; but the estimated quantity of fuel that would have been consumed, calculated at the price current at the ship's last port of departure at the date of her leaving, shall be credited to the general average.

Rule X. Expenses at port of refuge etc.

(*a*) When a ship shall have entered a port or place of refuge or shall have returned to her port or place of loading in consequence of accident, sacrifice or other extraordinary circumstances, which render that necessary for the common safety, the expenses of entering such port or place shall be admitted as general average; and when she shall have sailed thence with her original cargo, or part of it, the corresponding expenses of leaving such port or place consequent upon such entry or return shall likewise be admitted as general average.

When a ship is at any port or place of refuge and is necessarily removed to another port or place because repairs cannot be carried out in the first port or place, the provisions of this Rule shall be applied to the second port or place as if it were a port or place of refuge and the cost of such removal including temporary repairs and towage shall be admitted as general average. The provisions of Rule XI shall be applied to the prolongation of the voyage occasioned by such removal.

(*b*) The cost of handling on board or discharging cargo, fuel or stores whether at a port or place of loading, call or refuge, shall be admitted as general average, when the handling or discharge was necessary for the common safety or to enable damage to the ship caused by sacrifice or accident to be repaired if the repairs were necessary for the safe prosecution of the voyage, except in cases where the damage to the ship is discovered at a port or place of loading or call without any accident or other extraordinary circumstances connected with such damage having taken place during the voyage.

The cost of handling on board or discharging cargo, fuel or stores shall not be admissible as general average when incurred solely for the purpose of restowage due to shifting during the voyage unless such restowage is necessary for the common safety.

(*c*) Whenever the cost of handling or discharging cargo, fuel or stores is admissible as general average, the costs of storage, including insurance if reasonably incurred, reloading and stowing of such cargo, fuel or stores shall likewise be admitted as general average.

But when the ship is condemned or does not proceed on her original voyage storage expenses shall be admitted as general average only up to the date of the ship's condemnation or of the abandonment of the voyage or up to the date of completion of discharge of cargo if the condemnation or abandonment takes place before that date.

Rule XI. Wages and maintenance of crew and other expenses bearing up for and in a port of refuge, etc.

(*a*) Wages and maintenance of master, officers and crew reasonably incurred and fuel and stores consumed during the prolongation of the voyage occasioned by a ship entering a port or place of refuge or returning to her port or place of loading shall be admitted as general average when the expenses of entering such port or place are allowable in general average in accordance with Rule X(*a*).

(*b*) When a ship shall have entered or been detained in any port or place in consequence of accident, sacrifice or other extraordinary circumstances which render that necessary for the common safety, or to enable damage to the ship caused by sacrifice or accident to be repaired, if the repairs were necessary for the safe prosecution of the voyage, the wages and maintenance of the master, officers, and crew reasonably incurred during the extra period of detention in such port or place until the ship shall or should have been made ready to proceed upon her voyage, shall be admitted in general average.

Provided that when damage to the ship is discovered at a port or place of loading or call without any accident or other extraordinary circumstance connected with such damage having taken place during the voyage, then the wages and maintenance of master, officers and crew and fuel and stores consumed during the extra detention for repairs to damage so discovered shall not be admissible as general average, even if the repairs are necessary for the safe prosecution of the voyage.

When the ship is condemned or does not proceed on her original voyage, wages and maintenance of the master, officers and crew and fuel and stores consumed shall be admitted as general average only up to the date of the ship's condemnation or of the abandonment of the voyage or up to the date of completion of discharge of cargo if the condemnation or abandonment takes place before that date.

Fuel and stores consumed during the extra period of detention shall be admitted as general average, except such fuel and stores as are consumed in effecting repairs not allowable in general average.

Port charges incurred during the extra period of detention shall likewise be admitted as general average except such charges as are incurred solely by reason of repairs not allowable in general average.

(*c*) For the purpose of this and the other Rules wages shall include all payments made to or for the benefit of the master, officers and crew, whether such payments be imposed by law upon the shipowners or be made under the terms or articles of employment.

(*d*) When overtime is paid to the master, officers or crew for maintenance of the ship or repairs, the cost of which is not allowable in general average, such overtime shall be allowed in general average only up to the saving in expense which would have been incurred and admitted as general average, had such overtime not been incurred.

Rule XII. Damage to cargo in discharging, etc.—Damage to or loss of cargo, fuel or stores caused in the act of handling, discharging, storing, reloading and stowing shall be made good as general average, when and only when the cost of those measures respectively is admitted as general average.

Rule XIII. Deductions from cost of repairs.—Repairs to be allowed in general average shall not be subject to deductions in respect of 'new for old' where old material or parts are replaced by new unless the ship is over fifteen years old in which case there shall be a deduction of one third. The deductions shall be regulated by the age of the ship from 31 December of the year of completion of construction to the date of the general average act, except for insulation, life and similar boats, communications and navigational apparatus and equipment, machinery and boilers for which the deductions shall be regulated by the age of the particular parts to which they apply.

The deductions shall be made only from the cost of the new material or parts when finished and ready to be installed in the ship.

No deduction shall be made in respect of provisions, stores, anchors and chain cables.

Drydock and slipway dues and costs of shifting the ship shall be allowed in full.

The costs of cleaning, painting or coating of bottom shall not be allowed in general average unless the bottom has been painted or coated within the twelve months preceding the date of the general average act in which case one half of such costs shall be allowed.

Rule XIV. Temporary repairs.—Where temporary repairs are effected to a ship at a port of loading, call or refuge, for the common safety, or of damage caused by general average sacrifice, the cost of such repairs shall be admitted as general average.

Where temporary repairs of accidental damage are effected in order to enable the adventure to be completed, the cost of such repairs shall be admitted as general average without regard to the saving, if any, to other interest, but only up to the saving in expense which would have been incurred and allowed in general average if such repairs had not been effected there.

No deductions 'new for old' shall be made from the cost of temporary repairs allowable as general average.

Rule XV. Loss of freight.—Loss of freight arising from damage to or loss of cargo shall be made good as general average, either when caused by a general average act, or when the damage to or loss of cargo is so made good.

Deduction shall be made from the amount of gross freight lost, of the charges which the owner thereof would have incurred to earn such freight, but has, in consequence of the sacrifice, not incurred.

Rule XVI. Amount to be made good for cargo lost or damaged by sacrifice.— The amount to be made good as general average for damage to or loss of cargo sacrificed shall be the loss which has been sustained thereby based on the value at the time of discharge, ascertained from the commercial invoice rendered to the receiver or if there is no such invoice from the shipped value. The value at the time of discharge shall include the cost of insurance and freight except insofar as such freight is at the risk of interests other than the cargo.

When cargo so damaged is sold and the amount of the damage has not been otherwise agreed, the loss to be made good in general average shall be the difference between the net proceeds of sale and the net sound value as computed in the first paragraph of this Rule.

Rule XVII. Contributory values.—The contribution to a general average shall be made upon the actual net value of the property at the termination of the adventure except that the value of cargo shall be the value at the time of discharge, ascertained from the commercial invoice rendered to the receiver or if there is no such invoice from the shipped value. The value of the cargo shall include the cost of insurance and freight unless and insofar as such freight is at the risk of interests other than the cargo, deducting therefrom any loss or damage suffered by the cargo prior to or at the time of discharge. The value of the ship shall be assessed without taking into account the beneficial or detrimental effect of any demise or time charter-party to which the ship may be committed.

To these values shall be added the amount made good as general average for property sacrificed, if not already included, deduction being made from the freight and passage money at risk of such charges and crew's wages as would not have been incurred in earning the freight had the ship and cargo been totally lost at the date of the general average act and have not been allowed as general average; deduction being also made from the value of the property of all extra charges incurred in respect thereof subsequently to the general average act, except such charges as are allowed in general average.

Where cargo is sold short of destination, however, it shall contribute upon the actual net proceeds of sale, with the addition of any amount made good as general average.

Passenger's luggage and personal effects not shipped under bill of lading shall not contribute in general average.

Rule XVIII. Damage to ship.—The amount to be allowed as general average for damage or loss to the ship, her machinery and/or gear caused by a general average act shall be as follows:

(*a*) When repaired or replaced,

The actual reasonable cost of repairing or replacing such damage or loss subject to deduction in accordance with Rule XIII;

(*b*) When not repaired or replaced,

The reasonable depreciation arising from such damage or loss, but not exceeding the estimated cost of repairs. But where the ship is an actual total loss or when the cost of repairs of the damage would exceed the value of the ship when repaired, the amount to be allowed as general average shall be the difference between the estimated sound value of the ship after deducting therefrom the estimated cost of repairing damage which is not general average and the value of the ship in her damaged state which may be measured by the net proceeds of sale, if any.

Rule XIX. Undeclared or wrongfully declared cargo.—Damage or loss caused to goods loaded without the knowledge of the shipowner or his agent or to goods wilfully misdescribed at time of shipment shall not be allowed as general average but such goods shall remain liable to contribute, if saved.

Damage or loss caused to goods which have been wrongfully declared on shipment at a value which is lower than their real value shall be contributed for at the declared value, but such goods shall contribute upon their actual value.

Rule XX. Provision of funds.—A commission of two per cent. of general average disbursements, other than the wages and maintenance of master, officers and crew and fuel and stores not replaced during the voyage, shall be allowed in general average, but when the funds are not provided by any of the contributing interests, the necessary cost of obtaining the funds required by means of a bottomry bond or otherwise, or the loss sustained by owners of goods sold for the purpose, shall be allowed in general average.

The cost of insuring money advanced to pay for general average disbursements shall also be allowed in general average.

Rule XXI. Interest on losses made good in general average.—Interest shall be allowed on expenditure, sacrifices and allowances charged to general average at the rate of seven per cent. per annum, until the date of the general average statement, due allowance being made for any interim reimbursement from the contributory interests or from the general average deposit fund.

Rule XXII. Treatment of cash deposits.—Where cash deposits have been collected in respect of cargo's liability for general average, salvage or special charges, such deposits shall be paid without any delay into a special account in the joint names of a representative nominated on behalf of the shipowner and a representative nominated on behalf of the depositors in a bank to be approved by both. The sum so deposited together with accrued interest, if any, shall be held as security for payment to the parties entitled thereto of the general average, salvage or special charges payable by cargo in respect to which the deposits have been collected. Payments on account of refund of deposits may be made if certified to in writing by the average adjuster. Such deposits and payments or refunds shall be without prejudice to the ultimate liability of the parties.

Appendix H

The Hamburg Rules

ANNEX I

Preamble

THE STATES PARTIES TO THIS CONVENTION,
HAVING RECOGNIZED the desirability of determining by agreement certain rules relating to the carriage of goods by sea,
HAVE DECIDED to conclude a Convention for this purpose and have thereto agreed as follows:

PART I. GENERAL PROVISIONS

Article 1. Definitions

In this Convention:

1. 'Carrier' means any person by whom or in whose name a contract of carriage of goods by sea has been concluded with a shipper.

2. 'Actual carrier' means any person to whom the performance of the carriage of the goods, or of part of the carriage, has been entrusted by the carrier, and includes any other person to whom such performance has been entrusted.

3. 'Shipper' means any person by whom or in whose name or on whose behalf a contract of carriage of goods by sea has been concluded with a carrier, or any person by whom or in whose name or on whose behalf the goods are actually delivered to the carrier in relation to the contract of carriage by sea.

4. 'Consignee' means the person entitled to take delivery of the goods.

5. 'Goods' includes live animals; where the goods are consolidated in a container, pallet or similar article of transport or where they are packed,

353

'goods' includes such article of transport or packaging if supplied by the shipper.

6. 'Contract of carriage by sea' means any contract whereby the carrier undertakes against payment of freight to carry goods by sea from one port to another; however, a contract which involves carriage by sea and also carriage by some other means is deemed to be a contract of carriage by sea for the purposes of this Convention only in so far as it relates to the carriage by sea.

7. 'Bill of lading' means a document which evidences a contract of carriage by sea and the taking over or loading of the goods by the carrier, and by which the carrier undertakes to deliver the goods against surrender of the document. A provision in the document that the goods are to be delivered to the order of a named person, or to order, or to bearer, constitutes such an undertaking.

8. 'Writing' includes, inter alia, telegram and telex.

Article 2. Scope of application

1. The provisions of this Convention are applicable to all contracts of carriage by sea between two different States, if:

(a) the port of loading as provided for in the contract of carriage by sea is located in a Contracting State, or

(b) the port of discharge as provided for in the contract of carriage by sea is located in a Contracting State, or

(c) one of the optional ports of discharge provided for in the contract of carriage by sea is the actual port of discharge and such port is located in a Contracting State, or

(d) the bill of lading or other document evidencing the contract of carriage by sea is issued in a Contracting State, or

(e) the bill of lading or other document evidencing the contract of carriage by sea provides that the provisions of this Convention or the legislation of any State giving effect to them are to govern the contract.

2. The provisions of this Convention are applicable without regard to the nationality of the ship, the carrier, the actual carrier, the shipper, the consignee or any other interested person.

3. The provisions of this Convention are not applicable to charter-parties. However, where a bill of lading is issued pursuant to a charter-party, the provisions of the Convention apply to such a bill of lading if it governs the relation between the carrier and the holder of the bill of lading, not being the charterer.

4. If a contract provides for future carriage of goods in a series of shipments during an agreed period, the provisions of this Convention apply to each shipment. However, where a shipment is made under a charter-party, the provisions of para 3 of this Article apply.

Article 3. Interpretation of the Convention

In the interpretation and application of the provisions of this Convention regard shall be had to its international character and to the need to promote uniformity.

PART II. LIABILITY OF THE CARRIER

Article 4. Period of responsibility

1. The responsibility of the carrier for the goods under this Convention covers the period during which the carrier is in charge of the goods at the port of loading, during the carriage and at the port of discharge.
   2. For the purpose of para 1 of this Article, the carrier is deemed to be in charge of the goods
   (a) from the time he has taken over the goods from:
       (i) the shipper, or a person acting on his behalf; or
       (ii) an authority or other third party to whom, pursuant to law or regulations applicable at the port of loading, the goods must be handed over for shipment;
   (b) until the time he has delivered the goods:
       (i) by handing over the goods to the consignee; or
       (ii) in cases where the consignee does not receive the goods from the carrier, by placing them at the disposal of the consignee in accordance with the contract or with the law or with the usage of the particular trade, applicable at the port of discharge; or
       (iii) by handing over the goods to an authority or other third party to whom, pursuant to law or regulations applicable at the port of discharge, the goods must be handed over.
   3. In paras 1 and 2 of this Article, reference to the carrier or to the consignee means, in addition to the carrier or the consignee, the servants or agents, respectively of the carrier or the consignee.

Article 5. Basis of liability

1. The carrier is liable for loss resulting from loss of or damage to the goods, as well as from delay in delivery, if the occurrence which caused the loss, damage or delay took place while the goods were in his charge as defined in art 4, unless the carrier proves that he, his servants or agents took all measures that could reasonably be required to avoid the occurrence and its consequences.
   2. Delay in delivery occurs when the goods have not been delivered at the port of discharge provided for in the contract of carriage by sea within the time expressly agreed upon or, in the absence of such agreement, within the

time which it would be reasonable to require of a diligent carrier, having regard to the circumstances of the case.

3. The person entitled to make a claim for the loss of goods may treat the goods as lost if they have not been delivered as required by art 4 within 60 consecutive days following the expiry of the time for delivery according to para 2 of this Article.

4. (a) The carrier is liable

    (i) for loss of or damage to the goods or delay in delivery caused by fire, if the claimant proves that the fire arose from fault or neglect on the part of the carrier, his servants or agents;

    (ii) for such loss, damage or delay in delivery which is proved by the claimant to have resulted from the fault or neglect of the carrier, his servants or agents, in taking all measures that could reasonably be required to put out the fire and avoid or mitigate its consequences.

(b) In case of fire on board the ship affecting the goods, if the claimant or the carrier so desires, a survey in accordance with shipping practices must be held into the cause and circumstances of the fire, and a copy of the surveyor's report shall be made available on demand to the carrier and the claimant.

5. With respect to live animals, the carrier is not liable for loss, damage or delay in delivery resulting from any special risks inherent in that kind of carriage. If the carrier proves that he has complied with any special instructions given to him by the shipper respecting the animals and that, in the circumstances of the case, the loss, damage or delay in delivery could be attributed to such risks, it is presumed that the loss, damage or delay in delivery was so caused, unless there is proof that all or a part of the loss, damage or delay in delivery resulted from fault or neglect on the part of the carrier, his servants or agents.

6. The carrier is not liable, except in general average, where loss, damage or delay in delivery resulted from measures to save life or from reasonable measures to save property at sea.

7. Where fault or neglect on the part of the carrier, his servants or agents combines with another cause to produce loss, damage or delay in delivery the carrier is liable only to the extent that the loss, damage or delay in delivery is attributable to such fault or neglect, provided that the carrier proves the amount of the loss, damage or delay in delivery not attributable thereto.

Article 6. Limits of liability

1. (a) The liability of the carrier for loss resulting from loss of or damage to goods according to the provisions of art 5 is limited to an amount equivalent to 835 units of account per package or other shipping unit or 2·5 units of

account per kilogramme of gross weight of the goods lost or damaged, whichever is the higher.

(b) The liability of the carrier for delay in delivery according to the provisions of art 5 is limited to an amount equivalent to two and a half times the freight payable for the goods delayed, but not exceeding the total freight payable under the contract of carriage of goods by sea.

(c) In no case shall the aggregate liability of the carrier, under both sub-paras (a) and (b) of this paragraph, exceed the limitation which would be established under sub-para (a) of this paragraph for total loss of the goods with respect to which such liability was incurred.

2. For the purpose of calculating which amount is the higher in accordance with para 1(a) of this Article the following rules apply:

(a) Where a container, pallet or similar article of transport is used to consolidate goods, the package or other shipping units enumerated in the bill of lading, if issued, or otherwise in any other document evidencing the contract of carriage by sea, as packed in such article of transport are deemed packages or shipping units. Except as aforesaid the goods in such article or transport are deemed one shipping unit.

(b) In cases where the article of transport itself has been lost or damaged, that article of transport, if not owned or otherwise supplied by the carrier, is considered one separate shipping unit.

3. Unit of account means the unit of account mentioned in art 26.

4. By agreement between the carrier and the shipper, limits of liability exceeding those provided for in para 1 may be fixed.

Article 7. Application to non-contractual claims

1. The defences and limits of liability provided for in this Convention apply in any action against the carrier in respect of loss or damage to the goods covered by the contract of carriage by sea, as well as of delay in delivery whether the action is founded in contract, in tort or otherwise.

2. If such an action is brought against a servant or agent of the carrier, such servant or agent, if he proves that he acted within the scope of his employment, is entitled to avail himself of the defences and limits of liability which the carrier is entitled to invoke under this Convention.

3. Except as provided in art 8, the aggregate of the amounts recoverable from the carrier and from any persons referred to in para 2 of this Article shall not exceed the limits of liability provided for in this Convention.

Article 8. Loss of right to limit responsibility

1. The carrier is not entitled to the benefit of the limitation of liability provided for in art 6 if it is proved that the loss, damage or delay in delivery resulted from an act or omission of the carrier done with the intent to cause

such loss, damage or delay, or recklessly and with knowledge that such loss, damage or delay would probably result.

2. Notwithstanding the provisions of para 2 of art 7, a servant or agent of the carrier is not entitled to the benefit of the limitation of liability provided for in art 6 if it is proved that the loss, damage or delay in delivery resulted from an act or omission of such servant or agent, done with the intent to cause such loss, damage or delay, or recklessly and with knowledge that such loss, damage or delay would probably result.

Article 9. Deck cargo

1. The carrier is entitled to carry the goods on deck only if such carriage is in accordance with an agreement with the shipper or with the usage of the particular trade or is required by statutory rules or regulations.

2. If the carrier and the shipper have agreed that the goods shall or may be carried on deck, the carrier must insert in the bill of lading or other document evidencing the contract of carriage by sea a statement to that effect. In the absence of such a statement the carrier has the burden of proving that an agreement for carriage on deck has been entered into; however, the carrier is not entitled to invoke such an agreement against a third party, including a consignee, who has acquired the bill of lading in good faith.

3. Where the goods have been carried on deck contrary to the provisions of para 1 of this Article or where the carrier may not under para 2 of this Article invoke an agreement for carriage on deck, the carrier, notwithstanding the provisions of para 1 of art 5, is liable for loss of or damage to the goods, as well as for delay in delivery, resulting solely from the carriage on deck, and the extent of his liability is to be determined in accordance with the provisions of art 6 or art 8 of this Convention as the case may be.

4. Carriage of goods on deck contrary to express agreement for carriage under deck is deemed to be an act or omission of the carrier within the meaning of art 8.

Article 10. Liability of the carrier and actual carrier

1. Where the performance of the carriage or part thereof has been entrusted to an actual carrier, whether or not in pursuance of a liberty under the contract of carriage by sea to do so, the carrier nevertheless remains responsible for the entire carriage according to the provisions of this Convention. The carrier is responsible, in relation to the carriage performed by the actual carrier, for the acts and omissions of the actual carrier and of his servants and agents acting within the scope of their employment.

2. All the provisions of this Convention governing the responsibility of the carrier also apply to the responsibility of the actual carrier for the

carriage performed by him. The provisions of paras 2 and 3 of art 7 and of para 2 of art 8 apply if an action is brought against a servant or agent of the actual carrier.

3. Any special agreement under which the carrier assumes obligations not imposed by this Convention or waives rights conferred by this Convention affects the actual carrier only if agreed to by him expressly and in writing. Whether or not the actual carrier has so agreed, the carrier nevertheless remains bound by the obligations or waivers resulting from such special agreement.

4. Where and to the extent that both the carrier and the actual carrier are liable, their liability is joint and several.

5. The aggregate of the amounts recoverable from the carrier, the actual carrier and their servants and agents shall not exceed the limits of liability provided for in this Convention.

6. Nothing in this Article shall prejudice any right of recourse as between the carrier and the actual carrier.

Article 11. Through carriage

1. Notwithstanding the provisions of para 1 of art 10, where a contract of carriage by sea provides explicitly that a specified part of the carriage covered by the said contract is to be performed by a named person other than the carrier, the contract may also provide that the carrier is not liable for loss, damage or delay in delivery caused by an occurrence which takes place while the goods are in the charge of the actual carrier during such part of the carriage. Nevertheless, any stipulation limiting or excluding such liability is without effect if no judicial proceedings can be instituted against the actual carrier in a court competent under paras 1 or 2 of art 21. The burden of proving that any loss, damage or delay in delivery has been caused by such an occurrence rests upon the carrier.

2. The actual carrier is responsible in accordance with the provisions of para 2 of art 10 for loss, damage or delay in delivery caused by an occurrence which takes place while the goods are in his charge.

PART III. LIABILITY OF THE SHIPPER

Article 12. General rule

The shipper is not liable for loss sustained by the carrier or the actual carrier, or for damage sustained by the ship, unless such loss or damage was caused by the fault or neglect of the shipper, his servants or agents. Nor is any servant or agent of the shipper liable for such loss or damage unless the loss or damage was caused by fault or neglect on his part.

Article 13. Special rules on dangerous goods

1. The shipper must mark or label in a suitable manner dangerous goods as dangerous.

2. Where the shipper hands over dangerous goods to the carrier or an actual carrier, as the case may be, the shipper must inform him of the dangerous character of the goods and, if necessary, of the precautions to be taken. If the shipper fails to do so and such carrier or actual carrier does not otherwise have knowledge of their dangerous character:

(a) the shipper is liable to the carrier and any actual carrier for the loss resulting from the shipment of such goods, and

(b) the goods may at any time be unloaded, destroyed or rendered innocuous, as the circumstances may require, without payment of compensation.

3. The provisions of para 2 of this Article may not be invoked by any person if during the carriage he has taken the goods in his charge with knowledge of their dangerous character.

4. If, in cases where the provisions of para 2, sub-para (b), of this Article do not apply or may not be invoked, dangerous goods become an actual danger to life or property, they may be unloaded, destroyed or rendered innocuous, as the circumstances may require, without payment of compensation except where there is an obligation to contribute in general average or where the carrier is liable in accordance with the provisions of art 5.

PART IV. TRANSPORT DOCUMENTS

Article 14. Issue of bill of lading

1. When the carrier or the actual carrier takes the goods in his charge, the carrier must, on demand of the shipper, issue to the shipper a bill of lading.

2. The bill of landing may be signed by a person having authority from the carrier. A bill of lading signed by the master of the ship carrying the goods is deemed to have been signed on behalf of the carrier.

3. The signature on the bill of lading may be in handwriting, printed in facsimile, perforated, stamped, in symbols, or made by any other mechanical or electronic means, if not inconsistent with the law of the country where the bill of lading is issued.

Article 15. Contents of bill of lading

1. The bill of lading must include, inter alia, the following particulars:

(a) the general nature of the goods, the leading marks necessary for identification of the goods, an express statement, if applicable, as to the dangerous character of the goods, the number of packages or pieces, and the weight of the goods or their quantity otherwise expressed, all such particulars as furnished by the shipper;

(b) the apparent condition of the goods;

(c) the name and principal place of business of the carrier;

(d) the name of the shipper;

(e) the consignee if named by the shipper;

(f) the port of loading under the contract of carriage by sea and the date on which the goods were taken over by the carrier at the port of loading;

(g) the port of discharge under the contract of carriage by sea;

(h) the number of originals of the bill of lading, if more than one;

(i) the place of issuance of the bill of lading;

(j) the signature of the carrier or a person acting on his behalf;

(k) the freight to the extent payable by the consignee or other indication that freight is payable by him;

(l) the statement referred to in para 3 of art 23;

(m) the statement, if applicable, that the goods shall or may be carried on deck;

(n) the date or the period of delivery of the goods at the port of discharge if expressly agreed upon between the parties; and

(o) any increased limit or limits of liability where agreed in accordance with para 4 of art 6.

2. After the goods have been loaded on board, if the shipper so demands, the carrier must issue to the shipper a 'shipped' bill of lading which, in addition to the particulars required under para 1 of this Article, must state that the goods are on board a named ship or ships, and the date or date of loading. If the carrier has previously issued to the shipper a bill of lading or other document of title with respect to any of such goods, on request of the carrier, the shipper must surrender such document in exchange for a 'shipped' bill of lading. The carrier may amend any previously issued document in order to meet the shipper's demand for a 'shipped' bill of lading if, as amended, such document includes all the information required to be contained in a 'shipped' bill of lading.

3. The absence in the bill of lading of one or more particulars referred to in this Article does not affect the legal character of the document as a bill of lading provided that it nevertheless meets the requirements set out in para 7 of art 1.

Article 16. Bills of lading; reservations and evidentiary effect

1. If the bill of lading contains particulars concerning the general nature, leading marks, number of packages or pieces, weight or quantity of the goods which the carrier or other person issuing the bill of lading on his behalf knows or has reasonable grounds to suspect do not accurately represent the goods actually taken over or, where a 'shipped' bill of lading is issued, loaded, or if he had no reasonable means of checking such particulars,

the carrier or such other person must insert in the bill of lading a reservation specifying these inaccuracies, grounds of suspicion or the absence of reasonable means of checking.

2. If the carrier or other person issuing the bill of lading on his behalf fails to note on the bill of lading the apparent condition of the goods, he is deemed to have noted on the bill of lading that the goods were in apparent good condition.

3. Except for particulars in respect of which and to the extent to which a reservation permitted under para 1 of this Article has been entered:

(a) the bill of lading is prima facie evidence of the taking over or, where a 'shipped' bill of lading is issued, loading, by the carrier of the goods as described in the bill of lading; and

(b) proof to the contrary by the carrier is not admissible if the bill of lading has been transferred to a third party, including a consignee, who in good faith has acted in reliance on the description of the goods therein.

4. A bill of lading which does not, as provided in para 1, sub-para (k) of art 15, set forth the freight or otherwise indicate that freight is payable by the consignee or does not set forth demurrage incurred at the port of loading payable by the consignee, is prima facie evidence that no freight or such demurrage is payable by him. However, proof to the contrary by the carrier is not admissible when the bill of lading has been transferred to a third party, including a consignee, who in good faith has acted in reliance on the absence in the bill of lading of any such indication.

Article 17. Guarantees by the shipper

1. The shipper is deemed to have guaranteed to the carrier the accuracy of particulars relating to the general nature of the goods, their marks, number, weight and quantity as furnished by him for insertion in the bill of lading. The shipper must indemnify the carrier against the loss resulting from inaccuracies in such particulars. The shipper remains liable even if the bill of lading has been transferred by him. The right of the carrier to such indemnity in no way limits his liability under the contract of carriage by sea to any person other than the shipper.

2. Any letter of guarantee or agreement by which the shipper undertakes to indemnify the carrier against loss resulting from the issuance of the bill of lading by the carrier, or by a person acting on his behalf, without entering a reservation relating to particulars furnished by the shipper for insertion in the bill of lading, or to the apparent condition of the goods, is void and of no effect as against any third party, including a consignee, to whom the bill of lading has been transferred.

3. Such letter of guarantee or agreement is valid as against the shipper unless the carrier or the person acting on his behalf, by omitting the reservation referred to in para 2 of this Article, intends to defraud a third party, including a consignee, who acts in reliance on the description of the

goods in the bill of lading. In the latter case, if the reservation omitted relates to particulars furnished by the shipper for insertion in the bill of lading, the carrier has no right of indemnity from the shipper pursuant to para 1 of this Article.

4. In the case of intended fraud referred to in para 3 of this Article the carrier is liable, without the benefit of the limitation of liability provided for in this Convention, for the loss incurred by a third party, including a consignee, because he has acted in reliance on the description of the goods in the bill of lading.

Article 18. Documents other than bills of lading

Where a carrier issues a document other than a bill of lading to evidence the receipt of the goods to be carried, such a document is prima facie evidence of the conclusion of the contract of carriage by sea and the taking over by the carrier of the goods as therein described.

PART V. CLAIMS AND ACTIONS

Article 19. Notice of loss, damage or delay

1. Unless notice of loss or damage, specifying the general nature of such loss or damage, is given in writing by the consignee to the carrier not later than the working day after the day when the goods were handed over to the consignee, such handing over is prima facie evidence of the delivery by the carrier of the goods as described in the document of transport or, if no such document has been issued, in good condition.

2. Where the loss or damage is not apparent, the provisions of para 1 of this Article apply correspondingly if notice in writing is not given within 15 consecutive days after the day when the goods were handed over to the consignee.

3. If the state of the goods at the time they were handed over to the consignee has been the subject of a joint survey or inspection by the parties, notice in writing need not be given of loss or damage ascertained during such survey or inspection.

4. In the case of any actual or apprehended loss or damage the carrier and the consignee must give all reasonable facilities to each other for inspecting and tallying the goods.

5. No compensation shall be payable for loss resulting from delay in delivery unless a notice has been given in writing to the carrier within 60 consecutive days after the day when the goods were handed over to the consignee.

6. If the goods have been delivered by an actual carrier, any notice given under this Article to him shall have the same effect as if it had been given to

the carrier, and any notice given to the carrier shall have effect as if given to such actual carrier.

7. Unless notice of loss or damage, specifying the general nature of the loss or damage, is given in writing by the carrier or actual carrier to the shipper not later than 90 consecutive days after the occurrence of such loss or damage or after the delivery of the goods in accordance with para 2 of art 4, whichever is later, the failure to give such notice is prima facie evidence that the carrier or the actual carrier has sustained no loss or damage due to the fault or neglect of the shipper, his servants or agents.

8. For the purpose of this Article, notice given to a person acting on the carrier's or the actual carrier's behalf, including the master or the officer in charge of the ship, or to a person acting on the shipper's behalf is deemed to have been given to the carrier, to the actual carrier or to the shipper, respectively.

Article 20. Limitation of actions

1. Any action relating to carriage of goods under this Convention is time-barred if judicial or arbitral proceedings have not been instituted within a period of two years.

2. The limitation period commences on the day on which the carrier has delivered the goods or part thereof or, in cases where no goods have been delivered, on the last day on which the goods should have been delivered.

3. The day on which the limitation period commences is not included in the period.

4. The person against whom a claim is made may at any time during the running of the limitation period extend that period by a declaration in writing to the claimant. This period may be further extended by another declaration or declarations.

5. An action for indemnity by a person held liable may be instituted even after the expiration of the limitation period provided for in the preceding paragraphs if instituted within the time allowed by the law of the State where proceedings are instituted. However, the time allowed shall not be less than 90 days commencing from the day when the person instituting such action for indemnity has settled the claim or has been served with process in the action against himself.

Article 21. Jurisdiction

1. In judicial proceedings relating to carriage of goods under this Convention the plaintiff, at his option, may institute an action in a court which, according to the law of the State where the court is situated, is competent and within the jurisdiction of which is situated one of the following places:

(a) the principal place of business or, in the absence thereof, the habitual residence of the defendant; or

(b) the place where the contract was made provided that the defendant has there a place of business, branch or agency through which the contract was made; or

(c) the port of loading or the port of discharge; or

(d) any additional place designated for that purpose in the contract of carriage by sea.

2. (a) Notwithstanding the preceding provisions of this Article, an action may be instituted in the courts of any port or place in a Contracting State at which the carrying vessel or any other vessel of the same ownership may have been arrested in accordance with applicable rules of the law of that State and of international law. However, in such a case, at the petition of the defendant, the claimant must remove the action, at his choice, to one of the jurisdictions referred to in para 1 of this Article for the determination of the claim, but before such removal the defendant must furnish security sufficient to ensure payment of any judgment that may subsequently be awarded to the claimant in the action.

(b) All questions relating to the sufficiency or otherwise of the security shall be determined by the court of the port or place of the arrest.

3. No judicial proceedings relating to carriage of goods under this Convention may be instituted in a place not specified in paras 1 or 2 of this Article. The provisions of this paragraph do not constitute an obstacle to the jurisdiction of the Contracting States for provisional or protective measures.

4. (a) Where an action has been instituted in a court competent under paras 1 or 2 of this Article or where judgment has been delivered by such a court, no new action may be started between the same parties on the same grounds unless the judgment of the court before which the first action was instituted is not enforceable in the country in which the new proceedings are instituted;

(b) for the purpose of this Article the institution of measures with a view to obtaining enforcement of a judgment is not to be considered as the starting of a new action;

(c) for the purpose of this Article, the removal of an action to a different court within the same country, or to a court in another country, in accordance with para 2(a) of this Article, is not to be considered as the starting of a new action.

5. Notwithstanding the provisions of the preceding paragraphs, an agreement made by the parties, after a claim under the contract of carriage by sea has arisen, which designates the place where the claimant may institute an action, is effective.

Article 22. Arbitration

1. Subject to the provisions of this Article, parties may provide by agreement

evidenced in writing that any dispute that may arise relating to carriage of goods under this Convention shall be referred to arbitration.

2. Where a charter-party contains a provision that disputes arising thereunder shall be referred to arbitration and a bill of lading issued pursuant to the charter-party does not contain a special annotation providing that such provision shall be binding upon the holder of the bill of lading, the carrier may not invoke such provision as against a holder having acquired the bill of lading in good faith.

3. The arbitration proceedings shall, at the option of the claimant, be instituted at one of the following places:

(a) a place in a State within whose territory is situated:
    (i) the principal place of business of the defendant or, in the absence thereof, the habitual residence of the defendant; or
    (ii) the place where the contract was made, provided that the defendant has there a place of business, branch or agency through which the contract was made; or
    (iii) the port of loading or the port of discharge; or
(b) any place designated for that purpose in the arbitration clause or agreement.

4. The arbitrator or arbitration tribunal shall apply the rules of this Convention.

5. The provisions of paras 3 and 4 of this Article are deemed to be part of every arbitration clause or agreement, and any term of such clause or agreement which is inconsistent therewith is null and void.

6. Nothing in this Article affects the validity of an agreement relating to arbitration made by the parties after the claim under the contract of carriage by sea has arisen.

PART VI. SUPPLEMENTARY PROVISIONS

Article 23. Contractual stipulations

1. Any stipulation in a contract of carriage by sea, in a bill of lading, or in any other document evidencing the contract of carriage by sea is null and void to the extent that it derogates, directly or indirectly, from the provisions of this Convention. The nullity of such a stipulation does not affect the validity of the other provisions of the contract or document of which it forms a part. A clause assigning benefit of insurance of the goods in favour of the carrier, or any similar clause, is null and void.

2. Notwithstanding the provisions of para 1 of this Article, a carrier may increase his responsibilities and obligation under this Convention.

3. Where a bill of lading or any other document evidencing the contract of carriage by sea is issued, it must contain a statement that the carriage is subject to the provisions of this Convention which nullify any stipulation derogating therefrom to the detriment of the shipper or the consignee.

4. Where the claimant in respect of the goods has incurred loss as a result of a stipulation which is null and void by virtue of the present Article, or as a result of the omission of the statement referred to in para 3 of this Article, the carrier must pay compensation to the extent required in order to give the claimant compensation in accordance with the provisions of this Convention for any loss of or damage to the goods as well as for delay in delivery. The carrier must, in addition, pay compensation for costs incurred by the claimant for the purpose of exercising his right, provided that costs incurred in the action where the foregoing provision is invoked are to be determined in accordance with the law of the State where proceedings are instituted.

Article 24. General average

1. Nothing in this Convention shall prevent the application of provisions in the contract of carriage by sea or national law regarding the adjustment of general average.

2. With the exception of art 20, the provisions of this Convention relating to the liability of the carrier for loss of or damage to the goods also determine whether the consignee may refuse contribution in general average and the liability of the carrier to indemnify the consignee in respect of any such contribution made or any salvage paid.

Article 25. Other conventions

1. This Convention does not modify the rights or duties of the carrier, the actual carrier and their servants and agents, provided for in international conventions or national law relating to the limitation of liability of owners of seagoing ships.

2. The provisions of arts 21 and 22 of this Convention do not prevent the application of the mandatory provisions of any other multi-lateral convention already in force at the date of this Convention relating to matters dealt with in the said Articles, provided that the dispute arises exclusively between parties having their principal place of business in States members of such other convention. However, this paragraph does not affect the application of para 4 of art 22 of this Convention.

3. No liability shall arise under the provisions of this Convention for damage caused by a nuclear incident if the operator of a nuclear installation is liable for such damage:

(a) under either the Paris Convention of 29 July 1960, on Third Party Liability in the Field of Nuclear Energy as amended by the Additional Protocol of 28 January 1964, or the Vienna Convention of 21 May 1963, on Civil Liability for Nuclear Damage, or

(b) by virtue of national law governing the liability for such damage, provided that such law is in all respects as favourable to persons who may suffer damage as either the Paris or Vienna Conventions.

4. No liability shall arise under the provisions of this Convention for any loss of or damage to or delay in delivery of luggage for which the carrier is responsible under any international convention or national law relating to the carriage of passengers and their luggage by sea.

5. Nothing contained in this Convention prevents a Contracting State from applying any other international convention which is already in force at the date of this Convention and which applies mandatorily to contracts of carriage of goods primarily by a mode of transport other than transport by sea. This provision also applies to any subsequent revision or amendment of such international convention.

Article 26. Unit of account

1. The unit of account referred to in art 6 of this Convention is the Special Drawing Right as defined by the International Monetary Fund. The amounts mentioned in art 6 are to be converted into the national currency of a State according to the value of such currency at the date of judgment or the date agreed upon by the parties. The value of a national currency, in terms of the Special Drawing Right, of a Contracting State which is a member of the International Monetary Fund is to be calculated in accordance with the method of valuation applied by the International Monetary Fund in effect at the date in question for its operations and transactions. The value of a national currency in terms of the Special Drawing Right of a Contracting State which is not a member of the International Monetary Fund is to be calculated in a manner determined by that State.

2. Nevertheless, those States which are not members of the International Monetary Fund and whose law does not permit the application of the provisions of para 1 of this Article may, at the time of signature, or at the time of ratification, acceptance, approval or accession or at any time thereafter, declare that the limits of liability provided for in this Convention to be applied in their territories shall be fixed as:

12,500 monetary units per package or other shipping unit or 37·5 monetary units per kilogramme of gross weight of the goods.

3. The monetary unit referred to in para 2 of this Article corresponds to sixty-five and a half milligrammes of gold of millesimal fineness nine hundred. The conversion of the amounts referred to in para 2 into the national currency is to be made according to the law of the State concerned.

4. The calculation mentioned in the last sentence of para 1 and the conversion mentioned in para 3 of this Article is to be made in such a manner as to express in the national currency of the Contracting State as far as possible the same real value for the amounts in art 6 as is expressed there in units of account. Contracting States must communicate to the depositary the manner of calculation pursuant to para 1 of this Article, or the result of

the conversion mentioned in para 3 of this Article, as the case may be, at the time of signature or when depositing their instruments of ratification, acceptance, approval or accession, or when availing themselves of the option provided for in para 2 of this Article and whenever there is a change in the manner of such calculation or in the result of such conversion.

PART VII. FINAL CLAUSES

Article 27. Depositary

The Secretary-General of the United Nations is hereby designated as the depositary of this Convention.

Article 28. Signature, ratification, acceptance, approval, accession

1. This Convention is open for signature by all States until 30 April 1979, at the Headquarters of the United Nations, New York.
   2. This Convention is subject to ratification, acceptance or approval by the signatory States.
   3. After 30 April 1979, this Convention will be open for accession by all States which are not signatory States.
   4. Instruments of ratification, acceptance, approval and accession are to be deposited with the Secretary-General of the United Nations.

Article 29. Reservations

No reservations may be made to this Convention.

Article 30. Entry into force

1. This Convention enters into force on the first day of the month following the expiration of one year from the date of deposit of the 20th instrument of ratification, acceptance, approval or accession.
   2. For each State which becomes a Contracting State to this Convention after the date of the deposit of the 20th instrument of ratification, acceptance, approval or accession, this Convention enters into force on the first day of the month following the expiration of one year after the deposit of the appropriate instrument on behalf of that State.
   3. Each Contracting State shall apply the provisions of this Convention to contracts of carriage by sea concluded on or after the date of the entry into force of this Convention in respect of that State.

Article 31. Denunciation of other Conventions

1. Upon becoming a Contracting State to this Convention, any State party to the International Convention for the Unification of Certain Rules relating to Bills of Lading signed at Brussels on 25 August 1924 (1924 Convention) must notify the Government of Belgium as the depositary of the 1924 Convention of its denunciation of the said Convention with a declaration that the denunciation is to take effect as from the date when this Convention enters into force in respect of that State.

2. Upon the entry into force of this Convention under para 1 of art 30, the depositary of this Convention must notify the Government of Belgium as the depositary of the 1924 Convention of the date of such entry into force, and of the names of the Contracting States in respect of which the Convention has entered into force.

3. The provisions of paras 1 and 2 of this Article apply correspondingly in respect of States parties to the Protocol signed on 23 February 1968, to amend the International Convention for the Unification of Certain Rules relating to Bills of Lading signed at Brussels on 25 August 1924.

4. Notwithstanding art 2 of this Convention, for the purposes of para 1 of this Article, a Contracting State may, if it deems it desirable, defer the denunciation of the 1924 Convention and of the 1924 Convention as modified by the 1968 Protocol for a maximum period of five years from the entry into force of this Convention. It will then notify the Government of Belgium of its intention. During this transitory period, it must apply to the Contracting States this Convention to the exclusion of any other one.

Article 32. Revision and amendment

1. At the request of not less than one-third of the Contracting States to this Convention, the depositary shall convene a conference of the Contracting States for revising or amending it.

2. Any instrument of ratification, acceptance, approval or accession deposited after the entry into force of an amendment to this Convention, is deemed to apply to the Convention as amended.

Article 33. Revision of the limitation amounts and unit of account of monetary unit

1. Notwithstanding the provisions of art 32, a conference only for the purpose of altering the amount specified in art 6 and para 2 of art 26, or of substituting either or both of the units defined in paras 1 and 3 of art 26 by other units is to be convened by the depositary in accordance with para 2 of this Article. An alteration of the amounts shall be made only because of a significant change in their real value.

2. A revision conference is to be convened by the depositary when not less than one-fourth of the Contracting States so request.

3. Any decision by the conference must be taken by a two-thirds majority of the participating States. The amendment is communicated by the depositary to all the Contracting States for acceptance and to all the States signatories of the Convention for information.

4. Any amendment adopted enters into force on the first day of the month following one year after its acceptance by two-thirds of the Contracting States. Acceptance is to be effected by the deposit of a formal instrument to that effect, with the depositary.

5. After entry into force of an amendment a Contracting State which has accepted the amendment is entitled to apply the Convention as amended in its relations with Contracting States which have not within six months after the adoption of the amendment notified the depositary that they are not bound by the amendment.

6. Any instrument of ratification, acceptance, approval or accession deposited after the entry into force of an amendment to this Convention, is deemed to apply to the Convention as amended.

Article 34. Denunciation

1. A Contracting State may denounce this Convention at any time by means of a notification in writing addressed to the depositary.

2. The denunciation takes effect on the first day of the month following the expiration of one year after the notification is received by the depositary. Where a longer period is specified in the notification, the denunciation takes effect upon the expiration of such longer period after the notification is received by the depositary.

DONE at Hamburg, this thirty-first day of March one thousand nine hundred and seventy-eight, in a single original, of which the Arabic, Chinese, English, French, Russian and Spanish texts are equally authentic.

IN WITNESS WHEREOF the undersigned plenipotentiaries, being duly authorized by their respective Governments, have signed the present Convention.

ANNEX II

COMMON UNDERSTANDING ADOPTED BY THE UNITED NATIONS
CONFERENCE ON THE CARRIAGE OF GOODS BY SEA

It is the common understanding that the liability of the carrier under this Convention is based on the principle of presumed fault or neglect. This means that, as a rule, the burden of proof rests on the carrier but, with respect to certain cases, the provisions of the Convention modify this rule.

ANNEX III

RESOLUTION ADOPTED BY THE UNITED NATIONS CONFERENCE ON THE CARRIAGE OF GOODS BY SEA

'The United Nations Conference on the Carriage of Goods by Sea,

'*Noting* with appreciation the kind of invitation of the Federal Republic of Germany to the Conference in Hamburg,

'*Being aware* that the facilities placed at the disposal of the Conference and the generous hospitality bestowed on the participants by the Government of the Federal Republic of Germany and by the Free and Hanseatic City of Hamburg, have in no small measure contributed to the success of the Conference,

'*Expresses* its gratitude to the Government and people of the Federal Republic of Germany, and

'*Having adopted* the Convention on the Carriage of Goods by Sea on the basis of a draft Convention prepared by the United Nations Commission on International Trade Law at the request of the United Nations Conference on Trade and Development,

'*Expresses* its gratitude to the United Nations Commission on International Trade Law and to the United Nations Conference on Trade and Development for their outstanding contribution to the simplification and harmonization of the law of the carriage of goods by sea, and

'*Decides* to designate the Convention adopted by the Conference as the: "UNITED NATIONS CONVENTION ON THE CARRIAGE OF GOODS BY SEA, 1978", and

'*Recommends* that the rules embodied therein be known as the "HAMBURG RULES".'

Index